Bringing Human Rights Home

Pennsylvania Studies in Human Rights

Bert B. Lockwood, Jr., Series Editor

A complete list of books in the series is available from the publisher.

Bringing Human Rights Home

A History of Human Rights in the United States

ABRIDGED EDITION

Edited by
Cynthia Soohoo
Catherine Albisa
and
Martha F. Davis

PENN

UNIVERSITY OF PENNSYLVANIA PRESS

PHILADELPHIA

First published 2007 by Praeger Press, an imprint of Greenwood Publishing Group, Inc.

Published by
University of Pennsylvania Press
Philadelphia, Pennsylvania 19104-4112

Printed in the United States of America on acid-free paper

10 9 8 7 6 5 4 3 2 1

A Cataloging-in-Publication record is available from the Library of Congress

ISBN 978-0-8122-2079-7

Contents

Preface

> Where, after all, do universal human rights begin? In small places, close to home—so close and so small that they cannot be seen on any maps of the world. . . . Without concerted citizen action to uphold them close to home, we shall look in vain for progress in the larger world.
>
> *—Eleanor Roosevelt*

In the early 1990s, the term "U.S. human rights" would have probably elicited vague confusion and puzzled looks. Contemporary notions of human rights advocacy involved the criticism of rights abuses in *other* countries, and claims of human rights violations were *leveled by, not at,* the U.S. government. Although human rights documents and treaties purported to discuss universal rights obligations that applied to all countries, the prevailing wisdom was that the American people did not need human rights standards or international scrutiny to protect their rights. Many scholars and political scientists, who described themselves as "realists," expressed doubt that international human rights law could ever influence the behavior of a superpower such as the United States.

Yet segments of the American public have always believed that the struggle for human rights is relevant to the United States. One of the earliest uses of the term "human rights" is attributed to Frederick Douglass and his articulation of the fundamental rights of enslaved African Americans at a time when the United States did not recognize their humanity or their rights. At various times in U.S. history, the idea that all individuals have fundamental rights rooted in the concept of human dignity and that the international community might provide support in domestic rights struggles has resonated with marginalized and disenfranchised populations. Thus, it was no surprise that U.S. rights organizations, including the NAACP and American Jewish Congress, played a crucial role in the birth of the modern human rights movement. Both groups helped to ensure that human rights were included in the UN Charter.

Following the creation of the United Nations, many domestic social justice activists were interested in human rights standards and the development of international forums. Human rights offered the potential to expand both domestic concepts of rights and available forums and allies for their struggles. In the late 1940s and 1950s, Cold War imperatives forced mainstream social justice activists to limit their advocacy to civil claims rights, rather than broader human rights demands for economic and social rights, and to forgo international forums or criticism of the United States. At the same time, isolationists and Southern senators, opposed to international scrutiny of Jim Crow and segregation, were able to effectively prevent U.S. ratification of human rights treaties that required U.S. compliance with human rights standards.

As a result of these pressures, by the 1950s, the separation between international human rights and domestic civil rights appeared complete. Human rights advocacy came to be understood as involving challenges to oppressive regimes abroad, and domestic social justice activists focused on using civil rights claims within the domestic legal system to articulate and vindicate fundamental procedural and equality rights. Recent scholarship by Mary Dudziak and others point out that during the 1950s and 1960s, the United States' civil rights agenda was strongly influenced by concerns about international opinion because Jim Crow and domestic racial unrest threatened to undermine U.S. moral authority during the Cold War. However, although international pressures may have encouraged and supported reform within the United States, the main engine for change was the domestic legal system. Federal civil rights legislation and Supreme Court cases ending de jure segregation, expanding individual rights, and protecting the interests of poor people through the 1960s seemed to support the perception that the United States did not need human rights.

Soon after, however, the political climate began to shift. Changes on the Supreme Court led to a retreat in domestic protections of fundamental rights. By the end of the 1980s, the assault on domestic civil rights protections was well underway, as illustrated by political attacks on affirmative action and reproductive rights. Political leaders undermined long-standing social programs. President Ronald Reagan demonized the poor, claiming that welfare recipients were primarily defrauding the system and that women drove away from the welfare offices in Cadillacs. This image of the "welfare queen" created the foundation for further attacks on the rights of the poor in the years to come.

From the 1990s to the present, the deterioration of legal rights for Americans continued. Congress and increasingly conservative federal judges narrowed remedies for employment discrimination and labor violations and restricted prisoners' access to the courts. The legislature and executive branch over time also allotted fewer resources, and even less political will, to government enforcement of laws protecting Americans from job discrimination, health and safety violations in the workplace, and environmental toxins. Funding for legal services was cut.

Alongside this gradual unraveling of rights in the United States, global events shifted dramatically with the end of the Cold War. With new global political alignments and international dialogue, the standard politicization of human rights no longer made sense. This opened an important window of opportunity for activists in the United States. Human rights—including economic, social, and cultural rights—could now be claimed for all people, even those within the United States, without triggering accusations of aiding communist adversaries.

As the relevance of international human rights standards grew within the United States, even the federal judiciary took note. The Supreme Court issued a series of decisions citing international human rights standards regarding the death penalty and gay rights. These opinions were sharply criticized by the most reactionary politicians and members of the Court itself. In 2002, Supreme Court Justice Clarence Thomas admonished his fellow justices not to "impose foreign moods, fads, or fashions on Americans." Reactionary pundits and scholars picked up on this theme arguing that compliance with human rights standards is antidemocratic because it overrules legislative decisions that constitute the will of the majority.

Nonetheless, the trend toward applying human rights in the United States continued to quietly and gradually deepen until a series of events jolted the American psyche and quickly moved the issue of human rights to the fore. These developments finally forced the mainstream public to consider what human rights had to do with us.

First, as the nation began to recover from the 9/11 attacks, many were shocked by the antiterrorism tactics of the Bush administration. To deflect criticism, the administration claimed that torture and cruel and degrading treatment were legal under U.S. law and that international law prohibitions on torture and cruel treatment were not relevant. Voices both within the United States and from the international community challenged the Bush administration, pointing out that torture is a universal human rights violation, no matter where it occurs.

Next, in 2005, Hurricane Katrina also provided a stark illustration that poor, minority, and marginalized communities need human rights protections and that domestic law falls well short of even articulating, much less remedying, a wide range of fundamental rights violations. This remains particularly true when affirmative government obligations to protect life, health, and well-being are involved. The government's abandonment of thousands of people too poor to own a car and the resulting hunger, thirst, chaos, and filth they suffered for many days and weeks after the storm shocked the conscience of Americans. People around the world were incredulous that the richest nation in the world failed to respond to the needs of its own people. Given an opportunity to rehabilitate its image after the storm, government actions instead deepened existing inequalities, oppression, and poverty of those affected. Katrina served as a wake-up call for the region's activists who have collectively embraced human rights as a rallying cry.

Post-9/11, the Supreme Court served to moderate the worst excesses of the Bush administration's war on terror and, in closely contested cases, brought the United States in line with peer democratic countries by abolishing the juvenile death penalty and criminal restrictions on consensual homosexual conduct. However, the widening gap between U.S. law and international human rights standards was made brutally clear by the Supreme Court's 2007 decision striking down voluntary school desegregation plans in Seattle and Louisville. The case effectively overturned a significant part of *Brown v. Board of Education* and signaled an abandonment of the Court's historic role as protector of the vulnerable and marginalized in society. In direct opposition to the UN Convention on the Elimination of All Forms of Racial Discrimination, which allows and in some cases requires affirmative measures to remedy historic discrimination, the *Seattle and Louisville* case held that school desegregation programs voluntarily adopted by school boards constitute unconstitutional racial discrimination. In 2007, the *Seattle and Louisville* case appeared as a harbinger of the battles yet to be fought on the much disputed territory of human rights in the United States.

This book tells the story of the domestic human rights movement from its early origins, through its retreat during the Cold War, to its recent resurgence and the reasons for it. It also describes the current movement by examining its strategies and methods. It is our hope that this book will provide greater understanding of the history and nature of the domestic human rights movement and in doing so respond to criticism that domestic human rights advocacy is foreign to U.S traditions and that it seeks to improperly impose the views and morals of the international community on the American people.

Although the history of U.S. involvement in the birth of the modern international human rights movement is well known, the parallel history of the struggle for human rights within the United States has been overlooked and forgotten. Part I reclaims the early history of the domestic human rights movement and examines the internal and external factors that forced its retreat. In Part II, we hope to provide a clearer picture of current human rights advocacy in the United States. Human rights work in the United States is often misunderstood because those who search for it tend to focus on legal forums, forays into international institutions, and human rights reports written by international human rights organizations. While such work is critically important and continues to grow, human rights education and organizing tends to get overlooked. As we tell the story of human rights advocacy in the United States and come to understand the current depth and diversity of the movement and its embrace by grassroots communities, the hollowness of antidemocratic criticism becomes clear. Rather than encompassing a set of foreign values that are imposed upon us, the fight for human rights in the United States is emerging both from the top down and the ground up.

Introduction to Part I

Martha F. Davis

In early 1942, just a few months after the attack on Pearl Harbor, the United States Office of Emergency Management dispatched fieldworkers around the country to conduct "man-on-the-street" interviews about the war. Interviewees were asked to address their remarks directly to President Roosevelt. The recordings were ultimately used in a radio program titled "Dear Mr. President," broadcast in May 1942, intended to highlight the voices of everyday people. However, in their raw form, the recordings provide direct and candid access to the views of Americans during a pivotal time in our history, one year after Roosevelt's Four Freedoms speech, shortly after the U.S. declaration of war on Japan, coinciding with the start of the Japanese internments, and hard on the heels of the inception, on January 1, 1942, of the United Nations.

Amid the professions of wholehearted support for the president and willingness to do whatever it takes to win the war, interviewees repeatedly sound notes of concern about the domestic impacts of the effort and, more pointedly, the contrast between the ideals expressed in the war effort and the realities facing some communities in the United States. In particular, in a nation where formal racial inequality was still widely accepted, many of the African American interviewees expressed dismay about the disjunction between the nation's wartime rhetoric and the struggles they faced in their own lives. A grocery clerk in Nashville, Tennessee, observed that "at the present, probably Mr. Hitler or Japan might not be the greatest enemy we have . . . [w]e've got to do something to curb the misunderstanding between minor [*sic*] groups and the groups which are oppressed and robbed of opportunities here in this country, which is a free country."[1] An African American private serving in the U.S. Army described the discrimination that he experienced in his position before observing that "the Negro hopes that when these things are over, when the war is over, that these promises that has been made to him and these promises that he's fighting for—the promises that he lives and hopes for—will all be made a reality."[2] An unidentified man on the street in New York City summed up these concerns in his message to President Roosevelt:

"As a black American I'm quite naturally interested in democracy. However, I do feel that what we should do is get a little democracy in America first. . . . We are busy trying to bring the four freedoms to the rest of the world, but yet here in America they don't exist. I cite as examples of this the lynching in Sykestown, Missouri, the other day. The brutal shooting of several Negro soldiers in Alexandria, Louisiana, a couple of weeks ago. And the ever-present and still continuing discrimination against Negro craftsmen in defense industries."[3]

These remarkably consistent interviews from around the nation show, among other things, how deeply into the American psyche the wartime message—of exporting democracy, equality, and President Roosevelt's "four freedoms"—had permeated. At the same time, the individual testimonies concerning racial discrimination and lack of economic opportunities demonstrate a keen awareness of how far the nation had yet to go to reach these same ideals domestically.

The chapters in this part take up the same theme raised by these "people on the streets" of America more than sixty years ago—that is, the contradictions between the United States' historic embrace of human rights principles on the international stage and its deep ambivalence about human rights at home. Written by historians and other scholars of human rights, these chapters train a human rights lens on U.S. history to help understand the historical backdrop for the growing U.S. human rights movement we see today. Collectively, these chapters illuminate several tensions that have, over decades and even centuries, moderated efforts to implement human rights in the United States and that continue to play a role in the human rights movement.

First, as Paul Gordon Lauren's chapter, "A Human Rights Lens on U.S. History," so effectively describes, the U.S. government and other influential institutions and leaders have many times embraced human rights principles, as in the Declaration of Independence, Roosevelt's Four Freedoms speech, and more recently, ratification of the International Covenant on Civil and Political Rights.[4] Indeed, as Lauren chronicles, throughout the nineteenth and early twentieth centuries, human rights movements did not stop at the U.S. border. Rather, ideas that developed abroad readily permeated the national consciousness and influenced similar movements within the United States. The nineteenth-century U.S. women's rights movement and the Declaration of Sentiments provide apt examples of these influences.

Yet almost simultaneously, the same government institutions that embraced human rights have had no compunction about rejecting human rights approaches when they might challenge the hegemony of the capitalist system, as Hope Lewis writes in her chapter, "'New' Human Rights?," on the challenges of implementing economic, social, and cultural rights in the United States.[5] The U.S. failure to ratify the International Covenant on Economic, Social and Cultural Rights, despite the U.S. government's central role in drafting the treaty, is a case in point. Not surprisingly, as Carol Anderson describes in her historical chapter on the NAACP's forays into human rights advocacy, titled "A 'Hollow Mockery,'" the U.S. government's positions influenced the strategic directions of nongovernmental leaders as well.[6] The government's deep ambivalence toward and at times opportunistic manipulation of human rights and the consequences of that ambivalence are central themes in the historical chapters here.

Second, these chapters chronicle the various modes of institutional and social change that affect the fluctuating status of human rights within the United States. On the one hand, Elizabeth Borgwardt's chapter, "FDR's Four Freedoms and Wartime Transformations in America's Discourse of Rights," brilliantly describes the role of nations and national leaders in developing and exploiting the language of human rights in the service of diplomatic and political, albeit progressive, ends.[7] Her account is one of insiders, such as Franklin Roosevelt, Winston Churchill, and Eleanor Roosevelt; as the "Dear Mr. President" interviews reveal, these actors played a determinative role in the public understanding and acceptance of human rights concepts and implementation in the critical period before, during, and after World War II.

Carol Anderson's engaging chapter on the NAACP's efforts to use international human rights mechanisms to address Jim Crow and other segregationist policies is particularly poignant in light of the "Dear Mr. President" interviews excerpted above. Relegated to a position as outsiders after World War II despite the promise of greater postwar democracy and equality at home as well as abroad, African American activists briefly turned to human rights rhetoric only find that they had been outmaneuvered by Cold War hawks and states' rights supporters. That these developments had such a significant and lasting impact on the status of human rights in the United States underscores the critical role that outsiders play in shaping national policies on these issues. Through the 1950s and 1960s, in the absence of sustained pressure from outside institutions like the NAACP, U.S. government attention to international human rights approaches languished.

Finally, it is worth noting the ways in which issues of race and poverty in America cut across the chapters in this part. Paul Gordon Lauren observes the critical roles that race and class issues played in the early development of human rights concepts. Indeed, as he and others note, abolitionist Frederick Douglass is often credited with coining the phrase. Elizabeth Borgwardt links both race and poverty issues after the Great Depression with FDR's conception of the New Deal and, particularly, his pledge of "freedom from want." Carol Anderson and Hope Lewis describe from differing perspectives the role of America's race problem in foreign relations and in its domestic stance on international human rights.

Of course, one of the central reasons for recounting history is to help us understand our current situation. In that respect, these chapters surely succeed. Having identified the U.S. government's awkward waltz with human rights concepts—a three-part dance of ambivalence, rejection, and embrace—these writers identify the critical roles that domestic vulnerabilities, particularly around race and poverty, have played in keeping human rights nearby but at arm's length. Similarly, they note the ways in which government and media manipulation of these concepts have been used in service of other, political ends. These insights can inform our understanding of contemporary events and of human rights developments yet to come. These historical accounts can also help shape strategies for the new human rights movement emerging in the United States.

The history of human rights in the United States is a difficult story to tell and to hear. But in many ways, the strains are all too familiar. To borrow a phrase from songwriter Paul Simon, it's an American tune. The chorus pits the American dream and lofty national ideals against harsher realities, telling a story of racial divides, economic class segregation, political maneuvering, and exceptionalism that the person-on-the-street in Nashville or New York City would have no difficulty believing and understanding, and might even tell as their own.[8] Perhaps once we recognize the contours of this story—including its very commonness—we can begin to test and transcend the boundaries set by our own history.

Notes

1. "Dear Mr. President," Nashville, Tenn., January or February 1942, AFS 6442B, available online at www.loc.gov.
2. "Dear Mr. President," Granbury, Austin, Hood County, and Fletcher County, Tex., January or February 1942, AFS 6431.
3. "Dear Mr. President," New York, N.Y., January or February 1942, AFS 6410A, Cut A3.
4. Paul Gordon Lauren, "A Human Rights Lens on U.S. History: Human Rights at Home and Human Rights Abroad," Chapter 1 in the current volume.
5. Hope Lewis, "'New' Human Rights? U.S. Ambivalence Toward the International Economic and Social Rights Framework," Chapter 4 in the current volume.

6. Carol Anderson, "A 'Hollow Mockery': African Americans, White Supremacy, and the Development of Human Rights in the United States," Chapter 3 in the current volume.

7. Elizabeth Borgwardt, "FDR's Four Freedoms and Wartime Transformations in America's Discourse of Rights," Chapter 2 in the current volume.

8. Paul Simon, "An American Tune," on *There Goes Rhymin' Simon,* released May 1973.

Chapter 1
A Human Rights Lens on U.S. History: Human Rights at Home and Human Rights Abroad

Paul Gordon Lauren

Throughout their history, from its very beginnings to the present and despite the language of the Declaration of Independence and the Bill of Rights, Americans have seriously argued and sometimes violently contested over human rights. While some have enthusiastically embraced the concept that all people are endowed with certain inalienable or natural rights and have worked to bring this principle into practice, for example, others have insisted that not all people are fully human and that whatever rights exist should be applied instead only to certain groups based upon gender, race, class, opinion, or some other form of distinction. Other contests have raged over whether human rights are all indivisible and possess equal value, or whether political and civil rights are much more important and should be given far more weight than economic and social rights. Americans also have vehemently clashed over the question of whether or not human rights within their own country should be tied in any way to human rights in the world at large.

This debate over the relationship between human rights at home and human rights abroad has been long and intense—and, as the world becomes increasingly interconnected, continues to be so. Historically, of course, only a few arguments existed over the issue of sending human rights overseas. The idea that American values and practices should be exported and thereby serve as the model for others in the world always has been a highly popular theme to invoke among the body politic. As pastor John Winthrop wrote in his famous sermon while crossing the Atlantic Ocean in the seventeenth century: "For we must consider that we shall be as a city upon a hill. The eyes of all people are upon us, so that if we shall deal falsely with our God in this work we have undertaken . . .

we shall be made a story and a by-word throughout the world."[1] This statement, and many others like it, evoked the possibilities of a shining new land of opportunity whose people enjoyed basic rights, free from the trappings of a feudal past, monarchical despotism and oppression, privilege, corruption, class divisions, and the prejudice and intolerance that plagued other, less fortunate, countries. They believed that America was uniquely favored and, consequently, that it should set the standard that served as the model and beacon of hope that all others around the world would admire, respect, and surely want to emulate. As U.S. Senator Alfred Beveridge articulated the mission at the end of the nineteenth century: "It is a glorious history our God has bestowed upon His chosen people; a history heroic with faith in our mission and our future; . . . a history of prophets who saw the consequences of evils inherited from the past and of martyrs who died to save us from them. . . . Shall free institutions broaden their blessed reign as the children of liberty wax in strength, until the empire of our principles is established over the hearts of all mankind? . . . It is ours to set the world its example of right and honor."[2]

It is not at all difficult to find similar expressions used within American domestic politics during our own day.

The most serious debates thus existed not about exporting human rights abroad, but rather over bringing human rights home. Intense arguments have raged within America over the question of whether there were any ideas, practices, mechanisms, or laws elsewhere that might be useful in establishing, extending, or protecting rights within the United States. There have always been those Americans, for example, who have clearly seen themselves as a part of the larger world, eager to learn from others beyond their own borders, to draw upon international norms and influences for advocacy in domestic politics, and to play a role and actively contribute what they could to developments in the broader evolution of international human rights.[3] There also have always been Americans who have been reluctant or ambivalent supporters of international human rights norms, accepting the value of some while simultaneously rejecting others. At the same time, there have always been Americans firmly opposed to establishing or honoring any international standards and norms at all, insisting that their country was so truly exceptional—so special, so superior, and so destined to be different—that it need not surrender its own national sovereignty by being bound by rules or scrutiny from the outside, and that it certainly did not need foreigners telling it what to do.[4]

These sharply contrasting opinions and tensions are evident not only in history but also in contemporary issues of human rights and continuing violations of human rights, as America continues to struggle with its relationship with the rest of the world and the global human rights system. The various chapters in this volume titled *Bringing Human Rights Home* will describe and analyze some the most significant of these in detail. But it is important to recognize that the patterns of contentious dispute and the sharply contrasting themes of America as advocate, as ambivalent or reluctant participant, and as determined opponent of international human rights efforts are all part of a long-standing legacy that can be discerned if one examines American history from its beginnings to the watershed experience of World War II through the revealing lens of human rights.

The Creation of the Republic, the Constitution, and the Bill of Rights

Early American colonists did not find it at all strange to borrow ideas and practices from England and from the broader European intellectual movement known as the Enlightenment.[5] They argued that they were the inheritors and beneficiaries of the rights that had evolved through the Magna Carta of 1215 on the limitations upon royal government and legal protections for certain individual liberties, the Habeas Corpus Act of 1679 establishing the right to be protected against arbitrary detention, and the landmark English Bill of Rights of 1689 with its specific provisions of civil and political rights such as free elections, freedom of speech, religious toleration, trial by jury, and prohibitions against cruel and unusual punishment. These rights, among others, they had read in the seminal *Second Treatise of Government* written by philosopher John Locke, were "natural rights" derived from "natural law." As such, they should apply not just to the continent of Europe, but to "common humanity" and "governments throughout the world." All people are born, Locke declared, with "a title to perfect freedom and uncontrolled enjoyment of all the rights and privileges of the law of nature equally with any other man or number of men in the world and have by nature a power not only to preserve his property—that is his life, liberty, and estate—against the injuries and attempts of other men, but to judge and punish the breaches of that law in others."[6]

From this premise it followed that people formed governments to preserve these rights, not to surrender them. As a consequence, governments received their powers from the governed with whom they signed a contract. Any government that acted in such a way as to violate these natural rights, wrote Locke in passages widely quoted with approval among colonists in North America chafing under English rule, therefore dissolved the contract and gave people a right to resist.

The ideas about natural law and natural rights articulated by Locke and by other philosophers and writers such as Jean-Jacques Rousseau,

Baron de Montesquieu, Marquis de Condorcet, Voltaire, and Denis Diderot from France, David Hume from England, Francis Hutcheson from Scotland, Immanuel Kant from Prussia, and Cesare Beccaria from Milan, among others, heavily influenced the thinking of many of the founders of the early American republic. They drew not only upon the general ideas, but sometimes even the specific language from the other side of the Atlantic. Delegates to the First Continental Congress of 1774, for example, borrowed the words of the philosophers of the Enlightenment about "the immutable laws of nature" and "the principles of the English constitution" to assert that the inhabitants of the colonies were "entitled to life, liberty, and property."[7] George Mason did the same in composing the celebrated Virginia Declaration of Rights, forcefully arguing that "all men are by nature equally free and independent, and have certain inherent rights."[8] Thomas Jefferson knew and utilized the same sources, especially when writing the memorable words of the Declaration of Independence of July 4, 1776: "We hold these truths to be self-evident, that all men are created equal, that they are endowed by their Creator with certain unalienable rights, that among these are life, liberty, and the pursuit of happiness. That to secure these rights, governments are instituted among men, deriving their just powers from the consent of the governed. That whenever any form of government becomes destructive of those ends, it is the right of the people to alter or to abolish it, and to institute a new government."[9]

These words helped to launch the American Revolutionary War. When that long and painful war finally ended, the task at hand was not to fight and destroy but rather to debate and create. More specifically, the critical undertaking was to institute a new government by consent and to provide for the protection of what were perceived to be the unalienable or natural rights of its citizens, although there was no precise agreement upon exactly what these might entail. The definition of "human rights" would be one that evolved through time and circumstance. The Constitution of 1787 began this process by establishing a federal government with a separation of powers and checks and balances and by enshrining the political rights of voting and of holding office. Many citizens throughout the new republic, however, believed that the Constitution, as it then stood, said far too little about protecting individual rights.[10] They worried not only about threats and abuses that might originate from the government, but also—and very significantly—from a tyranny of the majority. As one of the central founders James Madison expressed it: "In republican government the majority, however composed, ultimately give the law. Whenever therefore an apparent interest or common passion unites a majority, what is to restrain them from unjust violations of the rights and interests of the minority, or of individuals?"[11] Such questions, and the fears and concerns they expressed, as well as the Declaration of the Rights of Man and Citizen that appeared with the outbreak of the French Revolution in 1789,[12] energized rights advocates to mobilize a vigorous, contentious, and lengthy campaign throughout the new country for the purpose of adding amendments to the Constitution that specifically addressed and enumerated critical civil rights.

As a result of their efforts, the first ten amendments, collectively known as the Bill of Rights, were added to the Constitution in 1791.[13] They established the legal foundation for the protection of human rights in the United States. Unlike earlier declarations of rights that used words like "ought" and "should," the amendments employed the word "shall" as a command. Thus, the powerful First Amendment enumerated the freedom of conscience and expression by explicitly stating: "Congress shall make no law respecting an establishment of religion, or prohibiting the free exercise thereof; or abridging the freedom of speech, or of the press; or the right of the people peacefully to assemble; and to petition the Government for a redress of grievances." Other amendments established that people shall be secure in their persons and possessions against unreasonable searches and seizures; shall enjoy the right to a speedy and public trial, a trial by jury, and legal counsel; shall not be compelled to provide witness against themselves; shall not be deprived of life, liberty, or property without due process of law; and shall be protected against excessive fines or cruel and unusual punishment.

Those advocates who had actively campaigned on behalf of rights and supported the inclusion of the Bill of Rights into the Constitution could take justifiable pride in the fact that these protections now became an integral part of the law of the land. They could hardly know, of course, just how important or what kinds of controversies they would generate through time, especially when its provisions were invoked as a rallying cry by those who fell outside its protection and during periods of crisis, national emergency, or war.[14] Some Americans of the early republic even hoped that the provisions they had created would make a significant contribution to human rights by setting an example and inspiring others throughout the world to do the same. As Jefferson himself noted earlier, "a bill of rights is what the people are entitled to against every government on earth."[15]

At times, they did inspire. The early American articulation of human rights certainly went on to influence scores of Europeans of contemporary and subsequent generations, many Asians and Africans in the process of decolonization during the twentieth century, and a number of significant and more recent international efforts. At other times, however, they provided little inspiration for emulation at all, especially when it was clear that they were not fully applied in practice at home. Activists and observers at home and from abroad were quick to point out that the human rights provisions in the much-heralded Constitution and Bill of Rights, for example, did not apply to everyone. Among the many not protected were women, the unpropertied, slaves, indigenous peoples, and children.[16] This fact, they noted, demonstrated a glaring gap between early American vision and American reality.

The Slave Trade and Slavery

Nothing marked the chasm in America between vision and reality more starkly than the slave trade and the institution of slavery that it supplied. Nowhere were violations of human rights—however defined—more blatant or more brutal than in this debasement of living human beings into property. Indeed, it was precisely the discussion about human rights surrounding the American Revolution and the Bill of Rights in the Constitution that sparked unprecedented public debate at home and abroad about the issue of human bondage. Never before in history had so many people on both sides of the Atlantic so seriously questioned the moral character of political and economic policy and the meaning of human rights. As Christopher Leslie Brown recently observes in his book about British abolitionism titled *Moral Capital,* by invoking universal principles rather than established law or custom, by professing an intense interest in the good of humankind, and by describing liberty as the natural right of all people, Americans inadvertently opened themselves to criticisms about the justice of holding African men and women, girls and boys, in lifelong bondage and treating them as property rather than as human beings.[17] The American revolutionary Patrick Henry saw the same striking contrast between professed values and practice, and felt compelled to write: "Is it not amazing that at a time when the rights of humanity are defined and understood with precision, in a country, above all others, fond of liberty, that in such a country we find men . . . adopting a principle as repugnant to humanity as it is inconsistent with the Bible, and destructive to liberty?"[18]

Many of those who struggled on behalf of human rights at the end of the eighteenth and beginning of the nineteenth centuries, therefore, focused their attention and energies on abolishing the slave trade and slavery itself. In this effort, Americans both contributed to, and drew support and encouragement from, the broader endeavor of what has been called "the anti-slavery international."[19] The formation of the Society for the Relief of Free Negroes Unlawfully Held in Bondage by the American Quaker pastor and activist Anthony Benzenet and others in Philadelphia, for example, not only created perhaps the very first human rights nongovernmental organization, or NGO, in the world, but in the process served as an example for Thomas Clarkson and other deeply committed campaigners in Britain to establish the much larger and more influential Society for Affecting the Abolition of the Slave Trade. Through time, activists in many countries, including those in the United States, came to look to the British abolitionists for inspiration and for evidence that their own efforts might be successful.[20] Additional NGOs were created, for example, including the Society for the Suppression of the Slave Trade, the Association of Friends for Promoting the Abolition of Slavery, and the American Anti-Slavery Society in the United States; the Aborigines Protection Society and the British and Foreign Anti-Slavery Society in Britain; the Société des Amis des Noirs and the Société de la Morale Chrétienne in France; and the Confederação Abolicionista in Brazil, among others. Together, they learned from each other and in the process developed significant organizational skills and techniques of human rights activism still used today such as writing letters, organizing public lectures and meetings, delivering sermons and speeches, collecting signatures and sponsoring petition drives to pressure governments and diplomats, proposing legislation, conducting research, participating in consumer boycotts, launching press campaigns, publishing pamphlets and articles, printing newsletters, and translating and distributing books (like Clarkson's powerful *The Cries of Africa to the Inhabitants of Europe; Or, a Survey of That Bloody Commerce Called the Slave Trade*) to leading decision makers.

Through time, efforts such as these began to have a cumulative effect. By 1806, for example, President Thomas Jefferson finally felt compelled to declare publicly that it was time to end the slave trade explicitly acknowledged in the U.S. Constitution and urged lawmakers "to withdraw the citizens of the United States from all further participation in those violations of human rights which have been so long continued on the unoffending inhabitants of Africa, and which the morality, the reputation, and the best interests of our country, have long been eager to proscribe."[21] Shortly thereafter, and very much aware of the efforts of each other, the U.S. Congress passed the Act to Prohibit the Importation of Slaves and the British Parliament enacted the Act for the Abolition of the Slave Trade during the same month in 1807.[22] Although the United States was not a part of the Congress of Vienna following the Napoleonic wars, it nevertheless followed a number of the deliberations closely, and during exactly the same month in 1815 when the European powers signed the Eight Power Declaration opposing the slave trade, it joined Britain in declaring within the text of the Treaty of Ghent that the traffic in slaves was "irreconcilable with the principles of humanity and justice" and agreed to work toward abolishing the trade altogether.[23] In the years that followed, American administrations sometimes willingly cooperated with other countries in the remarkable and unprecedented campaign to successfully end this trade in human beings that had lasted for several centuries and had brought untold wealth to the West, and sometimes they refused to participate at all. This mixed record, of course, reflected not only America's ambivalent attitudes toward international endeavors on behalf of human rights in general, but also the extreme divisiveness within the nation over the specific practice that created the market for the slave trade in the first place—slavery at home.

During the first half of the nineteenth century, American abolitionists constantly looked abroad for assessment, inspiration, ideas, and support. Since they constituted a beleaguered minority at home, they found strength and comfort by standing shoulder to shoulder with like-minded people from outside the United States.[24] They carefully read the perceptive and critical judgment made by foreign observers like the Frenchman Alexis de Tocqueville in his famous *De la démocratie en Amérique* about the sharp contrast between rhetoric and reality when he noted that "The absolute supremacy of democracy is not all that we meet with in America." Here, he concluded, "the European is to the other races of mankind what man is to the lower animals;—he makes them subservient to his use; and when he cannot subdue, he destroys them. Oppression has, at once stroke, deprived the descendants of the Africans of almost all of the privileges of humanity."[25] Tocqueville's assessment was reinforced by his compatriot and traveling companion, Gustav de Beaumont, whose book *Marie, ou l'esclavage aux Etats-Unis* observed that Americans "who have perfected the theory of equality" nevertheless failed to heal what he described as "the great canker." "I see," he has his major character say with great sorrow, "in the midst of a civilized Christian society, a class of people for whom that society has made a set of laws and customs apart from their own; for some, a lenient legislation, for others a bloody code; on one side, the supremacy of law, on the other, arbitrariness; for the whites the theory of equality, for the blacks the system of servitude; two contrary codes of morals: one for the free, the other for the oppressed; two sorts of public ethics: these—mild, humane, and liberal; those—cruel, barbaric, and tyrannical."[26]

Of particular importance, when abolitionists in America looked overseas, they saw successful examples of other countries actually achieving their dream of abolishing slavery and emancipating slaves. These included Costa Rica, El Salvador, Guatemala, Honduras, Nicaragua, Britain, Argentina, Colombia, Peru, and Venezuela. They also witnessed Prussia, the Austro-Hungarian Empire, Russia, and Poland end serfdom and set serfs free. As Lucretia Mott (who would go on to play a leading role in the movement for women's rights in the United States) pointed out during a major meeting of the American Anti-Slavery Society, "When we look abroad and see what is now being done in other lands, when we see human freedom engaging the attention of the nations of the earth," she declared, "we may take courage."[27] Their desire to bring these examples home to America by strictly peaceful means of persuasion, however, failed. Resistance remained strong and determined. In the end, therefore, it took the American Civil War (which remains to this day the nation's bloodiest military conflict) to transfer power away from those unwilling to share it voluntarily and thereby make it possible to adopt the Thirteenth Amendment finally prohibiting slavery within the United States.

Women's Rights

The impact of the campaign against the slave trade and slavery extended to another area of human rights as well: Many of those who became leaders in the early crusade for women's rights in America began their activist careers in the abolitionist movement. Once awakened, a sense of justice is not easily contained and, as Adam Hochschild observes, can often cross the boundaries of race, class, and gender.[28] Some campaigners, of course, had been encouraged at a certain level by the earlier statements of Abigail Adams at home that women would not feel themselves bound by any laws in which they had no voice or representation as well as voices from abroad, including those of Mary Wollstonecraft from England in her impassioned book *A Vindication of the Rights of Woman* and of Olympe de Gouges from France in her Declaration of the Rights of Woman and Citizen, which shouted, "Women, wake up; the tocsin of reason sounds throughout the universe; recognize your rights!"[29] But it was in the movement for abolition that they first became conscious of the broader nature and interrelationship of human rights and the connection between race and gender, and where they learned how to mobilize themselves into action and to experience successes that gave them both hope and the courage of their convictions. If slaves should have rights, then why shouldn't women? This motivated them to depart from the historic roles and rules of "woman's assigned sphere" and to step out into public activism.[30] "In striving to strike his irons off," acknowledged Abby Kelly Foster referring to black slaves, "we found most surely, that we were manacled ourselves."[31] The deeply religious and committed abolitionist Angelina Grimké reached the same conclusion, arguing that the struggle was one for human rights—not man's alone, not woman's alone, but equal rights for all whatever their color, sex, or station. "This is part of the great doctrine of Human Rights," she wrote, "and can no more be separated from Emancipation than the light from the heat of the sun; the rights of the slave and the woman blend like the colors of a rainbow."[32]

Growing opportunities to publish in the nineteenth century provided the means by which these ideas could receive more detailed expression than in the past, and this encouraged a broader public discussion of women's rights than ever before. Sarah Grimké's highly influential manifesto *Letters on the Equality of the Sexes and the Equality of Woman* in 1838, explicitly comparing the exploitation of women with that of slaves, for example, received considerable attention.[33] This was followed several years later by Elisha Hurlbut's suggestive book *Essays on Human Rights.*[34] Some men joined in this endeavor of viewing women's rights within the larger context of human rights as well, including abolitionists like William Lloyd Garrison and Frederick Douglass in the United States and George Thompson in Britain who spread their views through publications like *The Liberator, The Genius for Universal Emancipation, Human Rights,* and *The Rights of All.*

It was in this setting that a major development in the evolution of women's rights occurred. During 1848, the same year that saw revolutions explode throughout the continent of Europe with all of their energies and possibilities, Elizabeth Cady Stanton and Lucretia Mott, among two other women, determined "to do and dare anything" by organizing the very first convention ever held on behalf of the rights of women.[35] They attracted nearly three hundred participants who assembled in the Wesleyan Chapel at Seneca Falls, New York. Their discussions and resolutions expressed a variety of strongly held religious, secular, and political beliefs, as well as a determined impulse for reform, sometimes separately and sometimes woven together, into new statements about women's rights and the desire to secure "the equality of human rights." This is particularly evident in their famous Declaration of Sentiments where they began by modeling their language after the most revolutionary document in American history—the Declaration of Independence—and proclaiming:

We hold these truths to be self-evident: that all men and women are created equal: that they are endowed by their Creator with certain inalienable rights; that among these are life, liberty, and the pursuit of happiness; that to secure these rights governments are instituted, deriving their just powers from the consent of the governed. Whenever any government becomes destructive of these ends, it is the right of those who suffer from it to refuse allegiance to it. . . . [W]hen a long train of abuses and usurpations, pursing invariably the same object evinces a design to reduce [those who suffer] under absolute despotism, it is their duty to throw off such government, and to provide new guards for their future security. Such has been the patient sufferance of the women under this government, and such is now the necessity which constrains them to demand the equal station to which they are now entitled.

The Declaration of Sentiments then transformed the eighteenth-century charges against the English monarch found in the Declaration

of Independence into nineteenth-century charges against men and pro-
ceeded to describe the long record of abuse. "The history of mankind,"
it asserted, "is a history of repeated injuries and usurpations on the part
of man toward woman, having in direct object the establishment of an
absolute tyranny over her." To support this proposition, the document
presented a lengthy list: Men prevented women from voting, from owing
property, from earning wages, from being an equal partner in marriage,
from having custody of children in cases of divorce, from entering professions, from obtaining a thorough education ("all colleges being closed
against her"), from being subject to the same moral code, and assigning
a narrow "sphere of action" deliberately designed to destroy a woman's
self-confidence, self-respect, and freedom. Because women, "one half of
the people of this country," "feel themselves aggrieved, oppressed, and
fraudulently deprived of their most sacred rights," the declaration continued, "we insist that they have immediate admission to all the rights
and privileges which belong to them as citizens of the United States."
This language was followed by statement that left no doubt about the determination of the signatories: "In entering upon the great work before
us, we anticipate no small amount of misconception, misrepresentation,
and ridicule; but we shall use every instrumentality within our power to
effect our object."[36]

As Stanton would write in her *History of Woman Suffrage*, press coverage of the Seneca Falls meeting and its resolutions and declaration far
exceeded her greatest expectations. The entire proceedings were published in major newspapers, prompting considerable editorial opinion
and subsequent letters to the editors. This widespread publicity and public discourse, and its accompanying growing women's consciousness, in
turn, led to the emergence of a whole new social movement and political activism within the United States. The first National Women's Rights
Convention took place in 1850, attracting more than one thousand participants, and others followed annually for most of the decade, often
deliberately held to coincide with state constitutional conventions. Many
women worked to gain more control over their own bodies and repro-
duction, to change laws regarding property and child custodial rights
that discriminated against them, to create more educational opportunities, and to free themselves from their assigned "spheres" and presumed
"natural order" of the past. The new tone was reflected when Elizabeth
Cady Stanton and Susan B. Anthony formed the American Equal Rights
Association with its own newspaper entitled *The Revolution* and published
with the motto: "Men, their rights and nothing more; women, their rights
and nothing less!"[37]

Such developments and forceful declarations and statements from
women in the United States contributed significantly to the struggle

for women's rights in other countries as well. They provided examples and encouragement to other campaigners during the second half of the nineteenth century who, isolated from their own national contemporaries, eagerly reached out to like-minded activists across borders by exchanging letters, visiting each other and attending conventions, sharing ideas and tactics, and reading a common body of published writings about gender and equality. They thus often considered themselves as working for a universal cause. "This great movement is intended to meet the wants, not of America only," announced Paulina Wright Davis at a women's rights convention in 1853, "but of the whole world."[38]

This larger transnational movement and its sense of solidarity could be seen in many ways. One thinks of the newspaper *Frauen-Zeitung* (Women's Newspaper), published by the German activist Louise Otto; *The Subjugation of Women*, written by John Stuart Mill and his wife Harriet Taylor in Britain; the advocacy of equality between men and women by Mírzá Husayn 'Ali, or Bahá'u'lláh, when founding the Bahá'í faith; the writings of Tan Sitong in China; the remarkable essay by Toshiko Kishida in Japan titled "I Tell You My Fellow Sisters"; and the journal *La Camelia* of Rosa Guerra, which championed the cause of equality for women throughout Latin America and confidently asserted, "We are entering an era of liberty and there are no rights which exclude us!"[39] Utilizing the nineteenth century's new technological inventions of trains and steamships for transportation and the electric telegraph and penny postage stamp for communication, activists like Jenny d'Héricourt of France, Margaret Bright Lucas of Britain, Fredricka Bremer of Sweden, Stanton and Anthony of the United States, and Kate Sheppard of New Zealand, among others, achieved international stature as speakers, writers, and advocates of women's rights. Together they refused to let their differences divide them or to let the gains they had made in their own countries remain isolated from the rest of the world by deliberately sharing their visions and experiences with others, looking for helpful models for advocacy, and creating networks beyond their own borders. Moreover, to give explicit expression to the global nature of their cause, crusaders from fifty-three American organizations and from eight countries, including India, organized the first International Council of Women in 1888. Here the participants sought not only to take stock of the progress already made in removing women from their "slave status" and "domestic bondage" of the past in such areas as divorce laws, educational opportunities, and property ownership, but also to lay the foundation for the future and what Stanton called the strength and vitality of the "universal sisterhood" among those who advocated women's rights around the world.[40]

Among these various rights sought by women, particular attention focused on the political right to vote. This is understandable, for without

the franchise, many women believed that they would never be free or
empowered in a democratic society to directly influence the process and,
therefore, the agenda of national politics.[41] American women looked initially toward the activities in Britain where they saw the appearance of
Harriet Taylor's influential essay on the "Enfranchisement of Women"
in 1851, the creation of the Women's Suffrage Committee in 1865, and
later the National Union of Women's Suffrage Societies led by Millicent
Garrett Fawcett. At home, they formed the National Woman Suffrage
Association and the American Woman Suffrage Association in 1869,
and then combined the two in 1890 with the creation of the National
American Woman Suffrage Association (NAWSA). A determined voice
was given to this effort with the publication of Elizabeth Cady Stanton's
hard-hitting and widely discussed book, *Woman's Bible*.[42]

Resistance and opposition within the United States to the right to
vote, however, remained fierce. Only gradually, only because of pressure
from feminist organizations, and only in a few states in the West did this
begin to change. Wyoming, Colorado, Utah, and Idaho were among the
first to extend the franchise to women. But at the national level, the
truly pioneering step was taken elsewhere. In 1893, after many years of
unswerving work by Kate Sheppard and her colleagues, New Zealand became the first country in the world to extend to women the right to vote.
Nevertheless, even by the end of the nineteenth century, New Zealand
stood alone. The dream of suffragettes within the United States, including Susan B. Anthony and Carrie Chapman Catt who took leadership
roles in creating and contributing to the International Woman Suffrage
Alliance with affiliates in many countries, of course, was to take this successful example from abroad and bring it home to America.

Economic and Social Rights

It was not at all uncommon in the nineteenth century to hear human
rights activists speak excitedly about their reformist impulse and advances as "the progressive spirit of the age."[43] The reason can be found
in the fact that during this particular period three great reform movements emerged in American history: ending the slave trade and abolishing slavery, campaigning for women's rights, and promoting economic
and social rights for those most seriously exploited. At times, efforts in all
three aspects of human rights came together and became intertwined.
Activists like William Lloyd Garrison, Frederick Douglass, Franklin San-
born, Elizabeth Cady Stanton, Susan B. Anthony, and Sojourner Truth,
among others, came to see each of them as different threads of a seam-
less tapestry and different facets of the same common problem created
by those with power and prejudice who denied the basic human rights

of others. They thus often drew upon their experiences in the abolition-ist movement, comparing the status and situation of women with that of black slaves and arguing that men and women workers and their families were the exploited victims of "wage slavery."

Wendell Phillips, the famous and outspoken public orator, certainly personified this interconnectedness and indivisibility of human rights. He labored tirelessly in the abolitionist campaign and in the effort to adopt the Thirteenth Amendment eliminating slavery, the Fourteenth Amendment providing equal protection under the law, and the Fifteenth Amendment giving black and former slave males the right to vote. He then worked in support of women's suffrage and against laws of gender discrimination. All of these experiences to advance political and civil rights, in turn, then led him to advocate economic and social justice. He was one of the very first Americans to call for an eight-hour workday and for an investigation of inhumane factory conditions. "I am fully con-vinced," he declared in one well-known speech against the concentra-tion of wealth, "that hitherto legislation has leaned too much—leaned most unfairly— to the side of capital. . . . The law should do all it can to give the masses more leisure, a more complete education, better oppor-tunities and a fair share of the profits."[44]

Phillips and his fellow activists and labor organizers, of course, did not operate in a vacuum. They often looked abroad for ideas and strate-gies. No industrialized country in the world depended so heavily upon immigrants for its manufacturing labor force as did the United States. These workers came with painful personal experiences with poverty and hardship overseas and brought their hurt and their anger with them. This applied with particular reference to those from Europe where class divisions were severe, where most of the immigrants to America had been born, where the radical political movement among workers in England known as Chartism championed the plight of the working and unemployed poor, and where so many of the benefits and so many of the tragedies of the Industrial Revolution first became dramatically apparent. There, booming factories, textile mills, and mines brought not only a vast accumulation of wealth to a very few, but also the emer-gence of a vast urban proletariat of working men, women, and children who suffered in wretched squalor, thick smoke and soot, disease-infested water, overcrowded slums, misery, and working conditions of oppression without any prospect of relief. The exploitation of these workers and the accompanying starvation, destitution, crime, prostitution, acute illness, and family dislocations became so tragic, in fact, that it simply could not be hidden. Personal observations, government inquiries, exposés, books like *The Condition of the Working Class in England* by Friedrich Engels and *A Voice from the Factory* by Caroline Norton, provocative commentaries from Karl Marx written for American newspapers, and the dramatizations of such widely read and translated novelists like Honoré de Balzac in *Les Paysans* or Charles Dickens in *Bleak House* and *Hard Times* all contributed to a growing public consciousness of the brutal and widespread extent of human suffering.

In America and throughout the industrializing world, such obvious and severe misery among the working class ignited new and profoundly serious questions about the very meaning of human rights. What good were the political rights of voting and holding office or the civil rights of freedom of speech and religion, asked those who suffered, to people like themselves who had no food to put on the table, no shelter to protect their families, no clothing, no medical care, or no prospect at all for themselves or their children to obtain a formal education? What were the benefits of freedom if the result was destitution? Were Karl Marx and Friedrich Engels correct when they wrote in *The Communist Manifesto* that liberal conceptions of political and civil rights, which sought to protect individuals by limiting the power of the state, were no more than narrow, "bourgeois rights" of the ruling classes? Did this mean that all the declarations and expressions of human rights up to this point in history merely represented the abstract ideas of philosophers, the flowery language of parchment prose, or the empty platitudes of politicians?

With these kinds of questions very much in their minds, many of the have-nots of the working class and their leaders increasingly began to speak out about the necessity of going beyond the "negative rights" or "freedom from" rights to be protected from unwarranted government interference. Given the circumstances of the time, they now forcefully advocated the "positive rights" or "freedom to" rights to receive help and secure assistance in areas such as minimum wage, health care, safe working conditions, and educational opportunities. This marked a significant development in the evolution of human rights, for it extended the meaning of rights beyond the first generation of political and civil rights by moving into the second generation known as economic and social rights.

Americans certainly played an important role and made a contribution to this evolution. In doing so, however, they often found themselves in a difficult dilemma. When they saw the enactment in Europe of laws designed to help the plight of the exploited poor such as those that regulated child labor, the most egregious working conditions, sanitation, minimum standards for food, and compulsory education, many wanted to bring these examples home to America. At the same time, most had no desire whatsoever of bringing home the European examples of factory sabotage, violent uprisings, or especially the massive revolutionary convulsions that exploded during 1830, 1848, and 1870. Efforts to secure economic and social justice in America would always be plagued by fears that violence and revolution would occur and by charges that in a country of laissez-faire capitalism any action on the part of government that interfered with individualism and the forces of the market were "un-American" and could lead only to the dangers of a welfare state, socialism, or, worse, communism and "class warfare."[45]

In order to protect themselves from exploitation, low wages, dangerous working conditions, and an erratic economy subject to the frequent onset of depressions, a number of workers lashed out against an economic and social order that robbed them of their humanity. They began to participate in petition drives, demonstrations, protests, and strikes. At first, these took place in neighborhoods or in particular factories. Through time, however, workers began to become more conscious of the need to combine and coordinate their collective efforts and therefore founded local unions or national organizations like the Knights of Labor in 1869 and the American Federation of Labor in 1886. Under the leadership of Samuel Gompers, the latter gained a membership of nearly one million by the turn of the century. Their efforts often remained peaceful, but not always. Indeed, sometimes they turned bloody. In 1877, for example, railroad workers staged the first and most violent nationwide industrial strike of the nineteenth century that resulted in over one hundred deaths. Further violence occurred during the 1886 Haymarket Riot in Chicago, the 1892 Homestead Strike in the steel mills near Pittsburgh, and the 1894 Pullman Strike in the railroad yards of Chicago.

These extreme and polarizing events did not always generate sympathy. In fact, they often provoked fear among those terrified that violence might spread. They also generated countervailing power in the form of opposition strikebreakers, private security forces hired by factory owners, and the deployment of federal troops. In addition, and despite the language of economic and social rights, it was well known that many of the organized unions rarely welcomed women, blacks, nonwhite immigrants, or Native Americans into their ranks. For all of these reasons, a number of Americans determined that violence would only beget more violence and therefore determined that they could best advance economic and social rights by turning instead to the path of reform. Indeed, the second half of the nineteenth century in America was marked by an unprecedented reforming impulse to help address the claims and the needs of the exploited poor victimized by the forces of seemingly unrestrained capitalism, industrialization, and urbanization as well as to counter the proponents of social Darwinism who argued that mass fortunes accumulated by a few were beneficial since they encouraged competition and thereby helped to weed out the weak and unfit.[46]

Many of the reformers were motivated not so much by their fear of violence and the extremes, but by their sense of justice and their faith in the capacity of human beings to effect peaceful change and by their strong religious beliefs. Henry George's highly influential 1879 book *Progress and Poverty* contributed much to this approach. By insisting that the "unalienable rights" of the Declaration of Independence would remain empty phrases so long as the right of laborers to the product of their labor was denied, he importantly argued that economic and social rights should be at the same level as political and civil rights in the American tradition.[47] At the same time he observed that wherever the highest degree of "material progress" had been realized, "we find the deepest poverty" with its resultant human costs and loss of Christian values.[48] As a consequence, he encouraged his readers to not fall victim to cynicism or inaction but instead to put their beliefs into action by seizing the energy of reform.

Others gave expression to the same impulses. Protestants found their consciences stirred by innumerable sermons and by one of the best-selling novels of the century, *In His Steps*, written by Charles Sheldon, who asked his readers to ask one simple question: "What would Jesus do?"[49] The answer, he believed, would lead them to become actively involved in alleviating the sufferings of the poor and the exploited. At the same time, Catholics found inspiration in the remarkable 1891 encyclical known as *Rerum Novarum* (Of New Things) issued by Pope Leo XIII, explicitly addressing what he described as "the natural rights of mankind." Here he warned that "the first concern of all is to save the poor workers from the cruelty of grasping speculators, who use human beings as mere instrument for making money. It is neither justice nor humanity so to grind men down with excessive labor as to stupefy their minds and wear out their bodies." For this reason, he declared, human rights "must be religiously respected wherever they are found; and it is the duty of the public authority to prevent and punish injury, and to protect each one in the possession of his own. Still, when there is question of protecting the rights of individuals, the poor and helpless have a claim to special consideration. Their richer population have many ways of protecting themselves. . . . [But] wage-earners, who are, undoubtedly, among the weak and necessitous, should be specially cared for and protected by the commonwealth."[50]

The sense of responsibility to assist those unable to care for themselves that motivated such thoughts as these increasingly came to be known as the Social Gospel. Its message, especially when coupled with emotions aroused by visual images made possible by the recent invention of photography, inspired many to adopt the path of reform. Scenes of impoverishment in slums and despair in the haunting eyes of those in destitution as starkly revealed by Jacob Riis in his 1890 collection *How the Other Half Lives*, inspired many of the upper- and middle-class women who began to create a wide variety of religiously oriented charitable organizations and movements. The largest women's organization in the country, the Woman's Christian Temperance Union, under the leadership of Francis Willard, for example, worked in a variety of ways to address issues of poverty, unemployment, alcohol abuse, dangerous labor conditions, and the plight of workers, especially women and children. Its members often worked with unions and other sympathetic supporters to campaign for particular candidates for public office, to develop building codes for tenements, to actively lobby to abolish child labor and secure a national labor contract law, and to successfully work for the passage of legislation to institute a Department of Labor as a part of the executive branch of the federal government. On other fronts, reforming women activists launched the settlement house movement in the 1890s, seeking to apply their sense of Christian responsibility to the needs of the suffering, working-class poor. These included Jane Addams, who founded Hull House in Chicago, Vida Scudder with Denison House in Boston, and Lillian Ward with her house on New York's Lower East Side. They and the growing number of their counterparts elsewhere provided shelter, food, day nurseries, kindergartens, and classes on cooking, health care, and the English language in order to assist newly arrived immigrant families, thereby making a number of incremental and very practical contributions toward economic and social rights.[51]

Efforts for Human Rights on a Variety of Fronts, 1900–1920

The turn of the twentieth century brought not only a sense of anticipation for the possibilities that might exist for advancing human rights, but also a greater awareness of the international dimensions and scope of the process. That is, with advent of such technological innovations as the wireless telegraph, steamships, railroads, and the exciting new invention of aircraft, previous notions about distance, geographical barriers, and national boundaries began to undergo a dramatic transformation as people and places once regarded as far removed became closer than ever before. Observers thus began to speak of "world politics," "global affairs," and the truly "international" aspects of their concerns.[52] This could be seen in many ways, not the least of which was the announcement of the nongovernmental organization known as the Ligue des Droits de l'Homme in its first publication in 1901 that it would promote human rights not just to those in France but "to all humanity."[53] For advocates of human rights in the United States, such a global perspective meant that the possibilities for making contributions to the rights of others in the world might increase dramatically, as would the possibilities for learning from others abroad and bringing some their ideas home to America.

Those who campaigned on behalf of women's rights within the United States, for example, often looked abroad for their inspiration. They observed with great interest the efforts of feminist leaders like Qiu Jin in China, Hideko Fukuda in Japan, Concepción in the Philippines, and Emmeline Pankhurst in Britain with her organization of the Women's Social and Political Union and their slogan of "Deeds, Not Words!," among others, willing to confront centuries of tradition.[54] They greatly admired New Zealand for becoming the first country in the world to grant women the right to vote and then excitedly watched as Australia, Finland, and Norway followed suit. During the course of World War I from 1914 to 1918 they further witnessed the extension of franchise to women, sometimes with certain restrictions, in Denmark, Canada, Austria, Estonia, Germany, Hungary, Latvia, Lithuania, Poland, Russia, Britain, and Ireland. Belarus, Belgium, Luxembourg, the Netherlands, and Sweden followed shortly thereafter, as did Albania, Czechoslovakia, and Iceland.[55]

American women and their male supporters looked with both admiration and envy at these international developments beyond their own borders. They frequently compared the successes overseas with their own lack of progress at home, noting that even the much-heralded Fourteenth Amendment on equal protection did not seem to apply to them. In 1916 a landmark was reached with the election of Jeannette Rankin from Montana as the first female ever elected to the U.S. Congress, but resistance remained strong. The continued frustration and anger over the lack of a national franchise led to the formation of the militant National Women's Party, founded by Alice Paul and Lucy Burns. Party members were willing to hold protest demonstrations outside the White House, to be arrested, and to serve prison time with forced feedings, all while shouting their rallying cry "How Long Must Women Wait For Liberty?"[56] Their actions, when combined with those of many others, the desire to acknowledge the significant contributions of women to the war effort, and the interest to appear more democratic before the eyes of the world, finally resulted in the passage of the Nineteenth Amendment to the U.S. Constitution in 1920. This gave women the right to vote, thereby enfranchising twenty-six million females of voting age within America for the very first time. Interestingly enough in terms of the relationship between human rights and home and human rights abroad, the National American Woman Suffrage Association used its remaining funds after the passage of this amendment to aid suffrage organizations in other countries.[57]

Advances in women's rights were paralleled, if not exceeded, in the area of economic and social rights. The growing number of problems associated with rapid industrialization and urbanization spawned a growing concern for social justice and led to the development of the first nationwide reform movement of the modern era: Progressivism. This movement—or, more accurately, movements—took many forms, but all were designed to alleviate the suffering of the poor and the exploited. A number of activists drew upon their anger and moral indignation over the dangers of untrammeled capitalism and political corruption exposed in books such as Robert Hunter's *Poverty*, Lincoln Steffens's *The Shame of the Cities*, and David Graham Phillips's *The Treason of the Senate*; in novels like Frank Norris's *The Octopus* and Upton Sinclair's *The Jungle*; and in the troubling and provocative photographs of Lewis Hine revealing exhausted children exploited in factories and mines. Others were motivated to take action by their religious beliefs, the momentum of the Social Gospel, and the message from highly influential books like *Christianity and the Social Crisis* in 1907 and *Christianity and the Social Order* in 1912 written by Walter Rauschenbush, a young minister from the Hell's Kitchen area of New York City. Still others found themselves inspired by the successful examples of advancing economic and social rights in the industrialized nations of Western Europe which were leading the way in passing legislation providing for old-age pensions and health and unemployment insurance, and wanted to bring these benefits home to America as well.

These and other motives worked in combination to move Progressives to take action in a number of different areas. Some labored to create organizations that would meet the needs of working women, such the International Ladies' Garment Workers' Union (ILGWU) founded in 1900 and the Women's Trade Union League in 1903. Other activists focused their efforts on the plight of exploited children and formed the National Child Labor Committee that successfully lobbied to enact legislation that regulated child labor by restricting the hours of work and establishing safer working conditions, governing compulsory education, and creating the Children's Bureau within the Department of Labor. Many reformers worked at the local, state, and national levels to establish better public housing and health care, create more educational opportunities for the disadvantaged, and institute unemployment insurance and workers' compensation. In addition, they helped to enact progressive tax and municipal reform and regulations to govern some of the most egregious and exploitative excesses of the largest corporations and railroads, banks, food processors, and drug manufacturers in ways that dramatically impacted American society.

The experience of World War I greatly affected efforts to advance economic and social rights, both by denying them in the name of wartime exigency and by enhancing them in the name of buttressing the "home front." The most innovative development, however, and the one in which America assumed the leadership position and made the most significant contribution, occurred in the area of humanitarian relief. No war in history up to this point had ever produced such staggering levels of civilian deaths, refugees pouring across borders, and human suffering caused by armed combat and naval blockades. The extent of the wounded, the starving, the homeless, the sick, and the dislocated and destitute simply overwhelmed the capacities of every existing private charity or relief organization. Moreover, no government fighting for its own survival during wartime possessed the resources to adequately deal with its own victims, let alone those of other countries.

Rather than falling victim to either apathy or despair over this catastrophe, a number of Americans determined to step into this breach and offer assistance to those abroad whom they regarded as having a human right to life, food, and care. Under the direction of Herbert Hoover, a businessman of Quaker background, they created the innovative Commission for Relief in Belgium. This body engaged in the monumental task of coordinating the work of five thousand separate volunteer committees in raising funds, cajoling national governments, fighting bureaucrats, collecting food and necessities from around the world, getting supplies through war zones and across belligerent frontiers, and then distributing them to those in desperate need. During the course of the war they distributed an estimated five million tons of food and expended one billion dollars in loans and private donations. Nearly four million signatures appeared on letters and scrolls sent directly to Hoover from grateful recipients of this relief.[58] In the end, this effort not only saved the lives of several million people but also contributed heavily to the development of a mechanism for the administration of international humanitarian relief and to a sense of responsibility to the human rights of those who suffer, irrespective of national borders.

Other efforts to advance human rights in the early twentieth century focused upon a particularly difficult problem for America: race. Although slavery had ended after the Civil War, racism and racial prejudice most certainly did not. In fact, the language about race intensified with widely repeated expressions about "superior whites," the "backward colored races," "inferior blacks," "savage reds," "ignorant browns," the "yellow peril," "racial purity," and possible "racial wars."[59] Always alert to the international aspects of this problem, and to the interconnectedness of America and the broader world, the talented intellectual and activist W. E. B. Du Bois issued his much-quoted prediction during the first Pan-African Congress in 1900 that "the problem of the twentieth century [will be] the problem of the color line—the relation of the darker to the lighter races of men in Asia and Africa, in America and the islands of the sea."[60] Horrified by the continuing practices of lynching and segregation, angry over the fact that racial minorities often found themselves excluded from many of the benefits of Progressivism, and frustrated over the lack of any progress toward racial equality, Du Bois joined with other activists like Mary White Ovington and Ida Wells-Barnett in 1909 to organize one of the most influential human rights NGOs within the United States, the National Association for the Advancement of Colored People (NAACP). On the occasion of its formation, Du Bois loudly and forcefully declared, "We will not be satisfied to take one jot or tittle less than our full manhood rights. We claim for ourselves every single right that belongs to a freeborn American, political, civil, and social, and until we get these rights we will never cease to protest and assail the ears of America . . . It is a fight for ideals, lest this, our common fatherland, false to its founding, become in truth the land of the thief and the home of the slave—a byword and a hissing among the nations for its sounding pretensions and pitiful accomplishment."[61]

During World War I, Du Bois and many others in the NAACP were willing to "close ranks" for the sake of military victory. They hoped that their contributions for the war effort would be rewarded and desperately wanted to believe President Woodrow Wilson when he proclaimed that America "puts human rights above all other rights" and that it was fighting for liberty, self-determination, and equality in order "to make the world safe for democracy."[62] But their hopes proved to be short-lived. When Wilson represented the United States at the Paris Peace Conference in 1919, they watched in astonishment and anger as he supported self-determination, democracy, and the protection of minorities in the treaties for Europe—but not among blacks or indigenous peoples in colonial possessions or in America. Indeed, he personally and publicly rejected the principle of racial equality as it was proposed for the Covenant of the League of Nations, even though a majority of other delegates supported it.[63] After all of the sacrifices and the contributions of black soldiers during the war, Du Bois felt overwhelmingly betrayed. "We stand again to look America squarely in the face," he thundered. "We *return*. We *return from fighting*. We *return fighting*. Make way for Democracy! We saved it in France, and by the Great Jehovah, we will save it in the U.S.A. or know the reason why!"[64]

Such determined and forceful statements gave encouragement to those who campaigned on behalf of human rights in America, but among others they provoked strong reactions in the opposite direction. The white-hooded and racist Ku Klux Klan, for example, increased in membership and vowed that they would never allow these demands for racial equality to ever be realized. The summer of 1919 thus saw a whole series of lynchings, cross burnings, floggings, and personal attacks, some of which occurred against blacks in military uniform. These, in turn, provoked violent race riots in Chicago, Knoxville, Omaha, and even the capital of Washington, D.C., among other cities, necessitating the use of police, troops from the Army, and members of the National Guard to quell what some described as nothing short of a "race war."[65] All this, writes the leading historian of race relations in America, John Hope Franklin, "ushered in the greatest period of interracial strife the nation had ever witnessed." Moreover, he tellingly observes, the racial violence was not confined to any particular section of the country, but occurred in the North, South, East, and West—"wherever whites and blacks undertook the task of living together."[66]

America not only failed to address the issue of race in human rights at the end of the war, but also refused to participate in the development of what would eventually become international criminal law. In preparation for what they hoped would be a period of peace and the rule of law, for example, a special Commission on the Responsibilities of the Authors of the War and Enforcement of Penalties composed of fifteen distinguished international lawyers from ten different countries issued their final report. Here they declared that "there is no reason why rank, however exalted, should in any circumstances protect the holder of it from responsibility when that responsibility has been established before a properly constituted tribunal. This extends even to heads of states. . . . If the immunity of a sovereign is claimed . . . it would involve laying down the principle that the greatest outrages against the laws and customs of war and the laws of humanity, if proved against him, could in no circumstances be punished. Such a conclusion would shock the conscience of civilized mankind."[67]

Their recommendation that an international criminal tribunal be created for this purpose, however, proved to be too radical for some. The United States, in particular, firmly resisted establishing any such tribunal or holding individual leaders personally responsible for their actions as setting a dangerous precedent that would inflict irreparable damage to their national sovereignty. Secretary of State Robert Lansing, in fact, issued a formal dissent and announced that he had no intention at all of ever bringing this matter of human rights home to America. "The essence of sovereignty," he declared in blunt and revealing language, "is the absence of responsibility."[68]

Continuing the Mixed Legacy Between Two Wars and Beyond

As America attempted to move beyond the experience of World War I and enter the period of what it hoped would be peace, there were signs of both hope and despair for human rights. Some advances during the first two decades of the twentieth century had marked major turning points in the history of the United States and would benefit generations to come, and many activists vowed that they would use these new years of peace to continue their efforts on behalf of human rights. On the other hand, the energy and sense of progress on behalf of human rights in certain areas had been weakened by the war. The desire to stimulate patriotic unity during wartime, for example, greatly exacerbated the desire to stamp out dissent or any other activities deemed to be "un-American" by creating such legislation as the 1917 Alien Act and the notorious 1918 Sedition Act which effectively suspended any number of provisions in the Bill of Rights in their abuse of civil rights. It was not known whether these would continue after the conclusion of the war or not. Moreover, continuing postwar political and economic turmoil at home and abroad generated fear, distrust, confusion, and even further intolerance. Many Americans turned against blacks, Catholics, foreigners, Bolsheviks, and others whom they regarded as radicals, as evident in the 1920s by the growth of superpatriotic societies and the Ku Klux Klan, raids against presumed communists, highly restrictive immigration laws specifically designed to bar Asians, and the highly publicized Sacco and Vanzetti case involving the trial and execution of two Italian anarchists.

The international criticism resulting from these events and developments, of course, was widely resented by many Americans who regarded it as outside interference in their own domestic affairs. As such, it once again raised the difficult issue of the relationship between human rights at home and human rights abroad. Should human rights within the United States be influenced by or tied in any way to efforts, institutions, or standards initiated and developed overseas or not? Many activists within America answered in the affirmative, wanting to engage in transnational networks and to participate in external international organizations in such a way as to frame the broader discussion about human rights, share ideas and methods of advocacy, encourage activism, and thereby bring home concrete changes.[69] But during the interwar years they represented a distinct minority.

The United States during this period by and large retreated into isolationism and turned its back on transnational and international efforts to advance human rights. This was seen in a number of areas but made particularly dramatic in the case of the League of Nations. Although the creation of this international organization had been championed by Woodrow Wilson, America refused to join in membership. As a consequence, it not only removed itself from many of the highly innovative and creative efforts of the League to protect human rights, but at times actually worked to oppose them. These included standards and

mechanisms designed to protect the rights of labor, religious and ethnic minorities, indigenous peoples, women and children, refugees, and
prisoners, as well as developing minimum standards of health care and
creating the Permanent Court of International Justice.[70] The speeches
in the U.S. Congress revealed instead an intense determination to reject
participation in such developments. Senator James Reed of Missouri, for
example, gave voice in unmistakable and uncompromising language to
what he regarded as the most serious problem: "Think of submitting
questions involving the very life of the United States to a tribunal on
which a nigger from Liberia, a nigger from Honduras, a nigger from
India . . . each have votes equal to that of the great United States."[71] His
colleague Henry Cabot Lodge, who led the fight for isolationism, declared bluntly, "We do not want a narrow alley of escape from jurisdiction of the League. We want to prevent any jurisdiction whatever."[72]

Only when disaster struck were the majority of Americans seriously
willing to take a new look at matters of human rights again. The outbreak
of the Great Depression in 1929 plunged the country and then much of
the industrialized world into a catastrophe of monumental proportions.
Economic collapse and its attendant factory closures, bank failures, fore-
closures, evictions and homelessness, unemployment, starvation, hardship, and dislocation all led to an acute focus on economic and social
rights. A number of radicals turned to communism and sought solutions
through violence and revolution in class struggle or to socialism and
the intense organization of discontented workers and calls for general
strikes and militant action. But most Americans were more moderate and
turned instead to religious and charitable organizations, to established
labor unions, and now especially significant, to government as the most
important means of securing rights to some basic level of food, housing,
employment, and medical care, among other necessities for life.

In this regard, the election of Franklin Roosevelt to the presidency in
1932 signaled the beginning of a dramatic transformation of the role
of the federal government in American history. Roosevelt, administration members like Francis Perkins, who had been deeply involved with
the settlement house movement and became the first woman ever appointed to a cabinet post, advisors like Harry Hopkins, who had been a
social worker, and Roosevelt's wife Eleanor, who was outspoken on the
rights of women, racial minorities, and the poor (and who would go on
to join the Board of Directors of the NAACP and to play a critical role
in the creation of the Universal Declaration of Human Rights) launched
what was called the New Deal. The first phase sought to address the immediate problems of recovery from the Depression and relief for the
poor and the unemployed, as indicated by the creation of the Federal
Emergency Relief Administration (FERA) to appropriate grants to cities

and states, the Civilian Conservation Corps (CCC) and the Public Works Administration (PWA) to provide employment and stimulate business activity, among a number of other new programs. The second phase attempted to address larger issues of social reform and social justice, as evident with the landmark Social Security Act of 1935 establishing unemployment compensation and old-age and survivor's insurance, aid to dependent children, and assistance for the care of the crippled and the blind. This was followed by the National Labor Relations Act (frequently described as "labor's bill of rights")[73] of the same year recognizing labor's right to organize and bargain collectively, the National Housing Act of 1937 authorizing low-rent public housing projects for the poor, and the Fair Labor Standards Act of 1938 establishing a minimum wage and a maximum workweek.

At exactly the same time that these developments during the course of the Depression helped to focus the attention of Americans on human rights at home, a growing number of ominous international events increasingly directed their sight to human rights abroad. The seizing of power by Benito Mussolini in Italy, Adolf Hitler in Germany, Joseph Stalin in Russia, Francisco Franco in Spain, and military leaders in Japan all brought about dictatorships willing to seriously abuse human rights. These abuses occurred first against their own people, and then, in many cases, against others, as tragically evident with the Italian war against Ethiopia in 1935–36, the Japanese attacks against innocent civilians in China and the notoriously brutal Rape of Nanjing in 1937, and Hitler's invasion of Poland and the deliberate launching of World War II in 1939. As such, these developments increasingly suggested to a growing number of observers an extremely important insight about the interconnectedness of human rights in the world: that is, that nations who abuse the human rights of their own people at home are much more likely to abuse the human rights of others abroad and thereby be a threat to global peace and security.

A clear indication of precisely this point about the connection between the domestic and the international dimensions of human rights was revealed in Roosevelt's annual message to Congress in January 1941. It was at this time that he delivered his famous Four Freedoms speech asserting that he and America ought to seek the freedom of speech and expression, the freedom of worship, the freedom from want, and the freedom from fear not only at home but "everywhere in the world." "Freedom," he declared, "means the supremacy of human rights everywhere. Our support goes to those who struggle to gain those rights or keep them."[74] As the war expanded and escalated, Roosevelt believed that it was important to say even more about this theme of human rights, even though the United States was technically still a nonbelligerent. He wanted to delineate a sharp contrast between the democracies and their adversaries, to declare a purpose for allied endeavors, and to provide principles around which people could rally. Toward this end, he organized a meeting with British Prime Minister Winston Churchill in August 1941. The result was the Atlantic Charter, a declaration boldly asserting their commitment to seek a broad system of peace and security in the world by support- ing, among other objectives, "the right of all peoples to choose the form of government under which they will live," the right to have "improved labor standards, economic advancement, and social security" in all na- tions, and the right of all people to "live out their lives in freedom from want and fear."[75]

The words of this declaration about human rights provided immedi- ately inspiration to others across the globe (one of whom was a young black lawyer in South Africa by the name of Nelson Mandela), but they assumed even greater importance when, a few months later in December, the United States was attacked by the Japanese at Pearl Harbor and then entered the war as a formal belligerent. On January 1, 1942, it joined with twenty-five other nations (the number eventually became forty-six) in signing the Declaration by United Nations, pledging to devote their full resources to the war effort, to refrain from negotiating any separate armistices or peace agreements with their enemies, and to adhere to the principles of human rights enunciated in the Atlantic Charter. Here they promised to engage in the "common struggle against savage and brutal forces seeking to subjugate the world" and to secure "decent life, liberty, independence, and religious freedom" for all people. Moreover, and of particular importance in recognizing the connection between human rights at home and human rights abroad, they solemnly pledged them- selves "to preserve human rights and justice in their own lands as well as in other lands."[76]

What the United States, its allies, and other countries would actually do to fulfill these promises about human rights, of course, was unknown. Their immediate task was to mobilize a coalition and successfully fight and win a war. In this lengthy, complicated, arduous, and at times brutal process, massive violations of human rights would occur and no country or side would be immune from conducting abuses. While declaring its com- mitment to human rights at home and abroad and while finding many in the world looking to it for leadership, for example, America neverthe- less would imprison citizens of Japanese descent in internment camps, do nothing to stop lynching or eliminate racial segregation in its own society and armed forces, refuse to admit many Jewish refugees seeking shelter to its shores, insist on exercising its own prerogatives and national sovereignty in negotiations over postwar policy, and, in the end and like its adversaries, deliberately attack and kill large concentrations of innocent civilians.

But in 1942 when the Declaration by United Nations with its language of human rights was first signed, the war that would be called "The People's War" was just beginning for America.[77] Neither its leaders nor its people—nor the world—knew precisely what lay ahead or that they stood poised on the very threshold of what would soon become a veritable revolution in human rights. So many abuses would be inflicted, so many human lives would be taken in combat and in the genocide known as the Holocaust, so much effort would be expended, and so many promises about human rights would be made during the course of the war that it was highly unlikely that people would ever go back to where the status of human rights had been prior to the outbreak of hostilities. In addition, the experience of the war often exposed the hypocrisy of the democracies, especially the United States, whose claims about honoring human rights did not always ring true, and thus forced serious self-reflection upon the nation. How could the country oppose the racism of the Nazis and the fascists, asked Gunnar Myrdal again and again as he compared America at home with America abroad for his monumental wartime study titled *An American Dilemma: The Negro Problem and Modern Democracy*, and yet support racist policies so vociferously at home?[78] "The defense of democracy against the forces that threaten it from without," acknowledged Wendell Willkie, the titular head of the Republican Party, in a remarkably revealing wartime message, "has made some of its failures to function at home glaringly apparent. Our very proclamations of what we are fighting for have rendered our own inequities self-evident. When we talk of freedom and opportunity for all nations the mocking paradoxes in our own society become so clear they can no longer be ignored."[79]

For all of these reasons, many individuals, NGOs, civic and religious organizations, groups of scholars, and public officials at home and abroad began to create what one observer described as a "vast movement of public opinion" that "spread and impressed the idea that the protection of human rights should be part of the war aims of the Allied Powers" and that, once the war was over, "the future peace would not be complete if it would not consecrate the principle of international protection of human rights in all States and if it would not guarantee this protection in an effective manner."[80]

*   *   *

The role that America, with all of the power and all of the prosperity that it possessed during and after the war, would play in this new and unfolding human rights revolution that would continue in the twentieth and twenty-first centuries was very much in question. This is not at all surprising. For those who had taken the time to examine American history up to this point through the lens of human rights, they would have seen a country whose practice did not always match its rhetoric and whose record was extremely mixed. There were times when the United States did serve as a leader, a powerful voice, and a significant contributor to human rights both at home and abroad. There were other times when it borrowed ideas and examples of human rights advances in other countries and sought to bring them home and apply them within the United States. There also were times when America was an ambivalent or even reluctant participant in human rights, begrudgingly signing agreements with reservations and derogation clauses or holding other countries to standards that it refused to apply to itself. Finally, there were times when America revealed itself as a determined opponent of human rights, rejecting both its own founding principles and newly emerging international norms and mechanisms. This mixed legacy of the past would be continued by America as it approached human rights at home and human rights abroad in the future that lay ahead.

Notes

1. John Winthrop, "A Model of Christian Charity" (1630), in Alan Heimert and Andrew Delbanco (eds.), *The Puritans in America: A Narrative Anthology* (Cambridge, Mass.: Harvard University Press, 1985), p. 91, and based upon the biblical text of Matthew 5:14–15.

2. Alfred Beveridge, "The March of the Flag," speech of September 16, 1898, in Alfred Beveridge, *The Meaning of the Times, and Other Speeches* (Indianapolis, Ind.: Bobbs-Merrill, 1908), pp. 47–57.

3. For more discussion of these broader developments, see Paul Gordon Lauren, *The Evolution of International Human Rights: Visions Seen* (Philadelphia: University of Pennsylvania Press, 2003); and Micheline Ishay, *The History of Human Rights* (Berkeley: University of California Press, 2004).

4. See Michael Ignatieff (ed.), *American Exceptionalism and Human Rights* (Princeton, N.J.: Princeton University Press, 2005).

5. For broad and stimulating discussions, see Michael Zuckert, *Natural Rights and the New Republicanism* (Princeton, N.J.: Princeton University Press, 1994); Samuel H. Beer, *To Make a Nation* (Cambridge, Mass.: Harvard University Press, 1993); Edmund S. Morgan, *Inventing the People: The Rise of Popular Sovereignty in England and America* (New York: Norton, 1988); Richard Tuck, *Natural Rights Theories: Their Origin and Development* (Cambridge: Cambridge University Press, 1979); and Henry May, *The Enlightenment in America* (New York: Oxford University Press, 1976).

6. John Locke, *Two Treatises of Government* (New York: Hafner Library of Classics, 1947), pp. 124, 128, 163.

7. Continental Congress, *Declaration and Resolves, October 14, 1774*, in United States, Continental Congress, *Journals of the Continental Congress, 1774–1789*, vol. 1 (Washington, D.C.: Government Printing Office, 1904–37), pp. 63–73.

8. "The Virginia Bill of Rights, 1776," in Benjamin Poore, *Federal and State*

Constitutions, . . . Colonial Charters, and Other Organic Laws, vol. 2 (New York: Franklin, 1972), pp. 1908–9.

9. Declaration of Independence, July 4, 1776, in John Garraty, *The American Nation,* vol. 2 (New York: HarperCollins, 1991), p. A-1. See also the discussion in Gary Wills, *Inventing America* (New York: Vintage, 1979).

10. Jack Rakove, *Declaring Rights* (Boston: Bedford Books, 1998); Lance Banning, *The Sacred Fire of Liberty* (Ithaca, N.Y.: Cornell University Press, 1995); and Robert Rutland, *The Birth of the Bill of Rights* (Chapel Hill: University of North Carolina Press, 1955).

11. James Madison, *Papers,* ed. William Hutchinson et al., vol. 9 (Chicago: University of Chicago Prcss, 1962–91), pp. 353–57.

12. For more discussion, see Lauren, *The Evolution of International Human Rights,* pp. 18–21; and Lynn Hunt (ed.), *The French Revolution and Human Rights* (Boston: Bedford Books, 1996).

13. See Neil Cogan (ed.), *The Complete Bill of Rights: The Drafts, Debates, Sources, and Origins* (New York: Oxford University Press, 1997).

14. See James MacGregor Burns and Stewart Burns, *A People's Charter: The Pursuit of Rights in America* (New York: Vintage, 1991), p. 61.

15. Thomas Jefferson to James Madison, December 20, 1787, in P. L. Ford (ed.), *The Writings of Thomas Jefferson,* vol. 4 (New York: Putnam, 1892–99), p. 477.

16. Among others, see Jan Lewis, "'Of Every Age, Sex, and Condition': The Representation of Women in the Constitution," *Journal of the Early American Republic* 15 (Fall 1995): 359–87.

17. Christopher Leslie Brown, *Moral Capital* (Chapel Hill: University of North Carolina Press, 2006), p. 105.

18. Patrick Henry to Robert Pleasants, January 18, 1773, as cited in *OAH Magazine of History* (Spring 1995): 40.

19. See David Brion Davis, *The Problem of Slavery in the Age of Revolution, 1770–1823* (Ithaca, N.Y.: Cornell University Press, 1975), pp. 213–54. See also Betty Fladeland, *Men and Brothers* (Urbana: University of Illinois Press, 1972).

20. See Adam Hochschild, *Bury the Chains* (Boston: Houghton Mifflin, 2005); and Seymour Drescher, *From Slavery to Freedom* (New York: New York University Press, 1999).

21. Thomas Jefferson, December 2, 1806, in James D. Richardson (ed.), *A Compilation of the Messages and Papers of the Presidents,* vol. 1 (Washington, D.C.: Government Printing Office, 1896–99), p. 408.

22. Act to Prohibit the Importation of Slaves, March 2, 1807, in United States, Congress, *Annals of Congress,* 9th Congress, 2nd Session (Washington, D.C.: Gales and Seaton, 1852), pp. 1266–70; and Act for the Prohibition of the Slave Trade, March 25, 1807, in Elizabeth Donnan (ed.), *Documents Illustrative of the History of the Slave Trade,* vol. 2 (Washington, D.C.: Carnegie Institution, 1930–35), pp. 659–69.

23. "Treaty of Peace and Amity," February 18, 1815, in United States, Department of State, *Treaties and Other International Agreements of the United States,* comp. C. Bevans, vol. 12 (Washington, D.C.: Government Printing Office, 1974), p. 47.

24. See Fladeland, *Men and Brothers,* pp. 257–58.

25. Alexis de Tocqueville, *Democracy in America,* trans. Henry Reeve, vol. 1 (New York: Schocken, 1961), pp. 393–95. For a more extended treatment of race, see Paul Gordon Lauren, *Power and Prejudice: The Politics and Diplomacy of Racial Discrimination* (San Francisco: HarperCollins/Westview, 1996).

26. Gustave de Beaumont, *Marie, or Slavery in the United States,* trans. Barbara Chapman (Stanford, Calif.: Stanford University Press, 1958), pp. 216, 73, 214, 230–31. For more discussion of the role of foreign observers on domestic human rights issues, see Paul Gordon Lauren, "Seen from the Outside: The International Perspective on America's Dilemma," in Brenda Gayle Plummer (ed.), *Window on Freedom* (Chapel Hill: University of North Carolina Press, 2003), pp. 21–43.

27. Dana Greene (ed.), *Lucretia Mott: Her Complete Speeches and Sermons* (New York: Edwin Mellen, 1980), p. 75.

28. Hochschild, *Bury the Chains,* pp. 352–53.

29. See Abigail Adams to John Adams, March 31, 1776, as cited in Diane Ravitch and Abigail Thernstrom (eds.), *The Democracy Reader* (New York: HarperCollins, 1992), p. 104; Mary Wollstonecraft, *A Vindication of the Rights of Woman* [1792] (New York: Norton, 1988); "Déclaration des droits de la femme et de la citoyenne, 1791," in Olympe de Gouges [Marie Gouze], *Œuvres* (Paris: Mercure de France 1986), pp. 99–112.

30. See Kathryn Kish Sklar and James Brewer Stewart (eds.), *Women's Rights and Transatlantic Slavery in the Era of Emancipation* (New Haven, Conn.: Yale University Press, 2007); and Kathryn Kish Sklar, *Women's Rights Emerges Within the Antislavery Movement, 1830–1870* (Boston: Bedford Books, 2000).

31. Abby Kelly Foster, as cited in Winthrop Jordan et al., *The United States* (Englewood Cliffs, N.J.: Prentice Hall, 1987), p. 267.

32. Angelina Grimké, as cited in Catherine Du Pre Lumpkin, *The Emancipation of Angelina Grimké* (Chapel Hill: University of North Carolina Press, 1974), p. 120.

33. Sarah Grimké, *Letters on the Equality of the Sexes and the Condition of Woman* (Boston: Knapp, 1838).

34. E. P. Hurlbut, *Essays on Human Rights* (New York: Greeley & McElrath, 1845).

35. As cited in Bonnie S. Anderson, *Joyous Greetings: The First International Women's Movement* (New York: Oxford University Press, 2000), p. 168.

36. "Declaration of Sentiments and Resolutions," Seneca Falls Convention of 1848, in Elizabeth Cady Stanton et al. (eds.), *History of Woman Suffrage,* vol. 1 (New York: Charles Mann, 1881), pp. 70–73.

37. Cited in Eleanor Flexner, *Century of Struggle* (Cambridge, Mass.: Belknap Press, 1975), p. 153.

38. Paulina Wright Davis, as cited in Anderson, *Joyous Greetings,* p. 2.

39. Rosa Geurra, as cited in Anthony Esler, *The Western World* (Upper Saddle River, N.J.: Prentice-Hall, 1997), p. 540.

40. Elizabeth Cady Stanton, as cited in Elisabeth Griffith, *In Her Own Right* (New York: Oxford University Press, 1984), p. 193.

41. See Ellen Carol DuBois, *Feminism and Suffrage: The Emergence of an Independent Women's Movement in America, 1848–1869* (Ithaca, N.Y.: Cornell University Press, 1978).

42. Elizabeth Cady Stanton, *Woman's Bible* (New York: European Publishing, 1895).

43. See Sklar, *Women's Rights Emerges Within the Antislavery Movement,* p. 68.

44. Wendell Phillips, as cited in Charles Madison, *Critics and Crusaders: A Century of American Protest* (New York: Ungar, 1959), p. 71. See also James Brewer Stewart, *Wendell Phillips* (Baton Rouge: Louisiana State University Press, 1986).

45. For an interesting discussion comparing the United States with other countries in the development of modern welfare, see Theda Skocpol, *Protecting Soldiers*

and Mothers: The Political Origins of Social Policy in the United States (Cambridge, Mass.: Belknap, 1992).

46. On social Darwinism, see Richard Hofstadter, *Social Darwinism in American Thought* (Boston: Beacon Press, 1992).

47. See Burns and Burns, *A People's Charter*, p. 227.

48. Henry George, *Progress and Poverty* (New York: Random House, 1938), p. 6, first published in 1879.

49. Charles Sheldon, *In His Steps* (New York: Hurst, 1897).

50. Pope Leo XII, *Rerum Novarum* [1891] (New York: Paulist Press, 1939).

51. For more discussion, see Michael Katz, *In the Shadow of the Poorhouse: A Social History of Welfare in America* (New York: Basic Books, 1996).

52. For further discussion, see Lauren, *The Evolution of International Human Rights*, pp. 71–72; and Paul Gordon Lauren, *Diplomats and Bureaucrats* (Stanford, Calif.: Hoover Institution Press, 1976), pp. 34–68.

53. Ligue des Droits de l'Homme, *Bulletin officiel*, as cited in Henri Sée, *Histoire de la Ligue des Droits de l'Homme* (Paris: Ligue des Droits de l'Homme, 1927), p. 11.

54. For further discussion, see Lauren, *The Evolution of International Human Rights*, pp. 78–80 and 86–87.

55. For a detailed world chronology, see www.ipu.org/wmn-e/suffrage.

56. As cited in Gary B. Nash et al., *The American People* (New York: HarperCollins, 1990), p. 772.

57. See Lee Ann Banaszak (ed.), *The U.S. Women's Movement in Global Perspective* (Lanham, Md.: Rowman & Littlefield, 2006), p. 21.

58. Based on the archival evidence in Hoover Institution Archives, Commission for Relief in Belgium, Boxes 1–11.

59. See Lauren, *Power and Prejudice*, pp. 50ff.

60. W. E. B. Du Bois, as cited in United Nations, Centre Against Apartheid, *International Tribute to W. E. B. DuBois* (New York: United Nations, 1982), p. 48.

61. W. E. B. Du Bois, in P. S. Foner (ed.), *W. E. B. DuBois Speaks: Speeches and Addresses* (New York: Pathfinder Press, 1970), pp. 170–71.

62. Woodrow Wilson, as cited in Norman Graebner, "Human Rights and Foreign Policy," in Kenneth Thompson (ed.), *The Moral Imperatives of Human Rights* (Lanham, Md.: University Press of America, 1980), p. 40.

63. For more discussion on this point, see Lauren, *Power and Prejudice*, pp. 82–107.

64. W. E. B. Du Bois, as cited in John Hope Franklin, *From Slavery to Freedom* (New York: Knopf, 1974), p. 335.

65. William Tuttle, Jr., "Views of a Negro During 'The Red Summer' of 1919," *Journal of Negro History* 51 (July 1966): 209–18.

66. Franklin, *From Slavery to Freedom*, p. 357.

67. Commission on the Responsibilities of the Authors of the War and Enforcement of Penalties, "Report," March 29, 1919, reprinted in *American Journal of International Law* 14 (1920): 95–154.

68. Robert Lansing, as cited in James Willis, *Prologue to Nuremberg* (Westport, Conn.: Greenwood, 1982), p. 74.

69. On this broader issue, see the thoughtful discussion in Margaret E. Keck and Kathryn Sikkink, *Activists Across Borders: Advocacy Networks in International Politics* (Ithaca, N.Y.: Cornell University Press, 1998).

70. For more discussion, see Lauren, *The Evolution of International Human Rights*, pp. 111–33.

71. James Reed, as cited in Ralph Stone, *The Irreconcilables* (Lexington: University Press of Kentucky, 1970), p. 88.

72. Henry Cabot Lodge, *The Senate and the League of Nations* (New York: Scribner's, 1925), p. 246.

73. Burns and Burns, *A People's Charter*, p. 250.

74. Franklin Roosevelt, Address of January 6, 1941, in Samuel Rosenman (ed.), *The Public Papers and Addresses of Franklin D. Roosevelt*, vol. 9 (New York: Random House, 1938–50), p. 672. For a discussion of the background to this speech, see "Five Freedoms Can Assure Peace, Says Roosevelt," *Daily Herald*, July 6, 1940.

75. The detailed documentation can be found in the Franklin Roosevelt Library, Franklin Roosevelt Papers, President's Secretary's File, Safe File, Box 1, File "Atlantic Charter (1)."

76. Declaration of the United Nations, January 1, 1942, in United States, Department of State, *Foreign Relations of the United States, 1942*, vol. 1 (Washington, D.C.: Government Printing Office, 1960), pp. 25–26.

77. Among many examples, see Angus Calder, *The People's War* (London: Panther, 1969).

78. His study eventually appeared as Gunnar Myrdal, *An American Dilemma: The Negro Problem and Modern Democracy*, 2 vols. (New York: Harper, 1944). See also Lauren, "Seen From the Outside: The International Perspective on America's Dilemma," in Plumber (ed.), *Window on Freedom*, pp. 21–43.

79. "Willkie Says War Liberates Negroes," *New York Times*, July 20, 1942.

80. René Brunet, *La Garantie Internationale des Droits de l'Homme* (Geneva: Grasset, 1947), pp. 93–94.

Chapter 2
FDR's Four Freedoms and Wartime Transformations in America's Discourse of Rights

Elizabeth Borgwardt

This chapter highlights 1940s-era transformations in the American discourse of rights. It seeks to complement the important contributions of Paul Gordon Lauren and Carol Anderson in particular by engaging in a discussion of 1930s antecedents. Major themes in this discussion include the international nature of rights talk in the 1940s; the importance of studying a "thin" or globalizing politics as well as offering localized, "thick" descriptions; the importance of nuance and qualification in the various definitions of "human rights" and "fundamental freedoms" to include voices advocating group rights or rights combined with duties; and finally, the use of rights talk as a vehicle for advocating decolonization in the 1940s and injecting an explicitly moral calculus into geopolitics.

Historical perspectives on human rights politics contribute to a larger, ongoing dialogue with activists, lawyers, sociologists, and political scientists. As the historian of ideas Kenneth Cmiel has reminded us, "historians of human rights can do much to further our understanding of global political discourse by not taking the term for granted, by carefully attending to its different uses, and by locating those uses in local, political contexts."[1] Such a deeply contextualized approach in turn anchors broader discussions of what we might learn from particular transformative moments in the past. This kind of expansive analysis helps us interrogate overly facile deployments of historical "lessons" even as it offers affirmative examples of a more capacious definition of the national interest—an approach that would define American values as incorporating ideas about human rights, however imperfectly realized in practice.

Rockwell Versus Roosevelt

Norman Rockwell was feeling rejected. Early in 1942, the well-known American illustrator was interested in making an artistic contribution to the Allied war effort. He hoped to go beyond the sentimental content of his World War I propaganda posters, with their images of well-scrubbed soldiers singing around the campfire. Rockwell hoped to paint something inspirational, ideally with an uplifting ideological message. "I wanted to do something bigger than a war poster," he later explained, in order to "make some statement about what the country was fighting for." Accordingly, Rockwell thought he might illustrate the principles of the August 1941 Atlantic Charter, a short Anglo-American statement of war and peace aims, "thinking that maybe it contained the idea I was looking for."[2]

But how to paint the ideas about self-determination, free trade, disarmament, and collective security articulated in the eight-point Roosevelt-Churchill Atlantic Charter? Rockwell eventually gave up. He noted in his autobiography that not only could he not *paint* the war and peace aims itemized in the Atlantic Charter; the 376-word document was so boring that he couldn't even bring himself to *read* it. "I hadn't been able to get beyond the first paragraph," he confessed. The artist then decided that although the ideas in the proclamation were doubtlessly very noble, he, Rockwell, was "not noble enough" to paint them. He concluded, matter-of-factly, "Besides, nobody I know was reading the [Atlantic Charter] proclamation either, despite all the fanfare and hullabaloo about it in the press and on the radio."

Nor were the Office of War Information officials whom Rockwell solicited particularly interested in employing the forty-eight-year-old illustrator, anyway. They were seeking someone younger and edgier for a 1942 war bond campaign. They insulted the notoriously thin-skinned artist by suggesting that his realistic style might better lend itself to illustrating a calisthenics manual.[3]

So what was a patriotic and publicity-hungry artist to do? Instead of illustrating an abstract international agreement, Rockwell went on to paint his famously homespun interpretation of a related initiative describing war and peace aims: a depiction of each of Roosevelt's Four Freedoms—freedom of speech and religion; and freedom from fear and want—a list drawn from FDR's State of the Union Address of January 1941.

Robert Westbrook's recent essay on Rockwell's contribution to the war effort favorably contrasts the illustrator's "salt-of-the-earth" rendition of the Four Freedoms, featuring scenes from the daily lives of the artist's Vermont neighbors, with the "brainy" and "dense" presentation of the Four Freedoms offered by the Roosevelt administration in a 1942 Office of War Information pamphlet. As Rockwell himself put it, "I'll express the ideas in simple, everyday scenes. . . . Take them out of the noble language of the [Four Freedoms] proclamation and put them in terms everybody can understand."[4]

Rockwell took the "thin" and universalist terms of the language from Roosevelt's Four Freedoms speech and "thickened" them by using a local, culturally specific idiom. Political theorist Benedict Anderson famously observed that it is easier to motivate citizens to fight and die for their country rather than for amorphous, transnational values or organizations such as Marxism, the Red Cross, or the United Nations. This phenomenon arguably continues to push expressions of personal loyalty and sacrifice toward a more and more local vernacular, where concrete images of home and hearth exert a more powerful grip than discussions of rights and ideas as symbols of "what we are fighting for."[5] Rockwell had reshaped the Four Freedoms vision into a format that was so culturally specific that his rendition was barely comprehensible even to many of America's anti-Axis allies. The artist noted that the starving and overrun European allies "sort of resented" the image of abundance in the "Freedom from Want" poster, for example, which featured a well-fed family eagerly anticipating consuming an enormous roast turkey.[6]

The major point of contrast between the Rockwell and Roosevelt visions of the Four Freedoms was the distance between a domestic and an international focus for U.S. war aims. While the text of Roosevelt's original Four Freedoms speech percussively highlighted the worldwide relevance of each "freedom," repeating the phrase "everywhere in the world" after each item to emphasize its universal application, Rockwell's Four Freedoms were an almost exclusively domestic affair, in both senses of that term. As the runaway success of Rockwell's vision soon suggested, it proved dramatically easier to sell "national goals which justify asking citizens to make the ultimate sacrifice" as a purely domestic, front-porch-style agenda.[7] Even the initial circulation of these images was privatized: Instead of creating his paintings as a government commission (as he had originally tried to do), Rockwell ended up selling them to his longtime client the *Saturday Evening Post.*

One result of the instant popularity of Rockwell's Four Freedoms series was that it was soon picked up by the Office of War Information anyway, as part of a war bond campaign. Repackaged as a series of posters adorning the walls of schools and other government buildings, Rockwell's Four Freedoms went on to become some of the most enduring images of the war years for many Americans on the home front. Other publicists and advertisers soon integrated references to the popular and recognizable Four Freedoms into portrayals of daily life, as a device for selling consumer goods by linking consumption to war aims. A 1943 advertisement for Wilson Sporting Goods equipment in *Life* magazine asked Americans to dedicate themselves "to the proposition that all men everywhere are entitled to Freedom from Fear, Freedom from Want, Freedom of Speech and Freedom of Worship. *But* let us also be a *Nation of athletes*—ever ready, if need be, to sustain our rights by the might of millions of physically fit sports-trained, freedom-loving Americans."[8]

There were other contrasts between the Roosevelt and Rockwell visions of this boiled-down set of war aims. Rockwell's rendition also neatly elided what might be called the "New Deal content" of the Four Freedoms, namely the way economic rights were mixed together with more traditional political and civil rights. Historian Lizabeth Cohen notes how "Rockwell depicted 'Freedom From Want' not as a worker with a job, nor as government beneficence protecting the hungry and homeless, but rather as a celebration of the plenitude that American families reaped through their participation in a mass consumer economy."[9] By setting his image of abundance in a private space—the family dining room— Rockwell avoided any implication that ensuring freedom from want was a governmental responsibility.

By contrast, the government-sanctioned message of the Four Freedoms posited "the foundation of a Global New Deal," in the words of historian Robert Westbrook, and implied a "reciprocal relationship" between state and citizen, where the state would be obliged "to provide and protect a minimal level of subsistence for the individuals who comprise it."[10] This mixing of political and economic provisions speaking with the sovereign voice of government was a New Deal–inspired phenomenon, and such provisions were stewed together in the terms of the 1941 Atlantic Charter, as well—the also-ran subject of Rockwell's wartime vision—which sketched a vision for the postwar world where "all the men in all the lands may live out their lives in freedom from fear and want." In a recent essay, the historian of ideas James Kloppenberg highlights "the gap between the privatized utopia of plenty portrayed in Norman Rockwell's rendition and Roosevelt's own more egalitarian conception of the Four Freedoms."[11]

The Genesis of FDR's Four Freedoms: Legacies of the Great Depression

This research traces the wider ideological and more immediate political origins of Franklin Roosevelt's famous Four Freedoms address of 1941, focusing on the evolution and transformation of the content of the phrase "freedom from fear and want." The resulting analysis attempts to recapture a human rights moment that is all but forgotten in many treatments of mid-twentieth-century America: before the advent of the full-blown

Cold War, when the ideologies of the mature New Deal were colliding with the politics of oncoming war, and when social and economic rights, along with more traditional civil and political rights, were widely touted as ideological weapons in an anti-Axis arsenal. For Americans in the early 1940s, the very concept of "security" had been reshaped by the broader impact of the Great Depression of the 1930s. America's Great Depression, as a national slice of a transnational phenomenon, shattered lives and often reshaped the worldview of those who experienced it. Over the course of a decade in which unemployment rates never fell below 14 percent, and often approached 50 percent in cities such as Detroit and Chicago, nearly half of all white families, and 90 percent of African American families, lived for some time in poverty. Even the marriage rate declined by almost one-fourth, as pessimistic young people faced an uncertain future.[12]

The American iteration of the Great Depression assumed a pivotal importance not only for the certainties it shattered and the improvisation and resourcefulness it called forth from so many individuals, but also for the scope and variety of institutional responses. As local charities and states with depleted coffers turned helplessly to Washington, it was federally sponsored programs that got the country moving again. The Works Progress Administration (WPA) employed some 8.5 million of the formerly jobless; the Civil Works Administration employed over 4 million; the Civilian Conservation Corps put 3 million more to work on forestry, flood control, and antierosion projects. The WPA and other programs had an impact far beyond the numbers of those directly employed: For example, over 30 million Americans saw the productions of the federal Theater Project, while the Federal Music Project sponsored over 200,000 performances by 15,000 musicians.[13]

Millions of Americans responded to the New Deal experiment with fervor. The White House received 450,000 letters during FDR's first week in office; seventy people were hired just to respond to the overwhelming volume of mail. President Hoover, by contrast, had managed with a lone mailroom employee during his entire tenure in office. Roosevelt had "altered the fundamental concept and its obligations to the governed," in the words of historian Isaiah Berlin, by initiating "a tradition of positive action." This tradition in turn fed new expectations that quickly ossified into perceived entitlements. Security for individuals—the dominant motif of the New Deal—would be permanently associated with "entitled benefits that only the federal government could confer."[14]

For policymakers, the lessons of the New Deal response to the Great Depression were twofold: first, that there was a connection between individual security and the stability and security of the wider polity; and second, that institutions of governance had "an affirmative responsibility" to help individuals achieve that security. After transborder armed conflict erupted in Europe in 1939, these lessons were readily extrapolated to the international level by Roosevelt's aides in the executive branch as well as by State, War, and Treasury Department planners, many of whom had served as New Deal administrators themselves.[15]

Roosevelt had mentioned an earlier version of the idea of a list of freedoms in a press conference on June 5, 1940, as a response to a question about how he might "write the next peace."[16] Originally framed in the negative, FDR had offered a checklist for "the elimination of four fears": "the fear in many countries that they cannot worship God in their own way"; "the fear of not being able to speak out"; "the fear of arms"; and "the fear of not being able to have normal economic and social relations with other nations."[17] The following month, another reporter's question elicited a list that added up to five protected qualities—freedom of information, religion, and expression, as well as freedom from fear and want—although the fifth one was in effect added by the questioner after the president had finished an initial tally:

Q [Mr. Harkness]:	Well, I had a fifth in mind which you might describe as "freedom from want"—free trade, opening up trade?
The President:	Yes, that is true. I had that in mind but forgot it. Freedom from want—in other words, the removal of certain barriers between nations, cultural in the first place and commercial in the second place. That is the fifth, very definitely.[18]

It is fascinating to trace the evolution of the content of the catchphrase "freedom from want" over the course of 1940–42. Freedom from want actually starts out as one of the labels for U.S. Secretary of State Cordell Hull's cherished reciprocal free trade agreements. By 1942 it stands in for a concept much closer to what we would now call a personal entitlement, with its internationalization as the key difference between the post–World War I and post–World War II vision of international order, at least for many U.S. wartime planners.

According to Roosevelt speechwriter Sam Rosenman, reports of contemporaneous debates over social welfare in Britain were a major source of inspiration for Roosevelt's evolving list of "fears" and "freedoms."[19] A clippings file that was maintained for the president on the general topic of an "economic bill of rights" and used for the preparation of the Four Freedoms speech contained a letter quoting *New York Post* columnist Samuel Grafton, whose book *All Out* had recently been published in Britain. The Grafton excerpt explained that "In September of 1940 the better sections of the English press began to debate the need for an 'economic bill of rights,' to defeat Hitlerism in the world forever by establishing minimum standards of housing, food, education, and medical care, along with free speech, free press and free worship."

Roosevelt's Four Freedoms speech file also contained a December 1940 clipping from the *New York Post*, quoting the joint proposals offered by Protestant and Catholic leaders in Britain, advocating

1. That extreme inequalities of wealth be abolished,
2. Full education for all children, regardless of class or race,
3. Protection for the family,
4. Restoration of a sense of divine vocation to daily work, and
5. Use of all the resources of the earth for the benefit of the whole human race.

These debates in Britain were part of a transatlantic surge of interest in the relationship of domestic social welfare provisions—individual security—to wider war and peace aims—international security.[20]

In Britain, these concerns about the economic contours of the postwar world found immediate political expression in 1941 with the commissioning of the extensive surveys underpinning the so-called Beveridge Report, which was not published until late 1942.[21] The Beveridge Report, a detailed proposal developed by the British economist and social welfare expert Sir William Beveridge, was "designed to abolish physical want" in Britain through social security programs, noting that "social security for the purpose of the Report is defined as maintenance of subsistence income."[22] When the Report was finally released, a year after the publication of the Atlantic Charter, it mentioned the charter explicitly and used the language of the Four Freedoms, as did the American and British press coverage analyzing it. The Beveridge Report was "put forward as a measure necessary to translate the words of the Atlantic Charter into deeds," concluded the Report's own official summary, which also explained that "Freedom from want cannot be forced on a democracy. . . . It must be won by them."[23]

American press coverage of the Beveridge Report referred to it as a British "blueprint for postwar New Deal," which would stand as "the first attempt to translate the four freedoms into fact" by giving life to "at least one of the rights specified in the Atlantic Charter—the right to live without hunger or destitution."[24] This use denotes a definite shift in the way Americans were deploying the phrase "freedom from want" from FDR's earlier articulation two years earlier, regarding the "fear of not being able to have normal economic and social relations with other nations." Linking individual security to international security was becoming a fresh way of framing U.S. national interests.

This nexus of ideas explicitly linking individual and international security had started to gain traction before 1941—examples would include the Philadelphia Conference of the Federal Council of the Churches of Christ in America, establishing the Commission to Study the Bases of a Just and Durable Peace, as well as Roosevelt's 1940 State of the Union Address of January 3, 1940 and Radio Address of January 19, 1940—but the logic of linkages between individual and international security did not receive wide attention in the United States until the 1941 Four Freedoms speech.[25] Part of the process of consolidating late Depression-era gains in individual security consisted in shifting the focus to continuing sources of insecurity, namely, the increasingly tense international scene after 1939.

Nor was this an especially American phenomenon: As of 1942, "[m]ore than sixty major statements on the nature of the postwar world have thus far been issued by religious groups in various countries," notes historian Lois Minsky, such as the much more radical Malvern Declaration of Church of England leaders from January 1941, which called for "removal of the stumbling block of private ownership of basic resources, urge[d] unemployment insurance, industrial democracy, equal educational opportunities for all, and the unification of Europe as a co-operative commonwealth." European social and labor movements in the 1930s, such as Leon Blum's French Socialist Party, called for a "social regime" to replace untrammeled individualism, while legal scholars such as Chile's Alejandro Alvarez called for an international bill of rights, and sociologists such as Emile Durkheim and Karl Mannheim called for increased social solidarity. Historian Kenneth Cmiel has left us an important unpublished essay about four "conscience liberals" who were all professionally active in the early 1940s, all of whom went on to make major contributions to the UN's Universal Declaration of Human Rights in 1948: China's Peng-chung Chang, Lebanon's Charles Malik, Panama's Ricardo Alfaro, and France's Jacques Maritain. All four theorized "security" in ways that included an important role for community, duty, and social bonds.[26]

By 1942 in the United States, such an expansion of the idea of security was taken for granted in Roosevelt administration policy statements and widely perceived to be one of the lessons of the Great Depression in an increasingly unsettled international environment. A September 1942 pamphlet from the National Resources Planning Board entitled "After the War—Toward Security: Freedom From Want" stated in its introductory note that its own postwar planning efforts were "designed to meet the challenge to our national security caused by lack or inadequacy of jobs or income." Explaining that "without social and economic security there can be no true guarantee of freedom," the agency asserted that these objectives are "indeed a fundamental part of national defense."[27]

Ideas about national security were expanding in the American domestic realm, as well. As a way of pressuring Roosevelt to sign an executive order prohibiting racial discrimination by defense contractors, labor leader A. Philip Randolph threatened a march of one hundred thousand African American workers on the White House in June 1941, while lawyer and activist Thurgood Marshall was urging that antilynching legislation should be "just as important as portions of the National Defense Program" for a nation that was "starved for military personnel, begging for factory workers, and striving for international credibility."[28]

The Four Freedoms, Atlantic Charter, and Britain's Beveridge Report were only three of the more visible crests in a transatlantic wave of advocacy generated by journalists, social welfare activists, academics, professionals, and church leaders as well as elected political leaders and bureaucrats in the early 1940s.[29] The editor of the London *Times*, Robert M. Barrington Ward, wrote an impassioned letter to Churchill in April 1942, proposing additional dramatic public declarations based on the Atlantic Charter: "The fundamental demand on the peace-makers," the editor explained, "from uncounted millions of mankind, will be for welfare and security. These twin aims sum up the essential purpose of the [Atlantic] Charter. They are aims which will more and more obliterate the distinctions once possible between domestic and foreign policy. The realization of the Charter can and must begin at home."[30] As part of a dialogue that crossed national boundaries, the broader policy context of the Four Freedoms and the Atlantic Charter highlights the reciprocal relationship between domestic and international politics, a still-underemphasized perspective in the study of foreign policy generally and in the study of the U.S. role in the world in particular.

An "Economic Bill of Rights"

Because of the way scholars commonly write about rights today, discussions of the Four Freedoms and the Atlantic Charter tend to separate the "political" from the "economic" provisions. Skipping ahead to the late 1940s, for instance, we can see how political rights—often known as "civil rights" during the interwar era and embodied, for example, in the U.S. Bill of Rights—had come to be anointed by U.S. analysts as essential fundamental freedoms defining the "free world" in opposition to its remaining totalitarian rival, the Soviet Union. By contrast, economic rights, such as a right to food, shelter, medical care, or employment, had by the early Cold War era come to be denigrated as initiatives that were not merely aspirational or utopian, but affirmatively un-American.[31]

Indeed, by 1949, former State Department official, Roosevelt speechwriter, Librarian of Congress, and unofficial poet laureate Archibald

MacLeish was warning that American politics operated "under a kind of upside-down Russian veto"—that is, whatever Moscow advocated must by definition be the opposite of the liberty-loving American approach.[32] Tainted by their association with the USSR, by the late 1940s economic, social, and cultural rights accordingly were being dismissed as anathema to free-enterprise visions of limited government.[33]

But such a polarization was not always the case, particularly at the historical moment in the early 1940s when the realities of oncoming war were colliding with the ideologies of the mature New Deal. For example, another section of Roosevelt's same 1941 Four Freedoms speech had spelled out FDR's ideas about the "basic things expected by our people of their political and economic systems."[34] Roosevelt's list, in turn, served as the basis for a more elaborate "Economic Bill of Rights" devised by the National Resources Planning Board and was widely reprinted as a pamphlet under the title *Our Freedoms and Rights*.[35] This Economic Bill of Rights was discussed by the Planning Board's vice-chair, University of Chicago professor Charles E. Merriam, in his 1941 Edwin Lawrence Godkin Lecture on Democracy at Harvard University. In this speech, Merriam outlined a list of "fundamentals which underlie a democratic program guaranteeing social justice":

For everyone equal access to minimum security as well as—to the adventures of civilization.
For everyone food, shelter, clothing, on an American minimum standard.
For everyone a job at a fair wage—if he is in the labor market—and a guaranty against joblessness.
For everyone a guaranty of protection against accident and disease.
For everyone a guaranteed education, adapted to his personality and the world in which he lives.
For everyone a guaranty of protection against old age.
For everyone an opportunity for recreation and the cultural activities appropriate to his time.[36]

This is an astonishing list! One measure of the extent to which our contemporary sensibilities have been shaped by later, Cold War–inspired shifts in the American political discourse of rights is the continuing power of such a New Deal–inspired catalogue to surprise us. In a commentary that could just as easily be about the Four Freedoms proclamation itself, Merriam explained:

There are two great objectives of democracies in the field of world relationships:

The security of a jural order of the world in which decisions are made on the basis of justice rather than violence.
The fullest development of the national resources of all nations and the fullest participation of all peoples in the gains of civilization.

Linking these two ideas together as a matter of public policy was arguably a New Deal–inspired contribution. Indeed, Roosevelt speechwriter Sam Rosenman referred to the 1941 Annual Message as a whole—which included articulations of innovative initiatives such as Lend Lease, the Four Freedoms, the Economic Bill of Rights—as the president's "renewed summation of the New Deal."[37] Part of what was new about it was its explicitly international focus, putting the New Deal on the path to becoming a war aim. Merriam framed his own speech with the hope that "[s]ome day it will dawn upon us that all the clauses in the Preamble to the Constitution are worth fighting for." He elaborated, "Justice was the first term in the [Constitution's] preamble and liberty the last, but between them came the general welfare, common defense, and domestic tranquility."[38]

Roosevelt's famous phrase that Dr. New Deal would have to give way to Dr. Win the War as the primary physician resuscitating the American body politic has led a number of historians to conclude that the New Deal had ended, or was winding down, under the impact of the war. An alternative framing would be to argue that the New Deal was transformed from a set of domestic programs into a war aim and infused with a new, explicitly human rights perspective as it was multilateralized by its reiterations in the Four Freedoms and Atlantic Charter.

As legal scholar Cass Sunstein observes, New Deal–infused commitments such as the Four Freedoms "came from a fusion of New Deal thinking in the early 1930s with the American response to World War II in the 1940s. The threat from Hitler and the Axis powers broadened the New Deal's commitment to security and strengthened the nation's appreciation of human vulnerability." In the early 1940s, a thinner and more rhetorical iteration of the New Deal was becoming nothing less than America's vision for the postwar world.[39]

Transformation and Reinvigoration of Human Rights Ideas

This chapter does not assert that "human rights" was somehow a new term born of World War II. A more precise formulation would be to argue that, as a figure of speech, "human rights" entered the lexicon of educated readers and influential commentators as a readily understood shorthand in the World War II era, both in the United States and internationally. More important, the term's meaning shifted as it entered general use.

Before the war, the phrase occasionally appeared as a somewhat disfavored variation of the much older locution, "rights of man."[40] In arguing that the basic conception of the rights of man first crystallized in the French revolutionary era, historian Lynn Hunt explains that such rights "require three interlocking qualities: rights must be natural (inherent in human beings); equal (the same for everyone); and universal (the same everywhere)." Even given this essential conceptual framework, however, up through the interwar era, the term "human rights" was seldom used in the United States. It appears occasionally as a synonym for what was then the narrower legal term "civil rights"—which in the interwar era in the United States usually meant controversies relating to the Bill of Rights or specialized fields such as labor rights.[41] By the end of World War II, however, the term "human rights" was serving as a caption for the so-called fundamental freedoms meant to differentiate the Allies from their totalitarian rivals.

Traditional civil rights such as freedom of speech and religion were a lesser, included subset of these fundamental freedoms, which drew on natural law concepts to paint a vision of what scholar of ethics and public affairs Paul Lauren calls "certain basic and inherent rights" to which all individuals were entitled "simply by virtue of being human."[42] For example, for the political theorist Hannah Arendt, the wartime encounter with totalitarianism "demonstrated that human dignity needs a new guarantee which can be found only in a new political principle, in a new law on earth, whose validity this time must comprehend the whole of humanity."[43] Legal scholar Richard Primus explains that what he calls a "resurgence of normative foundationalism" soon resulted in "a new vocabulary of 'human rights'" which linked wartime political commitments with "a broader idea rarely seen in the generation before the war but ascendant thereafter: that certain rights exist and must be respected regardless of the positive law." Lynn Hunt agrees that "human rights only become meaningful when they gain political content," and wartime America supplied the concrete political experiences to transform these much older ideas.[44]

While the precise measurement of such a sea change is necessarily inexact, one way of highlighting this shift in American political thought would be to examine the *New York Times Index* for the years 1936–56. In 1936, there is no "human rights" heading at all. In 1937, the term makes a tentative appearance with two articles, one on property rights and one on labor rights. By 1946, the term is listed as a separate heading, referring the reader to "civil rights," where there are approximately 150 articles we would recognize as addressing human rights–related topics. In 1956, the human rights heading is no longer cross-referenced to civil rights, but rather to a whole new conceptual universe, "freedom and human rights," under which heading there are over 600 articles.[45]

There is arguably something of a time lag for such an amorphous shift to be reflected in the index of a general-interest newspaper. Indeed, if there were a moment when the term acquired its modern meaning, a strong candidate would be the signing of the initial "Declaration by United Nations" on January 1, 1942. This document explicitly multi-lateralized the war aims of the August 1941 Atlantic Charter and was a product of the second major Churchill-Roosevelt summit, code-named Arcadia, held in mid-December 1941 to early January 1942. Immediately after the December 7 attack on Pearl Harbor, the prime minister proposed a Washington summit to formalize a "Grand Alliance" of Anglo-American military operations. In private at least, Churchill signaled that he no longer saw himself as the hopeful suitor in his relationship with the United States, commenting that "now that she is in the harem, we talk to her quite differently." (Churchill often used gendered or sexualized images not at all uncommon to his day. What is perhaps noteworthy about the prime minister's salty asides is the way they consistently tagged the United States and its leader with feminine imagery.)[46]

Churchill famously took up residence in the White House for fourteen days, keeping Roosevelt up all hours, charming the American press corps and Congress—and having a mild heart attack, kept secret due to its potential effect on Allied morale. In a widely acclaimed address to a joint session of Congress on December 26, 1941, the prime minister noted bluntly that "If we had kept together after the last war, if we had taken common measures for our safety, this renewal of the curse need never have fallen upon us." At the urging via cable of Deputy Prime Minister Clement Attlee, the two leaders agreed that, in order to emphasize "that this war is being waged for the freedom of the small nations as well as the great powers," their resulting statement of alliance should be broadened to include the twenty-six other nations then at war with the Axis.[47] FDR himself coined the term "United Nations" for this growing anti-Axis coalition: The president liked the way the term stressed common purpose and de-emphasized the military component.[48] (Churchill preferred "Grand Alliance.") Roosevelt was reportedly so taken with his choice of title that he interrupted Churchill's bath to tell the prime minister about it.[49]

In this January 1942 Declaration by United Nations, the twenty-six Allies began by affirming the "common program of purposes and principles . . . known as the Atlantic Charter." The United Nations coalition went on to assert that they were fighting to secure "decent life, liberty, independence, and religious freedom" as against the "savage and brutal forces seeking to subjugate the world." These nations pledged to cooperate in order "to preserve human rights and justice in their own lands as well as in other lands."[50]

The term "human rights" had been absent from the December 25 draft of the Declaration by United Nations. It was likely added in response to a memo from Harry Hopkins, who wrote that "another sentence should be added including a restatement of our aims for human freedom, justice, security, not only for the people in our own lands but for all the people of the world." He continued, "I think a good deal of care should be given to the exact words of this and I do not think the reference to the Atlantic Charter is adequate."[51]

Incorporating the Atlantic Charter by explicit reference, the final version of the Declaration by United Nations is the first multilateral statement of the four key elements of a new, anti-Axis reading of the term "human rights."[52] These four elements included (1) highlighting traditional political rights as core values; (2) incorporating a broader vision of so-called Four Freedoms rights, which included references to economic justice; (3) suggesting that the subjects of this vision included individuals as well as the more traditional unit of sovereign nation-states (by means of the Atlantic Charter phrase referencing "all the men in all the lands"); and finally, (4) emphasizing that these principles applied domestically as well as internationally.[53] This was a fresh formulation of a much older term, and all four of these elements continue to inform our modern conception of the term "human rights" today.[54]

There is, of course, a heartbreaking irony in the timing of the United Nations' ringing phrases, which were circulated worldwide during the same month in 1942 as the infamous Wannsee Conference was held among Nazi Germany's wartime leaders.[55] Again with bitter irony, January 1942 is also the very same month that federal officials decided forcibly to "relocate"—under what were effectively POW conditions—some 127,000 persons of Japanese ancestry in the continental United States, roughly two-thirds of whom were American citizens.[56] Such horrifying contrasts only emphasize why it is important continually to juxtapose discussions of words with an examination of lived realities. Reacting to the Declaration of the United Nations, Mohandas Gandhi wrote to Roosevelt in July 1942, "I venture to think that the Allied Declaration that the Allies are fighting to make the world safe for freedom of the individual and for democracy sounds hollow, so long as India, and for that matter, Africa are exploited by Great Britain, and America has the Negro problem in her own home." (Kenneth Cmiel reminds us that "Gandhi generally disliked rights-talk of all kinds, associating it with the self-indulgence of the modern age.")[57]

Gandhi's letter underscores how aware historical actors themselves often were of these yawning gaps between rhetoric and reality. In part, it is an awareness of such disjunctures—in the examples above, amounting to a cognitive dissonance so strong as to induce near vertigo—that may itself constitute an engine of historical change in its own right, precisely in order to narrow the gap. This dynamic may be described as a kind of feedback effect, induced by reading one's own press releases.[58]

This transformation of human rights as a label—from narrow and domestic ideas about civil rights to a broader and internationalized vision
of fundamental freedoms—is an unusually clear example of how a conceptual change may be reflected in a rhetorical shift.[59] In short, human
rights as a locution achieved what might be called a kind of "cultural
traction" in the United States during this era—a congruence with the
newly reshaped worldview not only of elite opinion makers, but also of
what was then a fairly recently identified demographic growing up between elite and mass opinion, a widening group of citizens known at the
time as "the attentive public."

The very demographic group designated as "the attentive public" had
itself changed composition considerably during the war. This heteroge-
neous group included people who occasionally read a "middlebrow" pe-
riodical such as *Reader's Digest* or the *Saturday Evening Post*, for example,
in addition to a daily metropolitan newspaper. Just a few percentage
points' increase in this group could consolidate the critical mass favoring an ever-broader construction of the Roosevelt administration's war
aims—a mass that was either absent or quiescent in the wake of World
War I. The very term "middlebrow" dates from the early 1940s, although
the cultural historian Joan Shelley Rubin traces its roots to the founding of the Book-of-the-Month Club and other developments in the late
1920s. Robert Westbrook describes America's World War II as "the first
American war to follow the consolidation of mass culture and social science," putting the formulators of U.S. policy in a position to act on the
systematic "investigation of the reflective life of less articulate men and
women," especially after the advent of scientific public opinion polling
in 1936.[60]

The infusion of these human rights ideas into traditional American
conceptions of the national interest resulted in something new under
the sun in mid-1940s America. The human rights ideas embedded in the
Four Freedoms and the Atlantic Charter—as well as in the 1942 Declaration of the United Nations, the document which further internationalized the Charter—had reshaped the concept of the national interest
by injecting an explicitly moral calculus. While international initiatives
infused with moralistic ideas were hardly a new development, now mobilized and mainstream constituencies were arguably paying attention and
reacting in a way they had not before. These vocal constituencies were
quick to shout about the betrayal of the "principles of the Atlantic Charter" when confronted with the cold realities of U.S. policies that ignored
British colonialism, strengthened status quo ideologies such as national
sovereignty, or facilitated racial segregation and repression.[61]

New Zealand Prime Minister Peter Fraser echoed many of America's
allies when he repeatedly invoked "the principles of the Atlantic Char-

ter" which "must be honoured because thousands have died for them." As he elaborated in a 1944 speech to the Canadian parliament linking the Atlantic Charter and the Four Freedoms, "Your boys, boys of New Zealand, South Africa, India, the United States and all the united nations have given their lives that the four freedoms—freedom of speech, freedom of religion, freedom from fear and freedom from want—may be established and the masses of the people given greater opportunities than ever before." He then warned, "Unless we strive to carry out those principles we shall be undoing in peace that has been won on the battlefield."[62]

Similarly, after an early four-power draft of the United Nations Charter was circulated in October 1944, one of the main objections by "smaller" countries not invited to these negotiations was the absence of an explicit discussion of a role for human rights, especially economic and social rights. Representatives of Australia and New Zealand met in Wellington in November 1944 and developed a joint proposal calling for a greater role for expanded provisions on economic and social rights; Poland and Denmark offered proposals to append the 1941 Atlantic Charter to the draft of the United Nations Charter; Norway wanted to append the 1942 "Declaration by United Nations," multilateralizing the Atlantic Charter and explicitly referencing human rights.[63]

Probably the most trenchant human rights–related critique of the draft world charter came from an assembly of nineteen Latin American nations convened at Chapultepec castle near Mexico City in February–March 1945, when Bolivia, Cuba, and Mexico sought to annex an international bill of rights to the UN's proposed "constitution." The delegation from Nicaragua admonished that "the peace and security of the world" now depended on "all nations, large and small, now adopting in their international relations . . . solid principles of equality and justice, of liberty and law," while the delegation from Cuba submitted an extensive "Declaration of the International Rights and Duties of the Individual" which the conference voted to append to the other suggestions to be forwarded to the inaugural San Francisco UN conference. Conference president Ezequiel Padilla, who had formerly served as Mexico's attorney general and as a revolutionary leader under Pancho Villa, explained that wartime solidarity needed to be converted "into a solidarity of peace; a solidarity that considers the poverty of the people, its social instability, its malnutrition."[64]

By the end of the war, the iconic status of the Four Freedoms and the Atlantic Charter had itself become a sort of "entangling alliance" in its own right, in the evocative image of historian Lloyd Gardner. Especially in the realm of social and economic rights, images of "war aims" and "what we are fighting for" contributed to both creating and raising expectations about the justice and legitimacy of any proposed postwar order, much to the inconvenience—and occasional annoyance—of the Allied officials charged with planning for a postwar world.[65]

Some Contemporary Resonances: Constructing a More Expansive Vision of the National Interest

In the wake of World War II, United States security became bound up with the collective security embodied by the United Nations system in a way that large groups of citizens as well as traditional policy elites could intuitively understand. In the words of a 1946 League of Women Voters pamphlet, "Even before this war had ended this nation had decided that singlehanded it could not ensure its own security, and that the only safety lay in working away from the old system of a world organized into intensely competitive nationalistic states working together for agreed-upon ends." American multilateralism became a way of using rules and institutions to entrench U.S. interests in the global arena beyond the war.[66]

This story suggests a correlation between multilateralism—solving problems in tandem with allies—and a globalized, integrated vision of human rights that would apply within national boundaries as well as across them. But in the contemporary world, the shadowy outline of a new and disturbing correlation has emerged on the international scene: an axis linking unilateralism with a *lack* of respect for human rights. Such a link has a certain intuitive traction; that decency itself might become a casualty of discarding what the U.S. Declaration of Independence calls "a decent respect for the opinion of mankind."[67]

Lack of comprehension of these dynamic processes of transformation may well be the pith of what is missing from contemporary neoconservative and "realist" analyses of international politics. Such approaches are too static. They tend to discount the processes for transformation that emerge through the workings of institutions, activism, ideas, education, and technology, and reactions to local or international events. The late-twentieth-century wave of what the international legal scholar Jonathan Greenberg calls "rule of law revolutions" in Eastern Europe, the Philippines, Chile, South Africa, South Korea, and Taiwan was a set of developments that realists' analyses completely failed to predict, for example. These revolutions drew much of their power from international human rights ideas and institutions. Astonishingly, they also unfolded without the cataclysmic violence one would have expected, given the entrenched regimes they overthrew or drastically modified. But no realist-dominated mode of inquiry has been able to explain this phenomenon.[68]

Equally important, standard realist approaches unrealistically discount the possibility of transformation in unwelcome directions, such as the creation of additional terrorists and the alienation of allies through poorly planned and incompetently executed unilateral interventions. A worldview that assumes that the pool of "evildoers" is fixed is just as erroneous as one which assumes that a good process is the same thing as a good result.

In 1941 the political scientist Harold Lasswell expressed his concern that as a democracy mobilized to fight its enemies, it might transform itself into a "garrison state." He feared the emergence of a technocratic dystopia where "the specialists on violence are the most powerful group in society," having usurped legislators and other representative groups who were merely "specialists on bargaining." In Hannah Arendt's iconic analysis of the origins of totalitarianism, the first, fatal step on this downward path was the advent of the device of "protective custody" for "undesirable elements . . . whose offenses could not be proved and who could not be sentenced by ordinary processes of law." Repression of traditional civil rights at home was combined with the creation of what Arendt called "a condition of complete rightslessness" in occupation zones abroad.[69]

Wartime political theorists also understood that the process of administering such a garrison state, at home and abroad, would have a transformative effect on individual citizens. The lawyer and sociologist David Riesman worried in 1942 that a kind of authoritarian politics might be possible even in America: "Like a flood," he wrote evocatively, such a collapse of democratic institutions "begins in general erosions of traditional beliefs, in the ideological dust storms of long ago, in little rivulets of lies, not caught by the authorized channels." The ends—order, elite control, and military mobilization—would somehow serve to justify the means— repression, squelching of civil liberties, and the sowing of suspicion among citizens.[70] In the twenty-first century, we are starting to see that transforming one's polity into an occupying power may have dramatic and deleterious effects on the people called upon to do the actual occupying. The cultural critic Susan Sontag examined how individuals take their moral cues from the system in which they are embedded. The U.S. torture scandal beginning in 2004 was "not an aberration," she explained, but rather "a direct consequence of the with-us-or-against-us doctrines of world struggle with which the [U.S.] administration has sought to change, change radically, the international stance of the United States and to recast many democratic institutions and prerogatives." Such an impact also translates transnationally: The international relations expert Rosemary Foot has recently noted how arrests under Malaysia's internal security act have spiked since September 11, 2001, as has internal repression against separatists in Indonesia, with officials in those countries justifying repressive measures against internal opponents explicitly on the basis of America's handling of its own detainees in the war on terror.[71]

Here again the human rights politics of the 1940s have something to tell us. Seeking a different kind of congruence between the internal and the external, Roosevelt in his Four Freedoms address explained that "just as our national policy in internal affairs has been based on a decent respect"—note the deliberate echo of the Declaration of Independence—"for the rights and dignity of all our fellow men within our gates, so our national policy in foreign affairs has been based upon a decent respect for the rights and dignity of all nations, large and small." While FDR's assessment may have been excessively optimistic, he captured a dynamic through which rhetoric may sometimes serve to reshape reality. Legally unenforceable ideals, such as those embodied in the Declaration of Independence or Atlantic Charter, might nevertheless serve "both as personal aspiration and as effective political fulcrum," in the words of legal scholar David Martin, offering an impetus for positive changes.

By contrast, cultivating a reputation as a bully who fails to show decent respect—who scorns the permission slip of multilateral legitimacy for interventionist policies—may turn out to be especially costly and ineffective when imprudently designed plans go awry. The veteran American journalist Walter Cronkite observed in the waning months of the formal U.S. occupation of Iraq that "in the appalling abuses at Abu Ghraib prison and the international outrage it has caused, we are reaping what we have so carelessly sown. In this and in so may other ways, our unilateralism and the arrogance that accompanies it have cost us dearly." Rather than "draining the swamp of terrorism," in the imagery of today's political strategists, such policies have instead drained the "gigantic reservoir of good will toward the American people"—the increasingly parched resource that Republican presidential candidate Wendell Willkie in the 1940s had termed "the biggest political fact of our time."[72]

This is not to say that rights are always trumps and that a free society can never take steps to protect itself, including bounded curtailments of liberties, as the political commentator Michael Ignatieff has recently argued. But Ignatieff also suggests that it is a significant blow to a free society—a win for the bad guys—when the very institutions underpinning a free society are reframed as a source of weakness. This dystopian narrative, the narrative of Lasswell's 1940s "garrison state," deflates the spacious concept of the national interest by disparaging and diminishing those very values and principles that other peoples might admire about the United States and even seek to emulate.[73]

Policy expert Joseph Nye has coined the term "soft power" for what he describes as "the ability to get what you want through attraction rather than coercion or payments. It arises from the attractiveness of a country's culture, political ideals, and policies." Nye's premier example of this phenomenon is "the impact of Franklin Roosevelt's Four Freedoms in Europe at the end of World War II," which he terms a classic instance of "when our policies are seen as legitimate in the eyes of others."[74] This analysis is even more pointed in an era in which human rights have once again become a vector for transformations in America's self-image and its role in the world.

Notes

1. Kenneth Cmiel, "Review Essay: The Recent History of Human Rights," *American Historical Review* 109(1) (2004): 117–35. The work of the late, great historian of ideas Kenneth Cmiel imbricates almost every point in this analysis, even though FDR's foreign policy per se is a topic that engaged Ken hardly at all. In purporting to summarize, consolidate, and modestly extend the growing field of human rights history, Cmiel basically invented it. The most important examples of his work in this field include "Review Essay: The Recent History of Human Rights"; "Human Rights, Freedom of Information, and the Origins of Third-World Solidarity," in Mark Philip Bradley and Patrice Petro (eds.), *Truth Claims: Representation and Human Rights* (New Brunswick, N.J.: Rutgers University Press, 2002), pp. 107–30; "The Emergence of Human Rights Politics in the United States," *Journal of American History* 86(3) (December 1999): 1231–50; and most heartbreakingly, the manuscript "The United Nations and Human Rights: Ambiguous Origins," tragically unfinished. The Department of History at the University of Iowa, where Cmiel was formerly chair, maintains a Web page from which many of his works may be downloaded free of charge and which also features clips of his readings and from his astonishing memorial service: www.uiowa.edu/~history/People/cmiel.html.

2. Atlantic Charter, August 12, 1941, telegram headed, in President Franklin Roosevelt's handwriting, "For delivery to press and radio at 0900 EST on Thursday August 14" and reprinted in Elizabeth Borgwardt, *A New Deal for the World: America's Vision for Human Rights* (Cambridge, Mass.: Belknap, 2005), pp. 303–4. This chapter expands on my discussion of Roosevelt's Four Freedoms address and the wartime transformation of American ideas about rights in *New Deal for the World*.

3. Norman Rockwell, *My Adventures as an Illustrator*, as told to Thomas Rockwell (New York: Doubleday, 1960), pp. 338–41; Stuart Murray and James McCabe, *Norman Rockwell's Four Freedoms* (New York: Gramercy Books, 1993), pp. 8, 37–38, 40; Atlantic Charter.

4. FDR, "Annual Message to Congress, Jan. 6, 1941," PPA 1940, p. 672; Office of War Information (OWI) pamphlet, n.a., "The United Nations Fight for the Four Freedoms: The Rights of All Men—Everywhere" (1942) (overseen and likely authored by Archibald MacLeish). See also the excellent discussion of the Four Freedoms paintings as depicting U.S. war aims in Robert B. Westbrook, "Fighting for the American Family: Private Interests and Political Obligation in World War II," in Richard Wightman Fox and T. J. Jackson Lears (eds.), *The Power of Culture: Critical Essays in American History* (Chicago: University of Chicago Press, 1993), pp. 194–221, and reprinted in Westbrook, *Why We Fought: Forging American Obligations in World War II* (Washington, D.C.: Smithsonian, 2004).

5. Benedict Anderson, *Imagined Communities: Reflections on the Origins and Spread of Nationalism*, rev. ed. (London: Verso, 1991), p. 10.

6. Rockwell, *Adventures*, p. 343.

7. Murray and McCabe, *Rockwell's Four Freedoms*, p. x. Indeed, the only reference to international affairs in Rockwell's Four Freedoms series is an oblique one: the partially obscured headline describing the bombing of London, in a newspaper held by a concerned and loving father, as he watches his children being safely tucked in bed. Westbrook, "Fighting for the American Family," p. 203.

8. *Life*, October 11, 1943, 73, emphasis in original. Rockwell's editor, Ben Hibbs, described the subsequent career of Rockwell's Four Freedoms paintings: "The result astonished us all," he wrote. "The pictures were published early in 1943 [in the *Saturday Evening Post*] . . . requests to reprint flooded in from other publications. Various Government agencies and private organizations made millions of reprints and distributed them not only in this country but all over the world. Those four pictures quickly became the best known and most appreciated paintings of that era. . . . Subsequently, the Treasury Department took the original paintings on a tour of the nation as the centerpiece of a Post art show—to sell war bonds. They were viewed by 1,222,000 people in 16 leading cities and were instrumental in selling $132,992,539 worth of bonds." Letter excerpted in Rockwell, *Adventures*, p. 343.

9. Lizabeth Cohen, *A Consumers' Republic: The Politics of Mass Consumption in Postwar America* (New York: Knopf, 2003), p. 56.

10. Westbrook, "Fighting for the American Family," p. 204. See also Cass R. Sunstein, *The Second Bill of Rights: FDR's Unfinished Revolution and Why We Need It More Than Ever* (New York: Basic, 2004), pp. 9–30.

11. See National Resources Planning Board, "After the War—Toward Security: Freedom From Want," September 1942, FDRPL, PSF, Postwar Planning, Introductory Note, 1, 8; FDR, "Annual Message to Congress, Jan. 6, 1941"; Atlantic Charter point six; James T. Kloppenberg, "Franklin D. Roosevelt, Visionary," review essay on Cass R. Sunstein, *The Second Bill of Rights* and on Borgwardt, *New Deal for the World* in *Reviews in American History*, p. 34 (December 2006), pp. 509–20.

12. U.S. Department of Commerce, "Historical Statistics of the United States, Colonial Times to 1970s"; Paul Webbink, "Unemployment in the United States, 1930–1940," *Papers and Proceedings of the American Economic Association* 30 (February 1941): 250.

13. Franklin D. Roosevelt, "Three Essentials for Unemployment Relief," March 21, 1933, PPA, pp. 80–81; Harry A. Hopkins, *Spending to Save: The Complete Story of Relief* (Seattle: University of Washington Press, 1972), pp. 114, 117, 120; William E. Leuchtenberg, *Franklin D. Roosevelt and the New Deal, 1932–1940* (New York: Harper & Row, 1963), p. 128.

14. Louis M. Howe, "The President's Mailbag," *American Magazine* (June 1934): 22; Leila A. Sussman, *Dear FDR: A Study of Political Letter-Writing* (Totowa, N.J.: Bedminister, 1963); Isaiah Berlin, "President Franklin Delano Roosevelt," reprinted in Berlin, *The Proper Study of Mankind: An Anthology of Essays,* ed. Henry Hardy and Roger Hausheer (New York: Farrar, Straus, and Giroux, 2000), p. 636; Michael Ignatieff, *Isaiah Berlin: A Life* (New York: Metropolitan Books, 1998), p. 132; David M. Kennedy, *Freedom from Fear: The American People in Depression and War* (New York: Oxford University Press, 1999), p. 27.

15. See Anne-Marie Burley (now Anne-Marie Slaughter), "Regulating the World: Multilateralism, International Law, and the Projection of the New Deal Regulatory State," in John G. Ruggie (ed.), *Multilateralism Matters: The Theory and*

Praxis of an Institutional Form (New York: Cambridge University Press, 1993), pp. 125, 126; Marquis Childs, *I Write from Washington* (New York: Harper, 1942), p. 23.

16. Franklin D. Roosevelt, "No. 649-A (June 5, 1940)," *Complete Presidential Press Conferences of Franklin D. Roosevelt* (New York: DaCapo, 1972), p. 498.

17. Ibid., p. 499. See also Laura Crowell, "The Building of the 'Four Freedoms' Speech," *Speech Monographs* 22 (1955): 268.

18. FDR, "No. 658 (July 5, 1940)," *Press Conferences*, pp. 18–22.

19. Samuel I. Rosenman, *Working with Roosevelt* (New York: Harper, 1952), pp. 263–64.

20. Samuel Grafton, *All Out: How Democracy Will Defend America, Based on the French Failure, the English Stand, and the American Program* (New York: Simon and Schuster, 1940), p. 60 (internal quotations omitted). Ickes' letter discussed in Rosenman, pp. 264–65. This proposal by religious leaders in Britain is also discussed in Louis Minsky, "Religious Groups and the Post-War World," *Contemporary Jewish Record* 5 (August 1942): 357–72. On the "economic bill of rights," see generally Sunstein, *The Second Bill of Rights*, pp. 9–30.

21. "Social Insurance and Allied Services, Report by Sir William Beveridge," Papers of William H. Beveridge (first Baron Beveridge), Archives of the London School of Economics and Political Science, Part 8, File 46, "Summary and Guide to [Beveridge] Report and Related Papers, 1941–44." See also Daniel T. Rodgers, *Atlantic Crossings: Social Politics in a Progressive Age* (Cambridge, Mass.: Belknap, 1998), especially his concluding chapter, "London, 1942."

22. Beveridge Report, "Summary and Guide," pp. 7–8.

23. Ibid., p. 8.

24. American Division, Ministry of Information, "Beveridge Report: American Survey" by cable from the British Press Service, New York, "Report of Friday, December 4, 1942," quoting the *Louisville Courier Journal* of December 3, 1942 and "Report of Saturday, December 5, 1942," quoting the *Atlanta Constitution* of December 3, 1942, in Beveridge Papers, Part 8, File 49, part 2.

25. PPA, 1940 vol., pp. 1, 53. See also Minsky, "Religious Groups," p. 362.

26. Minsky, "Religious Groups," p. 362; Special issue of the *Leiden Journal of International Law*, "Alejandro Alvarez and the Periphery," 19(4) (2006); Kenneth Cmiel, "An International Bill of Rights," unpublished essay.

27. National Resources Planning Board, "After the War—Toward Security: Freedom From Want," September 1942, FDRPL, PSF, Postwar Planning, Box 157, Introductory Note, pp. 1, 8.

28. Carol Anderson, *Eyes off the Prize: The United Nations and the African-American Struggle for Human Rights, 1944–1955* (New York: Cambridge University Press, 2003), pp. 11, 14. FDR signed the highly controversial Executive Order 8802, setting up the Fair Employment Practices Division, but declined to present antilynching legislation during the war; Randolph canceled the march on Washington.

29. On the British side, see, for example, Deputy Prime Minister Clement Attlee's speech notes for the International Labor Organization, November 16, 1941: "Undoubtedly the evils from which we are suffering today are to a large extent due to the economic conditions of the last two decades which by destroying the security of millions made them ready in despair to listen to the promises of gangster dictators"; Attlee speech notes, November 16, 1941, CHAR 20/23: 86, Churchill College Archives, where he also explains that the general text for his speech "must be Franklin D. Roosevelt's four freedoms and the clauses of the Atlantic Charter." Ibid., p. 87. See also Rodgers, *Atlantic Crossings*, pp. 485–501.

30. Robert M. Barrington-Ward to Churchill, April 14, 1942, CHAR 20/62: 9–10 (this letter with attached memo also mentions the not-yet-published Beveridge Report).

31. For a vivid example of this winnowing out of economic rights in the late 1940s, see Stuart J. Little, "The Freedom Train: Citizenship and Postwar Political Culture, 1946–1949," *American Studies* 34 (1979): 35–67. One measure of the disfavor into which economic and social rights had fallen is indicated by the decision of the conservative, private-sector sponsors of the Freedom Train exhibition to cut the text of the Four Freedoms speech from the original list of exhibits proposed by the staff of the National Archives. The text of the Four Freedoms address was removed, along with the Wagner Act, because, as one of the consultants on the project wrote in private correspondence in 1946, "I think a great number of people in this country are sick and tired of many of the New Deal ideologies." Ibid., p. 48.

32. Archibald MacLeish quoted in Studs Terkel, *"The Good War": An Oral History of World War II* (New York: Pantheon Books, 1984), p. 13. MacLeish, in 1941 the Librarian of Congress and coeditor of one set of Felix Frankfurter's papers, had headed the State Department's Office of Facts and Figures, an agency created in October 1941. He was also occasionally called in to polish FDR's speeches. In June 1942 the OFF was folded into a new agency, the Office of War Information. MacLeish resigned in January 1943 under attack from Congress for acting as a "propagandist for Roosevelt and his policies." See Arthur M. Schlesinger Jr., *A Life in the 20th Century: Innocent Beginnings, 1917–1950* (Boston: Houghton Mifflin, 2000) especially chapter 14, "Blowup at OWI." See also Robert E. Sherwood, *Roosevelt and Hopkins: An Intimate History* (New York: Harper & Bros., 1948), p. 215.

33. See generally Les K. Adler and Thomas G. Patterson, "Red Fascism: The Merger of Nazi Germany and Soviet Russia in the American Image of Totalitarianism, 1930's–1950's," *American Historical Review* 75 (April 1970): 1046–48; Hannah Arendt, *Between Past and Future: Eight Exercises in Political Thought* (New York: Viking Press, 1968), pp. 149–58.

34. FDR, "Annual Message to the Congress, January 6, 1941," PPA 1940, p. 672. For additional background on the drafting of the speech, see Rosenman, *Working with Roosevelt*, pp. 262–65; and Crowell, "The Building of the 'Four Freedoms' Speech," pp. 266–83.

35. Charles E. Merriam, *On the Agenda of Democracy* (Cambridge, Mass.: Harvard University Press, 1941); National Resources Planning Board, "After the War— Toward Security: Freedom From Want," September 1942, in President's Secretary's File, Subject File: Postwar Planning, Box 157, FDRPL, especially pp. 19–28; National Resources Planning Board, National Resources Development: Report for 1942, p. 3, as discussed in Rosenman, *Working with Roosevelt*, pp. 53–54.

36. Merriam, *Agenda*, pp. 98–99. See also Merriam, "The National Resources Planning Board: A Chapter in the American Planning Experience," *American Political Science Review* 38 (December 1944): 1075, 1079.

37. Rosenman, *Working with Roosevelt*, p. 264.

38. Merriam, *Agenda*, pp. 9, 52–53, 78; Sunstein, *Second Bill of Rights*, p. 4.

39. Sunstein, *Second Bill of Rights*, p. 1. Kenneth Cmiel argues that "historians should set aside their preoccupation with 'thick descriptions' of culture and ponder the uses of 'thin' cultural messages in our mass-mediated world." Cmiel, "The Emergence of Human Rights Politics," p. 1233.

40. Lynn Hunt traces the term to philosophical debates in mid-eighteenth-

century France, which then took on a more concrete quality in the French revolutionary era. See generally, Hunt, *Inventing Human Rights: A History* (New York: W. W. Norton, 2007). For an excellent summary of the recent literature focusing on 1940s-era transformations in the politics of human rights ideas, see Cmiel, "Review Essay," p. 117, 129n35.

41. Hunt, *Inventing Human Rights*, p. 20. On civil rights, see, for example, Henry J. Abraham, *Freedom and the Court: Civil Rights and Liberties in the United States*, 5th ed. (Oxford: Oxford University Press, 1988); Geoffrey R. Stone, "Reflections on the First Amendment: The Evolution of the American Jurisprudence of Free Expression," *Proceedings of the American Philosophical Society* (September 1987): 131; Samuel Walker, *In Defense of American Liberties: A History of the ACLU*, 2nd ed. (Carbondale: Southern Illinois University Press, 1999).

42. See Paul G. Lauren, *The Evolution of International Human Rights: Visions Seen* (Philadelphia: University of Pennsylvania Press, 1998), p. 1.

43. Hannah Arendt, *The Origins of Totalitarianism* (New York: Schocken, 2004), p. xxvii.

44. Primus, *Language of Rights*, pp. 179, 178; Hunt, *Inventing Human Rights*, p. 21; see also Hersch Lauterpacht, "The International Protection of Human Rights," *Académie de Droit International de la Haye, 70 Recueil des Cours 1947* (I): 1–108. For a discussion of the links between this changing conception of the sources of international human rights and what historian Peter Novick calls "Holocaust consciousness," see chapter 8 in Borgwardt, *New Deal for the World*, on the Nuremberg Charter. Novick, *The Holocaust in American Life* (Boston: Houghton Mifflin, 1999).

45. These six hundred articles are only a partial listing: they are limited merely to articles pertaining to human rights in the United States. Additional human rights articles focusing on other countries may be found under the separate country headings.

46. Churchill quoted in Arthur Bryant, *The Turn of the Tide, 1939–1943* (London: Grafton, 1986), p. 282.

47. Attlee cable quoted in *Roosevelt and Hopkins*, p. 446.

48. John Milton Cooper traces the phrase "united nations" to a 1915 speech given by, of all people, Woodrow Wilson's nemesis, Senator Henry Cabot Lodge. This appears to be a coincidence—Lodge was not using the phrase as a caption for anything specific, but was speaking in a general way of the need for great power unity: "The great nations must be so united as to be able to say to any single country, you must not go to war, and they can only say that effectively when the country desiring war knows that the force which the united nations place behind peace is irresistible." Lodge, "Force and Peace," speech of June 9, 1915 in Henry Cabot Lodge, *War Addresses, 1915–1917* (Boston: Houghton Mifflin, 1917), as quoted in John Milton Cooper, Jr., *Breaking the Heart of the World: Woodrow Wilson and the Fight for the League of Nations* (Cambridge: Cambridge University Press, 2001), p. 12. It seems unlikely that Roosevelt would have known of this isolated reference.

49. Roosevelt's personal secretary Grace Tully reported seeing the president shortly after this alleged encounter and having FDR confide to her that the prime minister was "pink and white all over." Tully, *FDR My Boss*, p. 305. It seems to have been rather commonplace for Churchill to have visitors during his twice-daily baths.

50. Declaration of the United Nations, January 1, 1942, FRUS 1942, 1: 25–26; see also U.S. Department of State, *Cooperative War Effort: Declaration by United*

Nations, Washington, D.C., January 1, 1942, and *Declaration Known as the Atlantic Charter, August 14, 1941, US Department of State Publication 1732, Executive Agreement Series 236* (Washington, D.C.: U.S. GPO, 1942), p. 3. Forty-six countries ultimately adhered to this Declaration. Roosevelt himself insisted that India and other dominion countries sign as independent entities and not under Great Britain's signature. Roosevelt, Papers as President, PSF Safe File, Box 1, Atlantic Charter (1), FDRPL. On Roosevelt's coining the term "united nations," see Churchill, *The Grand Alliance* (Boston: Houghton Mifflin, 1953), pp. 575, 577.

51. *Roosevelt and Hopkins,* p. 448. The phrase "in their own lands as will [*sic*] as in other lands" was added by Roosevelt and appears in his own handwriting in an undated draft of the Declaration. Declaration of the United Nations draft, PSF, Box 1, Atlantic Charter (1), FDRPL.

52. The first unilateral example of such a statement was, arguably, the Four Freedoms speech itself.

53. While this definition is my own formulation, these elements may be extracted from the introductory sections of most basic texts on the history, law, or politics of human rights. See, for example, Lauren, *Visions Seen*; Henry J. Steiner and Philip Alston, *International Human Rights in Context: Law, Politics, and Morals,* 2nd ed. (Oxford: Clarendon Press, 2000); Richard Pierre Claude and B. H. Weston (eds.), *Human Rights in the World Community,* 2nd ed. (Philadelphia: University of Pennsylvania Press, 1992).

54. See, for example, Amartya Sen, "Elements of a Theory of Human Rights," *Philosophy & Public Affairs* 32(4) (2004): 315–56; Sebastiano Maffettone, "Universal Duty and Global Justice," paper presented to Global Justice Working Group, Freeman Spogli Institute for International Studies, Stanford University, December 2006 (available online at www.globaljustice.stanford.edu).

55. Wannsee is widely cited as the meeting where the decision was made to implement the genocide of European Jews known as the "Final Solution." See Richard Breitman, *The Architect of Genocide: Himmler and the Final Solution* (New York: Knopf, 1991); Ian Kershaw, "Improvised Genocide? The Emergence of the 'Final Solution' in the Warthegau," *Transactions of the Royal Historical Society,* 6th series, 2 (1992): 51–78, although more recent accounts suggest earlier decisions. See Christopher R. Browning, *The Origins of the Final Solution: The Evolution of Nazi Jewish Policy, September 1939–March 1942* (Lincoln: University of Nebraska Press, 2003), which notes that Himmler commissioned concentration camps with gas chambers for mass killings three months earlier, in October 1941.

56. See, for example, Greg Robinson, *By Order of the President: FDR and the Internment of Japanese Americans* (Cambridge, Mass.: Harvard University Press, 2001); Roger Daniels, *Prisoners Without Trial: Japanese Americans in World War II* (New York, 1993); Eugene V. Rostow, "The Japanese American Cases—A Disaster," *Yale Law Journal* 54 (1945): 489–533.

57. Gandhi to Roosevelt, July 1, 1942, FRUS, 1942 (1): 678–679; Cmiel, "Review Essay," p. 120.

58. For example, diplomatic historian Lloyd Gardner has observed that in FDR's press conferences, the president "often confronted his own rhetoric." Gardner, "The Atlantic Charter: Idea and Reality, 1942–1945," in Douglas Brinkley and David R. Facey-Crowther (eds.), *The Atlantic Charter, Franklin and Eleanor Roosevelt Institute Series on Diplomatic and Economic History* (New York: St. Martin's, 1994), p. 48. See generally Primus, *Language of Rights,* pp. 7–8; Jürgen Habermas, *Between Facts and Norms: Contributions to a Discourse Theory of Law and Democracy* (Cambridge, Mass.: MIT Press, 1996); William E. Forbath, "Habermas's Con-

stitution: A History, Guide and Critique," *Law & Social Inquiry* 23 (Fall 1998): 969–1016.

59. A similar shift, including the time lag, is mirrored in the more detailed and specialized *Index to Legal Periodicals* for this era. Volume 6, covering August 1940 to July 1943, does not list human rights as a topic heading, although a total of roughly 24 articles under both civil rights and international law headings address a human rights topic explicitly. The same is true for Volume 7 (August 1943 to July 1946), where approximately 46 articles deal directly with human rights. Human Rights has its own heading for the first time in Volume 8 (August 1946 to July 1949), cross-referenced to civil rights for all article listings, which now number 146 specifically on human rights, (including 40 with the term human rights in the title, up from none in 1940–43 and 2 in 1943–46).

60. Robert Westbrook, "Fighting for the American Family"; for a discussion of the concept of the attentive public, see Gabriel A. Almond, *The American People and Foreign Policy*, 2nd ed. (New York: Harcourt Brace, 1960), pp. 139–43, 150–52, 233; see also Eugene R. Wittkopf, *Faces of Internationalism: Public Opinion and American Foreign Policy* (Durham, N.C.: Duke University Press, 1990); William L. Rivers, *The Opinionmakers* (Boston: Beacon, 1965). On the idea of "middlebrow" culture in America, see Joan Shelley Rubin, "Between Culture and Consumption: The Meditations of the Middlebrow," in Fox and Lears (eds.), *Power of Culture*, pp. 162–91; Virginia Woolf, "Middlebrow," in Woolf, *The Death of the Moth* (New York: Harcourt Brace Jovanovich, 1974), pp. 180–84; Russell Lynes, "Highbrow, Lowbrow, Middlebrow," *Harper's*, February 1949, 19–48. On the measurement of U.S. public opinion, see William A. Lydgate, *What America Thinks* (New York: Thomas Y. Crowell, 1944); Sarah Igo, *The Averaged American: Surveys, Citizens and the Making of a Mass Public* (Cambridge, Mass.: Harvard University Press, 2007); and Susan Herbst, *Numbered Voices: How Opinion Polling Has Shaped American Politics* (Chicago: University of Chicago Press, 1993).

61. See, for example, the *Christian Century* editorial, "President Roosevelt Sabotages the Atlantic Charter," beginning, "He intended to undermine still further any moral authority which that much flouted declaration might retain." *Christian Century* 62 (January 3, 1945): 3–4; Horace R. Clayton, "That Charter: We Seem to be Reneging on the Principles of the Atlantic Charter," *Pittsburgh Courier*, November 28, 1942, p. 12, as cited in Penny M. Von Eschen, *Race Against Empire: Black Americans and Anticolonialism, 1937–1957* (Ithaca, N.Y.: Cornell University Press, 1997), p. 198n15. For a fascinating description of the international backlash against the disappointed hopes raised by the moralistic U.S. foreign policy of the Wilsonian era, see Erez Manela, *The Wilsonian Moment: Self-Determination and the International Origins of Anti-Colonial Nationalism* (New York: Oxford University Press, 2007).

62. New Zealand Prime Minister Peter Fraser addressing the Canadian Parliament, Friday, June 30, 1944, Debates, House of Commons, Session 1944, vol. 5 (Ottawa: Edmond Cloutier, 1945), p. 4424.

63. Edward R. Stettinius, Jr., Papers, "Dumbarton Oaks Diary," Albert and Shirley Small Special Collections Library, University of Virginia; British Commonwealth Conference, *Yearbook of the United Nations 1946–1947, Department of Public Information, United Nations* (Lake Success, N.Y., 1947), p. 10; United Nations Conference on International Organization: Selected Documents, Department of State Publication No. 2490 (Washington, D.C.: GPO, 1946), pp. 94–99; Division of International Organization Affairs, "Comments and Suggestions by Other Governments," undated, Harley Notter Papers, RG 59, Box 164, NARA;

telegram from U.S. Embassy in Norway to State Department, March 2, 1945, Notter Papers, Box 185; Division of International Organization Affairs, "Comments and Suggestions on the Dumbarton Oaks Proposals," March 28, 1944, Box 214, Notter Papers.

64. "Synopsis of Essential Observations Made by the Mexican Delegation on the Dumbarton Oaks Proposals," Inter-American Conference on Problems of War and Peace (Chapultepec Conference), February 25, 1945, Conference File, Papers of Leo Pasvolsky, LC; Editorial in El Universal (Mexico) February 28, 1945. The Conference of Chapultepec consisted of the members of the Pan-American Union minus Argentina, where the fascist-leaning government of General Edelmiro Farrell had seized power in 1944. On human rights–related provisions, see also "Resolution XXX of the Inter-American Conference on Problems of War and Peace" *State Department Bulletin* 12 (March 18, 1945): 449–50; Committee II, "An Account of the Essential Comments Made by the Delegates to the Inter-American Conference on Problems of War and Peace Concerning the Bases of Dumbarton Oaks," Records of the Office of UN Affairs, RG 59, Box 30, NARA; "Proposals of the Delegation of Cuba for the Declaration of the International Duties and Rights of the Individual," Notter Papers, RG 59, Box 23, NARA; U.S. Department of State, "Report of the Delegation of the United States of America to the Inter-American Conference on Problems of War and Peace" (Washington, D.C.: GPO, 1946).

65. Gardner, "The Atlantic Charter: Idea and Reality, 1942–1945," in Brinkley and Facey-Crowther (eds.), *Atlantic Charter*, pp. 45–81.

66. Slaughter, "Regulating the World"; Clark M. Eichelberger, *Organizing for Peace: A Personal History of the Founding of the United Nations* (New York: Harper & Row, 1977), p. 197; National League of Women Voters, "Memorandum: The United Nations: The Road Ahead," undated pamphlet but likely Fall 1945, Seeley Mudd Library, Princeton, pp. 3–4.

67. For an excellent discussion of the meaning of this phrase in the context of colonial and revolutionary American politics, see David Armitage, *The Declaration of Independence: A Global History* (Cambridge, Mass.: Harvard University Press, 2007).

68. Jonathan D. Greenberg, "Arendt and Weber on Law, Violence and the State," paper presented at the annual conference of the Law & Society Association, June 4, 2005, Las Vegas; see also Jonathan Schell, *The Unconquerable World: Power, Nonviolence, and the Will of the People* (New York: Metropolitan, 2003); Jonathan D. Greenberg, "Does Power Trump Law?" *Stanford Law Review* 55 (May 2003): 1789–1820; Hannah Arendt, *On Violence* (New York: Harcourt, Brace and World, 1970).

69. Harold D. Lasswell, "The Garrison State," *American Journal of Sociology* 46 (January 1941): 455–68; Hannah Arendt, *The Origins of Totalitarianism* (1948; New York: Schocken, 2004), pp. 568, 375.

70. David Riesman, "Civil Liberties in a Time of Transition," in Carl J. Friedrich and Edward S. Mason (eds.), *Public Policy* (Cambridge, Mass.: Harvard University Press, 1942), p. 96.

71. Susan Sontag, "The Photographs Are Us," *Sunday New York Times Magazine*, May 23, 2004, 25–29, 42; Judith Butler, "Indefinite Detention," in *Precarious Life: The Powers of Mourning and Violence* (London: Verso, 2004), p. 50; Rosemary Foot, "Changing the Script of Modern Statehood: U.S. Human Rights Policy in Asia Post 9/11," paper presented at the Rothermere American Institute, Conference on the United States and Global Human Rights, November 11–13, 2004. (Foot

discusses how Indonesian officials have set up a facility deliberately modeled on the extraterritorial features of the U.S. detention complex at Guantanamo, for the indefinite detention without recourse to proper legal process of separatist fighters from Aceh province.) See also the account by social psychologist Philip Zimbardo, designer of the famous Stanford Prison Experiment and expert witness at the court-martial of one of the Abu Ghraib guards, *The Lucifer Effect: Understanding How Good People Turn Evil* (New York: Random House, 2007).

72. "Permission slip" phrase from George W. Bush, State of the Union Address, January 20, 2004, available online at www.whitehouse.gov/news/releases/2004/01; Walter Cronkite in the *Seattle Post-Intelligencer*, May 20, 2004, as quoted in Lisa Hajjar, "Our Heart of Darkness," Amnesty International, Amnesty Now, Summer 2004; Lexington, "The Fear Myth," *Economist* (November 18, 2004); Wendell L. Willkie, *One World* (New York: Simon & Schuster, 1943), pp. 134, 137.

73. Ignatieff tries to "chart a middle course between a pure libertarian position which maintains that no violations of rights can ever be justified and a purely pragmatic position that judges antiterrorist measures solely by their effectiveness." He further asserts, however, that "actions which violate foundational commitments to justice and dignity—torture, illegal detention, unlawful assassination—should be beyond the pale." For Ignatieff, the key corrective measures are transparency and openness, especially "the process of adversarial review that decides these matters. When democrats disagree on substance, they need to agree on process, to keep democracy safe both from our enemies and from our own zeal." Michael Ignatieff, *The Lesser Evil: Political Ethics in an Age of Terror* (Princeton, N.J.: Princeton University Press, 2004), p. viii.

74. Joseph S. Nye, Jr., *Soft Power: The Means to Success in World Politics* (New York: Public Affairs, 2004), p. x; Ryan Goodman and Derek Jinks, "How to Influence States: Socialization and International Human Rights Law," *Duke Law Journal* 54 (December 2004): 621–703; see also Zbigniew Brzezinski, *The Choice: Global Domination or Global Leadership* (New York: Basic, 2004).

Chapter 3

A "Hollow Mockery": African Americans, White Supremacy, and the Development of Human Rights in the United States

Carol Anderson

Compelled to state the obvious, Walter White, executive secretary of the National Association for the Advancement of Colored People (NAACP), explained to several congressional leaders that "Democracy doesn't mean much to a man with an empty belly."[1] Although the context of that discussion was on human rights in the emerging nations, White (and the NAACP) had earlier grasped that that particular maxim was equally applicable to the United States. From the organization's long, hard years battling Jim Crow, the association realized that political and economic rights had to converge. One could not carry the heavy burden of equality all alone. The NAACP fully recognized, nonetheless, that most people of color had never even experienced political democracy. For millions of African Americans, the right to vote, to participate in civil society, to enjoy the freedoms associated with checks on government abuse, and to benefit from the protection of civil rights had become articles of faith, pillars of hope, and the ephemera of dreams, but certainly not the substance of reality. Indeed, much of black life in America focused on how systematically and completely those basic civil rights were repeatedly denied, ignored, and trampled on.

A new, major study, for example, focuses on the NAACP's almost hundred-year-long battle to integrate African Americans into the political life of the United States.[2] In the early years, the white primary, election-day terrorism, and the poll tax had eliminated generations from the voting booth. Historian Manfred Berg, therefore, notes that by the time of the 1942 congressional elections one report "estimated that . . . only 3 percent of the total population of the seven poll tax states had cast their ballots, compared to 25 percent in the rest of the nation." In fact "[m]ore votes were cast in Rhode Island, the smallest state in the Union with roughly seven hundred thousand residents and two representatives, than for all of the thirty-seven representatives of Alabama, Mississippi, Georgia, Virginia, and South Carolina, with a total population of more than 11 million."[3] Yet, as important as the right to vote was and is, the quest for equality would require more than simply ending disenfranchisement. As Walter White indicated, if black life was really going to be about life and not just survival, there was something beyond civil rights that had to be achieved.

The NAACP, the nation's largest, oldest, and most influential civil rights organization, had, therefore, slowly but surely begun to grasp the power and importance of economic rights in the struggle for equality.[4] The first glint came during the Great Depression. That economic meltdown had brought a horrific spike in the killing of black America as the number of lynchings and the degree of sadistic, spectacle violence increased. The Depression had also led to scores of impoverished black sharecroppers being driven off the land so that plantation owners could reap multimillion-dollar windfalls from the New Deal. And, while the overall unemployment rate in the United States was a crushing 25 percent, the jobless rate in the black community hovered well above 50 percent overall and in some cities lingered at a death-defying 80 percent. The right to vote, or any other civil right, was not going to solve this alone. Stark, raving abject poverty had black America buckling under the strain.[5]

The onset of World War II did little, initially, to ease this burden. While the United States' emergence as the "arsenal of democracy" finally gave most whites freedom from the economic devastation of the Great Depression, rampant discrimination in the defense industries and, frankly, throughout most sectors of the employment market kept African Americans locked out and locked down. More than half of the defense industries surveyed by the United States Employment Service, for example, "stated flatly that they would not" hire an African American for any position.[6]

Thus, as the United States prepared to destroy regimes championing Aryan and Japanese supremacy, economic and political oppression continued to converge like a vise on black life in America. From education, to medical care, to housing, to employment, to the court systems, even to the hallowed ground of the vote, there was no escaping the fact that there was, indeed, a "flagrant disparity" between the lofty rhetoric and the actual practice of American democracy. Presidential candidate Wendell Willkie would call it the "mocking paradoxes."[7] The Japanese government was even more blunt. The American people, Emperor Hirohito's regime declared, have "'run amuck' in an orgy of Jim Crowism."[8]

The killing of Cleo Wright, less than a month after the attack on Pearl Harbor, was painfully illustrative. In January 1942, while the United States was spelling out for the entire world its postwar human rights vision, Wright was lynched in Sikeston, Missouri. There was no question that he had brutally assaulted a white woman. There was also no doubt that, while resisting arrest, the black laborer had slashed a cavernous hole through half of a deputy's face. And it was, therefore, equally certain that Cleo Wright, staggering under the effects of "bad whiskey," had just committed the ultimate transgressions, especially for a black man in Jim Crow America, in an area of the country where African Americans barely earned fifty dollars a year, where nearly one hundred African American families, denied access to new public housing, stayed in tents year-round, and where other blacks "lived in cabins behind the northeast homes of wealthy whites, or in . . . alley quarters . . . 'unfit for human habitation.' "[9]

The attempted rape of a white woman and the knifing of a sheriff led to a blistering counterattack. When it was over, Wright, bloodied, pistol-whipped, and suffering from at least eight gunshot wounds, was taken to the only available medical facility in the area, a "whites only" hospital, where, with no painkillers, the doctor patched, stitched, and plugged up what he could. An overnight stay was, of course, out of the question. Bandaged and hovering near death, Wright was eventually packed off to the local jail. Although the end was a foregone conclusion, either through his numerous wounds or Missouri's criminal justice system, the "good folk" of Sikeston had concluded that a plain, old, run-of-the-mill death was not going to be enough. Black men may have accounted for nearly 90 percent of all executions in the United States for the offense of rape, but there were some lessons that no judge, no jury, and no hooded executioner could ever deliver.[10] The criminal justice system was just not fast enough or brutal enough to compensate for the fact that "[t]hese damn niggers are getting too smart," "too cocky," and were "just looking for a lynching."[11]

In the twilight hours, angry whites stormed the jail, overpowered the state troopers, pulled an unconscious Wright from his cell, hooked his bullet-riddled body to the bumper of a car, and set out for the black neighborhood. After trolling Sikeston's black district that Sunday morning with their macabre bumper ornament in tow, his lynchers cut Wright's mangled body from the car, soaked him in five gallons of gasoline, and lit a match. Wright, somehow miraculously still alive, let out an agonizing wail. In his last grasp for life, Wright's flame-whipped arms "reached skyward as if pleading for a mercy that did not come" while the thick putrid smoke from his roasting carcass poured through the windows of the packed local black church.[12] "This was," of course, "not a matter of executing justice." The point, as the lynchers made clear, was "to terrify the Negro population and to show them who was boss."[13] The lessons, however, were still not over. Although it was well known who, precisely, had participated in every phase of the lynching—from the storming of the jail to tossing the lit match on the black man's gasoline-soaked body—a "federal grand jury refused to return any indictments" because although the murderers "had denied Wright due process, . . . they had committed no federal offense since Wright was either already dead or dying."[14]

The black press erupted, "Remember Pearl Harbor . . . and Sikeston, Missouri."[15] The NAACP's report, while more restrained, was in its own way equally incendiary. This was war. Although the battle against the Axis powers was evident, there was an equally important battle to be fought at home. African Americans (and whomever their allies may be) were going to have to eliminate, root and branch, the economic and political conditions that had led to the killing of Cleo Wright and all of the thousands of Cleo Wrights that had gone before him. "[N]o change in legal procedure alone will solve the problem," the NAACP concluded. "Its roots are buried too deep in racial feeling and in our economic set-up. In southeast Missouri today Negroes . . . have never had an opportunity to develop beyond their position as serfs." In fact, because blacks "were imported to pick cotton," the report continued, there had been a concerted, conscious effort to ensure that they would have "little education and little earning power." The general fear was that "if they were educated they" might actually refuse to toil for pennies a day in the plantation owners' fields and, as a consequence, just "might be more troublesome." The NAACP's investigators concluded that it was the economic system that had left African Americans mercilessly exposed to the political and economic ravages of white supremacy. As a result, the association insisted, there was only one way out of this abyss. "The change from feudalism to a system whereby Negroes can earn enough to stand independently on their own, can only come . . . when the Negro reaches a point where he merits and receives respect as an independent individual with human rights."[16]

The association, in short, recognized that that horrible moment in Missouri—a lynching designed to terrorize and remind the economically depressed and politically vulnerable African American population of its "place" in the racial hierarchy; a "whites only" hospital that virtually ignored the medical needs of thousands of its residents; a readily identifiable black part of town that reflected the housing segregation, substandard education, and poverty wages that haunted African Americans; an all-white political power structure that fretted over the excessive violence of the lynching but was more concerned about maintaining a cheap, exploitable labor supply; and a judicial system that weighed guilt and innocence on racially rigged scales that denigrated black life and privileged whiteness—was but a microcosm of the human rights violations that had dogged African American communities for centuries. Cleo Wright was no aberration.[17]

That had to change. For the NAACP, the right to education was the wellspring of that change.[18] Education could broaden employment opportunities, provide access to better-paying jobs, create the wherewithal for quality housing, break the back of and expose the racist underpinnings of literacy tests, poll taxes, and other tools of disenfranchisement, and develop the healthcare system to meet the needs of millions who had little or no access to decent medical treatment.

That kind of education, however, was decidedly unavailable, especially for blacks in the America of World War II. One report on the status of black America in the early 1940s noted that "[a]pproximately four-fifths of all Negroes in the United States have had access to none other than segregated schools for their public education. To thousands of Negroes in the South, not even segregated schools have been available."[19] And, to be clear, the education served up to black people may have been separate, as *Plessy* allowed, but it certainly lacked the equality, which *Plessy* required. The federal government estimated in 1941 that it would take the equivalent, in 2005 dollars, of more than $4.2 billion to equalize the black school system in the United States.[20] The NAACP noted that when it came to state investment in school facilities "252% *more* money was spent on *each* white child than was spent on *each* Negro child in the same community—ranging from 28.5% in Oklahoma to 731.9% in Mississippi. In some counties the difference is 1500%."[21] A newspaper in Jackson, Mississippi, was even compelled to remark on the staggering disparities. Although African American children comprised nearly 60 percent of the school-age population in Jackson, they received "only 9 percent of the budget."[22] This pattern repeated itself throughout the state like a debilitating refrain. By 1940, more than half of all African American adults in Mississippi had less than five years of formal education; almost 12 percent had no schooling whatsoever. The figures for the "mis-education of the Negro" were even higher in South Carolina, Louisiana, Georgia, and Alabama.[23]

The fact that there were millions of uneducated, barely educated, and miseducated people held major repercussions for nearly every sector of black life in America. The effect on the healthcare system was immediately apparent. There was a critical need for African American physicians throughout the United States' segregated healthcare system but there were only a few who could slog through the miasma of Jim Crow education to meet that overwhelming demand. This chronic shortage was, unfortunately, exacerbated by the discriminatory admissions policies of universities and medical schools throughout the United States. In Phila-delphia, for example, which housed five different medical schools, "only eighteen Negroes have been graduated . . . in twenty-seven years." In New York, "no Negro enrolled at Cornell University College of Medicine at any time between 1920 and 1942" and Columbia University destroyed its admissions records when asked to provide racial data on medical school applicants and enrollees. In fact, only "eighty-five colored students are currently enrolled in twenty Northern and Western schools, as against 25,000 whites. About fifteen Negroes are graduate from these schools each year."[24]

With the bulk of higher education closed to African Americans, two historically black universities, Howard University Medical School and Meharry Medical College, accounted for nearly "85 per cent of all the Negro doctors now in practice."[25] Despite their herculean effort, how-ever, those two medical colleges did not have the capacity to produce a sufficient number of doctors to meet the healthcare needs of a malnour-ished, impoverished population, whose life expectancy rate was nearly a decade less than whites and whose infant mortality rates were double. That is to say, while the American Medical Association had determined that the minimum ratio of doctor to population was one for every 1,500, the ratio in the black community was more than twice that. On average, in the 1940s, there was only one African American "doctor for every 3337 Negroes. . . . In Mississippi the ratio is one to 18,527."[26]

Dr. Roscoe Conkling Brown, chief of the Office of Negro Health Work for the United States Public Health Service, summarized the conditions that had created this crisis. "Poor housing, malnutrition, ignorance, and inadequate access to basic health essentials—hospitals, clinics, medical care—are among the social factors contributing to the Negro's health status. This racial group 'has a problem of such size and complexity,'" he noted, "'as to challenge the leadership of both the Negro and white races to intelligently, courageously, and persistently prosecute for the na-tion a definite program of general health betterment for all people with-out recrimination or discrimination.'"[27] The NAACP, whose chairman of the board was Dr. Louis T. Wright, chief of surgery at Harlem Hospital, decided that this challenge and all of the other challenges surrounding the human rights of African Americans had to be met.

The war and the language of war proved an important vehicle in the association's fight to make human rights a viable force in the United States. In 1941, before Pearl Harbor, and despite President Franklin Roosevelt's concerns as he watched one European nation after the next being mowed under by the German *Wehrmacht*, isolationists had effec-tively blocked American entry into the war. Although Britain now stood alone as the thin dividing line between the democratic West and the global domination of Nazi Germany, the isolationists, haunted by the legacy of World War I, dug in. Senator George Aiken (R-Vt.) summarized the sentiment best when he noted that "The farm and village folk of my State . . . would go all the way, down to the last dollar and the last man, to protect Canada. But they do not see why American boys should give their lives to define the boundaries of African colonies, or to protect American promoters or exploiters in Indochina or New Guinea. Neither do I."[28] This was the implacable resistance that President Roosevelt and British Prime Minister Winston Churchill had to overcome.

On August 14, 1941, they issued the Atlantic Charter to make clear that this was not like World War I. This was not about secret treaties, secret clauses, colonial swap meets, and territorial envy. Rather, the war against the Nazis was different. A victory this time would create a better, new world order. This brave new world, the Atlantic Charter proclaimed, would be predicated on justice, democracy, and human rights. Historian Elizabeth Borgwardt brilliantly lays out, though, that the message in the Atlantic Charter was, in fact, many messages. It had one specific meaning for the British, another for the American government, and a decidedly different one for those living under racial oppression.[29]

The Atlantic Charter's language was specific enough, eloquent enough, and vague enough to envelop a range of interpretations. African Americans clearly saw it as a way out of no way. The second and third points of the Atlantic Charter, for example, spoke of self-determination, that all people had the right to choose their own government. That bedrock principle of democracy would, ironically enough, prove particularly troublesome for the two leaders. The people who lived in Britain's colonial possessions did not have the right to vote, could not choose their leaders or what form of government they wanted. Was Churchill finally saying that Hitler's attack, besides bringing Britain to its knees, had also brought the nation to its senses? And in the United States, African Americans, particularly in the South, were systematically denied the right to vote, denied the right to choose their governmental officials and the right to have a political voice in shaping the conditions under which they lived, worked, and died. Did this pledge from the president of the United States mean that the federal government was now finally going to compel Mississippi, Alabama, South Carolina, Louisiana, and the rest of the states to adhere to the Constitution and the Atlantic Charter? The African American leadership certainly thought that it did.

The Atlantic Charter offered more than mere self-determination, however. The fifth point in that historic document truly seemed to be the dawn of a new world order. The United States and Britain pledged "to bring about the fullest collaboration between all nations in the economic field with the object of securing, *for all*, improved labor standards, economic advancement and social security."[30] The phrase "for all" was unintentionally but decidedly revolutionary. The leaders seemed to promise that the world's citizens would finally have human rights—better working conditions, better and increasing pay, and a safety net of economic security. The British and American leadership had grasped that it was the destabilization in the world markets, which had then avalanched into the Great Depression, that had made Hitler so appealing to the Germans. Roosevelt and Churchill were determined that never again would a nation's economy be so ravaged that the only way out of darkness was through a raving demagogue like Adolf Hitler. Although this may have been the intention of the president and prime minister, African Americans, whose living conditions were simply appalling, interpreted this as a pledge by the federal government to remove the barriers that had systematically prevented them from reaping the benefits from centuries of the unpaid and barely paid hard labor that had built the wealthiest nation on earth.

Moreover, this vision of a new world, where there would never, ever be another Cleo Wright, was, for African Americans, encapsulated in the sixth principle of the Atlantic Charter. Roosevelt and Churchill averred that "after the final destruction of the Nazi tyranny, they hope to see established a peace which . . . will afford assurance that all the men in all the lands may live out their lives in freedom from fear and want."[31] This, of course, was intended to put a halt to military invasions and all the Gestapo-like goon squads who abused power and terrorized people. But it meant more than that to African Americans. It was not the Nazis who terrorized them day after day. It was the Ku Klux Klan, it was the police and sheriff's departments, it was the lynch mob, it was racial oppression in the United States. Indeed, African Americans looked at Nazi Germany and saw an evil that was distinctly, painfully familiar. In 1941, after reviewing a series of Nazi edicts such as the sterilization of the mulatto "Rhineland bastards" and the application of the Nuremberg Laws to Germany's black population, *Pittsburgh Courier* journalist George Schuyler remarked that "what struck me . . . was that the Nazi plan for Negroes approximates so closely what seems to be the American plan for Negroes."[32] Walter White and NAACP board member Earl Dickerson echoed that sentiment by continuously pointing to the similarities between white supremacy in the United States and Aryan supremacy in Nazi Germany and the inevitable destruction that rained down on so-called marginal populations whenever either of those supremacist doctrines came into play.[33] Had this picture of racial oppression been frightening enough, like the portrait of Dorian Gray, to compel the American government to reclaim its soul and honor its oft-spoken commitment to equality and democracy?

The black leadership, of course, had no illusions that this reclamation project would or could happen overnight. The sobering and unforgettable false promises of World War I still resonated like a bitter refrain. African Americans' unrequited faith in democracy and misguided "patriotic" silencing of agitation for equality, had not helped make the world, or the United States for that matter, "safe for democracy." Instead, after World War I, African Americans felt the cold, malevolent embrace of a nation that had reified white supremacy, welcomed the resurgence of the Klan, and drowned America in the black blood of Red Summer. Hardened by that unflinching betrayal, African Americans learned an invaluable lesson. White House aide Philleo Nash immediately noticed the difference. The tenor and tone of the black community during World War II was like nothing he had ever seen before. "Negroes," he warned the Roosevelt administration, were not the Negroes of World War I. This time, he noted with alarm, they are "in a militant and demanding mood."[34] Indeed, one black soldier encapsulated that militancy best when he declared, "I'm hanged if I'm going to let the Alabama version of the Germans kick me around when I get home. . . . I went into the Army a nigger; I'm coming out a *man*."[35]

This was a new day. African Americans were demanding "freedom [and] rejecting [the] idea of racial inferiority." The language of the Atlantic Charter's Four Freedoms, particularly freedom from fear and freedom from want, meant that the "[c]ontinued humiliation to Negroes who are segregated in the armed forces," the perpetuation of persistently "[b]ad and inadequate housing," and rampant "[u]nemployment even where man-power shortages are present," were not going to be tolerated. Not this time.[36] A "war for the Four Freedoms," the NAACP declared, had erupted in black America.[37]

Therefore, when Churchill insisted that the Atlantic Charter, was, for all intents and purposes, a "whites only" affair, Walter White and other members of the black leadership repudiated the prime minister and called on President Roosevelt to issue a Pacific Charter "so that dark-skinned and colonial peoples may be given greater hope of real political democracy and freedom from economic exploitation." White then challenged Roosevelt to "prove to the colored peoples . . . that you are not hypocrites when you say this is a war for freedom. Prove it to us and we will show you that we can and will fight like fury for that freedom. But," White added, "we want—and we intend to have—our share of that freedom."[38]

The "moral cross roads of the war has been reached."[39] The communist-dominated National Negro Congress (NNC) saw it, as well. There "is no middle road today," the leadership asserted, "there are only two paths before us." One "strives to secure for mankind the four freedoms that characterize a democratic government—freedom of speech, freedom of worship, freedom from want, freedom from fear." For "15,000,000 American Negroes," the NNC insisted, "this spells freedom from oppression." The other pathway, as the Axis powers, as well as the lynchers in Sikeston, Missouri, had made abundantly clear, "drowns in bloodshed the lives, dignity and culture of minority peoples."[40] The African American leadership had seized upon the reality that the needs in black America had converged with the wartime language of human rights to provide the road map for freedom.

It is within this framework of the Four Freedoms and human rights that the African American leadership soon began "formulating a program of post war needs for the American Negro." At the top of that list was "first-class citizenship" as defined by "basic civil rights" such as "the right to vote in all parts of the country." There was also a recurring emphasis on "essential economic rights" such as the "right to compete in fields of employment on equal levels," "the right to work," "the right to remuneration for work on the basis of merit and performance," and "the right to advance in rank and salary in terms of ability and productive contribution." In addition, African Americans sought the right to "unsegregated and unrestricted housing" and the "right to live without the burdens and embarrassments that are provoked by the unwarranted segregation" in education, health care, and in public accommodations.[41] Yet, as the association leadership and its allies in the African American community continued to thrash out what a definitive platform for equality looked like, it soon became obvious that all the discussions, all the debates, all the meetings, and all the conferences would have little or no impact unless African Americans were at the peace table. Black people had to have a meaningful role in shaping this new world order. It was simply too important to leave to the British, the Soviets, and, yes, even the Americans.[42]

This point was made abundantly clear at Dumbarton Oaks, which was the British, American, and Soviet conference to determine the shape, power, and form of the new international organization, the United Nations. The shortcomings of the 1944 Dumbarton Oaks agreement sent a warning shot across the bow to the black leadership about the ways in which the supposed new world order was, if the Allies had their way, going to look painfully like the old world order. One of the most striking and glaring deficiencies was that despite the Atlantic Charter, despite Nazi atrocities, and despite Japanese brutality, human rights had barely—and just barely—made a cameo appearance in the draft plan for the United Nations.

Venerable scholar and NAACP cofounder, W. E. B. Du Bois, who had rejoined the association specifically to address the human rights and colonialism issues that World War II had so rawly exposed, leveled a searing critique at the Dumbarton Oaks plans for the United Nations. The weaknesses, he warned, were predicated on the continuation of white supremacy and if allowed to become embedded in the operating code of the proposed United Nations, would prove fatal not only to the organization but to the hundreds of millions of people of color throughout the globe.[43] Du Bois, therefore, began to lobby the State Department to have the NAACP attached as an official consultant to the U.S. delegation at the founding conference of the United Nations in San Francisco. Officially known as the United Nations Conference on International Organization (UNCIO), it was here where the organization's structure and powers would be finalized.

As incredibly unrealistic as Du Bois's demand may have seemed, the State Department had learned one key lesson from the debacle following World War I: Without popular support, no peace treaty could ever get through the Senate. Hence, the invitation to the NAACP and more than forty other major organizations to join the U.S. delegation in San Francisco. Hence, as well, the dilemma. For the United States the crafting of a new world order that denounced Aryan supremacy and all of its vestiges as abhorrent and unacceptable to civilized society while at the same time shielding, protecting, and privileging white supremacy in the United States was going to be a difficult feat. As one journalist noted, "It is easy to talk about freedom for all; but it isn't easy to mean it. *All* is a [mighty] big word."[44] And the United States government knew it. Caught between the bitter harvest of the Holocaust and the "Strange Fruit" of lynching, the United States searched desperately to find some way to "assert . . . [America's] moral leadership in [the] field" of human rights while still maintaining the status quo of Jim Crow and racial inequality.[45] That was the dilemma that the powerful Southern Democrats had no intention of solving for the United States. As far as the Southern Democrats were concerned World War II had not changed a thing; there was no "American Dilemma," no new world order, and no emerging human rights regime. There was only the sacred old order that white supremacy had established. Mississippi Senator James O. Eastland, in his own patriotic, Capra-esque moment, "explained that white southerners were fighting [in World War II] . . . 'to maintain white supremacy and control of our election machinery.'"[46] The Southern Democrats had, therefore, fought every piece of civil rights legislation that dared to come near Capitol Hill. They consistently blasted the NAACP as the "nigger advancement society," defended "lynching as necessary 'to protect the fair womanhood of the South from beasts,'" and foamed at the thought of "burr headed niggers" having equal opportunity in employment, education, or health care. This was no mere ranting from the ideological fringe. The Southern Democrats "dominate[d] more than sixty percent of the Senate and House Committees which determine[d] not only domestic legislation but foreign affairs and the shape of the post war world."[47]

Early on they flexed their political muscle in determining the U.S. response to the founding of the United Nations and the UN's human rights initiatives. The hostility to a strong UN Charter, with explicit guarantees of rights, emanated from the same supremacist swamp that drowned federal antilynching bills, anti–poll tax measures, Fair Employment Practices Committees, and other civil rights legislation. A major part of the clout they were able to exert came from Texas Senator Tom Connally, who chaired the Senate Foreign Relations Committee, and who had also been instrumental in scuttling three antilynching bills in Congress. Connally was now a key member of the U.S. delegation at the founding conference for the United Nations. State Department officials were well aware of this and even admitted that "when you had men like . . . Connally [on the U.S. delegation to the UN] . . . you didn't go sailing off into the blue. You had to keep your eye all the time on not putting too much limitation on American sovereignty."[48] For Connally, that translated into ensuring that states' rights would never be challenged or curtailed by any international treaty. States' rights were the sine qua non of the South's power. The region had effectively used the doctrine to enshrine white supremacy, bar African Americans from enjoying their rights as U.S. citizens, and ensure that, like *Dred Scott*, blacks "had no rights which the white man was bound to respect."[49]

At the UNCIO Connally immediately wielded his power in the cause of white supremacy. The senator, despite numerous pleas from other delegations and the consultants, refused to even entertain the notion that all people, regardless of race, had the right to education. If the cacophony continued and the United States gave in, he warned, any UN Charter with the right to education embedded in it would never pass through his committee. Connally, in short, was willing to scuttle the entire treaty in order to maintain the Jim Crow education that was essential to black political and economic disenfranchisement. This was a high-stakes, political game of chicken that the American delegates were not prepared to play. While Connally stood firm, they blinked. The Americans, therefore, worked overtime to quell the clamor at the UNCIO by presenting Connally's indefensible position as viable, logical, and politically feasible.[50] That scramble to shroud in reasonableness the totally unreasonable would repeat itself over and over again as the United States, with one eye always on the Southern Democrats, tried to craft human rights language that would leave white supremacy untouched.

This would not go unchallenged. With forty-seven other nations and a contingent of headstrong consultants, the United States could not keep human rights the nice symbolic, meaningless gesture that the State Department intended. The consultants, led by the NAACP and the American Jewish Congress, exposed this problem when they demanded, of all things, establishment of a human rights commission. The American delegation may have been appalled at the suggestion, but the horrors of the Holocaust and, frankly, the horrors of America compelled the Jewish and African American consultants to view an international commission as absolutely essential.[51]

Understanding the problem, the revulsion at Nazi atrocities on one hand and the need to maintain Jim Crow on the other, foreign policy guru John Foster Dulles was confident that he could devise a human rights plan that would pacify the consultants and satisfy the Southern Democrats. His solution was simple. Amid an unequivocal statement "guaranteeing freedom from discrimination on account of race, language, religion, or sex," Dulles inserted an amendment that "nothing in the Charter shall authorize . . . intervention in matters which are essentially within the domestic jurisdiction of the State concerned." This "domestic jurisdiction" clause meant that the United States could continue to use the rhetoric of "freedom" but would not "be put in a position of having matters of domestic concern interfered with by the Security Council." More specifically the clause would ensure that the UN could not "requir[e]" a state to "change [its] . . . immigration policy or [Jim Crow] legislation."[52] While the American and Soviet delegations immediately embraced Dulles's stroke of genius, the other nations and the consultants sent up a wail of protest.[53]

Dulles did not care.[54] He insisted that the United States had to protect itself. The future secretary of state then made it abundantly clear that the domestic jurisdiction clause was America's price for allowing human rights to seep into the UN Charter. This "is as far as we can go," he said. "If [the domestic jurisdiction clause] is rejected," Dulles warned, "we shall be forced to reexamine our attitude toward increases in the economic and social activities of this Organization." After Dulles clarified the American position, the debate stopped and the other nations agreed to accept the domestic jurisdiction clause. The United States had just won an important battle in keeping human rights from darkening America's doorstep.[55]

This battle, however, was far from over. The State Department, given the emerging Cold War and the depth of atrocities in the Soviet Union, was convinced that a key strategy in highlighting the moral bankruptcy of Marxism was to position America as "the tower of strength and the innovator and the pioneer in the field of human rights." Yet, no matter how hard the department tried, it simply could not do it.[56] The truth of the matter, one department official admitted, was that no nation had an exemplary human rights record—not even the United States. "[T]he United States with all its power," he explained to his supervisors, "has not yet been able even to get up on the first rung of the ladder, namely elections which are free enough to provide the prerequisite basis for the honoring of even the most tangible of human rights, which are the legal ones."[57]

Human rights, however, constituted too important a Cold War arena in which to concede defeat, especially to the Soviets. The goal, as novelist Ralph Ellison so eloquently stated, was to find a way to "reconcile democratic ideas with an anti-democratic reality."[58] That is, the United States had to find a way to fight for human rights to expose the sham of the Soviets' people's democracy, while doing so in a manner that left intact the racial inequality that kept the Southern Democrats firmly ensconced in the Senate and House of Representatives and blocked Jim Crow and all its progeny from international scrutiny.

This was going to be tricky. While, to be sure, the Soviet Union ruthlessly quashed civil liberties, constructed a lethal gulag system, and saw to the destruction of millions of "political opponents" through forced starvation, mock trials, and real executions; the United States had a thriving and harsh convict lease-labor system, rampant debt slavery, widespread political and economic disenfranchisement, and extensive legal and extralegal violence aimed at millions of minority citizens. Nonetheless, despite their track records, these flawed superpowers began playing their disingenuous human rights game.

The Americans made the first move; on their terms; on their turf—the First Amendment. Knowing that it would be beyond impossible for the Soviet-controlled organs *Izvestia* and *Pravda* to compare favorably to the *New York Times*, *Le Monde*, the London *Times*, and thousands of other independently owned newspapers throughout the West, the United States quickly arranged to have the United Nations investigate the status of freedom of the press throughout the globe. For the Kremlin, this looming international exposure could prove highly embarrassing.

The Soviets, therefore, quickly counterattacked at America's weakest point—Jim Crow. The USSR successfully urged the United Nations to form a Sub-commission on the Prevention of Discrimination and Protection of Minorities (MINDIS). With the Nuremberg Trials fully under way, the United States had no choice but to assent to the subcommission's creation. That grudging assent, however, was about as far as the United States was willing to go. In addition to trying to sabotage MINDIS outright by changing its membership and scuttling its meeting schedule, the State Department also filleted the definition of "minority" so finely that it automatically excluded African Americans from the subcommission's purview. Although MINDIS was created to address the plight of minorities, the State Department argued that, in actuality, "national minorities" were the targeted group. For the State Department, "national minorities" had a separate language, a separate culture, and separatist political aims. African Americans, the department reasoned, therefore, were not a "national minority." Nor did it appear were Mexican Americans, Asian Americans, and even Native Americans. In fact, the State Department concluded that "there probably are no national minorities in the United States."[59] In other words, national minorities—Kurds, Armenians, and Basques—were a European problem, not an American one.

The State Department also decided, as a self-protective measure, to take the lead on the drafting of the Covenant on Human Rights, which, unlike the Declaration, was a treaty. The U.S. delegation worked hard to navigate around the "obstacles to the United States support for a Covenant," which were the "'non-discrimination article'" and "[i]ts import for other articles of substance" such as provisions dealing with the right to education, health care, housing, voting, and employment. Equally important was the fact that "we don't want others meddling in our affairs."[60] Thus, in order to get this treaty through the Southern-dominated Senate, the Truman administration broke the covenant in two, separated civil and political rights from economic and social rights (which were seen as communistic), proposed removing the most "offensive" rights, like voting, from the covenant because it violated Southern electoral policies, and inserted a federal-state clause that meant that even though the federal government may sign and ratify the treaty, no state in the system would be bound by its tenets. In championing the federal-state clause, Eleanor Roosevelt, chair of the Commission on Human Rights (CHR), emphasized three key areas in which the current balance of federal-state power would be sacredly preserved. The federal government, she promised the South, would never interfere in "murder cases," investigate concerns over "fair trials," or insist on "the right to education." In essence, Eleanor Roosevelt had just assured the Dixiecrats that the sacred troika of lynching, Southern justice, and Jim Crow schools would remain untouched even with a Covenant on Human Rights.[61]

The State Department also decided to use the unimpeachable cachet of Eleanor Roosevelt as chair of the Commission on Human Rights to ensure that the CHR would not have the authority to do anything with the thousands of petitions the United Nations received. The last thing the United States wanted was a Commission on Human Rights with power. If the United States had its way, a key State Department official Durward Sandifer admitted, the commission would be "of little use" regardless of the extent of the human rights violation. Sandifer remarked that in his estimation even the "ghastly" treatment of the "natives of the Belgian Congo or the persecution of the Christian Armenians by the Turkish

Empire" would not have been enough to warrant international intervention. Given that nearly 90 percent of the Armenians in Turkey and 10 million Africans had been killed, Sandifer had set the bar for UN intervention at an extremely high and dangerously lethal level.[62]

All of this maneuvering to turn the CHR into "the most elaborate wastepaper basket ever invented" was driven by the State Department's concern that those who lived below the Mason-Dixon line would try to find redress for their "domestic maladjustments" at the United Nations. The State Department knew how unresponsive the American political arena was to black demands for equality. The "trinity of constitutional guarantees, judicial decisions and administrative support," the State Department admitted, had certainly proven impotent in breaking the shackles of African Americans' second-class citizenship.[63] "No other American group is so definitely subordinate in status or so frequently the victim of discriminatory practices" as the Negro, one State Department analysis averred. The report then detailed what those discriminatory practices were.

"Among the more important of these practices are: segregation legislation in Southern and border states; restrictive covenants which limit the residential mobility of Negroes in many of the municipalities of the United States; economic restrictions and vocational discrimination—about 80 percent of the complaints before the Fair Employment Practice Committee from July 1943 to December 1944 were from Negroes; lynching; restriction of the Negro's access to the courts and various limitations on his participation in political activities, particularly in reference to the use of the franchise and office-holding; unequal access to schools, public facilities, and social services generally; and the social restrictions placed on the Negro by custom and convention. These practices, many of which are nationwide, are obviously in conflict with the American creed of democracy and equality of opportunity for all."[64]

These conditions, the State Department understood, made the United States a prime candidate for a UN hearing. "There is an alert and intelligent public, composed of Negroes and whites, keenly aware of the disabilities suffered by the Negro. Elements within this public," the report warned, "may be inclined to press for consideration of the Negro's case before the Human Rights Commission." The State Department further realized that the goodwill intentions of American democracy were simply not enough to forestall a determined international inquest. Although in "theory discrimination is not allowable under the American constitution and law and segregationists legislation of Southern and border states has been interpreted in the courts as not discriminatory, on the assumption that the facilities and services provided Negroes . . . are not of necessity unequal. In fact, however, facilities are on an unequal basis; and this and other discriminatory practices may give us some trouble before an international body concerned with preventing discrimination."[65]

This was not a trivial matter because the Cold War had intensified America's "mocking paradoxes" and made the cost of exposure almost too much to bear.[66] "The peculiar disadvantage of the United States," one official wrote to the assistant secretary of state, "would be that with the seat of the United Nations in this country and with a freer flow of information here than elsewhere the United Nations could be flooded with petitions relating to United States abuses . . . thus giving the impression that the United States was the chief offender against rather than defender of civil liberties."[67]

In 1947, the State Department's worst nightmare came true. Following the example of the National Negro Congress, the NAACP decided to challenge the domestic jurisdiction clause. The association petitioned the UN Commission on Human Rights to investigate the conditions under which African Americans lived and died in the United States. In doing so the NAACP made the disastrous error of overestimating its allies and underestimating its opposition. The petition, however, was first-rate. *An Appeal to the World!*, written under Du Bois's leadership, stated that although "there is general agreement that the 'fundamental human rights' which" members of the "United Nations are pledged to promote . . . 'without distinction as to race,' include Education, Employment, Housing and Health" it is clear that "the Negro in the United States is the victim of wide deprivation of each of these rights." In his chapter of the petition, Washington Bureau chief and trained sociologist Leslie S. Perry began first and foremost with the right to education because, he noted, "those who would continue to exploit the Negro, politically and economically have first tried to keep his mind in shackles."[68]

The petition had, therefore, carefully documented the gross disparities in educational attainment, opportunity, quality, and funding. It had noted that in school districts where African Americans comprised over 75 percent of the school-age population, only $2.12 per capita was spent on them as opposed to $28.50 per white student. The association had further documented that in 1943–44, while the United States was at war with the Nazis, Southern states spent 111 percent more on white students than black. Mississippi led the way, of course, with a staggering 499 percent difference between its funding of black and white schools.[69] Moreover, because of the South's insistence on paying black teachers significantly less than white ones, African Americans lost $25 million per year in wages, which in 2005, would equal nearly $1.6 billion annually.[70] As statistic after statistic rolled through the pages of the NAACP's petition to the United Nations about state-sponsored racial inequality—in education, in employment, in housing, in health care—one U.S. diplomat at the United Nations insisted that the Jim Crow Leader of the Free World could not afford to be exposed as a "nation of hypocrites" and he used his influence to bury the petition deep within the UN bureaucracy.[71]

Additional opposition came from "friend of the Negro," NAACP board member, and chair of the UN Commission on Human Rights Eleanor Roosevelt. In an article and a series of letters that read like "The Education of Walter White" she emphasized that the NAACP had made a big mistake in going to the United Nations to air African Americans' grievances because the petition played into the Soviets' hands, and, she intimated, the only petitions the USSR ever supported were those authored by known communist-dominated groups. White also needed to understand, she continued quite sternly, that the U.S. delegation "could not let the Soviet [*sic*] get away with attacking the United States" and dodge having their own shortcomings exposed.[72] Roosevelt also warned Du Bois that the NAACP did not ever want to run the risk again of "exposing the United States to distorted accusations by other countries." She firmly believed that the "colored people in the United States . . . would be better served in the long run if the NAACP Appeal were not placed on the Agenda." Then, in the ultimate lesson, Roosevelt submitted her resignation from the NAACP board of directors. Although she did not mention the petition that she had helped squash, the timing of her resignation seemed to carry with it a very distinct, ominous message. White, of course, pleaded with her to reconsider. The association "would suffer irreparable loss if you were to resign." She held firm. He begged her again. "[U]nder no circumstances would we want you to resign from the Board. Your name means a great deal to us." His pleas, astutely, never mentioned the United Nations but only how much needed to be done domestically and how only she had the clout to make that happen. Roosevelt eventually agreed to stay. And White began to seriously rethink the NAACP's investment in the struggle for human rights.[73] Indeed, the following year, as part of the growing fissure between White and Du Bois, which was then buttressed by the hard, cold reality of Roosevelt's displeasure with *An Appeal to the World!*, White announced to a State Department official that the NAACP "had no intention" of pressing its case ever again before the United Nations.[74]

Even with all of that, by the time Dwight D. Eisenhower came to power in the early 1950s, a group of Republicans had joined with the Southern Democrats and decided that the Truman administration had not done enough to protect the United States from the United Nations and human rights. That "evil combination" of the GOP and Dixiecrats, as the NAACP called it, charged that the U.S. Constitution and America were under attack by human rights, human rights proponents, and the United Nations, as that foreigner-dominated organization set out to subvert American values with socialistic, even communistic, ideas about freedom and democracy.

To rescue America and its children from the United Nations, Republican Senator John W. Bricker of Ohio proposed the ultimate weapon—a constitutional amendment to alter the treaty approval process. This was an incredibly radical move for such an arch-conservative because it attacked the very foundational American heritage that he claimed he was fighting to preserve. From the days of the Founding Fathers, treaties had to be ratified by two-thirds of the U.S. Senate to become the "law of the land." But now, for the senator and his allies, that was no longer enough. With the United Nations and human rights stalking America's shores, threatening to breach the bridgehead of American sovereignty and states' rights, a mere two-thirds of the Senate seemed like an incredibly weak and permeable line of defense. The Bricker Amendment was, therefore, designed to reinforce significantly America's battlements against the foreign invasion of human rights law. Although the amendment would maintain the requirement that all treaties had to be ratified by two-thirds of the Senate, Bricker then added executive agreements as part of the package. The point of including these instruments of diplomacy was to keep the president from using them to bypass the legislative branch and congressional oversight. Yet that was only the beginning. After ratification by two-thirds of the Senate, the executive agreement or treaty would then need to pass both houses of Congress with enabling legislation. Despite the enormous difficulties of transforming a bill into a law, as the stillborn antilynching, poll tax, and fair employment bills demonstrated, America's rampart, in Bricker's opinion, was still not high enough. The isolationist wing of the GOP and Southern Democrats, therefore, determined that state legislatures would be the final, impenetrable brick in the wall that could stop these human rights initiatives, especially the much-dreaded Genocide Convention, dead in their tracks. The reliance upon the recalcitrance of state governments was not surprising. The Southern Democrats had repeatedly voiced their fears that the Genocide Convention, if ratified, could trump states' rights, transform lynching into an international crime, and obligate the federal government to prosecute those who had, heretofore, killed black Americans with impunity.[75] The Bricker Amendment, as a result, included the provision that *all* forty-eight state legislatures had to ratify treaties and executive agreements. The Ohio senator crowed that this amendment, with its multiple lines of defense—two-thirds of the Senate; majority votes in both Houses of Congress; and approval by all forty-eight state legislatures—would rein in the "eager beavers in the UN" and prevent "some Americans" from using UN treaties "as a substitute for national legislation on purely domestic matters."[76]

The much-heralded Bricker Amendment enjoyed the support of a number of conservative, "patriotic" organizations and, even more important, enough senators from both parties to ensure its ratification. With over sixty senators sponsoring the amendment and the Republican Party firmly behind Bricker, President Eisenhower realized that he had a fight on his hands because, although the target was clearly the United Nations' human rights treaties, the Bricker Amendment's language was broad enough to strip the executive branch of any real authority whatsoever in foreign policy. In order to preserve his presidential role in foreign relations, Eisenhower now desperately searched for some sort of compromise.[77]

The solution that Dulles and the president seized upon was the complete abandonment of both the Covenant on Civil and Political Rights, even though it was designed to mimic the U.S. Bill of Rights, and the Covenant on Economic, Social, and Cultural Rights, which in the State Department's estimation was no more than a Pandora's box filled with the "inarticulate Slavic desire for the economic well-being of the masses."[78] For good measure Secretary of State Dulles added the Convention on the Political Rights of Women and the Convention on the Abolition of Slavery.[79] In the process, Eisenhower particularly withdrew support for the Genocide Convention because, as Vice President Richard Nixon noted, that treaty was the primary catalyst for the Bricker Amendment. The Southern Democrats, everyone recognized, were afraid that the human rights treaties, in general, just "might affect the Colored question" and that the Genocide Convention, in particular, could become, in the hands of the NAACP's attorneys, "a backdoor method to a federal anti-lynching bill."[80] These were the burnt offerings that Eisenhower presented to the Senate in exchange for saving presidential power.

Walter White, who had been relatively quiet on the human rights front since Eleanor Roosevelt had taken him and the NAACP to the woodshed, was outraged. He asserted that the Bricker Amendment, with its proviso that all forty-eight state legislatures had to approve any treaty, would drag the United States down to the "moral and intellectual level of the most backward state of the nation." That frightening scenario, he exclaimed, meant "that as a nation we could take no higher moral ground than that permitted by states like Mississippi or South Carolina." But, of course, he added, that was the whole point. The NAACP chieftain stated that it was no accident that Senator Bricker's crusade gained momentum only after a California court ruled that a racially discriminatory law violated the Declaration of Human Rights. That ruling, White explained, caused "consternation in conservative circles lest our international moral commitments require us to live up to those commitments here at home."[81] The "more we study this amendment," he noted in an address to congressional leaders, "the more dangerous we believe it to be."[82] The Senate, however, would not budge.

Only an idolized World War II hero like Eisenhower could stop the Bricker juggernaut, and it took him nearly a year to muster the will to do so. When the president finally came out openly against the Bricker Amendment, the battle in the Senate began in earnest.[83] The old general knew that this was a campaign he could not afford to lose, and his considerable influence pulled several Republican supporters away from the senator. This loss of key votes led one version of the amendment after another to fail. But just when it looked like victory was imminent, into the breach stepped Senator Walter George (D-Ga.), who, as everyone knew, "commanded attention and got respect from members of the Senate."[84] That influence combined with his Southern Democrat values portended disaster. George, an ardent states' rights champion, made no secret of the fact that he was particularly concerned that the Genocide Convention "would bring within the area of Congressional power anti-lynching legislation." As a result, George wanted the Bricker Amendment to succeed at all costs. He introduced his own substitute proposal and, with his cachet and clout, immediately breathed new life into the amendment's sagging chances.[85]

As historian Duane Tananbaum noted, this was the "showdown." After intense debates, the voting began. "As the clerk began calling the roll that evening for the final vote . . . , the outcome remained uncertain." At one point, it "looked bleak" especially after several Eisenhower Republicans jumped ship and "voted with Bricker and George." But then, several Democrats, who had previously supported the amendment, swung to the other side. Back and forth it went until "as the vote was ending, 60 senators had voted for the amendment and only 30 had voted against it." Bricker had his two-thirds! But then out of the blue, or more accurately, out of the tavern, "staggered into the Senate chamber" Harley Kilgore, "a liberal Democrat from West Virginia." The drunken lawmaker was "propped up by various aides and colleagues" and when the clerk "asked for the senator's vote . . . a 'nay' was heard—whether from Kilgore or one of the others is uncertain." What was certain, however, was that the George resolution had just gone down to defeat—by one drunken vote.[86]

Although Eisenhower clearly felt vindicated, it was a Pyrrhic victory for African Americans. The fact that the president chose to confront the Bricker forces only at the very last minute and instead attempted, at least initially, to appease the right wing by auctioning off the human rights treaties, cost African Americans dearly. The administration's sacrifice of the covenants and Genocide Convention, the loss of real American involvement in the development of international human rights protocols, and, most important, the pervasive notion that there was something un-American and foreign, if not totally communistic and dangerous, about human rights converged to severely constrict the agenda for real black equality, particularly as its advocates got destroyed by the McCarthy witch hunts.[87]

In many ways, that retreat from human rights, particularly as the civil rights movement erupted in Alabama the next year in 1955, bequeathed an agenda for equality that was too restricted to even ask the right question, much less provide the answer, about the root cause of systemic and perpetual inequality.[88] Over the next decade, as one civil rights triumph after the next left virtually untouched the human rights catastrophe brewing in the black communities, the limits of the movement became painfully apparent.[89] In 1985, Bayard Rustin, the logistics genius behind the 1963 March on Washington, told a college audience that two decades after the apogee of the civil rights movement, all still was not well. The "problems of the early sixties . . . were more easily solved than our current dilemma," Rustin observed. "First of all, it did not cost the government billions of dollars to do away with segregation in public accommodations, to give us the right to vote, to integrate the schools." These gains, Rustin made clear, were not without costs. It "took the bombing of churches and the murder of innocents" but "it was fairly easy to get most Americans to understand that it was *un*-American to continue segregation." Rustin warned, however, that the next phase of the struggle would be even more trying because "We are now asking for education, medical care, jobs and housing."[90]

In many horrific ways, nearly a generation later, the disaster in New Orleans, Louisiana exposed how black Americans were still in search of those basic human rights. In 2005, Katrina, a Category Five hurricane, slammed into a city that was already below sea level and sinking. Of course, there were levees, but they had been put in place forty years earlier after the last disaster in 1965 with Hurricane Betsy. Since that time, the sole line of defense, that thin barrier between the sea and hundreds of thousands of human beings (two-thirds of whom were African American), remained chronically underfunded by Congress and virtually neglected by the Army Corps of Engineers.[91] As a result, those crumbling concrete guardians of New Orleans simply did not stand a chance against the power of a Category Five hurricane.

Neither did those who were trapped in a drowning city. Their fate was tied directly to an educational system that ranked near the bottom nationally in graduating students, to a separate and unequal health care system where 20 percent of the population had absolutely no insurance, and to a grinding poverty that led to more than one-third of the city's population being unable to afford basic transportation.[92] The result was that, although there was ample warning that a storm like none other was on the way, the city's evacuation plan was designed for those who had the fiscal wherewithal, including cars, to flee. Everyone else was essentially left to find his or her own way out—which was often blocked by the police or armed vigilantes who did not want black or poor people crossing the bridge into their "safe" neighborhoods. Blocked by gun-toting marauders guarding the high ground and praying that the creaking forty-year-old concrete that had been whipsawed by salt water and wind for decades could handle just one more torrential rainfall, one more burst of 160-mile-per-hour winds, the elderly, the infirm, babies, and the poor were up against it. It was not a fair fight.

The levees, just as the Army Corps of Engineers had predicted, gave way. The pumping stations stopped pumping. With a clear path and nothing to slow it down, the raging sea and nearly every tributary, creek, dam, and bayou poured into the city, particularly into the Ninth Ward, where working-class and lower-income African Americans lived. It became where they died. The images of black swollen bodies bobbing in the floodwaters, children clinging to rooftops begging for help, and thousands of African Americans trapped in sweltering government-designated evacuation centers with no drinking water, sanitation facilities, or food exposed to the world what America looked like for those without human rights.

Yet, in a toxic blend of arrogance and incompetence, U.S. government officials, such as President George W. Bush, Michael Chertoff, the secretary of homeland security, and Michael Brown, the head of the Federal Emergency Management Agency, seemed blissfully unaware of the magnitude of the devastation or the plight of those whom they were sworn to protect.[93] Similarly, state and local officials endlessly dithered, quibbled, and squabbled while Rome essentially drowned. Shortly thereafter, surveying the horrendous toll that this perfect storm of nature and governmental indifference created, then-Senator Barack Obama (D-Ill.) summarized it best when he intoned, "I hope we realize that the people of New Orleans weren't just abandoned during the hurricane." "They were abandoned long ago— . . . to substandard schools, to dilapidated housing, to inadequate health care, to a pervasive sense of hopelessness."[94]

Oddly enough, in 1952, U.S. Ambassador to the United Nations Warren Austin had told the NAACP that if the United States did not deal with human rights "at home, . . . all our Declarations on Human Rights would be a hollow mockery." This Cassandra-like prediction came true as Hurricane Katrina "exposed some shocking truths about" the United States: "the bitterness of its sharp racial divide, the abandonment of the dispossessed, the weakness of critical infrastructure. But the most astonishing and most shaming revelations has been of its government's failure to bring succour to its people at their time of greatest need."[95] Or, as Walter White said more than fifty years earlier, "Democracy doesn't mean much to a man with an empty belly."[96]

Notes

Parts of this chapter first appeared in Carol Anderson's *Eyes off the Prize: The United Nations and the African American Struggle for Human Rights, 1944–1955* (Cambridge: Cambridge University Press, 2003). Excerpts from *Eyes off the Prize*, © 2003 by Carol Anderson. Reprinted with permission of Cambridge University Press.

1. Walter White to Herbert Lehman, Dennis Chavez, and Leverett Saltonstall, telegram, July 11, 1950, Box A617, File "State Department: Point IV Program, 1949–54," Papers of the National Association for the Advancement of Colored People, Series II, General Office File, 1940–55, Library of Congress, Washington, D.C. (hereafter Papers of the NAACP).

2. Manfred Berg, *"The Ticket to Freedom": The NAACP and the Struggle for Black Political Integration* (Gainesville: University of Florida Press, 2005).

3. Berg, *Ticket to Freedom*, p. 105.

4. For the rationale behind the NAACP's initial rejection of economic issues during the organization's founding in 1909, see Berg, *Ticket to Freedom*, pp. 14–15.

5. David M. Kennedy, *Freedom from Fear: The American People in Depression and War, 1929–1945* (New York: Oxford University Press, 1999), pp. 87, 164, 186, 193; Robert S. McElvaine, *The Great Depression: America, 1929–1941*, 2nd ed. (New York: Times Books, 1993), pp. 187–95; Patricia Sullivan, *Days of Hope: Race and Democracy in the New Deal Era* (Chapel Hill: University of North Carolina Press, 1996).

6. Roi Ottley, *New World A-Coming* (1943; New York: Arno Press, 1968), p. 290.

7. Paul Gordon Lauren, *The Evolution of International Human Rights: Visions Seen*, 2nd ed. (Philadelphia: University of Pennsylvania Press, 2003), p. 150.

8. Philleo Nash to Jonathan Daniels, memo, August 15, 1944, Box 29, File "OWI-Files Alphabetical-Race Tension-Jonathan Daniels File-News Analysis," Philleo Nash Papers, Harry S. Truman Presidential Library, Independence, Mo.

9. Gary R. Kremer and Antonio F. Holland, *Missouri's Black Heritage*, rev. ed. (Columbia: University of Missouri Press, 1993), p. 161; Dominic J. Capeci, Jr., *The Lynching of Cleo Wright* (Lexington: University of Kentucky Press, 1998), pp. 5–6.

10. U.S. Bureau of the Census, *Historical Statistics of the United States, Colonial Times to 1970, Bicentennial Edition*, Part 1 (Washington, D.C.: GPO, 1975), p. 422. From 1940 to 1955, African Americans accounted for 234 out of 263 of those executed for rape.

11. "An Informal Report on Attitudes in Southeast Missouri Relative to the Lynching of Cleo Wright, Negro, January 25, 1942, for the NAACP by Mr. and Mrs. L. Benoist Tompkins, Saint Louis, Mo.," Box 42, File "Internal Security File: Treasury File—NAACP Misc (folder 2 of 2), Stephen J. Spingarn Papers, Harry S. Truman Presidential Library, Independence, Mo. (hereafter Spingarn Papers); Capeci, *Lynching*, pp. 13–37.

12. Capeci, *Lynching*, p. 23.

13. "An Informal Report," Spingarn Papers.

14. Kremer and Holland, *Missouri's Black Heritage*, pp. 158–59.

15. Ibid., p. 159.

16. "An Informal Report," Spingarn Papers.

17. See, for example, Philip Dray, *At the Hands of Persons Unknown: The Lynching of Black America* (New York: Random House, 2002); Grace Elizabeth Hale, *Making Whiteness: The Culture of Segregation in the South, 1890–1940* (New York: Pantheon, 1998); James Allen (ed.), *Without Sanctuary: Lynching Photography in America* (Santa Fe, N.Mex.: Twin Palms, 2000).

18. Also see NAACP, "Education in a Democracy," March 1, 1938, *Papers of William H. Hastie* (Frederick, Md.: University Publications of America, 1984), Part 2, Reel 33 (hereafter *Hastie Papers*).

19. Jessie Parkhurst Guzman (ed.), *Negro Year Book: A Review of Events Affecting Negro Life, 1941–1946* (Tuskegee, Ala.: Tuskegee Institute, 1947), p. 56.

20. In 1941, the U.S. Office of Education estimated that it would take $43 million to equalize schools. Using the relative GDP for 2005, that estimate equals $4,227,303,867.40. Available online at eh.net/hmit/compare/. For the initial report see Emery M. Foster to Walter White, December 2, 1941, Box B173, File "Statistics: Education of Negroes, 1941," Papers of the National Association for the Advancement of Colored People, Series B (Legal Files), Part III, 1940–55, Library of Congress, Washington, D.C.

21. NAACP, "Education in a Democracy," March 1, 1938, *Hastie Papers*, Part 2, Reel 33. Emphasis in original.

22. Quoted in Guzman, *Negro Year Book*, p. 57.

23. Guzman, *Negro Year Book*, p. 70. The actual percentages for African Americans age twenty-five and older with less than five years education are: Alabama, 54.1 percent; Georgia, 58.6 percent; Louisiana, 60.9 percent; Mississippi, 52.5 percent; and South Carolina, 62.4 percent. For comparison, the figures for whites in those states with less than five years education are: Alabama, 16.3 percent; Georgia, 16.6 percent; Louisiana, 21.9 percent; Mississippi, 10.3 percent; and South Carolina, 18 percent.

24. Henry F. Pringle and Katharine Pringle, "The Color Line in Medicine," *Saturday Evening Post,* January 24, 1948, found in Box 54, File "United Nations: Negro Question, 1947–1952," Papers of Warren Austin, University of Vermont, Burlington, Vermont (hereafter Austin Papers).

25. Ibid.

26. Guzman, *Negro Year Book*, pp. 324, 326, 331–32; "The Color Line," Austin Papers. To see the continuation of these health care disparities well into the civil rights movement, see Walter J. Lear, "Testimony of the Medical Committee for Civil Rights on the H.R. 7152, The President's Civil Rights Bill before the Judiciary Committee," July 17, 1963, *Bayard Rustin Papers* (Frederick, Md.: University Publications of America, 1988), Reel 4 (hereafter *Rustin Papers*).

27. Guzman, *Negro Yearbook*, p. 320.

28. Senator George Aiken in Opposition to Lend Lease, *Congressional Record,* February 25, 1941, pp. 1360–63. For World War I's unsavory colonial legacy, see Wm. Roger Louis, "The Repartition of Africa During the First World War," in *Ends of British Imperialism: The Scramble for Empire, Suez, and Decolonization* (London: I.B. Tauris, 2006), pp. 205–24.

29. Elizabeth Borgwardt, *A New Deal for the World: America's Vision for Human Rights* (Cambridge: Belknap Press of Harvard University Press, 2005), pp. 1–45.

30. The Atlantic Charter, Avalon Project of Yale Law School, available online at www.yale.edu/lawweb/avalon/wwii/atlantic.htm. Emphasis added.

31. Ibid.

32. Johnpeter Horst Grill and Robert L. Jenkins, "The Nazis and the American South in the 1930s: A Mirror Image?," *Journal of Southern History* 58(4) (November 1992): 668.

33. "Political Action for the Negro: Delivered by Earl B. Dickerson, at the Philadelphia 31st Annual Conference of the National Association for the Advancement of Colored People," June 19, 1940, *Papers of the National Association for the Advancement of Colored People* (Washington, D.C.: University Publications of America, 1982) (hereafter *NAACP*), Reel 10; Speech of Walter White . . . at the Mass Meeting of the March-on-Washington Movement, June 16, 1942, *Papers of Eleanor Roosevelt, 1933–1945* (Frederick, Md.: University Publications of America, 1986) (hereafter *Roosevelt*), Reel 19.

34. Quoted in Carol Anderson, *Eyes off the Prize: The United Nations and the African American Struggle for Human Rights, 1944–1955* (New York: Cambridge University Press, 2003), p. 10. Excerpts from *Eyes off the Prize*, © 2003 by Carol Anderson. Reprinted with permission of Cambridge University Press.

35. Quoted in Berg, *Ticket to Freedom*, p. 95.

36. Workshop on Race and Non-Violence: Sheet no. 5, The American Racial Scene Today, October 9, 1943, *Rustin Papers*, Reel 5.

37. "An Emergency Conference on the Status of the Negro in the War for the Four Freedoms," June 3–6, 1943, File "391B," Papers of Herbert Lehman, Herbert Lehman Suite, Columbia University, New York, N.Y. (hereafter Lehman Papers).

38. Resolutions of the 33rd Annual Conference of the NAACP, July 14–19, 1942, *NAACP*, Reel 11; Address of Walter White at the NAACP Annual Convention, July 19, 1942, ibid.; Walter White to Franklin D. Roosevelt, May 4, 1942, *Roosevelt*, Reel 19; Announcing the Eastern Seaboard Conference on the Problems of the War and the Negro People, April 10, 1943, Box 29, File "National Negro Congress, 1936–51," Papers of Asa Philip Randolph, Library of Congress, Washington, D.C. (hereafter Randolph Papers).

39. An Emergency Conference on the Status of the Negro in the War for the Four Freedoms, June 3, 1943, File "391B: Walter White," Lehman Papers.

40. Announcing the Eastern Seaboard Conference, Randolph Papers.

41. Julia Baxter to J. E. Magnuson, January 25, 1944, Box A439, File "NAACP Programs: Postwar 1943–44," Papers of the NAACP; Memorandum Presenting Suggestive Notes on "The Negro Worker and His Struggle for Economic Justice," Prepared for Miss Thompson, September 11, 1940, attachment to Ralph Bunche to Malvina C. Thompson, *Papers of Ralph Bunche* (Los Angeles, CA: University of California, Los Angeles, 1980), Reel 2 (hereafter *Bunche Papers*); Radio Talk for Station KGFJ, by Roy Wilkins, July 16, 1942, *NAACP*, Reel 11.

42. A. Phillip Randolph: Movement for International Peace Conference Seat sponsored by Negro League for Real Democracy, February 12, 1942, Box A507, File "A. Philip Randolph, 1942–55," Papers of the NAACP; Speech of Walter White, June 16, 1942, *Roosevelt*, Reel 19; Walter to the Board of Directors, memorandum, February 8, 1943, Box A466, File "Peace Conference Committee to Present Views of Negroes at Upcoming Peace Conference, 1943–44," Papers of the NAACP.

43. W. E. B. Du Bois, "The Negro and Imperialism," transcript of radio broadcast, November 15, 1944, Box 527, File "Speakers: W. E. B. Du Bois, 1944–48," Papers of the NAACP.

44. Herbert Agar, "What We Are Fighting For: United Nations Must Show They Seek Freedom for All," *PM*, July 24, 1942, found in file "Federal Council of

Churches, 1941 [34]," Papers of Channing Tobias: YMCA Collection, University of Minnesota, Minneapolis.

45. Harley Notter to Dean Rusk and Mr. Thompson, memo, March 14, 1947, Box 2187, Decimal File 501.BD/3-1847 (1945–49), General Records of the Department of State Record Group 59, National Archives II, College Park, Md. (hereafter RG 59).

46. Quoted in Berg, *Ticket to Freedom*, p. 96.

47. Quoted in White, *A Man Called White: The Autobiography of Walter White* (New York: Viking Press, 1948), pp. 108, 168; quoted in Harry S. Ashmore, *Civil Rights and Wrongs: A Memoir of Race and Politics, 1944–1994* (New York: Pantheon Books, 1994), p. 8; Address by Walter White, . . . at closing meeting of Wartime Conference, July 16, 1944, Reel 19, *Roosevelt*.

48. Durward Sandifer Oral History, Harry S. Truman Presidential Library, Independence, Mo.

49. *Dred Scott v. Sandford*, 60 U.S. 393, 19 How. 393, 15 L.Ed. 691 (1856), 14.

50. Hamilton Fish Armstrong to Tom Connally, July 30, 1945, Box 16, File "Connally, Tom, 1943, 1945, 1949," Papers of Hamilton Fish Armstrong, Seeley Mudd Manuscript Library, Princeton University, Princeton, N.J. (hereafter Armstrong Papers); Walter White's handwritten notes of meeting with Corps Com., 9:30 a.m. 68 Post St., ca. May 1, 1945, Box 639, File "United Nations: United Nations Conference on International Organization—General, 1945–July, 1946," Papers of the NAACP; Meeting of the American Delegation, April 27, 1945, Box 84, Folder 17, Armstrong Papers; Meeting of the United States Delegation: Summary Record, April 27, 1945, Box 84, Folder 18, ibid.; Hamilton Fish Armstrong's handwritten minutes of U.S. Delegates Meeting 5:30, May 2, 1945, Box 84, Folder 23, ibid.

51. Hamilton Fish Armstrong's handwritten minutes of U.S. Delegates Meeting 5:30, May 2, 1945, Box 84, Folder 23, Armstrong Papers.

52. "Report of the Secretary," May 1945, Part 1, Reel 7, *NAACP*; Walter White et al. to Stettinius, telegram, May 7, 1945, Reel 58, *Papers of W. E. B. Du Bois* (Sanford, N.C.: Microfilming Corporation of America, 1980), microfilm (hereafter *Du Bois*); Informal Consultation on Domestic Jurisdiction of the United States, the United Kingdom, and Australia, June 1, 1945, Box 216, File "UNCIO-Domestic Jurisdiction (General)," Files of Harley A. Notter: RG 59 (hereafter Notter). Excerpts from *Eyes off the Prize*, © 2003 by Carol Anderson. Reprinted with permission of Cambridge University Press.

53. "Proposed Article to be inserted as a new chapter in the Charter," May 3, 1945, Box 216, File "UNCIO-Domestic Jurisdiction (General)," Notter; Meeting of the Big Four, 12 noon, May 4, 1945, Box 84, Folder 25, Armstrong Papers; Meeting of the United States Delegation, 6:20 p.m., May 3, 1945, Box 84, Folder 24, ibid.; United Nations, "Amendments Proposed by the Governments of the United States, the United Kingdom, the Soviet Union and China," May 5, 1945, *United Nations Conference on International Organization San Francisco, 1945: Documents*, vol. 3, *Dumbarton Oaks Proposals Comments and Proposed Amendments* (London: United Nations Information Organizations, 1945), pp. 622–23. Excerpts from *Eyes off the Prize*, © 2003 by Carol Anderson. Reprinted with permission of Cambridge University Press.

54. "Summary of Debate on Domestic Jurisdiction: Joint Four-Power Amendment," June 1, 1945, Notter.

55. Ibid. Excerpts from *Eyes off the Prize*, © 2003 by Carol Anderson. Reprinted with permission of Cambridge University Press.

56. Donald C. Blaisdell Oral History, Harry S. Truman Presidential Library, Independence, Mo.

57. Harley Notter to Dean Rusk and Mr. Thompson, memo, March 14, 1947, Box 2187, Decimal File 501.BD/3-1847 (1945–49), RG 59. Excerpts from *Eyes off the Prize*, © 2003 by Carol Anderson. Reprinted with permission of Cambridge University Press.

58. Ralph Ellison, *Shadow and Act* (New York: Random House, 1964), p. 28. Excerpts from *Eyes off the Prize*, © 2003 by Carol Anderson. Reprinted with permission of Cambridge University Press.

59. "Discussion on Principles and Problems Relating to Minorities with a View to Prepare Instructions to the United States Delegate," SD/E/HR/MINDIS/D-3, August 27, 1946, Box 47, File "SD/E/HR/MINDIS/1-4," Lot File 82D211, RG 59; James Green to Durward Sandifer, May 21, 1953, Box 8, File "Ninth Session of the Commission," Lot File 55D429, RG 59. Excerpts from *Eyes off the Prize*, © 2003 by Carol Anderson. Reprinted with permission of Cambridge University Press.

60. [James Hendrick,] Covenant on Human Rights, draft letter, January 14, 1948, Box 2, File "Human Rights Memorandum," Papers of James Hendrick, Harry S. Truman Presidential Library, Independence, Mo. (hereafter Hendrick Papers).

61. Logan to White, memo, March 8, 1948, Box 181-8, Folder 3, Papers of Rayford Logan, Moorland-Spingarn Research Center, Howard University, Washington, D.C. (hereafter Logan-MSRC); James Simsarian to Eleanor Roosevelt, December 21, 1949, Box 4588, File "Human Rights Commission, 1949," Papers of Eleanor Roosevelt, Franklin D. Roosevelt Presidential Library, Hyde Park, NY (hereafter Roosevelt Papers). White to Rayford Logan, September 25, 1951, Box 181-8, Folder 3, Logan-MSRC; White to Rayford Logan, October 24, 1951, ibid.; "Statement to the Press by Mrs. Franklin D. Roosevelt on the 'Federal State' Clause of the Covenant on Human Rights," press release, June 6, 1952, Box 4588, File "Human Rights Commission, undated," Roosevelt Papers; Lowell Limpus, "UN Pact Won't Clash with States' Rights, Says Mrs. Roosevelt," June 9, 1952, found in Box 626, File "UN Secur. Council 'Commission on Human Rt of the Econ & Soc Coun,'" Republican National Committee Newspaper Clippings, Dwight D. Eisenhower Presidential Library, Abilene, Kans. (hereafter RNC); White to Jacob Javits, March 6, 1952, Box 117, File "Bills: McCarran Bill—General—1950-52," Papers of the NAACP. Excerpts from *Eyes off the Prize*, © 2003 by Carol Anderson. Reprinted with permission of Cambridge University Press.

62. Durward V. Sandifer to Mr. Green, Mr. Hiss et al., memo, May 21, 1946, Box 8, File "Human Rights: March 1945–December 31, 1947," Lot File 55D429, RG 59.

63. Quoted in Howard Tolley, Jr., *The U.N. Commission on Human Rights* (Boulder, Colo.: Westview, 1987), pp. 16, 18; Charles S. Murphy to D. V. Sandifer, memo April 14, 1948, Box 533, File "85-Q Human Rights Commission Folder," Papers of Harry S. Truman: Official File, Harry S. Truman Presidential Library, Independence, Mo. (hereafter Truman: OF); Durward V. Sandifer to Eleanor Roosevelt, April 16, 1948, Box 4595 (No File), Roosevelt Papers; Draft Memo of Conversation with Roosevelt, Sandifer, Hendrick on March 4, 1948, April 20, 1948, Box 2, File "Human Rights Memorandum," Hendrick Papers; "Human Rights and International Organization," n.d., Box 4588, File "Human Rights Commission, undated," Roosevelt Papers; Statement of the Position of the United States on Petitions by Individuals in Relation to a Covenant on Human Rights, April 30, 1948, Box 4593, File "Mrs. Roosevelt," ibid.

64. "Problems of Discrimination and Minority Status in the United States," January 22, 1947, Box 43, File "SD/E/CN.4/1-43," Lot File 82D211, RG 59.

65. Ibid.

66. Mary L. Dudziak, *Cold War Civil Rights: Race and the Image of American Democracy* (Princeton, N.J.: Princeton University Press, 2000); Thomas Borstelmann, *The Cold War and the Color Line: American Race Relations in the Global Arena* (Cambridge, Mass.: Harvard University Press, 2001).

67. "Commission on Human Rights, First Session of Full Commission, January 1947: Consideration of Communications Received," SD/CS.4/5, January 16, 1947, Box 4594, File "U.N. Human Rights Commission, 1946–June 1947," Roosevelt Papers; Robert McClintock to Robert A. Lovett, November 25, 1947, memo, Box 4595, File "Book I: Position Book for Second Session of Commission on Human Rights, Geneva, Switzerland, December 1–19, 1947," ibid.; Marginalia on Harley Notter to Dean Rusk and Mr. Thompson, memo, March 14, 1947, Box 2187, Decimal File 501.BD/3-1847 (1945–49), RG 59.

68. NAACP, *An Appeal to the World! A Statement on the Denial of Human Rights to Minorities in the Case of Citizens of Negro Descent in the United States of America and an Appeal to the United Nations for Redress* (New York: NAACP, 1947), pp. 62–63.

69. Ibid., pp. 64–65.

70. Ibid., p. 66. $25 million in 1943 is the equivalent in 2005 of $1,567,950,654.58 using the relative share of GDP. Comparison calculations available online at eh.net/hmit/compare.

71. Jonathan Daniels to James Hendrick, October 29, 1947, Folder 597, Papers of Jonathan Daniels, University of North Carolina, Chapel Hill (hereafter Daniels Papers).

72. Eleanor Roosevelt to White, December 8, 1947, Box 635, File "United Nations General Assembly, 1946–August 1948," Papers of the NAACP; Eleanor Roosevelt, "My Day: The Delegate from Lebanon Was Missing," December 5, 1947, found in Folder 603, Daniels Papers; Eleanor Roosevelt to Walter White, January 20, 1948, Box 3389, File "White, Walter, 1947–50," Roosevelt Papers. Excerpts from *Eyes off the Prize*, © 2003 by Carol Anderson. Reprinted with permission of Cambridge University Press.

73. Walter White to Eleanor Roosevelt, December 31, 1947, 1Box 3389, File "White, Walter, 1947–50," Roosevelt Papers.; Comment Paper: Discrimination Against Negroes in the United States, August 30, 1948, SD/A/C.3/75, Box 175, File "Background Book: Committee III (Social, Humanitarian, and Cultural), Volume IV," Records of the U.S. Mission to the United Nations, Record Group 84, National Archives II, College Park, Md. (hereafter RG 84); Walter White to Eleanor Roosevelt, January 10, 1948, Box 3389, File "White, Walter, 1947–50," Roosevelt Papers; Eleanor Roosevelt to Walter White, January 20, 1948, ibid.; Risa Lauren Goluboff, " 'Let Economic Equality Take Care of Itself': The NAACP, Labor Litigation, and the Making of Civil Rights in the 1940s," *UCLA Law Review* 52(5) (June 2005): 1393–1486. Excerpts from *Eyes off the Prize*, © 2003 by Carol Anderson. Reprinted with permission of Cambridge University Press.

74. Chester S. Williams to Mrs. Roosevelt et al., memorandum of conversation, September 9, 1948, Box 78, File "1948–49, Discrimination: Race," RG 84. For the political reasons behind the clash between White and Du Bois, see Anderson, *Eyes off the Prize*, pp. 113–65.

75. Frank Holman, *The Life and Career of a Western Lawyer, 1886–1961* (Baltimore: Port City Press, 1963), pp. 569–70; Fisher to Rusk, memo, January 19, 1950, Box 8, File "Genocide (folder 1 of 2)," Lot File 55D429, RG 59; Phleger to

Dulles, memo, March 30, 1953, Box 70, File "Re: Genocide Convention, 1953," Papers of John Foster Dulles, Seeley Mudd Manuscript Library, Princeton University, Princeton, N.J. (hereafter JFD-Princeton); Minutes of Cabinet Meeting, February 20, 1953, Box 1, File "Cabinet Meeting of February 20, 1953," Cabinet Series, Papers of Dwight D. Eisenhower: Ann Whitman Files, Dwight D. Eisenhower Presidential Library, Abilene, Kans. (hereafter Eisenhower: AWF).

76. "Bringing the Constitution Up-to-Date: Address by Senator John W. Bricker Before the Annual Convention of the Ohio State Bar Association at Cincinnati, Ohio," April 22, 1953, Box 160, File "2," Papers of John W. Bricker, Ohio Historical Society, Columbus, Ohio (hereafter Bricker Papers).

77. Eisenhower to J. Earl Schaefer, January 22, 1954, Box 5, File "DDE Diary January 1954 (1)," Diary Series, Eisenhower: AWF; quoted in Ambrose, *Eisenhower: The President*, vol. 2 (New York: Simon and Schuster, 1984), pp. 70, 155.

78. Caroline Pruden, *Conditional Partners: Eisenhower, the United Nations, and the Search for a Permanent Peace* (Baton Rouge: Louisiana State University Press, 1998), p. 202; James Hendrick to James Simsarian, July 27, 1948, Box 2, File "Human Rights Memorandum," Hendrick Papers; Committee Completes General Discussion on Human Rights, press release, May 4, 1948, SOC/504, found in Box 634, File "United Nations: General, 1948–49," Papers of the NAACP.

79. Pruden, *Conditional Partners*, p. 203.

80. Minutes of Cabinet Meeting, February 20, 1953, Box 1, File "Cabinet Meeting of February 20, 1953," Cabinet Series, Eisenhower: AWF; Memorandum from Ralph E. Becker [to Senator Thomas J. Hennings, Jr.], January 22, 1954, Folder 4772, Papers of Thomas J. Hennings, Jr., Western Historical Manuscript Collection, University of Missouri, Columbia, Mo. (hereafter Hennings Papers); Fisher to Rusk, memo, January 19, 1950, Box 8, File "Genocide (folder 1 of 2)," Lot File 55D429, RG 59.

81. Broadcast WLIB and Affiliated Stations: Walter White, April 9, 1953, Box 113, File "Bricker Amendment Press Releases, 1953–54,"Papers of the NAACP.

82. Walter White to Senator, April 16, 1953, Box 113, File "Bills: Bricker Amendment Correspondence, 1952–55," ibid.

83. Edward A. Conway, "'Darling Daughter' Amendment," *America*, January 23, 1954, found in Folder 4772, Hennings Papers; Eisenhower to Senator William F. Knowland, January 25, 1954, Box 5, File "DDE Diary January 1954 (1)," Diary Series, Eisenhower: AWF; Eisenhower to Earl Schaefer, January 22, 1954, ibid.; Notes on the Bricker Amendment from Donovan's book, *Eisenhower, The Inside Story*, Box 7, File "Bricker Amendment–Draft Talk (1)," Administration Series, ibid.

84. Francis O. Wilcox, Chief of Staff, Senate Foreign Relations Committee, 1947–55, Oral History, Interview #3, Congress and the Cold War, March 21, 1984, available online at www.senate.gov/learning/learn_history_oralhist_wilcox3. html, pp. 133, 148–49, accessed July 15, 2001.

85. Phleger to Dulles, memo, March 30, 1953, Box 70, File "Re: Genocide Convention, 1953," JFD-Princeton.

86. Tananbaum, *The Bricker Amendment*, pp. 179–80; Amendment to Constitution Relative to Treaties and Executive Agreements, roll call votes, *Journal of the Senate of the United States of America*, 83rd Congress, 2nd Session, p. 159. Excerpts from *Eyes off the Prize*, © 2003 by Carol Anderson. Reprinted with permission of Cambridge University Press.

87. Excerpts from *Eyes off the Prize*, © 2003 by Carol Anderson. Reprinted with permission of Cambridge University Press.

88. J. Mills Thornton III, *Dividing Lines: Municipal Politics and the Struggle for Civil Rights in Montgomery, Birmingham, and Selma* (Tuscaloosa: University of Alabama Press, 2002).

89. U.S. Riot Commission, *Report of the National Advisory Commission on Civil Disorders: What Happened? Why Did It Happen? What Can Be Done?* (New York, 1968).

90. Bayard Rustin speech at Grand Valley State College in Michigan, March 25, 1985, *Rustin Papers*, Reel 2, emphasis in original.

91. Nicole Gaouette and Richard A. Serrano, "Despite Warnings, Washington Failed to Fund Levee Projects," *Los Angeles Times*, September 4, 2005.

92. Stephen Maloney, "Leaks in 'Education Pipeline' Tied to State's Poverty Levels," *New Orleans City Business*, October 23, 2006; Diane Rowland, Executive Vice President, Henry J. Kaiser Family Foundation, testimony before Congress, "Post Katrina Health Care: Continuing Concerns and Immediate Needs in the New Orleans Region," March 13, 2007; Ricardo Alonso-Zaldivar, "New Orleans Is Sicker Than Ever," *Los Angeles Times*, March 14, 2007; Randal O'Toole, "Lack of Automobility Key to New Orleans Tragedy," *Seattle Times*, September 14, 2005.

93. James Oliphant, "Bush Never Recovered from Response to Katrina, Former Aides Say: Surveys Bolster the Officials' Views, Finding That the President's Ratings Went into a Free-Fall After the New Orleans Disaster, with Most Americans Summing Him up as 'Incompetent,'" *Los Angeles Times*, December 31, 2008; "Poll: Katrina Response Inadequate: Public Says Response to Katrina Too Slow; Confidence in Bush Drops," CBS News, September 8, 2005, http://www. cbsnews.com/stories/2005/09/08/opinion/polls/main824591.shtml, accessed January 5, 2009; "Chertoff: Katrina Scenario Did Not Exist: However, Experts for Years Had Warned of Threat to New Orleans," September 5, 2005, http://www. cnn.com/2005/US/09/03/katrina.chertoff/, accessed January 5, 2009; Spencer S. Hsu and Susan B. Glasser, "The Point Man: FEMA Director Singled Out by Response Critics," *Washington Post*, September 6, 2005.

94. Jonathan Alter, "The Other America: After Katrina II—Confronting Poverty & Migration," *Newsweek*, September 19, 2005. For the ongoing crisis in education and its effects on African Americans, see Jay P. Greene,Civic Report, November 2001, High School Graduation Rates in the United States (revised April 2002), Manhattan Institute for Policy Research, available online at www. manhattan-institute.org/html/cr_baeo.htm#08, October 20, 2005; Gary Orfield, Susan E. Eaton, et al., *Dismantling Desegregation: The Quiet Reversal of Brown v. Board of Education* (New York: New Press, 1996); for housing, see George Lipsitz, *The Possessive Investment in Whiteness: How White People Profit from Identity Politics* (Philadelphia: Temple University Press, 1998), pp. 13–14; Urban Institute, *Report Card on Discrimination*, pp. 35–37; Urban Institute, "A Foot in the Door?: New Evidence on Housing Discrimination (February 2003), available online at www. urban.org/publications/900625.html; for the health care crisis, see Kevin Watkins, *Human Development Report 2005: International Cooperation at a Crossroads, Aid, Trade, and Security in an Unequal World* (New York: United Nations Development Programme, 2005), p. 58; Dave Davis and Elizabeth Marchak, "Deadly Differences," *Cleveland Plain Dealer*, March 12, 2000; Dr. Adewale Troutman, "Unequal Treatment," PBS Online Newshour with Jim Lehrer, March 9, 2005; Institute of Medicine of the National Academies, "Unequal Treatment: Confronting Racial and Ethnic Disparities in Health Care," March 20, 2002; for employment and wealth, see Rakesh Kochhar, *The Wealth of Hispanic Households: 1996 to 2002* (Washington, D.C.: Pew Hispanic Trust, 2004), p. 2; Mariann Bertrand and Sen-

dhil Mullainathan, "Are Emily and Greg More Employable than Lakisha and Jamal? A Field Experiment on Labor Market Discrimination," Working Papers Series WP 03-22, Massachusetts Institute of Technology Department of Economics, 2003, available online at www.nber.org/papers/W9873; Devah Pager, "The Mark of a Criminal Record," *American Journal of Sociology* 108 (2003): 937–75; Andrew Hacker, *Two Nations: Black and White, Separate, Hostile, Unequal,* 2nd ed. (New York: Ballantine Books, 1995), pp. 112–38.

95. Warren Austin to Henry L. Moon, December 23, 1952, Box 54, File "United Nations: Negro Question, 1947–1952," Austin Papers; "The Shaming of America," *Economist,* September 10, 2005, p. 11.

96. Walter White to Herbert Lehman et al., telegram, July 11, 1950, Box A617, File "State Department: Point IV Program, 1949–54," Papers of the NAACP.

Chapter 4
"New" Human Rights?
U.S. Ambivalence Toward the International
Economic and Social Rights Framework

Hope Lewis

> It is not charity, but a right—not bounty but justice that I am pleading for . . . The confluence of affluence and wretchedness continually meeting and offending the eye, is like dead and living bodies chained together.
>
> —*Thomas Paine*[1]

> A Bill of Rights for the disadvantaged, applicable to white and Negro families alike . . . could mark the rise of a new era, in which the full resources of the society would be used to attack the tenacious poverty that so paradoxically exists in the midst of plenty.
>
> —*Dr. Martin Luther King, Jr.*[2]

Who Needs "New" Rights? The United States and the Outsider Status of Economic and Social Rights

Economic and social rights[3] (including rights to food, adequate housing, public education, the highest attainable standard of physical and mental health, fair wages, decent labor conditions, and social security) still occupy a second-class, "outsider" status in official U.S. domestic and foreign policy. This is no accident. The full recognition and implementation of such rights pose a direct threat not to democracy or "American values," as some believe, but to the deeply held view that our country has achieved a truly representative, human rights–based society.[4]

This chapter provides an overview of American engagement with the international economic and social human rights system. It particularly explores how and why the U.S. has been so deeply ambivalent about international economic and social rights. The chapter begins by reviewing the international context in which U.S. attitudes about human rights developed and early U.S. influences on the drafting and promulgation of core human rights instruments. As described below, the initial, and deep, official U.S. involvement with the international human rights framework was soon undermined. American racism, among other factors, resulted in an effective decades-long suspension of U.S. formal acceptance of internally applicable international human rights treaties. Further, Cold War politics played a key role in the ultimate division of a single UN Covenant on Human Rights into two separate treaties. This period helped entrench fear and distrust of the domestic application of human rights which surface in some circles even today.

Although the United States signed the treaties in the International Bill of Rights in the late 1970s in preparation for ratification, domestic and foreign policy concerns undermined or voided entirely the practical legal application of international human rights standards in the United States. With few exceptions, that ideological legacy, including the formal rejection of economic and social rights, continues to impact U.S. government policy into the twenty-first century.

Nevertheless, there is room for optimism. The chapter ends by briefly highlighting some contemporary efforts that may help overcome the disappointing history of American ambivalence and make socioeconomic rights a reality in the United States.[5] Among those opportunities is the growing awareness of, and attention to, economic and social rights among grassroots groups, leading nongovernmental organizations, and other U.S. human rights advocates. Rejecting U.S. ambivalence, these entities grapple with such "domestic" U.S. problems as racial and ethnic discrimination, poverty, homelessness, abuses of workers' rights, and lack of access to health care by invoking international economic and social human rights standards.

Everything Old Is "New" Again: International Contexts for the Recognition of Socioeconomic Rights

Political precursors to contemporary socioeconomic rights were in the air during the U.S. postrevolutionary period. By the 1790s, the French constitution provided for free public education and maintenance of the poor and Thomas Paine was promoting his views on the redistribution of land and wealth in *Agrarian Justice*.[6] Rights to land and cultural integrity of indigenous peoples, resistance to the enslavement of African Americans, the theft of their labor, prohibitions on their literacy and violent interference with the enjoyment of family, religion, or cultural life, calls for recognition of the inheritance and employment rights of women, the rights of workers to a fair wage under safe conditions and to bargain collectively, the rights of Asian and European immigrants to enter the country and live decent lives—all represented early forms of economic, social, and cultural rights advocacy in the United States.[7] And, of course, the right to property was enshrined in our Declaration of Independence, if only for free white men who already owned property.[8]

The title of this chapter, " 'New' Human Rights?," however, reflects the common perception that socioeconomic rights concepts were new to the United States during the post–World War II period in which the international human rights instruments were being drafted. The United States and the major European powers were said to be most familiar with the liberal tradition of individual civil and political rights such as those elaborated in the French Declaration of the Rights of Man, the U.S. Declaration of Independence, and the U.S. Bill of Rights. This led some in the United States to define civil and political rights as the equivalent of "human rights." For them, it seemed self-evident that individuals needed protection against a state's abuse of its power: torture, arbitrary arrest, detention, and execution, as well as arbitrary restrictions on freedom of movement, freedom of religious belief and political conscience, freedom of speech, and the right to political participation. Such "negative" rights, it was argued, were clearly defined and had a long and well-developed comparative jurisprudence analyzing their scope and implementation. Courts would adjudicate them primarily as protections against state abuse of power over individual autonomy or the state's failure to appropriately protect individuals from certain private abuses.

In this strong form of Western liberal rights analysis, food, housing, education, and health care seemed "private" concerns that could or should be negotiated in the marketplace as matters of individual responsibility. To the extent that poverty or other deprivations led to lack of access to such goods, religious and other private charities could step in. Government could also address such social problems, but in the form of voluntary benefits rather than as legal claims that the state was obligated to fulfill.[9]

Further, some argued, economic and social rights are "positive" in nature and therefore require affirmative actions by the national state, as well as the significant expenditure of state resources, to fulfill. Such public expenditures should be authorized by legislative process and administered by the executive. It was considered antidemocratic and an infringement on the separation of powers for courts to step in except if such rights were being unconstitutionally or unfairly recognized or applied by the other branches.[10] Such a liberal philosophical view largely defined U.S. federal approaches to the rights of individuals while the fundamental international human rights instruments were being drafted and beyond.[11]

On the subnational level, however, a number of state constitutions took a different approach. For example, many state governments recognized the importance of a broad-based right to public education as important for a representative democracy. A number recognized subsistence, health, or other social welfare rights as well.[12] Yet even such state constitutional socioeconomic rights provisions tend to be narrowly construed.

The United States was not alone in its criticism and caution. Developing countries were also concerned that national state responsibility for implementation of economic and social rights would severely disadvantage poor countries by imposing significant costs that they would be unable to bear. Historians have charted in detail how the recognition of individual economic and social rights, nondiscrimination rights, and the right to the self-determination of peoples was to become part of a global political game in the period following the founding of the UN and in the Cold War to follow.[13]

Despite the post–World War II U.S. and international concerns about socioeconomic rights outlined above, concepts associated with socioeconomic justice are not entirely "new"—even to American political and social contexts. Economic and social rights originate from very old beliefs about the inherent claims of individuals on society and the obligations of that society to provide the fundamentals necessary to protect human dignity. Such concepts originated from both non-Western and Western sources.[14] Although the formal international human rights legal framework is a product of twentieth-century norm creation in the United Nations and in American and European regional bodies, there were many precursors to contemporary human rights systems in non-Western contexts. For example, certain communitarian cultural traditions among Asian and African peoples required the effective redistribution of wealth and material assistance to the poor, the sick, widows and orphans, and strangers to the community. Nevertheless, the provision of such assistance was generally structured as a duty rather than as the right of those in need.[15]

These varied religious, philosophical, and political influences were represented to some extent at the United Nations' founding and during the drafting of the International Bill of Rights although the traditions as interpreted by the major powers at the end of World War II played the most dominant roles.[16]

But it was World War II itself and widespread revelations about the extent and moral implications of the Holocaust, carpet bombing, and the use of nuclear weapons that further undergirded calls for the recognition of international human rights, including economic and social rights. In addition to the sheer physical violence associated with global war, it was widely recognized that economic dislocation, rampant inflation and the inability to purchase food and other basic needs, massive unemployment, as well as existing racial and religious prejudice, created conditions ripe for the perverted philosophies of fascism and Nazism to take popular hold.[17]

The protection of economic and social human rights can be viewed as an additional security measure, aimed at the prevention of further global and domestic conflicts. Further, the sheer inhumanity that millions witnessed in newsreels and print demonstrated how starvation, enslavement, and horrific medical experiments could be used as weapons against civilian populations. Exposing such atrocities could also reveal how recognizing and protecting rights to food, appropriate working conditions and wages, and the right to the highest attainable standard of health could be linked directly to civil and political rights to life, prohibitions on slavery, and integrity of the person.

These realities led to popular demands (despite governmental fears about the undermining of state sovereignty) that the promotion and protection of all human rights and fundamental freedoms (including socioeconomic rights) should be a primary purpose of the new United Nations. Only in a world that recognized the importance of human rights could it hope to fulfill its promise as an international peace and security organization.[18] U.S. President Franklin D. Roosevelt had called for such a pride of place for human rights, including economic and social rights, and U.K. Prime Minister Winston Churchill had confirmed this view in the Atlantic Charter of 1941.[19]

Although the obligation to promote and respect human rights and fundamental freedoms was imposed on all UN member states by the legally binding Charter of the United Nations,[20] it remained necessary to specifically elaborate the content of those human rights. Thus, the first UN Commission on Human Rights was charged with drafting a bill of rights (to be partially modeled on domestic constitutional standards including the U.S. Bill of Rights) that would elaborate specific human rights standards for which member states were to be responsible. Economic and social rights were an important, though controversial, part of this set of norms from the beginning, and strong support from Latin American states, among others, made the inclusion of socioeconomic rights in the International Bill of Rights almost inevitable.[21]

From National to International Economic and Social Security: Roosevelt's Four Freedoms and the Universal Declaration of Human Rights

United States official foreign and domestic policy was to become distinctly unfriendly toward socioeconomic rights by the beginning of the Cold War. But, in the period leading up to the founding of the United Nations, the United States was, in fact, a leader in the articulation of such rights. Rather than being "alien" to American values, one of the early advocates of economic and social rights was none other than U.S. President Franklin D. Roosevelt.

During World War II, President Roosevelt eloquently described the principles that would come to be known as "the Four Freedoms." In his 1941 State of the Union Address, he described the universal necessity of recognizing freedom of speech and expression, freedom of worship, freedom from want, and freedom from fear. In part, the speech laid the groundwork for a framework for an international economic, social, and cultural human rights regime.[22]

Set forth during the midst of the violence plaguing Europe, Africa, and Asia, but prior to the U.S. entry into the war, Roosevelt's early iteration clearly delineates the interdependence and international character of all human rights. The "freedom from want," for example, which was to serve as a partial underpinning of many specific economic and social rights, is described as part of an international economic order necessary to allow for such a freedom to be protected.

Roosevelt's list extended beyond a traditional American concern with civil and political rights to include the poverty, unemployment, and lack of access to basic needs that his administration had sought to address in New Deal legislation.[23] By treating these freedoms as equally important and linked, Roosevelt rhetorically embraced the principle that civil, political, economic, social, and cultural rights are indivisible. Although most UN member states still fail to put it into practice, Roosevelt's acknowledgment of the interdependence of rights categories was later to be reiterated at important moments in the international human rights movement and even confirmed by U.S. officials.[24]

By articulating clearly that the freedoms applied "everywhere in the world," Roosevelt acknowledged that certain rights should be universal, rather than limited only to certain races, ethnicities, cultures, or political and economic systems.

A few years later, while the United States was fully engaged in the war, Roosevelt further developed the economic and social rights aspects of the Four Freedoms concept and highlighted the links between the international and domestic spheres by calling specifically for an "Economic Bill of Rights" in the United States.[25]

Roosevelt was clear that this call for a "second Bill of Rights" was in U.S. national security interests. The failure to protect such rights might well lead to civil unrest and even violence. The impact of the Great Depression's high unemployment rates and widespread poverty in the United States highlighted the importance of economic and social security. Although not explicitly rights-based, some of the administration's New Deal policies responded to actual or potential unrest among displaced workers and veterans.[26]

Roosevelt's further assertion that socioeconomic rights should be extended to all "regardless of station, race, or creed" certainly caused consternation among conservatives, but it also served national security and reputational interests. Civil rights efforts were growing stronger at the time, but most African Americans still faced a culture of racial violence and discrimination, along with deep poverty and lack of access to basic needs. It was feared that racial discrimination and related human rights abuses could affect national security interests by encouraging organized political resistance and by undermining U.S. foreign policy efforts to counter Soviet critiques of U.S. racial politics.[27]

Interestingly, Roosevelt also adopted a pro-business stance in which trade and markets figured prominently, arguing in the 1944 State of the Union speech for "rights" to free trade and the protection of business interests. Thus, even early on, modern human rights policy was linked to domestic and global economic agendas. The human rights effects of international economic policies and corporate activity has only grown more significant since, but so far has not served the majority of the world's peoples in the positive ways that Roosevelt imagined.

The Four Freedoms approach to rights was both a domestic and an international strategy. An important force behind the founding of the United Nations, Roosevelt hoped that the new organization would promote the kind of international peace and security that had eluded the League of Nations.[28] Unfortunately, Roosevelt did not see the culmination of this vision before he passed away in 1945. It was left to Eleanor Roosevelt, a civil rights activist and humanitarian in her own right, to move U.S. policy forward on international economic and social human rights.

Because of her status as the former First Lady, as well as her internationally renowned commitment to bettering the lives of the poor, workers, and women, President Harry S. Truman appointed Mrs. Roosevelt to lead the U.S. delegation to the United Nations and to act as the first chair of the Commission on Human Rights (now the Human Rights Council).

The discourse in its founding instruments suggested that the protection of human rights was to be a high priority on the UN agenda and central to the organization's mission.

The Charter of the United Nations specifies in its preamble and in Article 2 that the promotion and protection of "human rights and fundamental freedoms" is an important purpose of the organization. Moreover, Articles 55 and 56 together create a legal obligation on all member nations to promote and protect human rights.[29]

However, despite their inclusion among the purposes of the United Nations, the protection of human rights were not initially, in practical terms, a high priority for the United Nations.[30] The major powers built in to the structure of the charter a seemingly strong non-intervention provision protecting state sovereignty over internal affairs in Article 2(7).

Thus, the charter's text reflects a continuing tension in the international legal system, including the human rights system. On the one hand, governments understood that it was in the interest of most states to cooperate across borders and to make collective arrangements to ensure international peace and security. By doing so, they hoped to prevent future global wars and to address issues—such as poverty and socioeconomic development—that are of an international character. At the same time, both dominant and developing states also feared that the new organization would interfere with the political or economic policies considered internal to each country—creating an unacceptably strong form of "world governance."

Under contemporary analysis, the notion that human rights might be a solely domestic matter has been strongly rejected by most governments and international legal scholars. During the early days of the United Nations' existence however, and for decades to follow, the paper shield of "sovereignty" concerns was used by some to argue against international approaches to human rights violations—including violations of economic and social rights.

U.S. administrations were not immune to the desire to resist international scrutiny on sovereignty grounds. The United States resisted UN actions and policies—including language and interpretations of the international human rights instruments that might allow other major powers (or coalitions of small countries) to interfere in U.S. domestic policies. Of course, this position on sovereignty did not prevent the United States from adopting foreign policies throughout its subsequent history that interfered politically, economically, or militarily in the domestic affairs of other nations.[31]

By contrast, representatives of some smaller developing countries also feared that the new UN organization would be dominated by the major powers or that human rights might be used as an excuse for colonial or neocolonial military and economic interventions. The latter fear turned out to be prophetic.

Nevertheless, in the period shortly after World War II, a grassroots movement for international human rights had begun to flourish. Ordinary people around the world hoped that a new international organization, and the worldwide recognition of fundamental human rights, could be helpful tools in struggles against government abuses, racism, ethnic oppression, and colonialism.

Once the Commission on Human Rights was created, many saw it as a potential protector of the range of human rights against the powerful. Activist groups, including some within the United States, filed petitions alleging widespread human rights violations in their home countries. Delegates from some developing countries argued that the protection of human rights, including economic and social rights, must be taken seriously as a principal purpose of the new United Nations; they helped raise the profile of the issue.[32] Mrs. Roosevelt's own commitment to humanitarian causes also made human rights advocacy a high-profile matter.

Drafting Socioeconomic Rights Standards

Mrs. Roosevelt's record as a social justice activist stirred hope in many, including African American leaders, that she would be a strong advocate for guaranteeing the full range of human rights protections within the United States and abroad. As chair of the UN body that drafted the Universal Declaration of Human Rights (UDHR), Eleanor Roosevelt's place in history as a human rights leader is self-evident. Unfortunately, however, Mrs. Roosevelt's approach to economic and social rights (along with Truman administration policy) became increasingly circumscribed and cautious as Cold War concerns took priority.

The first task assigned to the Commission on Human Rights was to draft an "International Bill of Rights"—a statement elaborating what the "human rights and fundamental freedoms" described in the UN Charter were to consist of. It was to be no easy task. Among the concerns initially articulated was whether it was even possible to identify a set of rights norms that were common to all peoples, including those from different political and economic systems, cultural traditions, and racial and ethnic makeups.

Further, sovereignty concerns delayed the development of implementation and enforcement mechanisms for the new human rights framework. Instead of a binding treaty, a statement of (initially) nonbinding principles was deemed an achievable first step to allay fears about the potential impact of a legally binding instrument on the domestic affairs of powers like the United States and the Soviet Union.

Thus, the commission began to draft a "declaration" that would set forth fundamental standards common to all peoples everywhere. And although it was drafted and adopted as a declaration of principles, the instrument has proved to be one of the most influential human rights documents in its legal, moral, and political significance.[33]

Mary Ann Glendon describes in some detail the drafting process and the often complex relationship between official government policies and the individual visions and personalities of the delegates involved.[34] From the beginning, the makeup of the Commission ensured that both civil and political rights traditions (associated, arguably, with the U.S.–Western European bloc) and economic, social, and cultural rights traditions (associated, arguably, with the Soviet Union and Eastern bloc countries) were to be included in the UDHR.[35] Latin American states also were important supporters of the inclusion of economic and social rights, some having already recognized such rights in domestic contexts.[36]

Franklin Roosevelt's influential Four Freedoms appear in the preamble to the UDHR, which notes that a world in which they are protected is "the highest aspiration of the common people."

Such a "world made new"[37] was to include civil and political rights, economic and social rights, and, as specified in Article 28, an entitlement to "a social and international order in which the rights and freedoms set forth in this Declaration can be fully realized."

The Scope and Influence of the UDHR

The most highly regarded and widely recognized of the international human rights instruments, the UDHR includes both civil and political rights (Articles 1–21) and economic, social, and cultural rights (Articles 22–27). Setting the stage for important nondiscriminatory language common to all of the major international human rights instruments to follow, the UDHR provides that "everyone" is entitled to the enumerated rights without discrimination as to "race, colour, sex, language, religion, political or other opinion, national or social origin, property, birth or other status."

As noted above, Article 28 places this rights regime for individual human beings in the broader context of the society and the international community. Finally, Article 29 recognizes that, for such an individual rights regime to be effective, individual duties to the community and lawful limitations on rights are to be provided for.

Among the economic and social rights elaborated are the right to own property (Article 17), labor rights (Article 23), the right to rest and leisure (Article 24), the right to free primary public education (Article 26), and intellectual property rights and to "share in scientific advancement and its benefits" (Article 27).

Articles 22 and 25 set out some of the most significant general provisions on socioeconomic rights, providing for social security and an adequate standard of living, respectively.

Since the declaration was intended to be a statement of principles rather than a legally binding treaty, its substantive provisions are phrased in passive terms, in most cases without identifying a specific duty-bearer ("Everyone has the right to . . ."). The major drafting powers, including the United States, the United Kingdom, and the Soviet Union, all had significant interests in beginning the elaboration of international human rights in a form that was not legally binding. They were still suspicious of the potential implications of legally enforceable rights on their own policies. With regard to the inclusion of economic and social rights, however, the Soviets and Eastern bloc countries argued that the state should be clearly required to have primary responsibility for the protection of such rights.[38]

The UDHR was to become the primary statement of international human rights as well as the most widely disseminated and respected instrument on this issue. After much intense debate over its content, the final version was adopted by unanimous vote of the UN General Assembly on December 10, 1948, with few states abstaining.[39] Subsequently, the newly independent states that entered the UN system in the postwar period have, at least rhetorically, embraced it as an authoritative statement of fundamental rights and freedoms to be promoted and respected by all.

With President Truman's support, the United States adopted the UDHR in 1948 and agreed, at least as a moral and political matter, to respect its principles, including its provisions on economic and social rights.[40] Nevertheless, Eleanor Roosevelt expressed U.S. official discomfort with a strong form of economic and social rights protection, stating that such rights did not "imply an obligation on governments to assure the enjoyment of these rights by direct governmental action."[41]

For the human rights movement, for the peoples of developing countries, for the poor and racial, ethnic, and religious minorities in the United States, 1948 marked a unique moment of hope and possibility. Although that dream continues to have strong significance and commitment among many today, the realities of political and economic struggle also revealed the limits of rights discourse.[42]

The years following the adoption of the UDHR saw the outbreak of a full-blown Cold War and the devolution, in some circles, of human rights to the status of political football. Nothing illustrates this retrogression on effective human rights protection more clearly than the U.S. role in the creation and ultimate bifurcation of the legally binding Covenant on Human Rights that was intended to complete the International Bill of Rights.

A Divided World: Cold War Politics, the Threat of Socioeconomic Rights, and the Bifurcation of the Human Rights Covenant

The U.S. relationship with the international human rights framework, including that for economic and social rights, played a key political role in the Cold War.

Race was often at the center of the related controversies. The United Nations' international human rights instruments, reflecting as they did the closely felt experience of recent European genocide, all had clear nondiscrimination, equality, and cultural protection provisions with regard to race, ethnicity, and religious difference.

The American legacy of racism in all aspects of civil, political, economic, and social life, however, made the international recognition of such equality and nondiscrimination principles particularly troublesome for U.S. policymakers. In addition to the perceived threat of rising internal expectations among African Americans and other racially subordinated groups, the United States was beginning to be subject to external criticism from the newly (or soon to be) decolonized nations of the Global South and the stinging criticism of the Soviet Union as the Cold War intensified in the 1950s.

The Soviet Union used media reports about race riots, lynchings, and racial segregation in the United States very effectively as evidence of U.S. human rights hypocrisy.[43] How could the United States claim moral superiority if it countenanced the political and economic subordination of millions within its own borders?

The Race Petitions

This Cold War context created greater political risk for those domestic groups hoping to use the new UN system and the UN Charter to expose human rights violations and promote social justice. Even prior to the adoption of the UDHR, African Americans and U.S. civil rights organizations were among those submitting complaints and petitions to the Commission on Human Rights. The National Negro Congress filed a petition with the UN Economic and Social Council in 1946 asking that the United Nations examine, and take corrective action on, patterns of racial abuse in the United States.[44] In addition, leading intellectual, internationalist, and civil rights leader W. E. B. Du Bois coauthored an influential petition to the United Nations on behalf of the National Association for the Advancement of Colored People (NAACP) titled "An Appeal to the World: A Statement on the Denial of Human Rights to Minorities in the Case of Citizens of Negro Descent in the United States of America and An Appeal to the United Nations for Redress."[45]

Although Eleanor Roosevelt, herself a board member of the NAACP, initially seemed supportive of efforts to include racial injustices in the United States on the UN agenda,[46] the petition's biting analysis and broad foreign support raised the stakes beyond what U.S. officials could bear in the Cold War context. Du Bois had garnered the support of numerous other domestic civil rights organizations. Perhaps even more significantly, peoples in the emerging nations of South Asia, Africa, and the Caribbean saw the petition as additional moral and political support for an end to colonialism and the promotion of self-determination of peoples on an international scale.[47] India, which had placed South African apartheid on the UN agenda, was supportive of the petition's racial equality goals but feared that formally bringing the matter for debate might mean "participating in functions which deal with controversial domestic politics or with sectarian affairs."[48]

Because neither the United States nor India was willing to take the ultimate step of sponsoring the Du Bois petition for debate before the Commission on Human Rights, it was the Soviet Union that formally placed it on the commission's agenda.[49] In the tense international political atmosphere, Soviet support for the petition was treated as a political betrayal by U.S. officials and some in civil society as well. The organizations and individuals who filed the petition were subject to suspicion. Some within NAACP leadership, as well as conservative African American commentators, argued that African American criticism of the United States on the world stage was disloyal. Du Bois, in contrast, criticized Eleanor Roosevelt for bowing to State Department concerns about the political effect of the petition.[50] Ironically, however, the furor surrounding Soviet involvement hastened civil rights reforms under the Truman administration.

Keenly aware of the growing foreign and domestic criticism of civil rights and U.S. vulnerability to charges of human rights hypocrisy, Truman's legislative agenda attempted to blunt the criticism. Such efforts focused primarily on outlawing overt civil and political public discrimination (such as segregation within the military) rather than the equally devastating impact of racism on housing, education, working conditions, and health care.[51]

Even Truman's efforts at securing basic civil and political rights for African Americans, however, were sometimes stymied by a conservative and segregationist Congress, leaving the United States open to international and domestic criticism on racial (in)justice. For some in the Truman administration and the U.S. delegation to the United Nations, external criticism only underscored their call to circle the wagons. Fears about communist influence overrode even the brutality of American apartheid.[52]

In December 1951, William Patterson of the Civil Rights Congress (CRC), a radical civil rights organization, and W. E. B. Du Bois submitted an even more incendiary communication to the United Nations titled "We Charge Genocide." Patterson argued that the violations occurring against African Americans met the definition in the recently adopted Convention on the Prevention and Punishment of the Crime of Genocide. Particularly embarrassing for a Truman administration facing elections in 1952, the communication highlighted specific cases of racial brutality, segregation, and discrimination already being discussed in the press. Foreign delegates began to ask members of the U.S. delegation about domestic conditions facing blacks and other minorities.[53]

The convention defines "genocide" broadly to mean "acts committed with intent to destroy, in whole or in part, a national, ethnical, racial or religious group, as such," including killing or committing other forms of physical or mental violence against the group. In a phrase that is most telling for the socioeconomic rights violations experienced by blacks, genocidal acts were also defined to include "deliberately inflicting on the group conditions of life calculated to bring about its physical destruction in whole or in part."[54] Adopted by the General Assembly and opened for signature on December 9, the Genocide Convention was signed by President Truman almost immediately—on December 11, 1948.

Although it was criticized by Eleanor Roosevelt and others as exaggerated in light of the genocide that had just killed millions in Europe, the CRC stimulated significant interest throughout the world. A petition describing the historical atrocities and continuing legacies of American racism—an evil that had resulted in the murders, abuse, and social dislocation of millions—was finally being heard on the world stage. Individuals, indigenous peoples, and oppressed ethnic groups began to see the petition process as an effective route through which to bring publicity to long-ignored causes. Such grassroots efforts and public attention could not easily be ignored and helped pressure the commission to begin drafting several of the long-anticipated legally binding human rights treaties.[55] The possibility that the new commission, and the United Nations itself, would be inundated with individual or group petitions, and perhaps, the power of some of those petitions to persuade others of a cause, prompted renewed efforts to create and define legally binding, if deliberately circumscribed, mechanisms for human rights monitoring and review.

The economic and social status of African Americans and other subordinated groups was highlighted in the petitions and the African American and foreign press as well. The majority of African Americans lived and worked in segregated communities and was relegated to the poorest quality housing, schools, and other public accommodations; most suffered the effects of unemployment or underemployment, poverty, and lack of access to adequate health care. The Eastern bloc's emphasis on the state's role in improving economic and social conditions was a key point of rhetorical distinction to be drawn between U.S. and Soviet policies. Soviet and U.S. communists made the most of U.S. failure to protect the rights of its own minorities, while hiding the Soviet Union's own atrocities against ethnic and religious minorities.

The United States was an eager participant in the propaganda wars. Anticommunist African American leaders were brought into UN fora to condemn the Soviet and U.S. communist reports on the racial situation as hyperbole.[56]

Officials at both executive and congressional levels had recognized the country's potential vulnerability on charges of racial discrimination and abuse early on—even during the drafting of the UDHR. However, Mrs. Roosevelt, among others, defended against Soviet and other countries' critiques of the United States by arguing that lynchings and other forms of racial violence were at least prohibited under U.S. law and, presumably, punishable by criminal sanctions. By contrast, she argued that the religious and political persecution and executions occurring in the Soviet Union were matters of official policy and therefore of a different character.[57] U.S. critiques of Soviet programs, political and religious persecution, and travel restrictions were valid subjects of human rights condemnation. Nevertheless, Roosevelt's defense of the United States masked the legally and culturally enforced apartheid under which many civil, political, economic, and social rights were denied to African Americans and other groups. Even those protective laws on the books were only haphazardly enforced to protect African Americans in many jurisdictions.

The racial atmosphere and conditions in the United States also played a considerable role in congressional opposition to U.S. application of the international human rights regime in general. U.S. ratification of international treaties under Article II of the Constitution requires a two-thirds majority vote of the Senate after presidential signature before the treaty can become U.S. law. Isolationist opposition in the U.S. Senate to the Treaty of Versailles had previously stymied President Woodrow Wilson's efforts to build and sustain a strong League of Nations in the aftermath of World War I.

The shadow of that failure strongly influenced U.S. administrations thereafter, including State Department officials. U.S. delegates to the United Nations were wary of possible Senate opposition to international human rights treaties. The Senate's formal rejection of an important human rights treaty supported by the administration would send a strong negative signal to the world community. In the Cold War context, such a failure would both embarrass the administration on a world stage and might well undermine the impact of the United Nations human rights system as a whole.

Cold War opposition to the ratification of human rights treaties was led by Senator John Bricker (a Republican from Ohio) and Southern segregationist senators.[58] Their opposition was said to be based on isolationism, federalism, and concerns about potential violations of U.S. sovereignty, but the question of race lay at the heart of the matter.

If existing and proposed international human rights treaties became U.S. law, racist senators feared that African Americans, Asian Americans, Native Americans, Latinos, and other disfavored minorities would use the law's nondiscrimination provisions to attack the system of segregation that the senators so dearly cherished. Indeed, U.S. litigants and courts had already begun to cite to the Charter of the United Nations in civil rights litigation.[59] Conservative fears about the meaning of international human rights in the United States certainly included the extension of economic and social rights to African Americans, who were particularly disadvantaged with regard to housing, employment, education, and health care. Senator Bricker and his supporters therefore sought to put a halt to efforts to establish human rights in the United States by introducing a series of proposed legislative initiatives (known as the "Bricker Amendments") that would amend the U.S. Constitution so as to prevent international human rights treaties from having significant internal impact in the United States.[60]

After the election of Republican President Dwight D. Eisenhower in 1952, Secretary of State John Foster Dulles attempted to nullify the threat to presidential powers and foreign policy flexibility posed by the Bricker Amendments. He proposed a "compromise." Dulles conveyed to the recalcitrant senators the administration's position that it would not seek further ratifications of international human rights treaties in return for the withdrawal of the Bricker Amendments. This capitulation to racial animus effectively undermined the formal application of international human rights to the significant racial, ethnic, gender, and economic challenges facing the United States for many years.[61]

Cold War brinksmanship occasionally had a salutary effect on domestic human rights struggles even during this period of early pessimism about the internal application of international human rights standards. Mary Dudziak argues, for example, that the 1954 Supreme Court case legally ending educational segregation, *Brown v. Board of Education*, was influenced by U.S. government attempts to counter Soviet propaganda about official U.S. racism.[62] And, as noted above, Truman's earlier domestic civil rights agenda was invigorated, in part, by the fear that the Soviet propaganda mill could influence African Americans (and devel-

oping nations that were closely observing progress on race relations in
the United States).

Dividing the Covenant on Human Rights

Despite the failure to formally recognize some of the civil and political
rights of blacks and other minorities in the United States until the 1960s
and 1970s, the Truman and subsequent U.S. administrations were at least
relatively more comfortable with the civil and political provisions of the
UDHR and a proposed UN Covenant on Human Rights. They, like many
in the U.S. legal community saw international civil and political rights as
more reflective of U.S. constitutional and liberal law and values than economic and social rights. Some such civil rights were already elaborated
in the Constitution in the Bill of Rights, and the U.S. civil rights movement of the 1940s and early 1950s seemed to be making some headway
toward the end of legal segregation.

On the other hand, the United States was concerned that economic
and social rights provisions might be drafted so as to require the kind of
centrally planned forms of government established by the Soviets and
other communist countries. The historical U.S. commitment to the right
to private property, a (seemingly) laissez-faire economic policy, and democratic traditions, it argued, were inconsistent with a strong form of "positive" economic and social rights obligations imposed on the state. Less
explicitly stated, of course, was the perceived threat that the legal recognition of economic and social rights in U.S. law might lead to fundamental changes in the socioeconomic order. Such rights, after all, might lead
to the redistribution of wealth from powerful elites to millions of poor or
subordinated Americans. The implications seemed revolutionary.

By contrast, the Soviet Union feared the implications of a strong civil
and political rights regime providing for freedom of political thought
and dissent, freedom of the press, freedom of religion, freedom of movement, and the rights of asylum seekers. They emphasized that their political and economic system provided the majority of their people with
access to free public education, health care, housing, and collective
agricultural and distributional systems for food security. Yet Soviet officials refused to acknowledge the contradictions of their claims toward
a utopian society—why was political dissent and freedom of expression
considered such a threat if socioeconomic needs were appropriately provided for?

Thus, despite the two superpowers' evident failure to live up to their
own public pronouncements about each system's superior ability to protect the rights of their citizens, the two nations each pressed for their own
set of prioritized rights in a planned Covenant on Human Rights. This

conflict ultimately resulted in the bifurcation of the covenant into two separate treaties. Between 1949 and 1951, the Commission on Human Rights worked to produce a single legally binding Covenant on Human Rights. But given growing pressure from the United States and other Western democracies, the commission finally prevailed upon the General Assembly to authorize the creation of two separate treaties.[63]

There were both theoretical and practical reasons supporting division of the covenant. At a practical level, some advocates of bifurcation hoped that the best way to get around the Cold War stalemate was to create separate instruments. One would provide largely for civil and political rights and another would address economic, social, and cultural rights. That way, each state could choose for itself which document was most consistent with its political and economic views and traditions. The goal was to achieve as widespread ratification as possible for at least one of the legally binding human rights treaties.

But there were deep-rooted ideological and philosophical reasons as well that continue to cause controversy about the indivisibility and implementation of the full range of rights to this day. According to annotations to the draft text of what was originally a single International Covenant on Human Rights:

Those in favour of drafting two separate covenants argued that civil and political rights were enforceable, or justiciable, or of an "absolute" character, while economic, social and cultural rights were not or might not, be; that the former were immediately applicable, while the latter were to be progressively implemented; and that, generally speaking, the former were rights of the individual "against" the State, that is, against unlawful and unjust action of the State, while the latter were rights which the State would have to take positive action to promote. Since the nature of civil and political rights and that of economic, social and cultural rights and the obligations of the State in respect thereof, were different, it was desirable that two separate instruments should be prepared.[64]

Arguments over the nature and implementation of economic and social rights, further complicated by Cold War competition for the loyalties of the newly emerging postcolonial states, delayed the drafting process considerably. Final texts for the binding instruments in the International Bill of Rights were not adopted by the General Assembly until 1966. The impact of the Bricker Amendment and the Eisenhower/Dulles compromise proved devastating to U.S. involvement in the drafting and negotiating efforts as well.

In announcing the Dulles compromise, the Eisenhower administration not only suspended plans for any future U.S. ratification of international human rights treaties, it also "refused to reappoint Eleanor Roosevelt to the Commission on Human Rights, even though she still had two years remaining before the end of her term."[65] The impact of this position was clear. Rather than have its sins and shortcomings exposed to scrutiny on the world stage, one of the most powerful actors had picked up its marbles and gone home.

Even after the formal adoption and opening for signature of the International Covenant on Civil and Political Rights (ICCPR) and the International Covenant on Economic, Social, and Cultural Rights (ICESCR), it still took another decade before the two covenants received a sufficient number of ratifications for entry into force in 1976.[66] Ironically, it was the adoption of another human rights treaty on racial discrimination that broke the international impasse on international human rights treaties.

The racial and ethnic context in which the United Nations itself was founded and which undergirded and lent false legitimacy to colonialism itself, led many newly emerging Third World states to a shared sense that an end to racial discrimination was of primary importance if the UN enterprise was to move forward. Therefore, an International Convention on the Elimination of All Forms of Racial Discrimination (ICERD) was adopted in 1965—even prior to the adoption of the covenants.[67] Significantly, ICERD includes the full panoply of socioeconomic rights as well as civil and political rights in its overall prohibitions on racial discrimination. It therefore creates legally binding international obligations with regard to economic and social rights. Predictably, however, the United States did not ratify ICERD until the 1990s, and then only with significant limitations on its domestic application.[68]

Despite the hobbling impact of the Dulles compromise, U.S. silence on its own human rights responsibilities was undermined by significant domestic human rights–related unrest and political activism. The Kennedy, Johnson, Nixon, and Ford administrations presided over a time of unprecedented social justice activism in the United States, often in resistance to administration policies. The African American civil rights movement, the women's rights and gay rights movements, anti–Vietnam War activism, labor unionism, and antipoverty and welfare rights efforts all contributed to a broader sense among the population (and some policymakers) that a human rights analysis might be relevant to U.S. problems.[69] Policymakers recognized that the Dulles compromise had limited U.S. effectiveness with regard to international human rights influence. Reflecting regrets about the foreign policy implications of the compromise, antiwar sentiments, and labor union pressures, Congress even enacted legislation in the early 1970s that linked various forms of U.S. economic foreign assistance to "internationally-recognized" human rights and labor standards.[70]

Some of this popular activism focused on economic and social issues and linked domestic struggles to international contexts[71]—including U.S. foreign policies affecting the poor and subordinated groups in other countries. This increased both internal and external pressure for the reestablishment of a more active official U.S. engagement with the international economic and social rights framework as well as human rights as a whole.

Domestic Human Rights as U.S. Foreign Policy Imperative? Flirting with (and Rejecting) the Indivisibility Paradigm

Official U.S. passivity with regard to international human rights lasted until the 1970s, although there were attempts at reform under the Kennedy administration.[72] However, President Jimmy Carter signaled an important shift in U.S. international human rights policy. Carter, at least in part because of concerns about the image and influence of the United States abroad, rejected the Dulles compromise legacy.

Carter, and other Democratic and Republican administrations in the decades to follow, recognized that the United States was open to charges of hypocrisy when it failed to ratify important international human rights treaties while attempting to impose human rights standards on others. Similarly, U.S. rejection of human rights treaty ratification might well undermine its efforts to hold the line, especially in the Third World, against communist influence. At first, it even appeared that Carter also appreciated the relationship between civil and political and economic, social, and cultural rights. In a famous articulation of administration policy on rights categorization, Secretary of State Cyrus Vance described "human rights as falling into three broad categories: rights that protect the integrity of the person; rights that guarantee fulfillment of basic economic, and social needs; and rights that protect civil and political liberties." The administration promoted protection of all categories of rights as being complementary and mutually reinforcing.[73]

In 1977, President Carter signed the International Covenant on Civil and Political Rights, the International Covenant on Economic, Social, and Cultural Rights, the International Convention on the Elimination of All Forms of Racial Discrimination, and the American Convention on Human Rights and submitted them to the Senate for advice and consent to ratification in early 1978.[74] The ICESCR was included as the companion treaty to the ICCPR and as an important component of the International Bill of Rights.

Despite this promising development for U.S. human rights advocates, the administration, with the advice of the State Department, transmitted the treaties to the Senate with significant "reservations, understandings, and declarations" (RUDs) intended to clarify the supremacy of U.S. constitutional law interpretations and to limit the practical implementation of the human rights treaties in the United States, including as a cause of

action. In some sense, the package of RUDs, and the even more restrictive limitations to be imposed on subsequent treaties by later administrations were the lasting legacy of the Bricker Amendments.

The most important such limitation, attached to all subsequent international human rights treaties, was a provision declaring even ratified
human rights treaties to be "non-self-executing." In the administration's
view, only implementing legislation passed by Congress would allow the
treaties to be given full effect in U.S. courts.

In addition to the non-self-executing declaration, Carter attached
substantive, and controversial, reservations and understandings to the
ICESCR. The most significant of these made explicit the Cold War hard-
ening of attitudes about the nature of socioeconomic rights: "The United
States understands paragraph (1) of Article 2 [the general obligations
provision of the ICESCR] as establishing that the provisions of Article 1
through 15 of this Covenant describe goals to be achieved progressively
rather than through immediate implementation."[75]

The transmittal letter then goes on to reject the international economic cooperation many in the UN system had contemplated as a necessary condition for the realization of socioeconomic rights: "It is also
understood that paragraph (1) of Article 2, as well as Article 1, which
calls for States Parties to take steps individually and through international cooperation to guard against hunger, import no legally binding
obligation to provide aid to foreign countries."[76]

The administration's interpretation of the ICESCR, apparently intended to make ratification more palatable to Senate decision makers,
instead had the effect of reasserting American exceptionalism and undermining a strong interpretation of the ICESCR's requirements internationally.[77] But even a watered-down version of the ICESCR was not
enough to overcome significant opposition to its U.S. ratification. The
ICESCR was, and is, still largely perceived to be a threat to "American
values." This led some supporters of ratification to adopt a stealth approach that would argue strategically that ratification would have only a
symbolic foreign policy effect. Such an approach resonated with the administration's view that the ICESCR's provisions were "for the most part
in accordance with United States law and practice."[78] Philip Alston, a
chair of the UN Committee that later administered the ICESCR, rejected
such an approach by U.S. activists in subsequent years, arguing instead
for a "robust" public debate on ratification. He argued that "the starting
point for such a debate must be recognition of the fact that a significant
range of obligations would flow from ratification."[79]

Carter's transmittal of the treaties and subsequent congressional activities in human rights did reinvigorate the debate about the application of
human rights to the United States and their role in U.S. foreign policy.

Unfortunately, the Senate Foreign Relations Committee, which held hearings in 1979 on the four human rights treaties transmitted by Carter, did not support them. Similarly, Carter's signature of the newly adopted Convention on the Elimination of All Forms of Discrimination Against Women (CEDAW) in 1980 was allowed to quietly languish in the Senate Foreign Relations Committee until the 1990s.[80] It was not until the Reagan and Bush (I) administrations that the Genocide Convention, signed by Truman in 1948, was finally ratified by the U.S. in 1989, signaling a new period of optimism that the United States would once again begin to engage with international human rights treaties in a domestic context.

Other ratifications of major human rights treaties followed in subsequent years as the Cold War ended and the United States fought for global influence among the newly emerging post–Cold War democracies. The ICCPR was finally ratified by the George H. W. Bush administration in 1992; the ICERD was ratified by the Clinton administration in 1994, as was the Convention Against Torture. Notably, the ICESCR, CEDAW, and the Convention on the Rights of the Child, although signed, have still not been ratified as of the time of this writing. Even though all of the treaties transmitted by Carter suffered from Senate inaction and opposition, the ICESCR was the most controversial human rights treaty for the United States and remains so today.

As the Cold War drew to a close in the late 1980s and early 1990s, the world saw another shift in U.S. government attitudes toward international human rights. As the Soviet Union collapsed and relatively peaceful popular democratic movements asserted themselves U.S. officials and some political economists trumpeted the triumph of democratic and neoliberal political and economic systems as dominant in the new global economy. The Bush (I) administration's ratification, for example, of the ICCPR was argued to be a strong signal to the rest of the world about the supremacy of U.S. liberal democratic values.

Nonetheless, that administration clung strongly to the philosophy of non-self-execution of international human rights treaties. After all, officials argued, the United States was a world leader in the protection of civil and political rights, already had significant federal and state laws on the subject, and should serve as a model for the rest of the world rather than be subject to its criticisms. Complaints by activists and some U.S.-focused NGOs about race and class discrimination in application of the death penalty, police brutality, voting rights abuses, and continuing discrimination in housing, health care, education, and employment fell on deaf ears.

The Controversial Nature of Economic and Social Rights

Why were and are the rights outlined in instruments like the ICESCR so controversial within U.S. official and civil society circles? They seem so clearly to codify the Four Freedoms and the "second bill of rights" envisioned in the 1940s by President Roosevelt. Clues can be found in Mrs. Roosevelt's statement in support of bifurcating the ICCPR from the ICESCR. Although at least rhetorically acknowledging that civil and political rights should have the same normative status as economic, social, and cultural rights, she accepted the view that the two categories of rights were different in nature and required different mechanisms of implementation. The Commission on Human Rights had failed to attach the kind of implementation machinery to economic and social rights that were included for civil and political rights provisions in a draft Covenant on Human Rights. Mrs. Roosevelt noted the following:

> It was felt by those with whom I discussed the matter in the Commission that this machinery is not appropriate for the economic, social, and cultural rights provisions of the Covenant, since these rights are to be achieved progressively and since the obligations of states with respect to these rights were not as precise as those with respect to the civil and political rights. These members of the Commission thought that it would be preferable with respect to the economic, social, and cultural rights, to stress the importance of assisting states to achieve economic, social, and cultural progress rather than to stress the filing of complaints against states in this field. [81]

As she noted, Mrs. Roosevelt was not alone in the view that socioeconomic rights were to be treated differently in the international human rights legal regime. But the differences were sometimes exaggerated or misunderstood in order to protect the international or domestic balance of power. Both West and East feared the implications of strong economic, social, and cultural rights enforcement. The text of the ICESCR reflected such concerns, but it also reflected strong pressure from the peoples of the world to hold their governments and the international community accountable for poverty and social injustice. As discussed below, the U.S. ratification debate largely tracked the legal requirements of the ICESCR itself.

Legal Obligations of Parties to the ICESCR

Despite the early protestations about the indivisibility and interdependence of all human rights, whether civil and political, or economic, social, and cultural, the ICESCR reflected the controversial nature of ESC rights in its very structure. For example, the ICESCR, like the ICCPR, is a legally binding treaty. As such, states could choose (or not) to ratify the treaty and take on the legal obligations described. However, at first glance, the legal obligations created under the ICESCR seem vague and less immediate than the obligations of the ICCPR. This reflected the ideological divide not only between East and West, but also among those who questioned whether economic and social rights could, or should, properly be called "human rights" at all.

Like the UDHR and the ICCPR, the ICESCR begins with a preamble, setting forth the purposes and rationale of the document, and general articles with legal principles such as the all-important self-determination of peoples provision in Article 1, and the equally important nondiscrimination provision in Article 2(2).

Such provisions caused official United States discomfort, not least because they might strengthen the cause of indigenous advocates for substantive fairness and equality, but also because of the long history of abuses against African Americans and other minority groups. Of course, the civil rights movement of the 1950s and 1960s had helped motivate changes in federal and state discriminatory laws and policies with regard to voting, desegregation of education and housing opportunity, and other civil rights. However, the potential for new obligations providing for substantive legal rights to food, housing, education, health care, work and fair working conditions, and social security seemed to be another matter. But what, exactly, did the ICESCR require?

Article 2 of the covenant sets forth the general legal obligations of the parties and serves as an interpretive guide to the other substantive provisions:

Each State Party to the present Covenant undertakes to take steps, individually and through international assistance and co-operation, especially economic and technical, to the maximum of its available resources, with a view to achieving progressively the full realization of the rights recognized in the present. Covenant by all appropriate means, including particularly the adoption of legislative measures.

Unlike the ICCPR, provision was not made for the creation of a separate implementing body for the ICESCR. Rather, states parties were to submit reports on the status of ESC rights in their countries to the UN's Economic and Social Council, the UN political body with responsibility for oversight of human rights as well as other broadly mandated social issues. This omission reflected the initial distrust among many, including the United States, about the implementation of ESC rights. Such misgivings about the potential role of human rights monitoring and implementation bodies had been expressed even during the drafting of the UDHR because of fears about the impact on traditional notions of state sovereignty. Although this resistance was overcome with the inclusion of a Human Rights Committee to implement the ICCPR, and the creation of other human rights bodies such as subcommissions, working groups, and special rapporteurs under the authority of the Commission on Human Rights, the implementation of the ICESCR was to be maintained in a second-class status at least until the 1980s.

Article 2 as Limitation and Opportunity

As drafted, the text of Article 2(1) seems a masterpiece of bets-hedging. Rather than a more straightforward guide to the legal obligations of states parties, its phrasing incorporates the pressing concerns expressed both by developing countries and by the United States and other Western powers about the "different" nature of economic, social, and cultural rights.

"Take steps, individually and through international assistance and co-operation, especially economic and technical"

This language makes a promising beginning to the article. The undertaking required obligates the parties to the Covenant to "take steps"— implying positive action by the states parties. Nevertheless, it also indicates that the drafters believed that all or some of the obligations set forth might require a multilevel process over time—steps on the way to some higher attainable standard. The phrase "individually and collectively" evidences the understanding that economic, social, and cultural rights such as food and health care could not effectively be protected solely within national borders and through national measures—international cooperation along the lines contemplated at the founding of the UN itself, would be necessary.

Article 23 set forth language defining, but not limiting, what such international action could include:

The States Parties to the present Covenant agree that international action for the achievement of the rights recognized in the present Covenant include such methods as the conclusion of conventions, the adoption of recommendations, the furnishing of technical assistance and the holding of regional meetings and technical meetings for the purpose of consultation and study organized in conjunction with the Governments concerned.

The responsibility to provide international economic assistance and fair terms of trade, for example, remained a point of considerable controversy, and led, in the United States, to Carter's attempt, through an "understanding," to limit the interpretation of the provision. Newly independent Third World states, in the majority at the United Nations, had begun to make political and moral demands for a "New International Economic Order" (NIEO) and a "right to development" that surfaced the responsibilities of wealthy nations to developing countries.

"To the Maximum of Its Available Resources"

This phrase evidenced a key concern and conflict that had arisen in the debate over social and economic rights at the United Nations. Developing countries, although smaller in number at the time of the United Nations' founding, had been quite vocal about the often vast differences in economic wealth among states between the industrialized and colonizing states and the developing states. If rights such as food, housing, free primary education, and health care were to be guaranteed by the state, it was argued that limits needed to be recognized based on differences in resources. On this point, the developing countries succeeded in building such a limitation into the covenant. Western critics of social and economic rights also argued that the failure to recognize resource limitations would result in the rights provided for in the treaty being undermined as empty promises. Of course, the key interpretive question was, and is, the meaning of "available." Should this mean, for example, that if a state sets aside an amount for public housing in its overall budget, the maximum of that set-aside should be used? Or, does it mean that the state has an obligation to maximize and prioritize budget allocations to fulfill the enumerated rights?

U.S. critics on both the left and the right were concerned about resource and allocation issues. While it should seem self-evident that one of the wealthiest countries in the world would have less concern about the availability of resources to protect the rights of poor, homeless, or sick people within its borders, conservatives worried that a rights approach would lead to inappropriate expectations and a lack of initiative on the part of those seeking a "handout." Market-based or other private sector approaches, they argued, would ultimately do the most good for the most people and do so more efficiently than could central government. Those on the left were concerned that the elevation of socioeconomic needs to "rights" might be misleading and divert attention and resources away from more effective strategies.[82] Might not homeless or poor people simply be wasting precious resources or time by attempting long, complex, and expensive judicial remedies to which only a lucky few could gain access?

Similar concerns were raised about allocation. Once it was determined that health is a "human right" on the domestic level, for example, and judges had the discretion to interpret that right, might not judges abuse or misapply that power? How, for example, would a court's decisions to direct allocation of public health resources between cancer treatments or diabetes prevention be constrained? Should that decision not be better left to a democratically elected legislature and executive?[83]

Finally, some questioned whether "available resources" might not also include external sources such as international aid. Would such a requirement interfere inappropriately with a sovereign state's decisions about how to use foreign aid?

"With a view to achieving progressively the full realization of the rights recognized"

The concept of "progressive realization" was intimately related to the resource problem discussed above. As the United Nations grew in membership with the progress of decolonization, newly independent developing states emphasized that time and resources were needed to adequately fulfill social and economic rights. Having become responsible in the postcolonial period for problems such as massive unemployment, trade imbalances, poverty, racial, ethnic, and religious conflict, and disease, many developing states argued that social and economic rights could not be implemented immediately in the same way as so-called negative rights (civil and political rights) which, it was said, only required the state to refrain from abusive actions against individuals under its jurisdiction.

Such a clear theoretical divide between "negative" and "positive" rights is subject to challenge, however.[84] The right to political participation, for example, not only requires that the state refrain from creating roadblocks to voting, it may also require that the state create elaborate and expensive primaries, voting sites, accessible voting machines, ballots, counting systems, and so on. By contrast, some could interpret a right to housing as a "negative" right in the sense that it could be narrowly interpreted only to prohibit the state from interfering with one's own efforts to purchase or build a home, rather than the more expansive and "positive" obligation of the state to provide housing for those who cannot otherwise obtain it.[85]

Still, the ideological divide remained strong and the limitation of "progressive realization" became an important aspect of the covenant. Even wealthy Western states saw progressive realization as a pragmatic response to differences in economic status among states. Recognizing that fulfillment might take time, progressive steps might lend greater credibility to the legal status and legitimacy of social and economic rights concepts. Both wealthy and developing states, however, tended to read the provisions as narrowly as possible, hoping to limit the extent of their potential economic obligations.

"By all appropriate means, including particularly the adoption of legislative measures"

The final phrase in Article 2(1) raised the question of implementation of social and economic rights. Like all major international human rights treaties, the ICESCR relies on the states as sovereign powers to provide for the primary means of implementation and protection of the rights listed in the Covenant. This is a fundamental irony of the international human rights movement: that states, often the most egregious violators of human rights at the time of the drafting of the International Bill of Rights, were also to be relied on as the primary and most powerful protectors of human rights. The drafters of the UDHR avoided this question by focusing primarily on the rights and duties of individuals and groups rather than which entities, individuals, or groups bore responsibility for implementing and enforcing them. Article (2)1 clearly identifies legislation as an "appropriate means" of national implementation. But the underlying controversy, which was to remain the key question for promoters of social and economic human rights, was whether or not such rights were "justiciable."

If so-called rights could not be adequately or appropriately protected in courts and by judicial process, some argued, could they still legitimately be called "rights" at all? Was it not more appropriate to think of them as social goods or benefits that a state or other entity could choose to distribute if it had the resources? To the extent such benefits intersected with civil rights, it was said that they should be distributed in a nondiscriminatory way,[86] but the United States largely rejected the notion that social and economic rights could or should be appropriately adjudicated in national or international courts or constitutionalized at the federal level.[87]

The controversies inherent in the legal framework created for the IC-ESCR and others were all implicated in the internal debates over ratification of the ICESCR that occurred within the United States after the treaty's submission to the Senate in 1978.

The Struggle Continues: New Realities and the Struggle to Make Space for the "Other" Human Rights in the United States

The disappointing history of U.S. encounters with the economic and social human rights framework so far evidences an important ideological barrier to the future recognition and implementation of socioeconomic rights in the United States. In addition, the George W. Bush administration's post-9/11 wholesale backtracking on the applicability of international law and especially international human rights and humanitarian law created an atmosphere in which the domestic recognition of human rights in general was thrown into question. As this new edition goes to press, it is likely that the new administration of Barack Obama, the first African American president of the United States, will adopt a more human rights–friendly foreign and domestic policy. It remains to be seen, however, whether such new policies will include the full recognition of economic and social rights in the United States.

There are also many signs of hope and progress in civil society. Such groups and institutions operate outside official U.S. government policy and seek to reflect the hopes and aspirations of ordinary Americans. This concluding section briefly outlines some of the areas in which such U.S. activism and advocacy around economic and social rights has been reasserted over the decades since Carter's signing of the ICESCR. Subsequent chapters discuss many of these human rights strategies in more detail

UN Elaboration of the Content and Implementation of ESC Rights: The Work of the Committee on Economic, Social, and Cultural Rights

The perception that economic and social rights are more vaguely defined than the civil and political rights with which they are more familiar remains a key sticking point for U.S. officials and some American activists.[88] Commentators have pointed out that some civil and political rights are also broadly and vaguely defined in the texts of international instruments and in national constitutions as well, often resulting in years or decades of interpretive litigation. Despite those interpretive problems with regard to civil rights, many agree on their importance, if not their sufficiency in achieving social justice. However, for some time there was relatively little jurisprudence and formal interpretation by authoritative international bodies on the meaning and content of economic and social rights.

Perhaps no other international institution has done more to address this situation than the UN Committee on Economic, Social and Cultural Rights (CESCR). Although the ICESCR was deliberately created without a specific monitoring and implementing body, advocates for ESC rights and experts on such issues were able to prevail upon the UN Economic and Social Council to create such a body in 1986. A committee could review and provide Concluding Observations on the reports submitted by states parties to the covenant, and, through the mechanism of "General Comments," could provide authoritative interpretations of, and specificity to, the substantive provisions of the ICESCR.[89]

International experts on economic, social, and cultural rights met in Limburg (The Netherlands) in 1986 to adopt unofficial recommendations with regard to the interpretation and implementation of the IC-

ESCR. The groundbreaking "Limburg Principles" resulting from the meeting strongly influenced the CESCR's interpretation of the nature and content of socioeconomic rights and their implementation.[90] A decade later in 1997, a similar expert consultation in Maastricht resulted in the highly influential "Maastricht Guidelines on Economic, Social, and Cultural Rights."[91] Among other things, the guidelines grappled with the thorny questions raised in U.S. objections and elsewhere about indivisibility and the relationship of socioeconomic rights to civil and political and collective rights, the justiciability of ESC rights, the legal obligations of states parties to the covenant, minimum core obligations, immediate obligations of states versus the principle of progressive realization, creating benchmarks for the realization of rights, and addressing the question of resource limitations in fulfilling the rights.

Most significantly, the Guidelines and the "General Comments" issued by the committee have specified the substantive and theoretical content of many ESC rights and state obligations to "respect, protect, fulfill and ensure" them. They therefore reveal that economic and social rights themselves have "negative" and "positive" aspects which may involve state action (or a requirement that a state refrain from acting) and the requirement that a state provide the legal and social circumstances in which a right can be fulfilled. It also reveals the actual or potential role of nonstate actors such as private individuals and groups, corporations and other business enterprises, and international trade or financial institutions.

The committee adopted a cooperative approach to administration of the ICESCR, working with states parties to recommend methods of improving compliance and collaborating with UN specialized agencies and other bodies to build expertise and technical assistance on specific issues such as the right to housing and the right to food. This growing body of interpretive material can act as an important response to the continued U.S. arguments about the vagueness and indeterminacy of socioeconomic rights. To be sure, all international human rights are elaborated at a certain level of breadth and indeterminacy; their meaning must constantly be contested in the political realm rather than through textual interpretation in isolation from political and historical context. But the process of working to define socioeconomic rights in practical and concrete contexts will likely contribute to their legitimization and ultimate protection. The danger remains, of course, that as the substantive obligations created by the fulfillment of economic and social rights are more specifically defined, resistance to their domestic application might intensify in the U.S. Congress and in the administration.[92] Most recently, on the sixtieth anniversary of the adoption of the UDHR, the UN General Assembly further strengthened and legitimized the implementation of the ICESCR by adopting an Optional Protocol. The Protocol provides an individual and group communications mechanism for complaints to the CESCR.[93]

The Influence of Comparative Jurisprudence on Economic and Social Rights Awareness in the United States

One unfortunate consequence of official U.S. exceptionalism about socioeconomic human rights is that the United States has been left behind as other countries work to define and implement these rights in domestic contexts. Over the past decade, there have been increasing measures internationally to constitutionalize economic and social rights or to interpret civil and political rights in ways that are protective of such concerns. Some U.S. legal scholars and jurists have taken note of this comparative jurisprudence in considering whether to apply such principles to U.S. law.

The postapartheid jurisprudence of the South African Constitutional Court has been particularly prominent in this regard. The 1996 Constitution of South Africa enshrines economic, social, and cultural rights protections as well as civil and political rights in its text. It also explicitly acknowledges the interpretive relevance of international law and comparative law. The court has therefore engaged in (sometimes controversial) efforts to give meaning and substance to constitutional protections for economic and social rights. Leading decisions have included interpretations of the right to health and to emergency care[94] and the right to adequate housing.[95] The constitution provides for a "reasonableness" standard against which state action or inaction is to be measured with regard to the protection of some socioeconomic rights. In interpreting this standard, the court has struggled with separation of powers issues and the appropriate extent of judicial engagement with economic and social rights.[96]

Courts in India, interpreting the "directive principles" approach of their constitution, have similarly responded to "social action litigation" strategies aimed at homelessness and other rights violations against the poor.[97] European and Latin American courts and human rights bodies have interpreted rights traditionally identified as civil and political (such as the right to life) to have socioeconomic application as well.[98] Such judicial analysis has undermined official U.S. arguments that economic and social rights are nonjusticiable.

NGO Strategies

As discussed above, some major international human rights NGOs based in the United States resisted application of ESC rights in the United

States. Some feared that limited financial and staff resources might be diverted from monitoring and advocacy for important civil and political rights, which seemed much more attainable than the seemingly ill-defined and impractical economic and social rights. Others feared that the prioritization of economic and social rights might mask existing violations of civil and political rights.[99] Still others remained unconvinced about the justiciability of socioeconomic rights in U.S. courts and the general lack of familiarity with such rights among Americans.

With the end of the Cold War, such attitudes among major U.S. human rights NGOs began to break down significantly. Leading human rights NGOs like Human Rights Watch, Amnesty International, and Lawyers Committee for Human Rights (now Human Rights First) reversed their original positions and began to monitor and document violations of economic and social rights, including violations in the United States. Such NGOs prepared reports on violations of the rights of U.S. workers in the meatpacking industry, violations of the rights of domestic workers, and violations of the rights of undocumented workers. In addition, grassroots activists began to focus on the abusive effects of welfare reform and lack of access to affordable and adequate housing and health care as human rights issues. Southern NGOs began to combine traditional civil rights strategies with economic and social rights approaches to address racial violence, discrimination, and economic injustices against workers.[100]

These grassroots campaigns often avoid the legal barriers to U.S. implementation of socioeconomic rights by engaging in multilevel strategies involving documentation and monitoring, community organizing, popular education, direct action (protests, occupation of abandoned housing), publicity, and formal international and regional human rights complaints mechanisms alleging U.S. violations of economic and social rights.[101]

Many such projects build on the theory that many poor or otherwise disadvantaged Americans already have some sense that they have a "right" to food, health care, education, and other basic needs, but that they have not previously been exposed to the language and legal status of the international instruments outlining those rights.

Perhaps most encouraging, some NGOs were specifically formed to focus on economic and social human rights, such as the Center for Economic and Social Rights, EarthRights International, Physicians for Human Rights, the Center on Housing Rights and Evictions, and the National Economic and Social Rights Initiative. Such organizations contribute to the continuing effort to dispel the myths surrounding the undefined nature of economic and social rights by monitoring and identifying violations, advocating for social change, and educating the public and policymakers. Some work with international coalitions, such as the International Economic, Social, and Cultural Rights Network, to create cross-border alliances. Coalitions of activists and NGOs, such as the U.S. Human Rights Network, prominently include economic and social rights in their literature and analysis. The USHRN also helped organize a successful shadow report to the United Nations on U.S. failures to comply with its obligations under ICERD. EarthRights International and the Center for Constitutional Rights have both attempted to push the boundaries of U.S. litigation under the Alien Tort Statute to hold multinational corporate actors accountable for violations of the rights of workers and communities adversely affected by corporate activity.

A recent colloquy between the executive director of Human Rights Watch (Kenneth Roth) and Physicians for Human Rights (Leonard S. Rubenstein) on the roles of NGOs in addressing economic and social rights revealed significant differences about approach, but it also revealed a shared sense that many human rights NGOs will have to take account of such issues in today's globalized world.[102] The implications for U.S. policy at home and abroad are significant.

These NGO and grassroots movements are likely to have at least two important effects on the U.S. encounter with the international human rights framework in coming years: (1) They are likely to galvanize popular awareness of, and support for, an economic and social rights–based approach to U.S. economic and social problems in conjunction with existing approaches; and (2) they are likely to create pressure for, and lend additional legitimacy to, judicial interpretive efforts, legislative efforts, and administrative interpretations of the recognition and promotion of socioeconomic rights.

This broad overview of the U.S. encounter with the international economic and social rights framework argues that U.S. fears and misconceptions about the nature and legal implications of socioeconomic rights are largely misplaced. The protection and implementation of such rights is indeed complicated, and will require careful democratic, judicial, and executive decision making. The protection of civil and political rights has been equally complex. But the national commitment to the latter rights has made the continuing effort worthwhile. Until we see the reality of discrimination, homelessness, malnutrition, educational disparities, and lack of health care as of similar priority, we will not be willing to expend that effort. The inspiring and continuing activism, legal work, and international and comparative leadership in giving meaning to such rights are important indicators that future U.S. encounters with the ESC framework will be more positive.

Notes

I greatly appreciate the assistance of Kyle Courtney, Professor Martha Davis, Saikon Gbehan, Caitlin McAteer, Jan McNew, Kaleema Nur, Forest O'Neill-Greenberg, David Pitler, Amy Senier, Blossom Stephenson, Stephanie Woldenberg, Dr. Cynthia Young and the Boston College African and Diaspora Studies Program, and the Northeastern University School of Law Faculty Research Fund.

1. Thomas Paine, "Agrarian Justice" (1792), excerpted in Jeanne M. Woods and Hope Lewis (eds.), *Human Rights & the Global Marketplace: Economic, Social, and Cultural Dimensions* (Ardsley, N.Y.: Transnational Publishers, 2005), p. 62.

2. Martin Luther King, Jr., "The Time Is Always Right to Do Right" (speech presented at Syracuse University, New York, July 15, 1965), available online at students.syr.edu/osvp/drkingaddress.html, accessed February 15, 2007.

3. This chapter refers interchangeably to "economic and social rights" and "socioeconomic rights." It focuses primarily on individual economic and social rights as elaborated in international standards rather than cultural and religious rights. See Articles 1–2, 22–26, 28, Universal Declaration of Human Rights, G.A. res. 217A (III), U.N. Doc A/810 at 71 (1948); Articles 1–14, International Covenant on Economic, Social and Cultural Rights, G.A. res. 2200A (XXI), 21 U.N.GAOR Supp. (No. 16) at 49, U.N. Doc. A/6316 (1966), 993 U.N.T.S. 3, entered into force January 3, 1976.

4. Philip Alston, "U.S. Ratification of the Covenant on Economic, Social and Cultural Rights: The Need for an Entirely New Strategy," *American Journal of International Law* 84 (1990): 365, excerpted in David Weissbrodt, Joan Fitzpatrick, and Frank Newman (eds.), *International Human Rights: Law, Policy, and Process*, 3rd ed. (Cincinnati, Ohio: Anderson Publishing, 2001), p. 134.

5. On activist support for economic and social rights in the United States, see, e.g., Alston, "An Entirely New Strategy"; Frank Deale, "The Unhappy History of Economic Rights in the United States and Prospects for their Creation and Renewal," *Howard Law Journal* 43 (2000): 281; Ford Foundation, *Close to Home: Case Studies of Human Rights Work in the United States* (New York: Ford Foundation, 2004); Rhoda E. Howard-Hassmann and Claude E. Welch (eds.), *Economic Rights in Canada and the United States* (Philadelphia: University of Pennsylvania Press, 2006); Barbara J. Stark, "Economic Rights in the United States and International Human Rights Law: Toward 'an Entirely New Strategy,'" in David P. Forsythe (ed.), *The United States and Human Rights: Looking Inward and Outward* (Lincoln: University of Nebraska Press, 2000); Cass R. Sunstein, *The Second Bill of Rights: Franklin D. Roosevelt's Unfinished Revolution and Why We Need It More Than Ever* (New York: Basic Books, 2004); United States Human Rights Network, *Something Inside So Strong: A Resource Guide on Human Rights in the United States* (Washington, D.C.: United States Human Rights Network, 2003).

6. "Declaration of the Rights of Man and Citizen," in Frank Maloy Anderson (ed.), *Constitution of the Year 1* (1793), *The Constitution and Other Selected Documents Illustrative of the History of France 1789–1901*, p. 170 (1904), excerpted in Jeanne M. Woods and Hope Lewis (eds.), *Human Rights and the Global Marketplace: Economic, Social, and Cultural Dimensions* (Ardsley, N.Y.: Transnational Publishers, 2005), p. 53; Paine, *Agrarian Justice*, in Woods and Lewis, *Human Rights*, p. 60. See also Paul Gordon Lauren, *The Evolution of International Human Rights: Visions Seen* (Philadelphia: University of Pennsylvania Press, 1998), pp. 18–20.

7. Woods and Lewis, *Human Rights*, pp. 43–67.

8. See, e.g., Barbara J. Stark, "Deconstructing the Framers' Right to Property: Liberty's Daughters and Economic Rights," *Hofstra Law Review* 28 (2000): 963, 967, excerpted in Woods and Lewis, *Human Rights*, p. 850.

9. See generally Chapter 10, "The United States of America: Federal Rejection, State Protection," in Woods and Lewis, *Human Rights*, pp. 841–930; Herman Schwartz, "The Wisdom and Enforceability of Welfare Rights as Constitutional Rights," *Human Rights Brief* 8(2) (2001), available online at www.wcl.american.edu/hrbrief/08/2rights.cfm.

10. See *San Antonio Independent School District v. Rodriguez*, 411 U.S. 1 (1973) ("Education is not among the rights afforded explicit protection under our Federal Constitution. Nor do we find basis for saying it is . . ."), excerpted in Woods and Lewis, *Human Rights*, pp. 868, 871.

11. As chair of the commission drafting the Universal Declaration of Human Rights (UDHR), Eleanor Roosevelt expressed the "wholehearted support" of the United States for its socioeconomic rights provisions. "The United States did not, however, consider them to 'imply an obligation on governments to assure the enjoyment of these rights by direct governmental action.'" Mary Ann Glendon, *A World Made New: Eleanor Roosevelt and the Universal Declaration of Human Rights* (New York: Random House, 2001), p. 186.

12. "Since neither the U.S. Constitution nor international law have yet been construed to create federal minimum welfare guarantees, we must go back to the original protector of the poor-state law. Historically, state and local governments have played the primary role in assuming responsibility for those unable to care for themselves. This continues to be the case today. The language of state statutory and constitutional law often contains explicit intentions to provide minimum welfare guarantees. These have frequently provided the basis for court decisions upholding state economic rights." Deale, "The Unhappy History," p. 320.

13. See, e.g., Carol Anderson, *Eyes off the Prize: The United Nations and the African American Struggle for Human Rights, 1944–1955* (Cambridge: Cambridge University Press, 2003); Mary Dudziak, *Cold War Civil Rights: Race and the Image of American Democracy* (Princeton, N.J.: Princeton University Press, 2000); Paul Gordon Lauren, *Power and Prejudice: The Politics and Diplomacy of Racial Discrimination*, 2nd ed. (Boulder, Colo.: Westview Press, 1996); Brenda Gayle Plummer, *Rising Wind: Black Americans and U.S. Foreign Affairs* (Chapel Hill: University of North Carolina Press, 1996).

14. Woods and Lewis, *Human Rights*, pp. 43–67.

15. Ibid., pp. 64–67.

16. For early criticism of Western dominance in elaborating "universal" human rights standards, see, e.g., American Anthropological Association, "Statement on Human Rights," *American Anthropologist* 49(4) (1947): 539, excerpted in Henry J. Steiner and Philip Alston, *International Human Rights in Context: Law, Politics, Morals*, 2nd ed. (Oxford: Oxford University Press, 2000), pp. 372–74. In later years, the association issued statements modifying its 1947 position and embracing a culturally sensitive human rights approach. Ibid., p. 374; Woods and Lewis, *Human Rights*, p. 80. Prior to the adoption of the UDHR, however, UN representatives did make efforts to draw on diverse religious and cultural traditions in determining common standards. Mary Ann Glendon, *A World Made New*, p. 17 (describing advocacy by U.S. religious, legal, labor, and civil rights groups for the U.S. Department of State to take an approach to international human rights that

would be inclusive on the basis of race, ethnicity, religion, and economic status); Lauren, *Evolution of International Human Rights*, pp. 223–25 (noting the influence of "150 prominent individuals from a variety of cultures and fields" as well as "an expert Committee on the Philosophic Principles of the Rights of Man . . . composed of leading scholars, jurists, and religious leaders of the day"). The range of rights enumerated as recognized throughout the world included a range of economic and social rights. Ibid., p. 225.

17. The Treaty of Versailles (1919), drafted by the victorious powers at the end of World War I, imposed massive reparations obligations on Germany, among other things. The economic dislocations resulting from World War I, the Great Depression, and ethnic and religious intolerance set the stage for the rise of fascism and nationalism in Europe and Asia and ultimately the catastrophe of World War II. See Versailles Treaty (June 28, 1919). (See especially Articles 227–30 [Penalties] and 231–47 [Reparations], available online at history.sandiego. edu/gen/text/versaillestreaty/vercontents.html, accessed March 27, 2007.)

18. Glendon, *A World Made New*, pp. 10, 13.

19. But see generally Makau Mutua, *Human Rights: A Political and Cultural Critique* (Philadelphia: University of Pennsylvania Press, 2000) (arguing that the International Bill of Rights was insufficiently influenced by the perspectives of peoples from the Third World); Franklin D. Roosevelt and Winston S. Churchill, The Atlantic Charter (August 14, 1941); Lauren, *Evolution of International Human Rights*, p. 142.

20. Charter of the United Nations. June 26, 1945, 59 Stat. 1031, T.S. 993, 3 Bevans 1153, entered into force October 24, 1945.

21. See, e.g., Paolo G. Carrozza, "From Conquest to Constitutions: Retrieving a Latin American Tradition of the Idea of Human Rights," *Human Rights Quarterly* 25, no. 2 (2003): 281, excerpted in Woods and Lewis, *Human Rights*, pp. 72–74 (Latin American influences); Mary Ann Glendon, "The Sources of 'Rights Talk,'" *Commonweal* 28(17) (October 13, 2001): 11, excerpted in Woods and Lewis, *Human Rights*, pp. 84–85 (Latin American and Asian influences).

22. Franklin D. Roosevelt, Four Freedoms Speech, 87-1 Cong. Rec. 44, 46–47 (1941), excerpted in Weissbrodt, Fitzpatrick, and Newman, *International Human Rights*, p. 86.

23. Sunstein, *Second Bill of Rights*, pp. 1, 18–19 (describing FDR's call for a second bill of rights as linked to the experiences of the Great Depression and New Deal policies).

24. "All human rights are universal, indivisible, and interdependent and interrelated. . . . [I]t is the duty of States, regardless of their political, economic and cultural systems, to promote and protect all human rights and fundamental freedoms." Vienna Declaration and Programme of Action, Adopted by the World Conference on Human Rights, Vienna, June 25, 1993 (A/CONF. 157/24 [Part I] chap. 111), excerpted in Woods and Lewis, *Human Rights*, p. 89.

25. Roosevelt, "1944 State of the Union Address," in Woods and Lewis, *Human Rights*, pp. 75–77.

26. Sunstein, *Second Bill of Rights*, pp. 10–11.

27. Anderson, *Eyes off the Prize*, pp. 16–17.

28. Lauren, *Evolution of International Human Rights*, p. 124.

29. Article 56 requires member states "to take joint and separate action in cooperation with the Organization for the achievement of the purposes set forth in Article 55." As a UN member state, the United States was, and is, therefore under such a general obligation, however vaguely defined in the charter's text.

Because its human rights provisions are so vaguely stated, legislators and courts in the United States subsequently treated the charter as non-self-executing; it therefore could not serve as the sole basis for a cause of action in U.S. courts absent implementing legislation. Bert B. Lockwood, Jr., "The United Nations Charter and United States Civil Rights Litigation: 1946–1955," *Iowa Law Review* 901 (1984): 69. See also *Sei Fujii v. State of California* (1952) 38 Cal.2d 718, 729 [242 P.2d 617] (finding that the human rights provisions of the UN Charter are non-self-executing and therefore do not automatically void conflicting U.S. law despite the status of duly ratified international treaties as part of the supreme law of the land).

30. Louis Henkin, "International Law, Politics, Values and Functions," in *Collected Courses of The Hague Law Academy of International Droit*, vol. 4 (1989), pp. 215, 216, excerpted in Steiner and Alston, *International Human Rights in Context*, p. 141.

31. See, e.g., Military and Paramilitary Activities in and against Nicaragua (*Nicaragua v. United States of America*), Merits, Judgment, ICJ Reports 1986, p. 98, para. 186.

32. Glendon, "Sources of 'Rights Talk,'" in Woods and Lewis, *Human Rights*, pp. 84–85 (noting involvement of delegates from Lebanon, the Philippines, and China, among other non-Western countries in negotiation and drafting of UDHR).

33. Steiner and Alston, *International Human Rights in Context*, pp. 138–39.

34. See generally Glendon, *A World Made New*. Among the influential members of the first UN Commission on Human Rights were Chair Eleanor Roosevelt of the United States, Charles Malik of the Lebanon, and Rene Cassin of France. Steiner and Alston, *International Human Rights in Context*, p. 138.

35. The legacy of Franklin Roosevelt's Four Freedoms speech, a draft submission by the American Law Institutes, and the support of Mrs. Roosevelt helped ensure the inclusion of economic and social rights in the UDHR. Steiner and Alston, *International Human Rights in Context*, p. 244. "Egypt, several Latin American countries (particularly Chile), and . . . the (Communist) countries of Eastern Europe" also supported socioeconomic rights provisions during the drafting of the UDHR. Australia, the United Kingdom, and South Africa were opposed, "arguing that such rights represented desirable goals, rather than rights as such." Further, they expressed the fear that the level of state control necessary to ensure the fulfillment of such rights would lead to totalitarianism. Ibid.

36. Glendon, "Sources of 'Rights Talk,'" in Woods and Lewis, *Human Rights*, pp. 84–85; Constitution of Mexico (1917), excerpted in Woods and Lewis, *Human Rights*, p. 71; Paolo G. Carrozza, "From Conquest to Constitutions," excerpted in Woods and Lewis, *Human Rights*, pp. 72–74.

37. "Save us from ourselves and show us a vision of a world made new." Eleanor Roosevelt, "Eleanor Roosevelt's Nightly Prayer," from Elliott Roosevelt and James Brough, *Mother R.*, reprinted in Glendon, *A World Made New*, p. ix.

38. "All of the Communist countries gave priority to social and economic rights, wanted them to be accompanied by corresponding civic duties, and insisted that the state should be the primary enforcer." Glendon, *A World Made New*, p. 43.

39. "The UDHR was adopted by the UN General Assembly on December 10, 1948. Forty-eight states voted in the affirmative, eight states abstained (Byelorus, Czechoslovakia, Poland, Saudi Arabia, South Africa, the Soviet Union, Ukraine, and Yugoslavia)." *Evolution of International Human Rights*, p. 345, n. 129. See also ibid., pp. 238–39 (discussing concerns raised by the abstaining states as primarily

related to the protection of sovereignty). But see Steiner and Alston, *International Human Rights in Context*, p. 138 (discussing South Africa's stated concern that the inclusion of economic and social rights might lead to totalitarianism).

40. See, e.g., Steiner and Alston, *International Human Rights in Context*, pp. 142–43.

41. Glendon, *A World Made New*, p. 186.

42. Mutua, *Political and Cultural Critique*. Mutua criticizes the International Bill of Rights as an unfulfilled and limited promise for the peoples of the Third World and the poor.

43. See, e.g., Mary L. Dudziak, "Desegregation as a Cold War Imperative," *Stanford Law Review* 41 (1988): 61; Mary Dudziak, *Cold War Civil Rights: Race and the Image of American Democracy* (Princeton, N.J.: Princeton University Press, 2000); Lauren, *Evolution of International Human Rights*, p. 227.

44. Gay McDougall, "Shame in Our Own House," *The American Prospect* (October 2004): A23–A24.

45. The petition was drafted by W. E. B. Du Bois, Milton Konvitz, Rayford Logan, and Earl B. Dickerson. Brenda Gayle Plummer, *Rising Wind: Black Americans and U.S. Foreign Affairs, 1935–1960* (Chapel Hill: University of North Carolina Press, 1996), pp. 180–81.

46. Plummer, *Rising Wind*, p. 179.

47. Lauren, *Evolution of International Human Rights*, pp. 226–27; Plummer, *Rising Wind*, p. 179.

48. Plummer, *Rising Wind*, p. 182.

49. Ibid., pp. 182–83.

50. Ibid., pp. 183–84.

51. Ibid., p. 183.

52. Anderson, *Eyes off the Prize*.

53. Plummer, *Rising Wind*, pp. 202–3. U.S. President Reagan signed the Genocide Convention in November 1988 (it entered into force at the beginning of the first Bush administration in 1989) following the adoption of domestic implementing legislation in 1987. Weissbrodt, Fitzpatrick, and Newman, *International Human Rights*, p. 124.

54. Plummer, *Rising Wind*, pp. 202–3.

55. Ibid.

56. Anderson, *Eyes off the Prize*, pp. 203–6.

57. Glendon, *A World Made New*, pp. 99–100.

58. Weissbrodt, Fitzpatrick, and Newman, *International Human Rights*, p. 117.

59. Lockwood, "United States Civil Rights Litigation," 901.

60. Art. VI of the U.S. Constitution provides that international law, along with federal law, is the "supreme law of the land." In addition, a leading U.S. Supreme Court decision (with the Court sitting as a prize court) states that "international law is part of our law." In cases of conflict, the Constitution itself is supreme, with federal statutes and ratified international treaties sharing the same level of priority. Federal courts have taken the view that federal statutes and U.S.-ratified international treaties should, as far as possible, be interpreted consistently, but in case of unavoidable conflict, the "later in time" instrument prevails. Detlev F. Vagts, "The United States and Its Treaties: Observance and Breach," *American Journal of International Law* 95 (2001): 313, 320. "International law is part of our law, and must be ascertained and administered by the courts of justice of appropriate jurisdiction, [. . .] as often as questions of right depending upon it are duly presented for their determination. For this purpose, where there is no treaty,

and no controlling executive or legislative act or judicial decision, resort must be had to the customs and usages of civilized nations; and, as evidence of these, to the works of jurists and commentators, who by years of labor, research and experience, have made themselves peculiarly well acquainted with the subjects of which they treat. Such works are resorted to by judicial tribunals, not for the speculations of their authors concerning what the law ought to be, but for trustworthy evidence of what the law really is." Paquete Habana, 175 U.S. 677 (1900), excerpted in Woods and Lewis, *Human Rights*, pp. 67, 70.

61. The desire to preserve U.S. racialism at almost any cost even went so far as efforts to promote the exclusion of African Americans and other U.S. religious or ethnic groups from the international human rights mechanisms aimed at the protection of minority rights so as to exclude (at least as they interpreted it) African Americans. Gay J. McDougall, "Shame in Our Own House," *The American Prospect* (October 2004): A22.

62. Dudziak, *Cold War Civil Rights*; Brown v. Board of Education, 347 U.S. 483 (1954).

63. Annotations on the Text of the Draft International Covenant on Human Rights, UN Doc. A/2929 (1955), p. 7, excerpted in Steiner and Alston, *International Human Rights in Context*, pp. 244–45.

64. Ibid. See also "Statement by Mrs. Franklin D. Roosevelt," *Department of State Bulletin*, pp. 1059, 1064–66 (December 31, 1951), excerpted in Woods and Lewis, *Human Rights*, pp. 85–88 (accepting the equal importance of socioeconomic rights, but elaborating her views with regard to the distinct nature of states obligations with regard to economic and social rights).

65. Lauren, *Evolution of International Human Rights*, pp. 245–46.

66. International Covenant of Civil and Political Rights, G.A. res. 2200A (XXI), 21 U.N. GAOR Supp. (No. 16), p. 52, U.N. Doc. A/6316 (1966), 999 U.N.T.S. 171, entered into force March 23, 1976; International Covenant on Economic, Social, and Cultural Rights, G.A. res. 2200A (XXI), 21 U.N. GAOR Supp. (No. 16), p. 49, U.N. Doc. A/6316 (1966), 993 U.N.T.S. 3, entered into force January 3, 1976.

67. Lauren, *Evolution of International Human Rights*, pp. 253–54.

68. See Periodic Report of the United States of America to the United Nations Committee on the Elimination of Racial Discrimination Concerning the International Convention on the Elimination of All Forms of Racial Discrimination (April 2007), available online at www.ushrnetwork.org/pubs/CERD%20Report%204-07.pdf (second report of the United States).

69. See, e.g., Malcolm X, February 21, 1965 speech to the Organization of Afro-American Unity (OAAU). Available online at www.malcolmx.org/docs/gen_oaau.htm (advocating for placing the status of African Americans on the UN human rights agenda and linking with the struggles of other subordinated groups cross-culturally).

70. See sections 116 and 502B of the Foreign Assistance Act of 1961 (FAA), as amended, and section 504 of the Trade Act of 1974, as amended. See also David P. Forsythe and Eric A. Heinze, "On the Margins of the Human Rights Discourse: Foreign Policy and International Welfare Rights," in Howard-Hassmann and Welch (eds.), *Economic Rights in Canada and the United States*, pp. 55, 58; Weissbrodt, Fitzpatrick, and Newman, *International Human Rights*, pp. 530–31.

71. Just prior to Martin Luther King's 1968 assassination in Memphis, Tennessee, he was working in support of a local garbage workers' "I am a Man" campaign for decent wages and working conditions. Most of the workers were African Amer-

ican. See, e.g., "I Am a Man: An Exhibit Honoring the 1968 Memphis Sanitation Workers' Strike," available online at www.reuther.wayne.edu/man/1intro.htm. In addition to civil rights, King began a "Poor Peoples' Campaign" in which he echoed FDR's calls for a "second Bill of Rights." Martin Luther King, Jr., "The Time Is Always Right to Do Right" (speech presented at Syracuse University, New York, July 15, 1965), available online at students.syr.edu/osvp/drkingaddress.html.

72. Weissbrodt, Fitzpatrick, and Newman, p. 118.

73. Cyrus Vance, "Human Rights and Foreign Policy," *Georgia Journal of International & Comparative Law* 7 (1977): 223, excerpted in Weissbrodt, Fitzpatrick, and Newman, *International Human Rights*, p. 141.

74. "Four Treaties Pertaining to Human Rights: Message From the President of the United States," 95th Cong., 2nd Sess., pp. VIII–XI (1978), excerpted in Weissbrodt, Fitzpatrick, and Newman, *International Human Rights*, p. 142.

75. Weissbrodt, Fitzpatrick, and Newman, *International Human Rights*, p. 143 (quoting transmittal letter).

76. Ibid.

77. Burns Weston, "U.S. Ratification of the International Covenants on Economic, Social and Cultural Rights: With or Without Qualifications?" in Richard B. Lillich (ed.), *U.S. Ratification of the Human Rights Treaties: With or Without Reservations?* (1981), pp. 30–38, excerpted in Weissbrodt, Fitzpatrick, and Newman, *International Human Rights*, pp. 145–48.

78. "Four Treaties Pertaining to Human Rights: Message From the President of the United States," 95th Cong., 2nd Sess., pp. VIII–XI (1978), excerpted in Weissbrodt, Fitzpatrick, and Newman, *International Human Rights*, p. 142.

79. Phillip Alston, "Entirely New Strategy," excerpted in Weissbrodt, Fitzpatrick, and Newman, *International Human Rights*, p. 138. See also Barbara J. Stark, "Economic Rights in the United States and International Human Rights Law: Toward 'an Entirely New Strategy,'" in David P. Forsythe (ed.), *The United States and Human Rights: Looking Inward and Outward* (Lincoln: University of Nebraska Press, 2000) (discussing proratification activist strategies during the Clinton administration).

80. Weissbrodt, Fitzpatrick, and Newman, *International Human Rights*, p. 128.

81. "Statement by Mrs. Franklin D. Roosevelt," Department of State Bulletin, pp. 1059, 1064–66 (December 31, 1951), excerpted in Woods and Lewis, *Human Rights*, pp. 85, 87.

82. See, e.g., David P. Forsythe and Eric A. Heinze, "On the Margins of the Human Rights Discourse: Foreign Policy and International Welfare Rights," in Howard-Hassmann and Welch (eds.), *Economic Rights in Canada and the United States*, pp. 55, 58; David Beetham, "What Future for Economic and Social Rights?," *Political Studies* 41 (1993): 443, excerpted in Steiner and Alston, *Human Rights in Context*, pp. 255–56; Herman Schwartz, "The Wisdom and Enforceability of Welfare Rights as Constitutional Rights," *Human Rights Brief* 8(2) (2001), available online at www.wcl.american.edu/hrbrief/08/2rights.cfm; Barbara Stark, "Economic Rights in the United States and International Human Rights Law: Toward an Entirely New Strategy," *Hastings Law Journal* 44 (1992): 79; Barbara J. Stark, "Economic Rights in the United States and International Human Rights Law: Toward 'an Entirely New Strategy,'" in David P. Forsythe (ed.), *The United States and Human Rights: Looking Inward and Outward* (Lincoln: University of Nebraska Press, 2000).

83. See, e.g., Schwartz, "Welfare Rights."

84. Ibid.

85. See generally Henry Shue, *Basic Rights: Subsistence, Affluence, and U.S. Foreign Policy*, 2nd ed. (Princeton, N.J.: Princeton University Press, 1996).

86. *Goldberg v. Kelly*, 397 U.S. 254 (1970).

87. Schwartz, "Welfare Rights."

88. U.S.-based human rights advocates from major human rights organizations or foundations such as Human Rights Watch, Physicians for Human Rights, and the Open Society Institute have debated the substantive or practical merits of economic and social rights approaches. See, e.g., Aryeh Neier, "Social and Economic Rights: A Critique," *Human Rights Bulletin* 13(2) (Winter 2006): 1; Kenneth Roth, "Defending Economic, Social and Cultural Rights: Practical Issues Faced by an International Human Rights Organization," *Human Rights Quarterly* 26 (2004): 63–73; Leonard S. Rubenstein, "How International Human Rights Organizations Can Advance Economic, Social, and Cultural Rights: A Response to Kenneth Roth," *Human Rights Quarterly* 26 (2004): 845–65.

89. See United Nations, Office of the High Commissioner for Human Rights, Committee on Economic, Social, and Cultural Rights, available online at www.ohchr.org/english/bodies/cescr/.

90. Limburg Principles.

91. Maastricht Guidelines.

92. A recent attack on the idea of economic and social rights in the pages of the U.K. magazine *The Economist* (March 22, 2007) illustrates the kind of retrenchment and debate that is already happening in Europe. Despite the provenance of economic and social rights and significant recent global activity on them, articles criticized Amnesty International's decision to further highlight such rights. This caused a significant response among the large network of activists, academics, and international diplomats who champion international economic and social rights. For the original articles and a range of responses to them, see, e.g., Amnesty International, "Economic, Social and Cultural Rights are Human Rights," available online at web.amnesty.org/pages/economist-response-index-eng (regularly updated Web site).

93. Stephanie Farrior, "UN Adopts Optional Protocol to the Covenant on Economic, Social, and Cultural Rights," IntLawGrrls (11 December 2008), available at http://intlawgrrls.blogspot.com/2008/12/un-adopts-optional-protocol-to-covenant.html

94. *Minister of Health and Others v. Treatment Action Campaign and Others* 2002(5) S.A. 721 (CC).

95. *Government of Republic of South Africa and Others v. Grootboom and Others* 2000 (11) BCLR 1169 (CC).

96. Woods and Lewis, "Chapter Eight: South Africa: The Bill of Rights Approach," in *Human Rights*, pp. 715–80.

97. Woods and Lewis, "Chapter Seven: India: The 'Directive Principles' Approach," in *Human Rights*, pp. 653–713.

98. Woods and Lewis, "Chapter Nine: The Council of Europe: A Blending of the Categories," in *Human Rights*, pp. 781–839; Alicia Ely Yamin, "The Future in the Mirror: Incorporating Strategies for the Defense and Promotion of Economic, Social, and Cultural Rights into the Mainstream Human Rights Agenda," *Human Rights Quarterly* 27 (2006): 1200–1244 (on Latin America).

99. Cf. Rhoda Howard-Hassmann, "The 'Full-Belly' Thesis: Should Economic Rights Take Priority over Civil and Political Rights? Evidence from Sub-Saharan Africa," *Human Rights Quarterly* 5(4) (1983): 467–90.

100. See, e.g., Mississippi Worker's Center for Human Rights, available online atwww.msworkerscenter.org/.

101. See, e.g., Woods and Lewis, *Human Rights*, pp. 923–30; Ford Foundation, *Close to Home*; U.S. Human Rights Network, *Something Inside.*

102. Roth, "Defending Economic Rights"; Rubenstein, "A Response to Kenneth Roth."

Introduction to Part II

Catherine Albisa

There is a growing movement with a core commitment to holding the United States accountable to human rights. This growing movement is not entirely unified and faces many challenges both external and internal. This part covers the political, legal, and social evolution of this movement, as well as examines its current limits and potential. It tracks the roots of the latest manifestation of the U.S. human rights movement, in particular the period from 1990—the "end of the Cold War"—to the present day through thematic chapters. It scans the landscape of this work across the country and examines watershed moments that resulted from the impact on human rights of the September 11, 2001, attacks on the World Trade Center and the devastation of Hurricane Katrina in August 2005.

One clear outcome of these events has been the increasing use and relevance of international human rights standards. For example, "The Impact of September 11 and the Struggle Against Terrorism on the U.S. Domestic Human Rights Movement" by Wendy Patten and "Bush Administration Noncompliance with the Prohibition on Torture and Cruel and Degrading Treatment" by Kathryn Sikkink carefully detail the environment in which progressive activists found themselves after September 11, 2001, and their fierce efforts to prevent and curtail some of the worst governmental abuses using every tool in their arsenal, particular universal international human rights standards.

In the post-9/11 landscape, however, Americans have sacrificed far more than specific human rights directly linked to the "war on terror." Indeed, this costly "war" has direct budgetary repercussions for issues such as health care, education, and economic security, all of which are basic human rights.

These rights, as noted in Chapter 6, "Economic and Social Rights in the United States: Six Rights, One Promise," have never been fully recognized or adequately protected in the United States, although there was a period of time in which public and government support was far greater than it is now.

In the face of such profound social ills and such an abject failure on a nationwide level to respect human dignity and freedom, activists have—not surprisingly—turned to less traditional approaches for their advocacy. In particular, they are undertaking domestic human rights work. Human rights work in the United States is multifaceted and involves educators, organizers, artists, musicians, Web activists, lawyers, scholars, policy advocates, economists, and other activists. But as Dorothy Q. Thomas explains in "Against American Supremacy: Rebuilding Human Rights Culture in the United States," regardless of what specialty human rights activists come from, the work is fundamentally about challenging supremacy in all its forms and demanding equality and social inclusion. The work is also supranational from a legal perspective in that it lays claim to a body of law that is not dependent on national legislation or constitutions.

U.S. activists have—as detailed in Margaret Huang's " 'Going Global': Appeals to International and Regional Human Rights Bodies"—increasingly brought domestic issues to the international stage, including holding hearings and bringing cases to the Inter-American Commission on Human Rights, working with UN experts on global reporting, appearing at the annual UN Human Rights Council meetings, and filing "shadow" reports when the United States has to report to a UN treaty body. Activists have found new potential, but also limitations, in bringing the fruit of these international interventions back to their localities. Other activists, as put forth by Martha F. Davis in "Thinking Globally, Acting Locally: States, Municipalities, and International Human Rights," have adopted an inverse strategy, bringing international human rights standards to the local level through municipal ordinances and resolutions. Additionally, Cynthia Soohoo in "Human Rights and the Transformation of the 'Civil Rights' and 'Civil Liberties' Lawyer" describes the struggle of activist lawyers to embed human rights values and standards into the U.S. legal system. Finally, Lance Compa in "Trade Unions and Human Rights" provides a cogent analysis and example of how human rights strategies and approaches have begun to intersect with other major movements, such as the labor movement.

Together these chapters paint a picture of a growing body of work that may yet significantly influence the political landscape in the coming decades. This movement is unique in the breadth of its scope and audacious in its aspirations. In short, it is idealistic. It seems we are just emerging out of a moment in history in which to have ideals was suspect. Better—some very recently argued—to accept that some rights, such as freedom from torture, are not absolute when we are afraid, and others, such as health care, are only commodities that serve market interests.

This volume brings you the voices of those who argue, intensely and passionately, that this view cannot and must not prevail. The authors argue that we must hold on to the best of what is inherent in our identity and ideals as a country and heal ourselves of the systemic dysfunctions that lead to widespread violations of dignity, equality, and freedom. The disease is easy to identify: violence, inequality in all its forms, greed, exclusivity, cruelty, indifference, ignorance, and poverty. The upcoming chapters explore a growing movement that believes that human rights are the cure.

Chapter 5
Against American Supremacy: Rebuilding Human Rights Culture in the United States

Dorothy Q. Thomas

Is this America?
—*Fannie Lou Hamer*

Where We Begin

The contemporary movement for human rights in the United States arises out of a struggle over the identity of the nation, its people, and each and every individual within its jurisdiction. It takes place simultaneously at the personal and the political level, unfolding as much within the confines of the individual, the community, and the group as it does in the corridors of the Congress, the White House, or the nation's highest courts. Like any effort at self-definition, the U.S. human rights struggle is irreducible to any particular period, or exclusive type or single strand; it is intergenerational, multidimensional, and mixed. This chapter traces the development of the contemporary movement for human rights in the United States, analyzes its evolving character, and recommends ways to strengthen its voice in the struggle to determine what America stands for in the eyes of its own people and of the world.

Before discussing the origins, nature, and future of the contemporary U.S. human rights movement in detail, it is important to understand what precipitates it. At its core is the question of racism or, more broadly, supremacy. Its nearest roots lie in the sharp conflict of the mid-1940s and 1950s between the principles of human rights and the practice of discrimination based on race. At the time, the U.S. government chose explicitly and aggressively to protect domestic racial segregation at the cost of its own adherence to human rights, despite the origin of those rights in much of its own leadership and tradition.[1] The contemporary U.S. human rights movement is, perhaps more than anything else, a renewed expression of the global struggle against structural and individual racism in the world and a resurgent voice in the effort to reclaim the United States as a nation which eschews supremacy for equality and favors dignity over oppression in both domestic and foreign policy.

Even as the struggle for human rights in the United States is about strengthening the fight against structural racism in America and elsewhere, it is also about situating race in the context of systematic inequality more generally. This wider analysis is what makes the U.S. human rights movement so complex, so powerful and, for some, so threatening. In trying to relink the struggles for civil and human rights, it seeks to connect the fight against racism to the often parallel fights against class, sex, nationality, or other status-based discrimination not only in this country but elsewhere.[2] It also seeks to reconnect the struggle for civil and political liberty with that for economic, social, and cultural equality. As noted by the Reverend Martin Luther King, Jr., in a 1966 speech at Howard University, "Now we are grappling with basic class issues between the privileged and the under privileged. In order to solve this problem, not only will it mean restructuring the architecture of American society, but it will cost the nation something. . . . If you want to call it the human rights struggle, that's all right with me."[3]

Often the contemporary U.S. human rights movement is criticized for this all-embracing framework, for what is called its "kitchen-sink" quality, that is, its seeming dilution of the significance of particular rights abuses or of particular abused groups in the name of promoting all human rights for everyone. This critique arises most virulently from the conservative, corporate right, which in any case contests the legitimacy of all but the most narrow rights claims.[4] But it also resonates quite deeply with respected human rights leaders who question its effectiveness and a wide range of progressive social justice movements that identify themselves with single issues or groups or both. In sum, opposition to or concern about the U.S. human rights movement is as wide-ranging as the movement itself. This, as I will discuss throughout, has had a significant effect on the movement's development, its character, and its strategy.

Before we take a closer look at the most recent ancestry of the contemporary human rights movement in the United States, the fate of that early work, the various arenas in which it currently unfolds, the culture surrounding it, its most pressing challenges, and, finally, how it might go forward, we would do well to remember one simple fact about human rights: They belong to us. They don't belong to any one of us, or any group of us, or any political party of us, or any nation of us, or any continent of us, or any hemisphere of us. Human rights belong to all of us, everywhere. If the movement for human rights in the United States is about anything, it is about reaffirming this simple fact. It reminds us all that if the most powerful country in the world is allowed to slip uncontested outside the vision and system of human rights, nothing less than the affirmation of our common humanity and the recognition of our shared fate are at stake.

Where We Are From

> *Freedom means the supremacy of human rights everywhere.*
> —*Franklin Delano Roosevelt*

A full discussion of the origins of the contemporary human rights movement in the United States would require a review of American and world history taken up, in part, in Part I of this volume. Here, I have confined myself to a more abbreviated discussion of the contemporary movement's proximate intellectual and political antecedents in order to set the stage for my discussion of that movement's current form.

The contemporary U.S. human rights movement's nearest intellectual relative is the fight against fascism. The movement takes as its premise the belief that assertions of supremacy, whether in the international or interpersonal sphere, are anathema to fundamental principles of equality and dignity. It assumes as its mantle the long American tradition of distrust of any form of government that sets itself above the will of the people or doubts the integrity of the common woman or man. It claims as its anthem Franklin Delano Roosevelt's 1941 assertion of the Four Freedoms: from fear, from want, to think, and to believe,[5] which were subsequently given fuller expression in the Universal Declaration of Human Rights of 1948. It asserts as its mission the restoration of what the Reverend Martin Luther King, Jr., called "the era of human rights."

As much as the contemporary U.S. human rights movement takes its inspiration from the fight against fascism, its activism—even its very existence—arises out of the contradictions in that same tradition, especially in its American iteration. "It's tragic," then-president of the National Association for the Advancement of Colored People (NAACP) Walter White noted in 1944, "that the Civil War should be fought again while we are waging a World War to save civilization." He found it incomprehensible, Carol Anderson tells us, "that the United States could fight 'a war for freedom' with a Jim Crow army." White's determination to resolve this contradiction in favor of freedom for all people drove the

NAACP and more than forty other domestic groups to demand a place at the 1945 conference in San Francisco to establish the United Nations. "On behalf of the negroes not only of America but of Africa, the West Indies and other parts of the world," White said that the NAACP was going to make its "voice heard."

In San Francisco, the coalition of domestic groups fought hard for the inclusion of human rights in the UN Charter, an unequivocal commitment to decolonization and the creation of a human rights commission. Under the leadership of W. E. B. Du Bois, the NAACP's San Francisco delegation reached out to the organization's membership and mobilized pressure on the United States to stand against colonialism and for greater enforcement powers with respect to human rights. Du Bois later told a Chicago reporter "We have conquered Germany, but not [its] ideas. We still believe in white supremacy, keeping negroes in their place and lying about democracy, when [what] we mean [is] imperial control of 750 million human beings in the colonies."[6]

The domestic groups' unified efforts to link the fight against colonialism abroad with the struggle against racism at home provoked the very supremacist and nationalist forces they sought to defeat. As noted in *Eyes Off the Prize,* Secretary of State Edward Stettinius, who headed the U.S. delegation, avowed that his "job in San Francisco was to create a charter . . . not to take up subjects like . . . 'the negro question' or to allow something so 'ludicrous' as a delegation of American Indians . . . to present a plea . . . for recognition for the independence of the Six Nations (The Iroquois)."[7] Stettinius was equally lackluster in his support for decolonization. And John Foster Dulles ultimately saved the day for Southern segregationists by drafting an amendment to the charter to ensure that nothing within it would "authorize the United Nations to intervene in matters which are essentially within the domestic jurisdiction of any state."[8]

The conflict within the United States about the relevance of human rights to domestic racial, economic, and other injustice reached a fevered pitch over the next decade, exacerbated greatly by the politics of the Cold War. As noted above, I do not intend to restate this history here, which in any case has been much better told by Carol Anderson, Thomas Jackson, and others. My aim instead is to establish that the struggle for human rights in the United States, whether then or now, does not arise out of a battle *between* America and the rest of the world. Instead, it is a product of contradictions *within* the country's own political and legal tradition. Far from being a "foreign" problem, the relation of human rights to U.S. culture is a quintessentially domestic concern. It defines who the United States is as a nation and what it stands for in the eyes of its people and of the world.

How We Got Lost

> *[The] era of . . . domestic, social and economic "reforms" through international treaties is at an end.*
>
> —*John Foster Dulles*

Still, it seemed throughout most of the Cold War that the early movement for human rights in the United States had come to naught. Beginning with Dulles's insertion of the "domestic jurisdiction" clause in the UN Charter right up until the ratification of the Genocide Convention in 1988, the U.S. government forestalled any significant application of human rights to itself. In the 1950s, the Eisenhower administration protected its treaty-making power by assuring Southern democrats there would be no ratifications challenging race discrimination. It wasn't until the Carter administration nearly twenty years later that any meaningful executive action with respect to human rights took place. Although the 1980s and 1990s witnessed U.S. ratifications of several key human rights treaties, in many cases their approval was accompanied by reservations and understandings that sharply limited their effect on domestic law and practice.[9]

Some notable exceptions to this trend did occur, but largely on the part of civil society. For example, in the 1960s, in the context of anti-colonialism and the war in Vietnam, Malcolm X and the Reverend Martin Luther King, Jr., both reiterated the need to link the civil and human rights struggles and adopt a more comprehensive and internationalized approach to social and economic justice. In the 1980s, U.S. civil and other rights activists joined in the global campaign to end apartheid. In securing the passage of U.S. sanctions against South Africa, this coalition and its congressional allies handed Ronald Reagan the most significant foreign policy defeat of his presidency. These examples speak to an undercurrent of sustained resistance to the split between civil and human rights, as well as domestic and international advocacy. They also illustrate the linkage's enduring value for effective work for social change in the United States and other countries.

These telling exceptions, however, could not sufficiently counter the cumulative effect of several U.S. administrations' sustained resistance to the domestic application of human rights. Despite their historic links to domestic thought and advocacy, human rights came to be constructed as utterly foreign to the nation's internal life and the United States proclaimed itself as essentially above the law that it argued should apply to every other country. This "negative exceptionalism," as Harold Koh calls it,[10] not only separated the United States from the international community, but also divided it from itself. The unity of vision and purpose reflected in the human rights–related advocacy of the U.S. civil, women's, and workers' rights groups in the early period, for example, was largely lost to the polarizing effects of the Cold War and its internal and external progeny. Domestic antiracist, antisexist, and antipoverty movements, separated not only from their counterparts in the rest of the world, but also from each other. Efforts via human rights to reconnect them in whatever sphere were and often still are decried as *un*-American. Nonetheless, the early phase of U.S. human rights work accomplished a lot. More than anything else, it exposed the world to the internal contradictions in the character and conduct of the United States, helping to generate pressure for federal reform and to spur domestic change.[11] During the U.S. government's long course of self-inoculation from human rights, the domestic civil, women's, workers', and other social justice movements flourished as did the international movement for human rights. Both these developments arose, at least in part, out of the U.S. government's willingness to improve rights at home and defend them abroad in order to shore up its Cold War status as the "leader of the free world." Instead of working together to shape progressive U.S. policy on both fronts, however, these movements were now for all ideological and practical purposes distinct.

Our Worlds Fell Apart

> *How is a black man going to get "civil rights" before he first wins his human rights?*
> —Malcolm X

This is the bifurcated world of social justice activism into which I, and most of my contemporaries, was born: civil rights on one side, human rights on the other. The one was domestic, the other foreign. Most U.S. social justice organizations were of one type or the other, as were the programs that funded them.[12] Not surprisingly, the situation within the Congress, the courts, and the executive branch was much the same. There were, and still are, separate congressional committees for civil and human rights, elaborate barriers between international and domestic law, and a profound disconnect between the rights machinery at the Department of Justice and that at the Department of State. The recent Bush administration did more than virtually any other to ensure that these movements, systems, and mechanisms remained apart.

Given this present context and past experience, many observers have argued that contemporary activists who seek to relink the struggle for civil and human rights should leave well enough alone. They suggest that although the various domestic social justice and international human rights groups operate in separate spheres, they have undeniably accomplished a lot; that the matters of interest to the civil and human rights committees of Congress are manifestly distinct; that the relationship between international and domestic law is fraught; and that Justice and State have different mandates. The effort required to interconnect all these separate spheres is monumental and, if the past is prelude, risky.

The content of this critique is accurate, but its aim is not. The goal of the contemporary U.S. human rights movement, as I understand it, has never been to confuse these distinct arenas or to collapse them. Instead it seeks to challenge the legitimacy of assuming (and institutionalizing) their innate separation. To Du Bois's generation the split between human and civil rights represented a mortal threat to everything they held dear. They saw in it a defense of white and American and other forms of supremacy that imposed significant limitations on the struggle for equality and freedom at home and in the world. To mine, a scant fifty years later, this exact same split was, more or less taken as a given. In whatever movements we were most active, we largely operated within the very limitations on the nature of our struggle (separated not unified), the scope of our rights (civil not economic), and the shape of our movement (domestic not international) that our forbearers were determined to resist. I was a human rights professional for nearly a decade before I ever worked on my own country. I'll never forget the words of the first domestic rights activist I reached out to for an investigation on the sexual abuse of women in U.S. prisons. "Where the hell," she asked me, "have you all been?"

To me this felt (and feels) like a legitimate question, especially as it was one she also asked herself. And it has become one that an increasing number of U.S. activists, communities, and groups, whatever their interests and in a variety of forms, are now asking each other: Why are we so separate? Whose interests does this separation serve? Does this really reflect who we are and for what we stand? Can we get back together?

We Rediscover and Rebuild Ourselves

> There is simply no better way to broaden all our struggles for social justice then through human rights.
>
> —Loretta Ross

The contemporary movement for human rights in the United States reemerged out of a growing awareness, particularly among those most affected by the denial of rights, that the old divisions between civil and

economic or citizen and alien or domestic and international no lon-
ger made much sense. Some of its earliest leaders, including Catherine
Albisa, Sandra Babcock, Willie Baptist, Ajamu Baraka, Larry Cox, Lisa
Crooms, Krishanti Dharmaraj, Mallika Dutt, Heidi Dorow, Fernando Garcia, Steve Hawkins, Jaribu Hill, Monique Harden, Paul Hoffman, Cheri
Honkala, Ben Jealous, Keith Jennings, Ethel Long-Scott, Leni Marin,
Brenda Smith, Deborah LaBelle, Sid Mohn, Catherine Powell, Loretta
Ross, and me, were all deeply embedded and engaged in domestic civil,
political, environmental, women's, workers', immigrant, prisoner, welfare, and gay rights advocacy. We saw the divisions between these movements as unresponsive to the experiences of the people we represented
and unequal to the threats we faced.

The biggest challenge to this new U.S. human rights leadership—
aside from the visceral opposition of the U.S. government—was that
we ourselves were largely of a generation for which all these issues and
strategies and arenas were ideologically and practically distinct. We understood from the beginning, therefore, that the contemporary human
rights movement in the U.S. could and would not be built from the top
down. It would have to come from within: within ourselves, within our
communities, within our organizations, within our movements, within
our government, and ultimately, within our country. As such, it would require a sustained community education and organizing effort, a push for
the internal transformation of existing institutions and movements, a systematic reintegration of human rights into domestic law and policy, and
the cultivation of new organizations, skills, and leadership to support this
change. These insights lie at the heart of the approach to and strategy
for rebuilding the U.S. human rights movement and culture that is outlined below, under subheadings drawn from the poetry of T. S. Eliot.

Home Is Where One Starts

The contemporary movement for human rights in the United States
begins with people in community. Many of its early leaders were of the
same communities in which they worked. We were determined to de-
molish the divide between professional advocates and affected groups
that had become quite pervasive in U.S. social justice advocacy more
generally. These efforts amounted to a ground-level assault on the mini-
supremacies of privilege and mini-nationalisms of identity that had
trickled down from similar trends in U.S. legal and political life more
generally. "To me," Fernando Garcia of the Border Network for Human
Rights once said, "human rights are about equality and dignity. I felt the
people themselves should make the decisions and do the work."

Garcia was not alone. Activists like Albisa, Dharmaraj, Hill, and Ross, for example, all created new projects or organizations, like WILD for Human Rights or the Mississippi Workers' Center for Human Rights, in which the work was determined by and the leadership drawn from the community itself. The aim was never to create a new set of institutions to compete with established civil, women's, or other rights groups, but to renew the human rights voice and vision within and across these existing movements. Human rights, whether in the United States or in any other part of the world, does not function as a substitute for civil, women's, immigrant, gay, or other work. Instead they arise out of and reinforce such distinct work and connect it to similar activism in other issue areas and parts of the globe.

Still, these early U.S. human rights leaders and groups looked and felt like interlopers in their own communities. The by-now ingrained perception of human rights as "foreign," however contrary it may have been to the history, values, and aims of U.S. social justice groups, colored many of these groups' profound skepticism with respect to the domestic human rights endeavor. One of my most respected professional mentors, for example, told me that the idea of reintegrating human rights into U.S. social justice activism "was a loser" and its potential "miniscule." This experience was not unique. U.S. human rights activists consistently report that they face substantial criticism from people and organizations with whom they were usually allied. This has had a profound effect on the movement's development and the mindset of its leadership.

The Wisdom of Humility Is Endless

The tendency of some U.S. human rights leaders when faced with criticism from within their own communities, organizations, and movements was to become defensive. I myself spent a long time avidly denouncing "American exceptionalism," before I ever acknowledged my own grandiosity in this regard. By contrast, the most effective human rights work and leadership within the United States involves a patient exercise in humility, a debunking from the inside out of the ideas of personal or racial or sexual or economic or national supremacy which have come to characterize the country despite its roots—however twisted—in the declaration of freedom and equality.

The point is that the contemporary movement's rebuilding strategy must encompass as much its own constitution and leadership as it does the country's. As noted in *Making the Connections*, "If human rights is to live up to its promise, the individuals that lead the movement and organizations that support it must consistently and deliberately examine our own conduct and ensure that the principles we hold up to others are ones that we uphold ourselves."[13] This level of self-discipline does not come easily to any human being, including one dedicated to the promotion of human rights. It requires not only a fairly unusual organizing strategy, but also a unique form of leadership.

It may seem counterintuitive to adopt humility as an organizing strategy, but for U.S. human rights activists it makes perfect sense. At the level of principle, as Garcia pointed out, human rights require an egalitarian approach. At the level of practice, no other method for rebuilding a domestic human rights movement will succeed. To assert the primacy of human rights would be to reaffirm their separation from existing U.S. social justice work. On the other hand, to reintroduce human rights as a way to respect and strengthen that work is to reclaim their inherent (and inherited) connection to the pursuit of lasting social change. Once the connection to human rights is rediscovered within domestic social justice work it becomes less treacherous to navigate its resuscitation in the internal political, legal, and popular culture of the country overall.

And All Is Always Now

In pursuit of this broader transformation, the U.S. human rights movement aims to link its in-depth education, training, and organizing work in particular areas or communities with outreach to social justice activists and movements more generally. It also functions cross-sectorally, connecting work at the community level with activism at the level of the U.S. judiciary and even of the international community. It also deploys multiple methodologies, linking its education and organizing efforts with participatory fact-finding work, policy advocacy, and legal change. Obviously, the enormity of this task frequently overwhelms the fledgling movement's capacity. Nonetheless, the disaffection from human rights and the addiction to supremacy so pervades U.S. identity that the appeal of human rights must be reinvigorated at all these levels simultaneously. Otherwise progress at one level will be, and often is, preempted at another.

Still one has to question the advisability or even conceivability of pursuing a movement-building strategy of such inordinate ambition and complexity. To pursue such changes in consciousness and action within a single-issue movement is challenging enough. To do so in a cross-issue effort is exponentially more difficult. Not surprisingly, the contemporary U.S. human rights movement is under constant pressure, from within and without, to narrow its focus: to emphasize a single issue, prioritize a particular sector, or choose a single method. By and large, this pressure to self-limit is one that, in principle at least, the contemporary movement resists. Whether it should continue to do so—given the degree to which its current resources are overstretched—is one of the most pressing strategic questions now facing it and will be discussed in more detail in the section below on challenges. As it stands now, significant work across a wide range of communities, issue areas, sectors, and methods is taking place and, as discussed in the remainder of this section, it increasingly takes a better capacitated and more coordinated form.

The Detail of the Pattern Is the Movement

So much is happening at once in contemporary human rights work that it can be difficult to discern the movement's overall shape or even its actual existence. The fact that it does not yet entirely cohere, however, does not mean that it isn't there. In fact, it's popping up everywhere, from international, national, state, and local groups, to a wide range of issue areas, across a variety of sectors and methods and with respect to advocacy at both the domestic and international level.

International, national, state, and local groups.   U.S.-based international human rights organizations like Amnesty International U.S.A (AIU.S.A), Global Rights, Human Rights Watch, Human Rights First, and Physicians for Human Rights, which once focused almost exclusively outside the country, have expanded their U.S. programs and reestablished their relationships with domestic social justice groups. National civil and other rights organizations with state and local counterparts, like the American Civil Liberties Union (ACLU) and the Leadership Conference on Civil Rights, increasingly see human rights as a dimension of their own work, rather than something carried out by other organizations focused elsewhere. Additionally, new national organizations have been founded to address the needs of the field, including the National Center for Human Rights Education, the National Economic and Social Rights Initiative (NESRI), the Opportunity Agenda, and the U.S. Human Rights Network. A growing number of local and regional groups have also arisen, like the Border Network for Human Rights, the Mississippi Workers' Center for Human Rights, Montana Human Rights Network, the North Dakota Human Rights Coalition, WILD for Human Rights, the Women of Color Resource Center, or the Urban Justice Center Human Rights Project, all of which frame and carry out their U.S. work entirely in terms of human rights.

Work in different issue areas.   The contemporary human rights movement is diverse not only geographically, but also by issue area. For example, along with the Border Network, immigrant rights groups like CLINIC, Hate Free Zone, the National Network for Immigrant and Refugee Rights, and the Rights Working Group have all begun to integrate human rights into their education, organizing, and advocacy work. Similar work in criminal justice is being pursued by the Center for Community Alternatives, the Haywood Burns Institute, the Youth Law

Center, and groups working on juvenile sentences of life without parole in Michigan, Illinois, and Minnesota. Groups like Gender-Pac, Immigration Equality, IPAS, and SisterSong are building human rights into their gay and gender-based advocacy, including in the area of reproductive rights. The Indian Law Resource Center and the Western Shoshone all use human rights to advance the local work of Native Americans. Community Asset Development Redefining Education (CADRE), the Deaf and Deaf-Blind Committee for Human Rights, the Coalition of Immokalee Workers, the Miami Workers Center, the National Economic and Social Rights Initiative, National Law Center for Homelessness and Poverty, and the Poor People's Economic Human Rights Campaign increasingly work with local communities to demand access to housing, health care, decent work, and education. Advocates for Environmental Human Rights and other groups that are focused on the effects of Hurricane Katrina are using human rights to take an integrated, structural approach to issues like racism, sexism, environmental degradation, economic deprivation, and the right to return.

Multiple methodologies.   Current U.S. human rights work also takes place across a wide range of methods. Groups like the Border Action Network and Breakthrough are pioneering community-based education and organizing strategies that are gradually being adapted by other groups. AIU.S.A, NESRI, the Poor People's Economic Human Rights Campaign, the Urban Justice Center, and Witness are all developing participatory fact-finding methods that affected communities can themselves use to record and combat abuse. The ACLU, the Center for Constitutional Rights, Legal Momentum, and some state-level legal groups increasingly raise human rights claims in their briefs and arguments. Similar work has yet consistently to emerge regarding local-, state-, and national-level policy, but significant advocacy campaigns are underway with respect to the military commissions, the restoration of habeas corpus, and adherence to the norms prohibiting torture and cruel, inhuman, and degrading treatment.

Relinking domestic and international advocacy.   Increasingly this internal human rights work reconnects to advocacy at the international level. In June 2006, more than 140 U.S. organizations representing a wide range of issue areas and sectors participated in an unprecedented collaborative effort to challenge the U.S. report to the UN Human Rights Committee and to actively engage the international human rights process as a supplement to their domestic advocacy. Similar efforts are envisioned for the U.S. report to the UN Committee that monitors compliance with the treaty to eliminate race discrimination. Alongside these relatively episodic activities, groups such as AIU.S.A, Human Rights Watch, and other traditional human rights groups with expertise in international advocacy more regularly ally with their domestic counterparts to raise issues of mutual concern. Similarly domestic groups like Advocates for Environmental Human Rights, the Center for Constitutional Rights, or the Kensington Welfare Rights Union consistently link to their sister organizations in other countries.

Training and communications support. This interwoven tapestry of U.S. human rights activities can increasingly count on high-level and much-needed support from organizations and projects that have arisen to build domestic human rights capacity and effect via issue-, method-, and sector-specific training or communications strategy and support. For example, the ACLU's Human Rights Project, the Center on Housing Rights and Evictions, the National Center for Human Rights Education, the National Economic and Social Rights Initiative, and the U.S. Human Rights Network all offer regular trainings by issue area or method or both. These groups in turn increasingly receive assistance from law school and other university-based human rights centers including those at American, Berkeley, Columbia, Connecticut, Fordham, Georgetown, Harvard, New York, Northeastern, Northwestern, Seattle, and Yale. These groups can also count on ever more expert assistance to enhance their strategic communications through the groundbreaking work of the Border Human Rights Coalition, Breakthrough, Fenton Communications, the U.S. Human Rights Network, the Opportunity Agenda, Riptide, the Spin Project, and Witness, among others.

Networking and coordination. Finally, all of these groups are gradually finding ways to come together at local, regional, and national levels, and by issue area and sector, for both domestic and international advocacy. For example, the Atlanta-based U.S. Human Rights Network (and its issue and method based caucuses), the border-based Border Rights Coalition, the Chicago- and Minneapolis-based Midwest Coalition for Human Rights, the D.C.-based Rights Working Group, the Mississippi-based Southern Human Rights Organizer's Network, and the New York–based Bringing Human Rights Home Lawyers Network all bring their constituents together on a regular basis to develop both strategy and capacity.

As a result of these developments, the contemporary effort to relink civil and human rights in the United States has a far greater chance of gaining momentum than it did even a decade ago. International human rights, domestic human rights, and U.S. civil, economic, and other rights groups have joined the effort. The work is taking place at the local, state, regional, national, and international level, within a wide range of issue areas and via everything from popular education to litigation to academic scholarship. Although it remains markedly undercapacitated and underresourced in the depth of its work and the pattern of its relationships, a new movement for human rights in the United States has clearly emerged.

The success of the contemporary movement derives from the fact that it arises out of domestic social justice work rather than, as is often alleged, being imposed upon it. At the micro level, the renewal of human rights in the United States reflects the domestic movement's collective fatigue with being divided within itself and from its counterparts elsewhere. At the macro level, it responds to U.S. civil and human rights groups' growing recognition that an America which sets itself above the rest of the world poses a threat to equality and dignity not only abroad but also at home. These various groups remain largely distinct but they are no longer ideologically and practically disconnected. This is a significant accomplishment of the contemporary movement for human rights in the United States. The question for the next section is whether that movement can expand beyond itself and connect to the culture at large.

The Current Environment

> *A universal-feeling, whether well or ill-founded, cannot be safely disregarded.*
> —*Abraham Lincoln*

Even as the contemporary movement has expanded its influence, it has never lost sight of the fact that deference to human rights is no more ingrained in American identity than is defense of supremacy, perhaps even less so. What preoccupies the movement is the struggle between these two tendencies at every level of U.S. society. The hunger for supremacy in the United States may famish its craving for human rights, but it also fuels it. The question now facing U.S. human rights activists is how best to stoke the country's growing demand for human rights and at the same time dampen its appetite for the opposite. As a matter of survival, this means the movement must find ways to resonate with the broader legal, political, and popular culture, counter those who seek to eradicate it and, most important, attend to the needs the vast majority of people who fall somewhere in between.

There can be no doubt that the horrific events of September 11, 2001, and their aftermath accelerated, but also fueled resistance to, the uptake of human rights by mainstream legal and political culture in the United States. As the remainder of this section sets forth, powerful actors from the Supreme Court on down increasingly assert the relevance of human rights to domestic law and policy. Yet the White House, the attorney general, the former secretary of defense, and many other influential figures have asserted the exact opposite. In the middle there are ever more key stakeholders, including jurists, policy makers, academics, donors, and activists who reject the exceptionalist assertions of the executive but remain resistant to the domestic resort to human rights. Leaving aside for the moment its need to appeal to the general public, the contemporary movement must take heed of the concerns of these key stakeholders if it is to rebuild not only itself but a broader culture of respect for human rights. These various actors, from allies, to enemies, to skeptics are discussed in that order below.

Supreme Court Justices

The U.S. human rights movement boasts some extremely unlikely and perhaps unwitting allies, including several current and former justices of the United States Supreme Court. While they consistently argue that international law is "not controlling," Justices Breyer, Ginsburg, Souter, Stevens, O'Connor, and Kennedy have all defended its interpretive weight. For example, on March 1, 2005, when the Supreme Court cited human rights in its decision to overturn the juvenile death penalty, Justice Kennedy wrote, "It does not lessen our fidelity to the Constitution . . . to acknowledge that the express affirmation of certain fundamental rights by other nations and peoples simply underscores the centrality of those rights within in our own heritage of freedom." Similarly, in a speech on February 7, 2006, Supreme Court Justice Ruth Bader Ginsburg restated her belief that "the U.S. Supreme Court will continue to accord 'a decent respect to the opinions of [human]kind' as a matter of comity and in a spirit of humility."

Legal Scholars and Practitioners

Interest is also growing in the broader legal community. The Aspen Institute hosts annual programs to educate American judges about human rights and humanitarian law and Brandeis University sponsors convenings of U.S. and international judges to address issues related to international justice. Columbia, Fordham, Georgetown, Howard, and New York University law schools are all hosting conferences on the applied use of human rights in domestic legal thought and arguments with specific regard to immigration, civil rights, and criminal and economic justice. The American Society of International Law increasingly features debate on the domestic application of human rights in its annual meetings, and the American Constitution Society is developing a human rights dimension to its Constitution 2020 project.

Policymakers, Think Tanks, and Networks

Although outside the areas of torture, detention, and due process U.S. policymaker support for the reintegration of human rights remains weak, policy advocates, think tanks, and support group express growing human rights interest. The Migration Policy Institute, for example, released a 2006 report titled *America's Human Rights Challenge: International Human Rights Implications of US Immigration Enforcement Actions Post-September 11.* The Center for American Progress joined the campaign against the military commissions at Guantánamo Bay and for the restoration of habeas corpus. The Western States Center integrated human rights into its effort to strengthen regional social justice movements. The Applied Research Center has expressed interest in researching the historic and current links between civil and human rights. By contrast, MoveOn.Org told a May 2006 meeting of U.S. human rights activists hosted by Breakthrough that human rights is not a language that resonates very well at the moment with its membership. This remains characteristic of opinion in this sector.

National Civil and Other Rights Organizations

Given the United States' utter determination to shield itself from meaningful legal accountability to human rights, it is notable that a growing number of public-interest legal organizations are developing their capacity to deploy human rights. The Center for Constitutional Rights has a historical and sustained commitment to this approach and the ACLU has more recently developed a sophisticated human rights unit. The Asian American, Mexican American, and NAACP Legal Defense Funds, the Center for Reproductive Rights, and Legal Momentum have all, to varying degrees, made use of human rights arguments in domestic litigation, and they increasingly express an interest in developing their internal knowledge and expertise in this area. Legal Momentum is also in the process of developing a program to provide training to U.S. judges with respect to the domestic application of human rights.

Media

Domestic human rights work has never attracted much attention from the mainstream media. But via the leadership of groups like the Border Network for Human Rights, the Kensington Welfare Rights Union, the Mississippi Worker's Center, the U.S. Human Rights Network, and others, U.S. human rights issues—and the movement itself—are attracting more attention from the ethnic, local, online, and, occasionally, national press. *The American Prospect*, for example, did a special supplement dedicated solely to the reemergence of a domestic human rights movement, which was also the sole focus of the spring 2007 issue of *YES!* magazine. The Opportunity Agenda, in cooperation with a wide range of advocacy and communications groups, is coordinating a national effort to poll American attitudes on human rights and the U.S. and to develop and disseminate more persuasive messages in this regard.

Donors

One of the great ironies of the resource-starved movement for human rights in the United States is that it is often charged with being "donor driven." This charge is frequently leveled at human rights movements in other countries as well. It implies that the domestic human rights movement in question is actually instigated by something foreign to itself. Here, as elsewhere, and now, as before, this is a very potent charge. In the case of the United States it is often leveled by observers with a genuine concern about the movement's bona fides. But it has the perhaps unintended effect of further obscuring the U.S. civil and other rights groups' historic links to human rights and of abetting the assault on domestic human rights activism as inherently un-American. It also effectively denies the existence and advocacy of the domestic human rights activists themselves.

Donors who support domestic human rights work, and their numbers are steadily growing, don't drive that work. Instead, they try to make way for it in their own programs or via collaborative funds. Quite often these donors are themselves undergoing a change in approach to the rights work being supported by their own institutions. They see a need, for example, to better link their international and domestic programs, to better connect their grant making across issue areas, or to strengthen their support for the defense of human rights across the board. Some donors, such as the Ford Foundation, the Libra Foundation, the Mertz Gilmore Foundation, the Otto Bremer Foundation, the Overbrook Foundation, and the Shaler Adams (for whom I work), frame and carry out a great deal of their U.S. grant making in human rights terms. Many others, like the Atlantic Philanthropies and the Open Society Institute support domestic human rights work when it most effectively intersects with their existing priorities. Increasingly these and other donors work together to respond to cross-cutting needs of the movement and strengthen its effect. In June 2005, for example, a number of donors founded the U.S. Human Rights Fund, a collaborative effort to respond to the self-expressed needs of the movement to enhance its capacity, connection, communications, and impact.

Staunch Opponents

One of the most encouraging, if frustrating, things about the contemporary human rights movement in the United States is that its most likely supporters are also its most loyal critics. To be sure, extreme opponents to relinking civil and human rights exist. Today's version of the supremacist and nationalist voices of the Cold War denounce the contemporary U.S. human rights efforts as foreign, a threat to American sovereignty, a vehicle for undue racial, sexual, and economic equality and, directly or indirectly, a sop to terrorists. On March 2, 2007, for example, the *Rocky Mountain News* decried the decision of the Inter-American Commission on Human Rights to take up a U.S. case involving severe, unremedied, and ultimately fatal domestic violence as "an attempt to undermine U.S. legal sovereignty."

The extreme opposition to human rights in the United States is well organized, well resourced, and emboldened by fifty years (or more) of dominance. For meaningful changes in U.S. policy and practice to occur it must be countered. But ideas of American or white or other supremacy will never be effectively challenged unless the contemporary U.S. human rights movement first successfully allies itself with those who also oppose such extreme exceptionalism but remain unconvinced that it can be effectively countered via the reintegration of civil and human rights. Such friendly critics abound in American legal and political life, in and out of government, among both elite and grassroots groups, representing both donors and activists. Their voices cannot and should not be rejected alongside those of the extremists who reject the domestic application of human rights altogether. The movement ignores its more tempered critics at its peril.

Loyal Opponents

Generally speaking, the views of what might be called the contemporary movement's loyal opposition reflect little disagreement with its basic premise: that the United States should uphold human rights. The loyalist critique is more pragmatic. It relies on two key assumptions: (1) that reinvigorating the domestic human rights movement will provoke a legal and political backlash which does more harm than good, and (2) that reintegrating human rights into U.S. legal and political culture will, in any case, have little meaningful impact. Movement supporters often counter that the more powerful the backlash the more substantial the impact. This may be true. But to those potential allies concerned about the best way to defend rights in the current context, provoking one's opponents without accruing immediate benefits seems a torturous and risky route.

If the movement is to broker the broader alliances which are necessary to its overall success, pervasive concerns about backlash and impact will have to be more thoroughly addressed.

Concerns about backlash are well founded. Justice Ginsburg, for example, revealed in February 2007 that she and Justice O'Connor had received death threats due to their use of foreign and international law in U.S. jurisprudence. Federal judges in general who cite to human rights and humanitarian law have been threatened with impeachment. Potential citation to the Geneva Conventions in the context of the so-called war on terror led the former attorney general to denounce them as "quaint" and "outmoded." U.S. activists who have raised domestic human rights concerns in the inter-American or UN systems report being personally reprimanded by representatives of the U.S. government. Their experiences recall those of Du Bois and his colleagues who, for all their troubles to bring the fate of black Americans to the attention of the United Nations, were denounced as pro-Soviet, and, in some cases, deprived of their passports. The early movement did not survive this backlash, hence the instinctive reaction of modern-day critics that its progeny will suffer the same fate.

In the intervening years, however, a more conducive environment for domestic human rights work has arguably emerged. In the past five years in particular two interrelated developments have helped to challenge the notion that adherence to human rights is bad for America. The first, as noted above, is the so-called war on terror. As result of the actions of the Bush administration and its allies, more and more people have seen the costs at home and abroad of America's double standard with respect to human rights and have from the military to the judiciary to the polity risen up to demand U.S. accountability to standards prohibiting torture and prolonged detention and requiring due process of law. While these voices might not all speak up for the reintegration of human rights into every other area of concern to domestic social justice advocates, they have opened up significant political space for the second main development of recent years: the increasingly trained, organized, and vocal domestic human rights movement. These two advantages were not ones enjoyed by Du Bois and his peers. If the contemporary movement can further expand its outreach and strengthen its effect it may be better able to withstand the withering attack on its legitimacy that is sure to come.

Herein, however, lies the rub. The contemporary movement for human rights in the United States cannot expand its outreach and impact without courting backlash. But backlash, or fear thereof, significantly constrains its breadth and effect. Although the environment has changed, the movement still operates within the ruling mindset that the domestic application of human rights to the United States is un-American or dangerous or ultimately and, for the government's purposes conveniently, without effect. Even if the first two assumptions can be successfully challenged, the last, if left unaddressed, is fatal. The contemporary movement for human rights in the United States must either better explicate and demonstrate its impact or the risk involved in rebuilding it will be taken only by those for whom it is a matter of necessity or conviction or both. At present these spirited U.S. human rights defenders, while increasingly numerous, do not constitute a large enough percentage of the American public or its elected leadership to reshape the country's identity, institutions, and culture to favor an inner allegiance to human rights. Additional proof of the "value-added" of human rights to U.S. social justice, however instrumental this may sometimes seem, is desperately needed if support for the movement is to grow.

Proving the value-added of human rights in a country that for more than fifty years has argued that human rights are the one value it need not add is tough. Despite an arguably more conducive legal and political and advocacy environment for the domestic reintegration of human rights, the instruments of such a broad cultural change, whether in the White House, or the Congress, or the courts, or the organizations, or the communities, or even the people themselves remain insufficiently mobilized for it. To engage them more actively in the movement's objectives requires, as discussed in some detail above, a simultaneous education, organizing, fact-finding, policy advocacy, litigation, and scholarship effort across issue areas, sectors, and localities which is simply not conducive to short term outcomes. Yet without such relatively immediate effects, and the infrastructure necessary to obtain them, the movement will never be able to build the momentum and membership necessary to deliver on the longer-term change. These issues of infrastructure and impact, raised in the context of the need for an overall strategy and concluding with a reflection on capacity, are discussed in the next section on current challenges.

Our Current Challenges

> What makes this hope radical is that it is directed toward a future goodness that transcends the current ability to understand what it is.
> —Jonathan Lear

The only way to move as much change as is envisioned by the U.S. human rights movement is to divvy up the labor in the context of a coordinated overall strategy that provides for both meaningful impact and requisite capacity. Sadly, and not for lack of trying, the movement as yet lacks a sufficient quantity of all four of the above areas. There are at present too few opportunities to devise coordinated strategy, not enough people and organizations to make it stick, insufficient impact, particularly with respect to policy, and underdeveloped capacity. The remainder of this section sets forth how some of these challenges are already being and might further be addressed.

Overall Strategy

The pursuit by U.S. human rights activists of a unified field-building strategy which works simultaneously across issues, methods, sectors, and localities far surpasses the current movement's infrastructure and capacity. As a result, it faces constant pressure, from within and without, to focus on this or that issue, one or another sector, a single method or place. By and large the movement has resisted this pressure to self-limit. But as it has grown, the tension between long-term mobilization and short-term effect has only gotten more and more acute.

No simple resolution of this dilemma exists. On the one hand, focused human rights work in a single-issue area or sector might deliver visible benefits in the short run even if they did not accrue to the entire movement. On the other hand, more widespread work to build the field as a whole might produce more pervasive change in the long run even if it was of little immediate assistance to the movement's various constituents. For the U.S. human rights activists, the answer thus far lies somewhere in between these two extremes. It involves both the retention and refinement of a long-term, unified movement-building strategy and, within that context, the setting of short-term, discrete priorities.

To its immense credit, the contemporary movement for human rights in the United States has already assembled the component parts of a unified strategy. The trouble is that, with the exception of the certain regular meetings like biannual convenings of the U.S. Human Rights Network or the Southern Human Rights Organizers Conference, it rarely has enough space or time to review its progress overall, identify gaps, and set priorities. Smaller issue- or sector-specific conferences also take place, but they are relatively infrequent and don't always connect up to a broader strategic process. If the movement is to be able to prioritize key initiatives without sacrificing overall progress, it will have to devote greater space and increased resources to the elaboration and dissemination of its overall strategy.

In the meantime, mounting pressure on the movement to adopt the very same issue-, sector-, method-, or region-specific divisions it arose to help heal is at once unforgiving and understandable. The contemporary movement for human rights simply is not yet at the stage where it can deliver the type of immediate results which existing social justice groups and their supporters need and expect. By the same token, it cannot afford to shortcut the movement-building process. Caught between this particular rock and hard place, the movement has no choice but to withstand the critique of its long-term base-building strategy and, at the same time, find ways to deliver short-term outcomes that benefit its constituents and foster its necessary alliances.

The challenge, assuming progress in the elaboration, dissemination, and implementation of an overall movement-building strategy, is how to set these short-term priorities. A recent assessment of the U.S. human rights field suggests that they are less likely to be defined by issue area than they are by sector, with priority given to community-based education, training, and organizing across issues and localities. This makes strategic sense. Any other approach inhibits the participation of affected groups and fuels the notion that human rights are foreign to American culture, come from the top down, or pertain only to certain groups. The rub is that education, training, and organizing work at the level of the community across both geography and issue area takes time. It does not always yield short-term changes in government policy, particularly at the federal level. Unless the necessary infrastructure is developed to link community education, training, and organizing to influencing related local, state, and federal policy, the tension between the U.S. human rights movement's long- and short-term work may emerge as its Achilles heel.

Infrastructure

The problem of linking local organizing and national policy is hardly unique to the U.S. human rights community. What is unique to this community is its intention to do so across issue areas and via the reintegration of human rights into work at all levels. To achieve this end, the movement has had to develop a set of organizations as a supplement to existing progressive infrastructure in the United States, which are designed to foster cross-issue work and help to develop human rights expertise at all levels. This U.S. human rights infrastructure, which has already been enumerated above, provides education and organizing support to local communities, trains advocates in key issue areas and sectors, builds essential communications skills and strategies, links U.S. human rights activists and groups to each other, and reaches out to social justice movements and other key stakeholders in the U.S. and elsewhere. In large measure, it serves as a map of the movement's current impact on U.S. culture and an itinerary for its future work. The variety of groups and the diversity of their locales, areas of interest, and sectors paints an encouraging picture of the movement's initial success and potential longevity.

Two areas in which this infrastructure is particularly underdeveloped, however, concern public interest litigation and policy advocacy—whether at the state, national, or international level—and grassroots organizing. Legal and policy work at all these levels does occur, but it could benefit from much more targeted research, sharper strategy, and technical support. Similarly, priority has been given to outreach and education at the grassroots level, but it needs to be accompanied by an increased focus on and capacity for community organizing. It may make sense in the coming phase for the movement to consider focused efforts in these two areas, in the context of its overall strategy, both by relying on existing infrastructure and developing any necessary supplementary capacity.

Impact

At the risk of contradicting everything I have said so far about the need for field-wide strategy and infrastructure, I am going to make an argument for the contemporary movement, in the context of an overall strategy and reliant on related infrastructure, to focus more intensively on issue-specific advocacy. I recognize that if we are after overall unity in a country and set of social justice movements characterized by its opposite, this may tempt fate. At an earlier stage of the movement's development, as proved true of its Cold War predecessor, too narrow a focus would have rendered it unsustainable. But given the contemporary movement's growth, its determined iteration of an overall strategy and the gradual emergence of a field-wide infrastructure, I believe it would be possible to develop coordinated efforts to advance short-term, single-issue campaigns in a way that would assist rather than derail the movement's overall advance.

Some likely candidates for such issue specific work have already emerged: These include U.S. adherence to the ban on torture and cruel, inhuman, and degrading treatment; the restoration of habeas corpus; an end to the practice of sentencing juveniles to life with no possibility of parole; the reinvigoration of judicial oversight of deportation; the recognition of the right to return, including to public housing, of those displaced by Hurricane Katrina; the right to non-discrimination, including with respect to asylum, on the basis of one's gender identity or HIV status; and finally, the right to accessible and accountable education and health care. These issues have several things in common: They affect a large number of people across a wide array of communities in different parts of the country, they lend themselves to multi-method and cross-sector advocacy, they have both grassroots and elite constituents, they are of great interest inside and outside the country, and they all have an inherent relationship to fundamental principles of human rights. Perhaps via the articulation of criteria such as these, the contemporary movement can ensure that as it responds to the demand for focused, short-term impact, it also advances its longer-term, field-building goals.

Capacity

I want to close this section on challenges with a brief reflection on the issue of capacity. The contemporary movement for human rights in the United States asks and expects a lot of itself, its potential allies, its government, and, ultimately, its country. I believe it does so in all humility and out of a conviction that one's inner commitment to human rights says a lot about who one is as a person or as a nation. For all this idea's simplicity, however, it involves an enormously complex cultural shift and one that must go head-to-head with the equally, if not more powerful notion that our identity depends on the assertion of our supremacy whether over other individuals or other countries. Such a struggle must be waged, however incrementally, at every level of American society. This requires a level of capacity that the contemporary movement and those who support or ally with it do not yet have.

At one level, this is obviously about resources. For example, the long-term movement-building effort and related work on overall strategy and infrastructure is *very difficult* to adequately resource. At the same time, the short-term issue- or sector-specific work is also remains underfunded. The donors, like the movement itself, need a grant-making strategy wherein they *both* pool their funds to advance the movement's long-term, field-wide efforts *and* use their own issue- or sector-specific programs to fund shorter-term human rights–inflected work in those discrete arenas. In my view, the movement itself needs to develop a parallel fundraising strategy and defend it collectively.

At another level, however, the question of capacity is much more about leadership than it is about money. In this respect, the contemporary movement is quite rich. Human rights, as the movement's mantra goes, begin in small places, close to home. Its leadership strives to be as principled, accountable, egalitarian, and diverse as the change it seeks. Such leadership, whether in this or any other movement, is a rare commodity and its development could do with some targeted attention and flexible support, particularly for younger activists whose generation already sees human rights as more integral to its culture than did, for example, my own.

Where Do We Go from Here?

Let America be America again.
Let it be the dream it used to be.

—*Langston Hughes*

The contemporary movement for human rights in the United States owes a huge debt to those early leaders like Mary McLeod Bethune, W. E. B. Du Bois, Fannie Lou Hamer, Martin Luther King, Jr., Eleanor and Franklin Roosevelt, Walter White, and Malcolm X who, in their own ways and with varying degrees of conviction and success, laid the groundwork for the present effort to reintegrate human rights into U.S. social justice work and American legal, political, and popular culture more generally. Now, as then, this is a complex and risky undertaking. It involves resisting the lure of national, or white, or other supremacies wherever they occur and choosing instead the promise of equality and dignity in every walk of public and private life. It requires a unified strategy across issue, method, sector, and place that is rooted in affected communities and links domestic social justice groups to each other and to their counterparts in other countries. It entails strategic alliances at all levels of American society with those who may not join the movement's ranks but nonetheless share in its aims. And it relies on supporters and leaders who reflect and enable this vision.

Given the inequality, polarization, deprivation, and disillusion that characterize so much of U.S. legal, political, and popular life at the current moment, such a vision may seem more like a dream. And so it is. Yet, inspired by its forbearers and instigated by their progeny, the contemporary movement for human rights in the U.S. has gradually become a reality. What remains going forward is to strengthen its strategy, infrastructure, impact, and capacity so as to give it a fighting chance to once again define the United States as a country which in the eyes of its own people and of the world stands for the idea that human rights belong to us all.

Notes

This chapter reflects many (some might say too many) long conversations on the subject of human rights in the United States with colleagues and friends including, among others, Carol Anderson, David Bank, Rini Banarjee, Michelle Coffee, Tanya Coke, Larry Cox, Lisa Crooms, Puja Dhawan, Heidi Dorow, Steve Hawkins, Michael Hertz, Taryn Higashi, Gara LaMarche, Adrian Nicole LeBlanc, Susan Osnos, Catherine Powell, and Eric Ward. I would like to thank Cathy Albisa in particular for her close reading of this chapter and my colleagues at the center, in particular Conor Gearty and Francesca Klug, for their support.

1. Carol Anderson, *Eyes off the Prize* (Cambridge: Cambridge University Press, 2003); Mary L. Dudziak, *Cold War Civil Rights* (Princeton, N.J.: Princeton University Press, 2000); Thomas F. Jackson, *From Civil Rights to Human Rights: Martin Luther King, Jr., and the Struggle for Economic Justice* (Philadelphia: University of Pennsylvania Press, 2006).

2. See, e.g., Women's Institute for Leadership Development for Human Rights and Shaler Adams Foundation 2000, *Making the Connections*, available online at www.fordfound.org/publications/recent_articles/docs/close_to_home/part3.pdf; U.S. Human Rights Network, *Something Inside So Strong: A Resource Guide on Human Rights in the United States*, 2002, available online at www.ushrnetwork.org.

3. Martin Luther King, Jr., Seventh Annual Gandhi Memorial Lecture, Howard University, November 6, 1966, cited in Jackson, *From Civil Rights to Human Rights*, p. 244.

4. See "Stand Up for Your Rights," *The Economist*, March 22, 2007, available online at www.economist.com/opinion/displaystory.cfm?story_id=8888856.

5. Franklin D. Roosevelt, Four Freedoms Speech to the 77th Congress, January 6, 1941, available online at www.presidentialrhetoric.com/historicspeeches/roosevelt_franklin/fourfreedoms.html.

6. Anderson, *Eyes off the Prize*, p. 51.

7. Anderson, *Eyes off the Prize*, p. 41 (quoting Edward Stettinius, diary, Box 29, week 8–14, April 1945).

8. Charter of the United Nations, Article 2, para. 7.

9. See, among others, Dorothy Q. Thomas, "Advancing Rights Protection in the United States: An Internationalized Advocacy Strategy," *Harvard Human Rights Journal* 9 (Spring 1996): 15.

10. Harold Hongju Koh, "Foreword: On American Exceptionalism," *Stanford Law Review* 55 (2003).

11. Dudziak, *Cold War Civil Rights*; Anderson, *Eyes off the Prize*.

12. See Dorothy Q. Thomas, *A Revolution of the Mind, Funding Human Rights in the United States*, a report to the Ford Foundation, 2002.

13. "Making the Connections: Human Rights in the United States," WILD for Human Rights and the Shaler Adams Foundation, 2000, p. 26.

Chapter 6
Economic and Social Rights in the United States: Six Rights, One Promise

Catherine Albisa

Few people would hesitate to condemn poor education systems, inadequate healthcare infrastructure, hunger, scores of families suffering from abject poverty and homelessness, wages that do not support a dignified life, and widespread economic insecurity. Nor would anyone plausibly deny that all of these are sharply evident in the United States. Yet the U.S. government steadfastly refuses to recognize fundamental economic and social rights to be free from such conditions and has failed to reform its legal and political system to protect people from the structural inequalities that amount to a systemic assault on human dignity.

It is a contemporary cultural paradox that the United States places immense value and emphasis on human freedom but simultaneously debases and discounts the human dignity that constitutes the foundation for any legitimate expression of freedom. To be free only to suffer deprivation and exclusion is no kind of freedom at all. Freedom inherently includes the ability to exercise choices, and that ability is fully dependent on a protective, effective, and rational social infrastructure.

Economic and social rights are the foundation for freedom. The United States has recognized this indisputable link at different points in history, most explicitly in recent history through the administration of Franklin D. Roosevelt. Roosevelt's well-known Four Freedoms speech permanently connected freedom from violence and war with freedom from want, and recognized that "necessitous men are not free men." This vision took root within an international human rights system that was born of the horrors of the Nazi genocide and was grounded in a belief that every human being had fundamental rights, including economic and social rights, simply by virtue of being human.

The Universal Declaration of Human Rights, drafted under the watchful eyes of Eleanor Roosevelt, was truly a revolution in values. Not only did it proclaim that every human being, without exception and irrespective of the position of his or her particular government, had fundamental rights regardless of race, sex, religion, or any other status, it also included among those fundamental rights access to adequate housing, education, food, and decent work, along with a right to health and social security.

These six rights were part of one large and visionary promise. A promise by all the participating nations in the United Nations to create a new world where no group of people could ever be so marginalized and unprotected that another genocide would occur. It is far from a secret that this historical promise remains painfully unfulfilled. The world has suffered from a multitude of genocides since World War II, including the genocides in Rwanda and Bosnia after which, once again, international tribunals were set up to deal with the grisly aftermath in the name of "accountability to human rights."

But the notion of accountability has limited meaning if it is confined to narrow legal criminal processes directed against a few individuals after the abuses occur. This notion of accountability is based on the flawed assumptions that violations are inherently individual in nature, when in fact the vast majority of violations across the globe have a structural component, referred to as *structural violence*. This is convincingly expressed in *Pathologies of Power* and other writings by Dr. Paul Farmer, as well as the argument that this structural component is often, although not exclusively, expressed in the form of social exclusion, economic oppression, and disempowerment.

The purpose of this chapter is not to provide an analysis of structural violence or structural racism, a closely aligned concept. Rather, this chapter is premised on the notion that a deeper accountability to all human rights, including civil and political rights, requires the recognition and implementation of economic and social rights and that the protection of this set of rights is a precondition for addressing structural violence and racism.

This concept that rights depend on each other to be realized—that is, the concept of interdependency—is clearly recognized in the foundational human rights conventions: the International Covenant on Economic, Social, and Cultural Rights and the International Covenant on Civil and Political Rights. Both of these conventions state in their preambles respectively:

Recognizing that, in accordance with the Universal Declaration of Human Rights, the ideal of free human beings enjoying freedom from fear and want can only be achieved if conditions are created whereby everyone may enjoy his economic, social and cultural rights, as well as his civil and political rights. (Preamble to International Covenant on Economic, Social, and Cultural Rights)

Recognizing that, in accordance with the Universal Declaration of Human Rights, the ideal of free human beings enjoying civil and political freedom and freedom from fear and want can only be achieved if conditions are created whereby everyone may enjoy his civil and political rights, as well as his economic, social and cultural rights. (Preamble to International Covenant on Civil and Political Rights)

Indeed, initially the first members of the United Nations had not planned to create two separate covenants, but rather one major human rights convention. Cold War politics intervened, however, and splitting the full range of rights into two covenants became the first volley in the degrading dynamic that has gone on for decades of using human rights as a manipulative tool of foreign policy. Western politicians would avoid responsibility for economic and social rights by claiming such rights were associated with communist regimes and repressive highly centralized economies.

But there are a variety of views as to why the United States is so resistant to economic and social rights, and Cold War politics figure prominently in only some of them. One view assumes that support for economic and social rights began to weaken after the civil rights movement succeeded in creating nondiscrimination laws and standards that would make it far more difficult to protect these rights only for the white community and required equal access to social support and services. Another perspective ascribes the resistance to some inherent individualistic tendencies within U.S. culture. Finally, yet another view is that because many social programs in the United States, such as Medicaid and Section 8, were designed only for the poor, the concept never took hold in the imagination of the middle class and had the necessary "buy in"—unlike similar social programs in Europe that benefited both the poor and middle class. This theory is buttressed by the recent outpouring of support for the social security public pension program in the United States after the second Bush administration threatened to privatize it.

All of these theories likely play some role in the unusual resistance economic and social rights engenders within the United States among elites and nonelites alike. People in the United States do express greater support for certain rights, such as health and education. Nonetheless, despite some pockets of support for specific rights, the one thing that remains certain is that the United States stands out among developed nations, in fact among all nations, in its hostility toward making commitments to assure that that its people are able to achieve an adequate standard of living consistent with human dignity, freedom, and equality.

The Door Opens

Human rights were held hostage to the Cold War for several decades. The West accused the East of violating civil and political rights, and the East accused the West of violating economic and social rights. And through this time, both sides used human rights as a foreign policy weapon in a manner far removed from the integrity inherent in the language and founding principles of the human rights system. Only after the disintegration of the Soviet Union was the human rights and social justice community able to take stock of the wreckage left in the wake of the ideological war. In the United States, in particular, there were at least six clear victims left in this wreckage: the right to housing, health, education, food, social security, and decent work.

Despite having provided critical leadership on economic and social rights early in the development of the human rights system, after the 1950s the United States consistently took the position at global conferences and other international venues that economic and social rights were in fact not really rights at all, but aspirations that were all but unrealizable.[1] By the 1990s, the United States had become the chief opponent of economic and social rights on the international stage. Even earlier, starting at least with the 1980s, opponents of economic and social rights were gaining ground at home. The U.S. Supreme Court, which came close to recognizing the "rights of the poor" in the 1960s and 1970s, changed direction after President Nixon added his Supreme Court appointees to the bench. While the country had an extensive social protection infrastructure, consisting of the welfare program, Section 8 housing program, Medicaid and Medicare health programs, social security pension system, minimum wage and other labor protections, and several other programs and policies, this infrastructure was severely underfunded and increasingly coming under political attack. Rhetorically the attack began under President Reagan and his references to "welfare queens" as single mothers defrauding the system. By the 1990s, even liberal Democrats, such as President Clinton, made vows such as "ending welfare as we know it."

The economic and social rights vision launched by Roosevelt that is detailed so elegantly in Cass Sunstein's book *The Second Bill of Rights* seemed effectively dead. For the average person in the United States, an explicit human rights strategy focusing on economic and social rights would not have seemed viable for improving human well-being and protecting human dignity and freedom. But the early activists of the human rights movement in the United States were far from average people. They were moved by a vision larger than themselves, which they promoted when and wherever possible. No venue was too small, no audience unimportant.

These very early conversations about economic and social rights as a necessary part of a "human rights platform" in the United States were held in car rides on journeys to meetings and demonstrations, in elevators, over dinner among activists, and "at the water cooler" among activist staff in nonprofit organizations that would ultimately come to embrace this vision. From these early conversations, committees formed, conferences were held, presentations and trainings developed and were taken "on the road," organizations sprung forth, and ultimately major institutions began to acknowledge the legitimacy of this vision.

This chapter does not pretend to document all the relevant actors and activities that have led to the still nascent but emerging economic and social rights wing of the human rights movement in the United States. While emerging networks and more consistent meeting venues have helped to link the various strands of the work, the efforts still remain too fragmented. It would require intensive study to identify all the pockets of movement and speculate as to how and whether they will converge. Rather, this chapter simply represents reflections based on the author's personal experiences and individualized perspective of a slice of these wonderful, underresourced, against-all-odds but compelling efforts.

These efforts can be found in every region of the country, and activists from each region have come into relationship with the economic and social rights movement in different ways. In the Southern United States, activists embraced this approach early and strongly emphasized the intersection of racism and economic and social rights. This region has had a national influence and birthed important national organizations. Activists originating in Philadelphia reached out to the middle of the country with a relentless focus on class. Surprising allies have emerged in the Midwest, including traditional service organizations that have taken up leadership in the movement. Pockets of intense activity can be found up and down the West Coast, and several initiatives in the Northeast reflect a sustained commitment from that region to build an economic and social rights movement. Finally, activists in the Gulf Coast have found themselves bound together after Katrina through their joint demands for a human right to return for poor and Black communities displaced by government action and the disaster. The next section details some of the work and perspectives found in each of these regions.

Interdependence of Rights in the South

Not surprisingly some of the earliest rumblings on reviving a human rights vision for the United States came from the cradle of Dr. Martin Luther King, Jr.'s work, the Southern United States. Today's generation of human rights leaders within the African American community have been meeting and discussing the potential of human rights for the movement for racial equality since the 1980s, even before the end of the Cold War. Activists such as Keith Jennings, Jaribu Hill, Ajamu Baraka, and Loretta Ross developed a political analysis not too dissimilar from activists from earlier eras. For African Americans to win the struggle for real equality, a human rights vision that recognized the full range of rights—civil, political, economic, social, and cultural—for everyone must take hold in the country.

These activists spoke widely, in small and large spaces, to the fact that we are a society that is still fractured by race and driven by perceived self-interest. They eloquently brought to the surface that in the United States, we have yet to embrace the moral imperative that human rights are universal and that only by ensuring and recognizing the rights of everyone regardless of race, class, or any other status can we truly ensure the rights of anyone. They argued that there was a desperate need to develop a political community that was grounded in human rights and solidarity to counter this dynamic and that we could not abolish poverty, sexism, and racism in separate struggles. Their point of view was, and is, that traditional civil rights approaches would not dismantle structural racism, which was significantly manifested in the social and economic sphere; mainstream feminism would not touch the lives of women of color; race-blind approaches to poverty would never guarantee the rights of communities of color; and until we successfully situated our specific struggles within a broader human rights effort, we wouldn't become part of the solution.

These visionary activists soon realized that they needed to create a political space to further develop this conversation. By the 1990s, organizers in the Deep South, under the leadership of Jaribu Hill (an outspoken civil rights attorney as well as an organizer), pulled together over thirty organizations in the spring of 1996 to plan the first Southern Human Rights Organizers' Conference (SHROC I). This conference was held at the University of Mississippi in Oxford in September 1996. Two hundred activists attended the conference, a large portion of which worked on economic justice. Indeed, Jaribu Hill is the director of the Mississippi Worker's Center for Human Rights. There have been six SHROC biannual conferences since 1996. The conferences are very much a community and grassroots affair, and intentionally so. With little concern for the more restrained approaches of self-identified elite institutions and organizations, SHROC approached the pervasiveness of human rights violations in the United States as an ongoing national emergency. SHROC is a space where civil disobedience is valued and appreciated as a necessary strategy to address the crisis.

SHROC has also been a space for a wide range of perspectives from the grass roots. Attending a SHROC conference you might find sitting on one side an AIDS activist who has been fighting hard for access to antiretroviral medications for her or his community and on the other an activist who believes that AIDS is a myth created by the white community to destroy African Americans. It is both a fascinating and inspiring experience to watch exchange on a range of disparate viewpoints mitigated through a human rights framework that holds people together through this common language and with the goal of identifying and connecting through common values.

At SHROC there is always a political demonstration or action organized to communicate the significance of a human rights approach, and it usually incorporates an economic and social rights element. During SHROC IV in 2002 in Miami, Florida, several hundred activists at the conference took to the streets for a direct action that targeted three community struggles—Haitian refugees seeking fair treatment on asylum issues; African Americans at Scott Carver Homes in their fight against urban removal and gentrification; and the Coalition of Immokalee Workers in their boycott against Taco Bell. It is rare for an event to pull together such disparate constituencies and issues—immigration policy, housing "redevelopment" policies, and supply chain issues affecting wages of farm workers—for what was a highly disciplined and powerful action in a place such as Miami, Florida. Yet these issues were linked under a broader umbrella of economic and social rights. Ultimately, SHROC has been an important space for activists to come together around the broad human rights frame, particularly on critical issues involving the intersection of race and poverty and the interdependence of civil/political and economic/social rights.

In addition to the SHROC gatherings, organizations were emerging in the 1990s that would ultimately spearhead the economic and social rights vision in this part of the country. The Mississippi Human Rights Worker's Center, the Coalition of Immokalee Workers, and the Miami Worker's Center are a few examples of that generational wave of post–Cold War organizations addressing economic and social issues as human rights as a significant part of their agenda. Many of these organizations have had surprising and important victories. Just some examples include the Coalition of Immokalee Workers' agreements with McDonald's and the parent corporation of Taco Bell, Yum! Brands Inc., that double the wages of tomato pickers and create participatory worker-led monitoring of labor abuses.

The Miami Worker's Center, after an extraordinarily impressive and creative struggle, forced the notoriously corrupt city of Miami to provide housing to poor African American families displaced and forcibly evicted by the destruction of public housing. The center is now striving to create a base in Liberty City, a historically black and poor neighborhood, of community leaders that would ensure that redevelopment efforts in their community benefit and meet the needs of the families that have been living there for generations. They have placed this effort within a human rights context. In particular, influenced by a global meeting in Barcelona, Spain, of civil society groups, they have spearheaded the development of a framework focused on every person's "human right to the city," which includes access to transportation, housing, and other necessary public infrastructure. This is an incredibly important concept as concentrated wealth returns to urban centers and gentrification threatens to push out entire communities from every major city in the country. Additionally, the National Center on Human Rights Education and the U.S. Human Rights Network are both based in Atlanta. Both of these national organizations, discussed in more detail below, emerged from the work in the South.

The organizations and people committed to a human rights vision in the South have painstakingly worked on building a movement for well over a decade now, almost two. Still the existing organizations remain small. With notable exceptions, attracting resources remains a serious challenge and obstacle to growing this work in the United States. SHROC and now U.S. Human Rights Network conferences are exciting and inspiring but still draw hundreds and not thousands of people. Most of the activists involved have invested years of their lives on the assumption that this is the beginning of a very long-term project that will truly bear fruit decades down the road, similar to the pattern of the civil rights movement in the twentieth century. Only time will tell whether "human rights in the U.S." was a temporary trend in activism or truly the foundation for the next burst of human progress toward universal freedom, dignity, and equality.

Class Unity Through Human Rights in the Rust Belt and Beyond

No campaign did more to bring attention to international economic and social rights as a strategy for social justice than the Poor People's Economic Human Rights Campaign (PPEHRC). This campaign emerged out of the work of the Kensington Welfare Rights Union (KWRU) in Philadelphia, Pennsylvania. Using guerrilla tactics, members of KWRU raised public awareness about the cruelly indifferent housing policies in Philadelphia by doing "housing takeovers" and moving homeless families (mostly women and children) into abandoned city-owned property. Naming these properties "human rights houses," KWRU put the city in a position where they had to either allow families to live in possibly dangerous subhuman conditions or forcibly and very publicly throw these families into the street. Neither option was very attractive, with the former highlighting the many empty city properties that the city had inexplicably failed to care for properly and make available to poor families to address the acute affordable housing crisis. Most of the time, the city found housing for the families.

These tactics were far from universally popular, and many housing advocates criticized KWRU for "grandstanding" and not doing anything that would solve the crisis for the city as a whole. While KWRU did not offer detailed and concrete policy alternatives, it is also the case that the more mainstream housing advocates were unable to push the city to solve the crisis. These tactics did bring to light the urgent nature of the crisis and reflected a decision to respond to it as a serious emergency. For families in the street, at risk of losing their children to city agencies that were ruthlessly efficient at the more expensive process of placing kids in foster care but seemingly incapable of the far less expensive alternative of housing these families, it was without question a severe emergency that called for desperate tactics. KWRU sought to establish the housing situation in Philadelphia as a human rights crisis, which justified civil disobedience. Facing criminal trials based on charges of trespassing and other petty crimes, KWRU members mounted a political "necessity defense," and none were convicted.

In the mid-1990s, KWRU, under the leadership of Cheri Honkala and Willie Baptist, decided to reach out nationally with their vision and approach. The analysis that the organization adopted was one grounded in the assumption that class was the issue that people in the United States needed to face and that issues of race had obfuscated a serious conversation about class to the detriment of poor people. The organization's stated goal was to unite the poor across color lines. This approach engendered some controversy among human rights activists, particularly those working on the intersection of race and class who felt that failing to talk about race was tantamount to accepting racism. KWRU was clearly antiracist and much of the leadership and membership was African American and Latino. It was often Willie Baptist, an African American leader in the organization with roots in the Black Power movement, who made the most impassioned arguments in favor of sidestepping the discussion on race as part of the strategy to win unity among and rights for the poor.

The other principle that KWRU sought to promote across the country was leadership by the most affected—that is, the poor. This is a principle espoused by many organizations with varying levels of success in actually implementing it. One of KWRU's strengths was its consistent fidelity to this principle in practice. Reaching out to a wide range of groups during bus tours and other organizing and education events, KWRU formed the PPEHRC.

PPEHRC used the United Nations as its symbolic rallying point, holding Truth Commissions across the street from the United Nations and
enlisting the support and gaining the admiration of high-level UN officials, such as Mary Robinson, the former High Commissioner of Human
Rights, and Kofi Annan, the former Secretary General. Similar to the
work in Philadelphia, PPEHRC was quite effective at raising the visibility
of the suffering created by poverty. It was less effective at creating a clear
infrastructure for the loose collection of groups that came into contact
through PPEHRC. While in more recent years PPEHRC lists members
publicly, there is no formal membership process, and some organizations and individuals are surprised to find themselves listed despite years
of not having had contact with PPEHRC. It has also declined to develop
a policy agenda. None of this takes away from the immense contributions it has made to bringing the human rights conversations to places
like Ohio, West Virginia, Utah, and other states. PPEHRC has been one
of the important forces in giving a far wider range of affected communities' ownership over these ideas and concepts.

PPEHRC's analysis and the deep political education it offered resonated strongly with poor people after President Bill Clinton dismantled
the entitlement to welfare. This was a period where, for example, state
agencies in Wisconsin had internal memos suggesting that case workers
tell their clients to rummage in garbage bins behind supermarkets if
they were short on food. It was a low point for compassion in the United
States and an even lower point for respecting basic rights to dignity and
social security. Poor people across the country visited by the PPEHRC
leadership were hungry for a counter-vision to the punitive policies they
faced daily. The campaign has since faced many challenges, but the most
recent and possibly strongest challenge came in the aftermath of Hurricane Katrina, which inextricably linked race and class in the United
States in the minds of people within our borders and around the world.
Today, PPEHRC retains its exclusive class-based analysis and vision of
"uniting the poor across color lines." Its mission statement still does not
refer in any way to discrimination or racism (or sexism). This approach
may prove increasingly challenging as the post-Katrina discourse has intensified the racialized nature of the activist conversation in a wide range
of fora.

Some of PPEHRC's most lasting work may be the result of its educational arm, the University of the Poor. Jointly led by Willie Baptist and
Reverend Liz Theo-Harris, the University of the Poor focuses on political
education for communities. Its key members and leaders travel around
the country for the kind of deep conversations at the community level
that are necessary precursors for successful movements. This mobile
and unorthodox university has spawned more traditional institutional

arrangements as well, as it provided the source of inspiration for the recently established Poverty Institute at the Union Theological Seminary in New York.

The Heartland's Emerging Alliance

In addition to PPEHRC's outreach work, a growing network in the Midwest links that region of the country to the national conversation. There has always been a human rights consciousness and an important coalition for human rights in the Midwest. The focus in the region has historically targeted civil and political rights with a strong emphasis on refugee and international issues. This is slowly changing, and long-standing groups like Minnesota Advocates for Human Rights are looking at domestic human rights issues like education in the United States. There has been particularly innovative work by one service organization—intentionally referenced in the subtitle for this section—the Heartland Alliance for Human Needs and Human Rights in Chicago under the leadership of Sid Mohn.

The Midwest is increasingly diverse and has always had major cities with the kinds of human rights concerns that inevitably arise in urban centers. Additionally, the Midwest faces poverty in both rural and urban areas and grapples with violence, hunger, homelessness, racism, xenophobia, and sexism among other social ills. The Heartland Alliance is a substantial social service organization addressing some of these social ills using traditional approaches such as soup kitchens and health clinics, as well as policy advocacy work. Several years ago, however, the organization intentionally underwent a transformation.

It still provides a range of social services and engages in policy advocacy, but it has refocused its identity and mission around a human rights mission. This transformation has impacted the dynamic between staff and clients whereby it is no longer simply a charitable endeavor, but one that raises consciousness and engages in ongoing human rights education. Staff members consider themselves human rights workers and opportunities are created and seized to share information about human rights with those coming to seek services.

Additionally, once you view poverty as a symptom of human rights violations, it is no longer adequate to seek to reduce or manage poverty, for it becomes imperative to abolish it. No one speaks about reducing torture or managing violations of free speech; the goal is to prevent these violations altogether. Human rights necessarily makes poverty abolitionists of us all, and when a large and important social service organization incorporates that vision it is bound to have effects both within and outside the organization.

The Midwest is an important bellwether for the direction of the country as a whole. What emerges from that region cannot easily be tarred as foreign or incompatible with U.S. culture. Leadership on human rights has emerged from states such as Illinois in the past. For example, once the death penalty had become a common form of punishment again in the United States, it was in Illinois that then-governor George Ryan began to question its legitimacy. In 2000, Governor Ryan imposed a moratorium on all executions, making Illinois the first of thirty-eight states with capital punishment to do so. This helped to reverse the trend toward this barbaric method of punishment and led to the banning of the juvenile death penalty by the U.S. Supreme Court.

Up and Down the West Coast

While the work in the Southern United States and in the center of the country on economic and social rights is linked together to some extent, the West Coast from California to Montana is following more of a model of each locality "doing its own thing." There are shining examples of work up and down the West Coast, but little communication among those efforts. Thus, it is more difficult to see the work as having a regional identity. Many of the organizations involved are more connected to national efforts than to each other.

In Los Angeles, Community Asset Development Redefining Education (CADRE) has incorporated human rights into its parent-led organizing in schools in South L.A. In partnership with the National Economic and Social Rights Initiative, CADRE has trained parents to engage in human rights documentation, conducted human rights tribunals, and developed human rights training materials for community members. CADRE has done in-depth organizing work and recently helped move the Los Angeles Unified School District to adopt a "positive discipline support policy." This policy requires each school to develop a plan as to how it will prevent disciplinary problems and support students who are struggling. Given the punitive and harsh disciplinary approaches to date, which have led to skyrocketing suspensions and soaring drop-out rates, this change of approach may turn out to be a crucial step toward protecting the human right to access education in the city. In this effort, CADRE has integrated its analysis of a "push-out" crisis in public education with human rights standards. This reframing has been very compelling for community members and has increased and motivated their organizing base. However, it has an indirect impact on how policymakers see the issue. While there has been an important policy gain through increased organizing using this approach, it has been far more difficult to persuade policymakers to see and formally recognize the human rights dimensions of these issues.

Further up the coast, activists in San Francisco have successfully taken the approach into the policy arena in explicit ways. San Francisco is unique among major urban centers in its openness to human rights approaches and the amount of human rights work taking place in the area. "Thinking Globally, Acting Locally" by Martha F. Davis in this volume describes the campaign leading to the local human rights ordinance in San Francisco. It is worth noting is that the work in San Francisco and the surrounding area (such as Oakland) generally looks at economic and social rights through the lens of discrimination. Thus, the local ordinance requires agencies to ensure there is no gender discrimination in any area of local government activity, which encompasses the economic and social sphere. The San Francisco ordinance does not, however, focus on the underlying minimum economic and social rights guarantees irrespective of any discrimination. It is typical to see campaigns and projects work from one perspective or another—that is, either looking at basic minimums or discrimination but rarely both at once. Integrating both approaches remains a challenge for the work across the country.

On a statewide level, the Women of Color Resource Center (WCRC) has had an interesting experience in developing its campaign to have California repeal its child exclusion law. The child exclusion law, also known as the family cap, prohibits a child from receiving welfare benefits if he/she is born into a family already on welfare. WCRC initiated its campaign with arguments about how the law impinged on women's reproductive freedom and discriminated against families of color. Bringing in human rights arguments added new dimensions, including the child's right to basic social security, freedom from hunger, and an adequate standard of living. Activists from WCRC report that policymakers have responded positively to the arguments focused on the rights of the child, and there is now pending a bill to repeal this policy. At the end of this effort, it will be interesting to assess whether WCRC shifted from antidiscrimination arguments to those focused on basic access to economic and social rights or whether it was possible to integrate both approaches to achieve success.

Up the coast, there has been much progressive work by Uplift in Seattle and surrounding areas on the human right to health. Using grassroots approaches such as petitions at farmers' markets, local coalitions (with technical assistance on human rights standards by Uplift) succeeded in having the city of Seattle adopt a human right to health resolution calling for universal access to care. Uplift hopes to expand this effort to other cities in Washington and possibly to Oregon. Washington and Oregon are relatively progressive states with an openness to issues such as health. What remains to be seen is whether these states can carry out such change within the framework of economic and social rights.

Another interesting development in the Northwest is the Montana Human Rights Network's growing interest in economic and social rights. The Network arose up in response to white supremacists and hate groups in the state but has now begun to address economic and social inequity. Given that Montana is a place known for its rugged individualism, how activists and communities approach issues that inevitably have a collective component will also yield important insights for the movement.

The Northeast

States and localities in the Northeast, as well as activists in the region, are receptive to at least discussing human rights approaches. In New York City, the Urban Justice Center (UJC), staffed first by Heidi Dorow, then Ramona Ortega, has promoted the development of policy through human rights at the local level. Specifically, it has been spearheading a local ordinance modeled upon the San Francisco effort. In addition to the work focused on nondiscrimination in the economic and social sphere, the UJC has worked from a basic access to economic and social rights perspective and developed innovative analysis on the right to food within the city's food stamp program and the right to welfare benefits. Housing activists have also been embracing the approach in the city, particularly with respect to the housing needs of those who are HIV positive. Additionally, an all-volunteer network called the Independent Commission on Public Education (ICOPE) has undertaken the mammoth task of working with communities to redesign the New York City school system to conform with human rights principles and develop policy proposals based on that redesign. ICOPE has set up five Independent Borough Education Commissions made up of local activists to run this conversation. Despite this growing activity, actual policy change from this perspective has been more difficult to come by than expected in the rough-and-tumble local politics of New York.

In Massachusetts and Pennsylvania, activists have persuaded the state legislatures to look at statewide human rights resolutions calling for review of state laws to assess whether they meet human rights standards. The Pennsylvania effort was undertaken as a partnership between the state social workers' association and the PPEHRC and has a clear economic and social rights focus. The Massachusetts effort emerged from the women's community and focused on gender discrimination, but the activists are making attempts to integrate a more general economic and social rights perspective. In Pennsylvania, the resolution has been adopted by the state House of Representatives and in Massachusetts it is still under consideration. The activists involved view these resolutions as organizing and education efforts targeting both legislators and communities. The question is whether the energy invested in this kind of broad-based political education on a range of issues will truly bear fruit in the long run, or whether energy is better spent on more targeted policy change using human rights standards. It is a strategic question that remains absolutely unresolved in the human rights community. Most people agree both are needed, but how much of each is anyone's guess.

The Gulf Coast

Although much of the United States is in a state of collective amnesia about the government abandonment of poor people left behind after the 2005 hurricane in the Gulf region, the situation in the Gulf Coast may yet become an important catalyst in demanding basic economic and social rights in the United States. This may turn out to be the case if only because rights most often spring from deep wrongs, and what has happened in the Gulf Coast is a striking example of brutal wrongs committed against the most vulnerable people in the region.

The Gulf Coast policies and practices after the storm were designed to purge poor people from the region and to privatize public systems and services such as schools and hospitals. This has a clear impact on how economically accessible such services are to middle-class and poor communities. People have been locked out of their public housing units despite very little damage from the storm, and as of the writing of this chapter, every neighborhood now has electricity restored except the historically poor and black Lower 9th ward.

Human rights language has resonated in a powerful way for affected residents in the Gulf Coast. Prior to the storm, Advocates for Environmental Human Rights (AEHR)—located in New Orleans—had undertaken important right-to-health campaigns, including a corporate accountability campaign targeting Shell Oil for its practices leading to environmental degradation and soaring cancer rates in a poor African American community. That campaign led to a settlement, which allowed the community to relocate. It also put the region on the map as one of the centers for innovative human rights advocacy.

After Katrina, AEHR teamed up with national organizations to do training on the human rights of hurricane survivors. Today, activists in the Gulf Coast are deeply committed to the concept of a "right to return," which is inclusive of basic economic and social rights. The right-to-return language has taken such a deep hold in the region that it has filtered up to major figures and institutions, such as Reverend Jesse Jackson and the Congressional Black Caucus.

Most significantly, activists and communities have lost all faith in domestic legal and political structures to protect basic human dignity in their still storm-affected communities. Turning to the international and universal arena of human rights not only makes perfect sense, but in many ways is the only refuge for communities facing chronic deprivation and abandonment. First left to die without food and water immediately after the storm, and now left to survive as they may in mold-infested damaged homes or inadequate trailers, without basic services, poor communities in the Gulf Coast have good reason to believe their government has not failed, but rather succeeded, in its attempt to erase or purge the poor from public consciousness and from any role in the rebuilding and redevelopment of the Gulf Coast. These are the unfortunate conditions from which human rights movements emerge.

New National Organizations

National organizations have also developed in order to support the range of local and regional work using human rights. There is a desperate ongoing need to build capacity within the United States on using the human rights approach in order to counter the view that human rights offers nothing more than superficial rhetoric and cannot be implemented in real and concrete ways. To strengthen human rights activism in the United States requires increased support for creative uses of the standards and analysis, greater coordination, persuasive public messages, and stronger links across this activist work. This requires support from the national level as local and regional organizations are often stretched beyond capacity in doing their existing work.

The first national organization created toward this end was the National Center on Human Rights Education (NCHRE) in Atlanta. The obvious first step in bringing human rights to the United States is actually ensuring that activists and others know what they are! NCHRE provided countless workshops at the community level to demystify human rights and give community leaders ownership over this framework. The role of human rights education in the development of the U.S. human rights movement cannot be underestimated. It is almost impossible to find an activist promoting human rights in the United States today that had not at some point heard Loretta Ross (former director of NCHRE) speak. She emerged from the Southern United States to criss-cross the country spreading the message of human rights, with a profound emphasis on the interdependence of economic and social rights on the one hand, and civil and political rights on the other.

Women's Institute on Leadership Development for Human Rights (WILD) was founded a decade ago in San Francisco to build leadership among young women of color in the human rights movement and has spearheaded a number of nationally relevant initiatives focused on human rights and identity. WILD played a significant role in linking the women's movement with economic and social rights activists and breaking down the barriers between identity-based and issue-based activism.

Three national organizations have emerged more recently to support the field as well.

The U.S. Human Rights Network, founded in 2003, is situated in Atlanta, Georgia. The Network is the first of its kind and seeks to provide an umbrella and collective voice for the diverse range of grassroots and national organizations that have committed to bringing a human rights vision and practice to the United States. The development and creation of this network is a very important part of the story of human rights in the United States. The network emerged from a series of meetings of extremely diverse activists—from high-profile national constitutional lawyers to impressive strategists organizing local communities working on every issue imaginable. Normally, it is rare for advocates against torture to be in discussion with education and housing advocates. The different activist communities simply never get a chance to exchange information and perspectives. It is worth noting that the U.S. Human Rights Network is unique in its integrated mission and membership reflecting the value placed on protecting a full range of rights.

The Network is a center for information sharing, training, and meeting, and there are hopes that in the future it may provide a space for joint strategizing for the movement. As a fairly new organization, it faces daunting challenges in its mission to serve an extremely large base covering a multitude of issues and communities. How to identify the cross-cutting threads and ideas that join together its disparate membership is one of its biggest and most important tasks.

The National Economic and Social Rights Initiative (NESRI) was formed in 2004 to support activists in the use of human rights as an integral part of their campaign strategies. NESRI's role is to demonstrate how human rights works in practical and concrete terms, and it works in partnership with activists to build new models of advocacy not typically used in the United States. The Opportunity Agenda (OA) was also founded in 2004 in order, among other things, to test and develop public messages using human rights. The goal of OA is to identify how the public views human rights in order to assist activists in influencing and moving those perceptions. With the exception of NESRI, none of these organizations are exclusively dedicated to economic and social rights, yet all of them have made this set of rights a central part of the agenda.

The development of these national organizations is indicative of the state of human rights within the activist community. It is no accident that the first national organization to arise on human rights in the United States focused on educating the community; knowledge is the foundation of building any field or movement. Leadership is the next obvious ingredient, and education and leadership building was the core of the work for the first decade. The newer organizations clearly focus on the next stage of development: building actual models of advocacy, creating ongoing and strong networks, and identifying public messages. When you put these national organizations together it is clear that activists are building the necessary components for a domestic human rights movement.

Institutional Paradigm Shifts

Another reflection of the increasing interest in and legitimacy of international economic and social rights in the United States is the ongoing shifts within major institutions. Amnesty International (AI) has both expanded its mandate to include economic and social rights and focused greater energies on the United States. AI is on the verge of launching its first global campaign against poverty, which should prove to be a historical milestone in this work. Moreover, it can be expected that AI will be working more closely and in concert with the U.S. human rights movement, in particular its economic and social rights wing.

Additionally, major organizations still very focused on civil and political rights have started to build relationships with economic and social rights activists and incorporate some issues into their work representing the intersection between civil/political and economic/social rights. For example, Human Rights Watch has issued major reports focused on the United States on worker health and safety, as well as one on discrimination in housing. The American Civil Liberties Union has created a human rights unit that works on, among other things, the abusive treatment of young people when sent to alternative schools or boot camps after expulsion from regular schools in Mississippi, which touches on important right-to-education issues.

Organizations and institutions in the health field have also taken significant steps to further the human rights approach. The FXB Center on Health and Human Rights at the Harvard School of Public Health, which once focused almost exclusively on international work, is partnering with U.S. advocates to map out human rights indicators for universal healthcare efforts at the state level. The National Health Lawyers Program, a forty-year-old organization that is domestically focused both in geography and approach, is one of FXB's partner organizations and is seriously exploring human rights strategies and approaches for its own work and to bring to its large network of members.

The National Law Center on Homelessness and Poverty (NLCHP), under the leadership of Maria Foscarinis, was one of the front-runners among national organizations developing a human rights approach. NLCHP has built a human-rights-to-housing caucus that it brought wholesale to the U.S. Human Rights Network. The caucus has held conferences, worked with the UN Special Rapporteur on Housing to bring attention to gentrification and displacement in Chicago, and organized training for hundreds of housing advocates. It has been more difficult for NLCHP to identify litigation opportunities to use human rights. Translating the enthusiasm for economic and social rights from the activist community to the courts may be a very long journey for groups like NLCHP. It seems an equally long journey to translate this enthusiasm to Capitol Hill, and few groups with a legislative focus have taken up the approach. Even NLCHP, when writing policy briefs targeting a Beltway audience, makes little or no mention of human rights.

Finally, it is important to note that some national rights organizations have always kept a twin focus on constitutional and human rights. In particular, the Center for Constitutional Rights (CCR) that has led the charge against abusive post-9/11 actions by the executive branch has a long-standing history that integrates a domestic and international approach. Despite CCR's broad mission and vision, it has not in recent years become involved in bringing economic and social rights to the United States. It is a notable absence in the field, but one that is understandable in light of the heavy demands placed on progressive litigators involved in curtailing post-9/11 abuses combined with the challenging nature of identifying litigation opportunities using economic and social rights standards.

These institutional paradigm shifts, where international economic and social rights standards are shaping the way major organizations are doing their work, show both the opportunities and limitations of the approach at present. On the one hand, some of these institutions are exploring new ways to do their work in order to promote economic and social rights, including more often using partnership with local communities to move their agendas forward. On the other, some of their standard strategies, such as litigation, present limited opportunities to move forward because there is still so much more to do to legitimate and integrate these standards into the political and legal fabric in the United States.

Identity-Based Movements and Human Rights

Some of the work of legitimating economic and social rights still needs to be focused on existing progressive movements in the United States. These movements are our natural allies; however, many of them have, at best, an ambivalent relationship with the U.S. human rights movement—

in particular its economic and social rights wing. Identity-based movements are a particularly interesting example. Does the universal nature of human rights make linking to these movements a challenge or an opportunity? Or does the strong emphasis on nondiscrimination in human rights standards make them natural partners?

A majority of the activists who have become part of the U.S. human rights movement have come from one of the many identity-based movements, such as the women's, racial justice, or lesbian/gay/bisexual/transgender movements. Let's examine one example—the women's movement. The women's movement radically changed some of the ways that we perceive social relations, yet stopped short of addressing structural economic issues that enabled much gender discrimination. These questions were more squarely at the center of the feminist agenda in the early years but were ultimately crowded out by a dominant approach focused on privacy, freedom from violence, and "free choice" to work with equality. How and why economic and social issues constrained free choice for or enabled violence against the average woman was relegated to side conversations among the most progressive feminists and in particular among women-of-color activists. Today, women's equality, such as it is, is often dependent on cheap nannies and domestic workers—in other words, on the oppression of an entirely different class of women. Some women-of-color activists argue that the feminist movement has made strides exclusively on the increasingly burdened and abused backs of women of color.

Several women's human rights activists, coming from both the international arena and the domestic sphere, sought to reach for a new vision that would unite the interests of women across both race and class and address the weaknesses in feminism today as a progressive vision. Analytical and conceptual leadership came from feminists such as Rhonda Copelon and Celina Romany while at CUNY Law School, Charlotte Bunch at the Center for Women's Global Leadership at Rutgers University, and Dorothy Q. Thomas, the first director of the Women's Division at Human Rights Watch. All these women have in common a deep involvement in the international arena paired with a background in the United States. They, with others such as Radhika Balakrishnan at Marymount College and Mallika Dutt now of Breakthrough, became key "importers" of the human rights approach from the international to the United States. Some played a role through mentoring future activists; others were phenomenal speakers who moved other women into the work through their inspiring presentations. Radhika Balakrishnan, a radical feminist economist, has made monumental efforts to bring a human rights framework to heterodox economists. And all these women contributed through their writings and convenings.

Other equally important key thinkers include Hope Lewis and Martha F. Davis, professors at Northeastern Law School. Hope Lewis has contributed intellectual leadership on the intersection of migration, development, and economy with regards to human rights. While legal director of Legal Momentum (formerly NOW LDF) Martha F. Davis was one of the consistent voices within the mainstream women's movement both for economic and social rights and for a human rights vision in the United States. Today, she is one of the most important legal scholars on the question of the relationship of human rights law to economic and social issues affecting women. Similarly, Lisa Crooms, a professor of law at Howard University, has written extensively on the intersection of race, gender, class, and human rights in the United States and hosted several key scholarly and activist conferences, including the one that launched the U.S. Human Rights Network.

The one consistent organizational voice from the gender perspective was WILD, headed by Krishanti Djamerah. Dorothy Thomas worked closely with WILD to organize a meeting of self-identified women's human rights activists in Mill Valley, California, in 1999. The decision emerging from this meeting to reach out to other U.S. human rights activists not working on gender issues was the first important step toward the creation of the U.S. Human Rights Network. The importance of Dorothy Thomas's role in linking the women's movement to other threads of the U.S. human rights movement cannot be understated.

Each of these women made different contributions and was instrumental in different ways in supporting the growth of a nascent U.S. human rights movement and its economic and social rights wing. Although it was professional feminists—among them Loretta Ross, mentioned earlier—who provided a great deal of the "fuel" for this kind of U.S. human rights work, with the exception of WILD, there are relatively few NGO voices on economic and social rights issues in the domestic human rights movement that are specifically "gendered" in their approach.

One exception already mentioned above is the Women of Color Resource Center. Sister Love, working on issues such as HIV among African American women, is also an organization that has embraced this approach since its inception. There are projects anchored in academic institutions, such as the International Women's Human Rights Law Clinic run by Rhonda Copelon at CUNY Law School, that take on domestic projects. But in terms of constituency-based groups, there are more active ones within PPEHRC that address women's issues, and the irony is that they have come to the human rights approach through an arm of the movement that discourages putting discrimination front and center as a primary issue. Similarly, domestic workers groups in New York have strongly embraced the approach, but the public education and organizing appear much more focused on issues of class than gender.

What is one to make of this anomaly where leadership by feminist women within the domestic human rights movement has somehow not directly translated to leadership explicitly on feminist issues at the grass-roots level? Is this simply a result of a less active grassroots movement on women's issues? Or are feminist leaders focusing on nonfeminist issues in the interest of the broader movement and to the detriment of issues affecting women (as some argue occurred during the civil rights movement)? One alternative possibility is that many activists on women's issues have been disappointed with the mainstream women's movement (it is often criticized as having a narrow agenda and vision, particularly because of an absence of an economic and social rights focus) and have joined other efforts rather than continue to try and reform their own movement. Human rights activism has recently transformed the public conversation on issues as diverse as death penalty, LGBTQ rights, and farm workers' wages and conditions of work. It will be interesting to see how or whether this approach will have an impact on the community of activists working on "women's issues" in the United States, particularly whether it will raise up the importance of economic and social rights within this community.

The World Responds: Solidarity Through Common Vision

The validity and value of an internationally grounded economic and social rights movement in United States may still be a subject of debate within progressive movements and sectors in the United States, but around the world the response has been decidedly different. Sitting across from an East African human rights advocate in a hotel restaurant in Antigua, Guatemala, during a global meeting held by the Ford Foundation, I first started to understand that the human rights movement in the United States was important to people in other places. It turns out that people in Africa and Asia, as well as most other parts of the world, have a strong interest in the success of this movement, in particular its economic and social rights wing. "What can we do for you, what can we do to help?" This is a question that has now been asked of me by activists from several regions.

With only moderate reflection, it becomes clear why. The refusal of the U.S. government to recognize the legitimacy of economic and social rights has repercussions all over the world. The dynamics that lead to public hospital closures in poor neighborhoods in the United States are not dissimilar to those that lead to such closures in poor parts of the world that are affected by international policies influenced and designed by the United States. U.S. policy is certainly not the only factor in deci-sions that deny scores of people access to health care, clean water, food, and decent jobs, but the U.S. government is clearly a powerful actor on the international stage and exercises disproportionate influence in such decisions.

What would the world be like if the United States took leadership in the *protection* of economic and social rights? Communities around the world would definitely like to know! But in order for this to happen, the United States has to begin recognizing the legitimacy of these rights for its own people. These activists are offering true solidarity, as they view our work as part of a common vision that serves our collective common interests.

It has become clear there is much we can learn from activists abroad. As this chapter is being written, plans are under way to bring a delegation from tsunami-affected areas of Thailand and Indonesia to the Gulf Coast to share strategies and insights with Gulf Coast activists. This is part of an ongoing exchange that could not have happened without the solidarity and hard work of the Asian Coalition for Housing Rights. Time and time again the coalition has asked, How can we help you? It is often difficult to identify specific actions that those outside the country can take to help those within it. But the first step is acknowledging that we need the help. The second is to understand that in our globalized world we really are "all in it together" in practical and concrete ways, and if we do not learn how to give strength to the extraordinary vision and system that led to human rights laws, the world will be a much poorer, more insecure place where human development and dignity remain at risk.

Conclusion

The future of economic and social rights in the United States remains uncertain. But the deepening commitment by activists and the show of solidarity across issues as well as borders create a feeling of hope and wonder that current circumstances otherwise defy. This emerging move-ment is not sui generis, however. It owes deep debts to leaders from other movements outside the United States that have become mentors and models, as well as provided inspiration, for this work.

Examples include Dr. Paul Farmer, cofounder of Partners in Health and the strongest voice for economic and social rights in the global health movement today. Paul Farmer has become an inspiration for scores of young activists that have committed their lives to economic and social rights in many countries, including the United States, as a result of his work. Partners in Health has also been a groundbreaking example of community-based and participatory human rights work. Nobel Prize–

winning economist Amartya Sen, while not having much of a direct link to the work in the United States, has deeply impacted many in the U.S. economic and social rights community with his brilliant analysis of development as a potential force for freedom. Both of these men also brought home that rights belong both in and beyond the province of law and must be embedded in almost every sphere of human activity if they are to truly become real for those currently suffering the worst violations.

The international women's movement has been an important source of innovation and leadership for this work as well. Charlotte Bunch at the Center for Women's Global Leadership has created some of the training ground for feminists entering the U.S. work. Similarly, Rhonda Copelon's insistence on the importance of U.S. work for those focusing on international concerns and the importance of human rights for those focusing on U.S. concerns has touched the lives of many activists. Additionally, Dorothy Q. Thomas and Larry Cox from Human Rights Watch and Amnesty International respectively are two examples of important leaders who have contributed to significant changes within the international human rights movement fueling both economic and social rights and human rights in the United States.

The economic and social rights movement in the United States and around the world also owes a great debt both for intellectual leadership and political inspiration to the antiapartheid movement in South Africa. The leadership of that movement not only beat extraordinary odds but also wrote and developed one of the world's most respected constitutions with economic and social rights as an integral component. Speaking to doubts expressed by U.S. colleagues at a high-level roundtable discussion in 1993, which was still early days for the conversation on human rights in the United States, Albie Sachs, justice of the South African Constitutional Court and widely admired antiapartheid activist, commented:

The rest of you have every right to be pragmatic, but we in South Africa are clinging to the right to be naïve . . . A pragmatic man in Nelson Mandela's position would have given up a long time ago and reconciled himself to second-class status in a racist society. *But Mandela was naïve, and Mandela was unpragmatic, and that is why he has attained so much.*

In the new South Africa, it is one of our major tasks to hold to that essential faith in justice and rightness, to believe that even these poor international documents might help us transform our world. If I'm less skeptical than some others in this room, it is due to our strong grassroots movement and our strong public consciousness of rights. In South Africa, we are seeking the political mechanisms to realize our ideals; here in the United States, around this table, we are groping for ideals to give substance to our institutions. The twain ought to meet.[2]

Yes, the two ought to meet. Those working today toward having our institutions meet our ideals are not the first within the United States to recognize the need for this vision. I cannot close this chapter without an acknowledgment of the giants upon whose shoulders we stand—the many leaders, martyrs, and other participants in the various strands of the civil rights and labor movements that burst through the public consciousness in the twentieth century in the United States. We owe an ultimate debt to those movements and those who gave their lives to take us this far. We also owe it to them to continue the work. As Reverend Martin Luther King noted toward the end of his life, "I think it is necessary to realize that we have moved from the era of civil rights to the era of human rights."

Notes

I would like to thank Cindy Soohoo, Dorothy Q. Thomas, Martha Davis, Laura Gosa, and Liz Sullivan for their insightful comments and assistance with this chapter.

1. Daniel J. Whelan, "The United States and Economic and Social Rights: Past, Present . . . and Future?," Working paper no. 26, p. 8, Graduate School of International Studies, University of Denver, presented at the 2005 International Studies Association Convention, on the panel "Human Rights as a Foreign Policy Goal: Rhetoric, Realism and Results," March 5, 2005, Honolulu, Hawaii, available online at www.du.edu/gsis/hrhw/working/2005/26-whelan-2005.pdf

2. "Economic and Social Rights and the Right to Health, An Interdisciplinary Discussion Held at Harvard Law School" (Human Rights Program, Harvard Law School; and the François-Xavier Bagnoud Center for Health and Human Rights, Harvard School of Public Health, Cambridge, 1993), Section III, transcript available online at www.law.harvard.edu/programs/hrp/Publications/economic2.html.

Chapter 7
Human Rights and the Transformation of the "Civil Rights" and "Civil Liberties" Lawyer

Cynthia Soohoo

Over the past few years, clear signs indicate that the wall between domestic social justice and international human rights work is crumbling:

- In 2005, six of the nine Supreme Court justices indicated that international human rights sources were relevant in determining whether the juvenile death penalty violated the Eighth Amendment of the U.S. Constitution. The same justices endorsed the use of international sources in a case striking down the criminalization of consensual sexual contact between two people of the same sex.[1]
- In 2006, over sixty-five U.S. lawyers and activists traveled to Geneva to participate in a UN review of U.S. compliance with an international human rights treaty—the International Covenant on Civil and Political Rights. These individuals were drawn from more than 140 U.S. organizations that were involved in the review process.
- In fall 2006, Harvard Law School made headlines by requiring that first-year law students take a course in international and comparative law.[2] Law students at the University of Michigan are also required to take a class in transnational law in order to graduate.[3]
- In 2004, the American Civil Liberties Union, the nation's largest civil liberties organization, officially created a human rights program.

As the world shrinks, domestic conversations on issues like the death penalty and the right to privacy are starting to include international human rights standards and consider information and experiences from abroad. Given improvements in communication wrought by the Internet and the recognition of globalization in other areas such as education and business, the internationalization of discussions about fundamental rights and social justice is not surprising.

Yet the law has long stood apart. Traditionally, U.S. lawyers arguing about and judges interpreting U.S. law did not see the need to look abroad. Among lawyers, "civil rights" and "human rights" were regarded as two distinct specialties. Civil rights lawyers worked in U.S. courts making arguments for social change in the United States based on U.S. law. Human rights lawyers used international human rights standards to make arguments for social change in other countries. These arguments were made in international forums such as the UN and regional human rights systems but also involved documentation of human rights abuses through "human rights reports" designed to focus international attention and leverage "shame and blame" to change local conditions. Despite this historic division, in recent years domestic lawyers are increasingly turning to human rights strategies—defined here as appeals to international human rights bodies, use of international human rights and comparative foreign law in U.S. courts, and broader activism using international pressure. Contemporary domestic human rights advocates also recognize economic and social rights as fundamental rights of equal stature and interdependent with civil and political rights.

A growing number of domestic lawyers are incorporating international sources and human rights arguments into their work. These arguments are reflected in and encouraged by increased consideration of such sources in judicial decisions. And even as these international sources seep into U.S. courts, U.S. lawyers are stepping outside U.S. courtrooms, bringing claims of U.S. rights violations to international forums within the United Nations and the inter-American human rights system. Lawyers are also adopting integrated strategies that combine litigation with grassroots organizing, documentation, and media work. At the beginning of the twenty-first century, U.S. lawyers and courts are reengaging and reinventing human rights strategies, both learning from international human rights advocacy strategies and expanding and adapting them to fit the domestic context.

The first part of this chapter examines progressive lawyers' early attempts to use human rights standards and international forums to promote social justice in the United States and the historic reasons that lawyers turned away from such strategies, creating a divide between domestic "civil rights" and international "human rights." The second part examines how contemporary human rights strategies emerged out of the work of a small number of lawyers in the 1970s and 1980s, who began to make human rights arguments in U.S. courts and international human rights bodies concerning issues such as the death penalty and indigenous and immigrant rights. Efforts in U.S. courts were aided by globalization, reflected in judges' increased familiarity with international sources and law schools' growing emphasis on international law. The third part of this chapter considers how the international human rights work of U.S. lawyers began to cross over into domestic work. Many of these "domestic international human rights" lawyers would become important bridges and translators of human rights strategies for the domestic civil rights/ civil liberties community. Their efforts to transform legal attitudes were aided by projects specifically designed to train and support domestic lawyers to use human rights and by the development of law school human rights clinics. The final part looks at how a changing legal and political environment made new approaches and forums more appealing to U.S. lawyers tackling domestic social justice issues. As U.S. lawyers faced growing conservatism and increased barriers to judicial relief at home, the international human rights system was both expanding to tackle issues of greater resonance to the United States, and building stronger mechanisms for accountability.

A Long History of Human Rights Legal Advocacy

As we try to understand the forces that drive the blurring of boundaries between civil and human rights, it is instructive to examine the historical roots of the divide. Following World War II, domestic lawyers, frustrated with the legacy of segregation and racial discrimination in the United States, were eager to use developing international human rights law. At the time, this may not have seemed novel. Many of the components of modern human rights advocacy could already be found in the U.S. legal system and in social justice activism. As discussed by historian Paul Gordon Lauren, international influence on U.S. conceptions of rights traces its roots back to the Declaration of Independence, and transnational advocacy played an important role in the abolitionist and women's suffrage movements.[4] A recent article by legal scholar Sarah Cleveland points out that the Supreme Court has traditionally understood constitutional interpretation to include consideration of international sources and that the practice of considering such sources dates back to Chief Justice Marshall.[5] Similarly as scholars and activists have written in recent works,[6] the modern human rights movement's recognition of social and economic rights can trace roots to FDR's Four Freedoms speech in 1941 and 1944 State of the Union Address, which both articulated a vision of social and economic rights for America.[7]

Given the context, it is not surprising that immediately following the creation of the UN, civil rights and civil liberties organizations like the American Civil Liberties Union (ACLU) and the National Association for the Advancement of Colored People (NAACP) saw the developing international human rights system as a vehicle for addressing rights violations in the United States, especially segregation and the continuing discrimination against African Americans. However, in the 1940s and 1950s, opponents of progressive reforms were able to exploit the Cold War context by portraying appeals to international human rights standards and forums as un-American. Human rights advocacy was criticized as undermining U.S. interests and reputation, and demands for social and economic rights were linked to communism. As a result, human rights claims were effectively excised from the agenda of progressive U.S. legal organizations until recently.

1940s–1950s: Early Attempts to Make Human Rights Arguments

Historian Carol Anderson writes that after World War II, African American leadership was interested in defining the struggle for equality as a fight for human rights. Anderson explains that human rights documents articulated a broader rights framework, which included economic and social rights, and offered the potential of internationalizing the struggle for equality. "[O]nly human rights could repair the damage that more than three centuries of slavery, Jim Crow, and racism had done to the African American community [and] had the language and philosophical power" to go beyond political and legal inequities and address "the education, health care, housing and employment needs that haunted the black community."[8]

In 1947, the NAACP, the nation's oldest civil rights organization, filed a petition with the United Nations entitled "An Appeal to the World," which denounced Jim Crow and racial discrimination in the United States.[9] However, Cold War politics provided a convenient way to deflect attention from the merits of the NAACP's claims. As chair of the UN Human Rights Commission, Eleanor Roosevelt refused to even introduce the petition. She was able to prevail upon the NAACP leadership to abandon the petition in order to preserve the NAACP's relationship with the Truman administration.[10] Although the Soviet delegation proposed investigation of the charges, the UN Human Rights Commission refused to take action.

By the 1950s, NAACP leadership had essentially given up on international human rights advocacy, focusing instead on domestic civil and political rights claims. Any demands for economic and social rights were left to the black left. When the Civil Rights Congress (CRC) filed a petition with the UN in 1951 based on many of the same underlying facts as the NAACP petition,[11] it failed to gain the support of the black community, and many prominent African Americans, including NAACP leadership denounced it.[12] The NAACP's decision to adopt a course that would not expose it to accusations of communist or anti-American sentiment resulted not only in a split with the black left, but also in a retreat from international advocacy and an economic and social rights agenda.

During the same period, U.S. lawyers also tried to incorporate international human rights law into legal arguments in U.S. courts. In a review of Supreme Court civil rights cases from 1946–55, legal scholar Bert Lockwood found that lawyers frequently raised the United States' human rights and antidiscrimination obligation under the UN Charter.[13] Briefs submitted by the U.S. government, progressive legal organizations such as the ACLU, and occasionally by the parties themselves argued that the UN Charter evidenced the high principles to which the United States had subscribed including public policy against discrimination.[14] Some briefs went further contending not only that the Court should consider the UN Charter in determining the content of U.S. law and constitutional provisions, but also that U.S. courts were bound to enforce the charter's human rights provisions as a matter of law. The U.S. government briefs opposing segregation also frequently emphasized the negative impact that segregation had on world opinion.[15] For example, in a case challenging segregated dining cars on railroads, the United States argued that "in our foreign relations, racial discrimination, as exemplified by segregation, has been a source of serious embarrassment . . . Our position and standing before the critical bar of world opinion are weakened if segregation not only is practiced in this country but also is condoned by federal law."[16]

The high-water mark for judicial recognition of UN Charter obligations came in the 1948 Supreme Court case *Oyama v. California*, in which the Supreme Court considered a challenge to California's Alien Land Law. The law prohibited aliens ineligible for citizenship from owning agricultural land, and, at the time, Japanese citizens were ineligible for naturalization. Four Supreme Court justices (one less than a majority), in two separate concurring opinions, indicated that the law was unconstitutional and inconsistent with the human rights obligations the United States undertook when it ratified the UN Charter.[17]

However, in 1950, a California appellate court went farther. In *Sei Fuji v. State*, the court issued a decision overturning the Land Law based on the UN Charter's human rights and nondiscrimination provisions, stating that the treaty invalidated conflicting state laws.[18] By suggesting that the UN Charter imposed enforceable legal obligations superseding inconsistent state law, the *Sei Fuji* decision played right into the hands of opponents of the United Nations such as Frank Holman, a former president of the American Bar Association, and Senator John W. Bricker of Ohio. Holman portrayed the United Nations and human rights treaties as threats to U.S. sovereignty and tools to erode states' rights. He argued that human rights treaties were a plot to promote communism and impose socialism on the United States.[19] *Sei Fuji* provoked an outpouring of criticism. Lockwood describes it as "the legal shot heard around the nation. Perhaps no other decision of a state appellate court received as much attention in the legal periodicals."[20] In 1952, the California Supreme Court responded by repudiating the appellate court's reasoning, stating that the charter "represents a moral commitment of foremost importance" but the human rights and nondiscrimination provisions relied on by the plaintiff "were not intended to supersede existing domestic legislation, and we cannot hold that they operate to invalidate the alien land law."[21]

The Bricker Amendment and Backlash Against U.S. Human Rights Treaties

The *Sei Fuji* case, the UN petitions, and opposition to U.S. ratification of the Convention on the Prevention and Punishment of the Crime of Genocide (Genocide Convention) fueled domestic backlash against the United Nations and human rights treaties in the 1950s led by Senator Bricker and Frank Holman.[22] Concerned about the potential of the UN Charter and future human rights treaties to impact domestic law, Bricker attempted to amend the Constitution to limit the president's power to ratify treaties. Support for the amendment was fueled by concern that human rights treaties would be used to dismantle segregation, which was being defended as a state prerogative.

The battle over U.S. ratification of the Genocide Convention in the 1950s was a focal point for this struggle. In the aftermath of the Holocaust, one of the first items on the international agenda was the drafting of the Genocide Convention. Despite a context in which a convention denouncing genocide would appear an appropriate undertaking by the international community, Southern senators adamantly opposed U.S. ratification because they feared it was a "back-door method of enacting federal anti-lynching legislation."[23] Holman belittled the Genocide Convention arguing that accidentally running over a "Negro child" could be grounds for an overseas trial for genocide and argued that the treaties could lead to the "nullifying of statutes against mixed marriages."[24]

The Bricker Amendment was narrowly defeated in the Senate. In order to head off further attacks on the president's foreign relations power, the Eisenhower administration agreed that it would not seek ratification of the Genocide Convention or any other human rights treaty.[25] The U.S. Senate did not take up ratification of human rights treaties until the waning days of the Cold War.

The Legacy of the Cold War and Senator Bricker

After World War II, the international community concluded that an international commitment to protect human rights was necessary to sustain peace and ensure fundamental rights. Progressive lawyers in the United States recognized the potential that the twin tools of universally recognized human rights standards and international pressure could have on social justice work in the United States, particularly on the issues of racial discrimination and segregation. In response to this threat to their interests, U.S. isolationists and defenders of a segregated South formed an effective alliance. In the context of the Cold War, they were able to both narrow the rights claims domestic activists could make and the venues in which they made them. As legal historian Mary Dudziak writes, "The primacy of anticommunism in postwar American politics and culture left a very narrow space for criticism of the status quo. By silencing certain voices and by promoting a particular vision of racial justice, the Cold War led to a narrowing of acceptable civil rights discourse. The narrow boundaries of Cold War–era civil rights politics kept discussions of broad-based social change, or a linking of race and class, off the agenda."[26]

Bricker and the Cold War had a lasting effect on the U.S. human rights movement that continues today. Although the United States ratified the Genocide Convention in 1988 and the International Covenant on Civil and Political Rights (ICCPR), the Convention Against Torture and Other Cruel, Inhuman, or Degrading Treatment or Punishment (Torture Convention), and the International Convention on the Elimination of All Forms of Racial Discrimination (Race Convention) in the early 1990s, as Louis Henkin writes, the ghost of Senator Bricker lived on in the reservations, understandings, and declarations ("RUDs") attached to the treaties as a condition of ratification, which "virtually achieve[d] what the Bricker Amendment sought, and more."[27] Most notably, each human rights treaty was ratified with a declaration stating that the treaty is not self-executing, which has been interpreted to mean that individuals cannot sue to enforce treaty provisions without separate congressional legislation. Thus, human rights treaties were ratified in a manner that essentially makes them toothless in domestic courts.

Ironically, while Bricker and his allies bristled at the idea of the U.S. being held accountable to any international organization, in the post–World War II context, the U.S. government remained acutely concerned about how its domestic problems played abroad. As argued forcefully by Mary Dudziak, the same Cold War pressures that successfully neutralized domestic legal organizations' appeals to international forums made the United States particularly sensitive to world opinion. Dudziak writes that U.S. diplomatic posts from places as far-flung as Fiji frequently reported foreign press coverage of racial problems in the United States, all of which were eagerly exploited by Soviet propaganda.[28] As the United States competed with the Soviet Union to win allies among former colonies composed of Africans and Asians, treatment of racial minorities within the United States began to be a major foreign policy concern. In this context, civil rights reform became not only morally right, but also politically expedient. Dudziak argues that the same concern for international opinion expressed in U.S. government briefs submitted in major civil rights cases was also reflected in civil rights legislation and reforms championed by Presidents Truman, Kennedy, and Johnson.

While the confluence of domestic civil rights struggles and the Cold War in the 1940s and 1950s was a unique time in U.S. history, the period captures a continuing tension with the use of international human rights law in the United States. The UN Charter (and later the human rights treaties ratified by the United States in the 1990s) created a legal and moral imperative for the United States to alter its conduct. In the 1940s and 1950s, this imperative intensified as the world watched to see how the United States would respond as segregation was challenged by the civil rights movement. At the same time, anti-internationalist sentiment and fear of the erosion of domestic sovereignty made it difficult for courts and the public to accept claims that the United States was legally bound to domestically enforce human rights treaties. As a result, any influence on Supreme Court decisions was indirect. As Lockwood states, "Courts, disposed to move in the direction of correcting the American dilemma, were on firmer ground to buttress the change with a domestic constitutional cloak of legitimacy than to rely on such a radical notion as international human rights law."[29]

Human Rights Strategies Reemerge

As U.S. lawyers and courts reengage human rights strategies today, they are profoundly influenced by the lessons learned from and the constraints imposed by the past. The legacy of the Cold War and the Bricker Amendments imposed real limitations on domestic legal strategies by reducing the UN Charter and subsequently ratified human rights treaties to the status of "non-self-executing" documents. When lawyers and activists began to rediscover human rights in the late 1990s, the RUDs forced them to develop different strategies, both forging new legal arguments within the courts and broadening the way they approached legal advocacy work. Similarly, while the end of the Cold War helped neutralize criticisms that any domestic application of human rights standards or appeal to international bodies is unpatriotic, opponents of such strategies still argue that they are aimed at undercutting American sovereignty.

Despite this legacy, since the end of the Cold War, three distinct factors have contributed to the resurgence of human rights strategies among U.S. lawyers: (1) globalization and increased receptiveness on the part of at least some U.S. judges and lawyers to international and foreign law; (2) a decline in the effectiveness of traditional civil rights legal strategies, opening the way for new strategies; and (3) the growth and development of the international human rights advocacy model, which is now being adapted for the U.S. context. These factors have spurred an increased emphasis on international and foreign law and human rights in legal education, which in turn has reinforced the openness of the courts and Bar to international human rights law.

As lawyers begin to incorporate human rights strategies again, these strategies look somewhat different than those employed in the 1940s and 1950s. The non-self-executing status of treaties has meant that in U.S. courts, the most productive use of international sources (here defined as treaties, other sources of international law, and foreign law) has been in the comparative or interpretative context.[30] These sources are used to help interpret fundamental rights recognized by U.S. law rather than as part of arguments that they are independently binding. Treaties constitute evidence of international consensus rather than binding authority, and foreign law (the decisions of courts of other countries) also becomes relevant.

Second, based on the less-than-binding status of human rights treaties in domestic courts as well as a broader reassessment of the efficacy of social justice strategies that rely solely on litigation, progressive lawyers began to adopt broader human rights strategies that look beyond domestic litigation. Many of these strategies and forums were developed by human rights lawyers and activists working on issues in other countries and are now being adapted to fit the U.S. context.

International Human Rights and Foreign Law in U.S. Courts

In the 2003 case *Lawrence v. Texas*, the Supreme Court struck down a Texas law criminalizing sexual conduct between two persons of the same sex. In reaching its decision, the Court discussed and considered a case from the European Court of Human Rights and the laws of other countries, stating, "[t]he right petitioners seek . . . has been accepted as an integral part of human freedom in many other countries. There has been no showing that in this country the governmental interest in circumscribing personal choice is somehow more legitimate or urgent."[31] Similarly in the 2004 case *Roper v. Simmons*, striking down the juvenile death penalty, the Supreme Court invoked world opinion to confirm the Court's holding that the death penalty for juvenile offenders constituted disproportionate punishment. To support his conclusion that "the United States now stands alone in a world that has turned its face against the juvenile death penalty," Justice Kennedy considered the number of countries that have ratified treaties prohibiting the juvenile death penalty, the practices of other countries, and U.K. law.

Of course, *Lawrence* and *Roper* were not the first cases in which the Supreme Court had considered international sources.[32] In addition to the civil rights–era cases cited by Bert Lockwood, the *Roper* decision cites cases going back to 1958, which referred to the law of other countries as part of the Court's analysis of what constitutes "cruel and unusual punishments" under the Eighth Amendment. Legal scholars have shown that international law has historically played an important role in U.S. constitutional jurisprudence.[33] Based on an exhaustive review of cases, Sarah Cleveland concludes "international law has always played a substantial, even dominant role, in broad segments of U.S. constitutional jurisprudence."[34] However, the two cases, along with an earlier death penalty case, seemed to signal a shift in which the Court appeared willing to expand its reliance on and consideration of international sources in cases concerning fundamental rights.

The use of international sources in *Lawrence* and *Roper* engendered heated debate among the justices and politicians. The political debate seemed to be fueled by the use of international sources in the controversial area of individual rights, especially since such sources were viewed as supporting more progressive interpretations of rights.[35] Indeed the reliance on international sources in *Roper* and *Lawrence*, two of the most controversial cases of their time, was not lost on conservative politicians. Following *Lawrence*, a House Resolution and bills in both the Senate and the House designed to curb judicial reliance on international or foreign sources were introduced.[36] In a press release, Congressman Tom Feeney of Florida, sponsor of the House Resolution, stated, "[t]he sovereignty of our nation is jeopardized when justices seek the laws of foreign nations to justify their decisions rather than the original intent of the Constitution." Rhetoric around the legislation from lawmakers and conservative Web sites went so far as to threaten judges who cite international materials with impeachment. In spring 2006, Justice Ginsburg revealed that she and Justice O'Connor received death threats following Internet postings criticizing their references to international sources as threats to "our Republic and Constitutional freedom" and urging that if patriots take action "those two justices will not live another week."[37]

These criticisms are reminiscent of the statements made by Senator Bricker and Frank Holman, but they are surprising given that the Supreme Court is well aware of the outcome of the Bricker debate and the fact that the United States ratified human rights treaties to be "non-self-executing." Current Supreme Court references to international sources do not suggest that U.S. courts are bound to comply with the decisions of foreign courts or with human rights treaty provisions, but instead merely take them into account in interpreting the Constitution.[38] In *Roper,* Justice Kennedy states, "the opinion of the world community, while not controlling our outcome, does provide respected and significant confirmation of our own conclusions."[39] Similarly, while the United States has ratified the ICCPR, which explicitly prohibits the juvenile death penalty, U.S. RUDs specifically reserved the right to execute juveniles and stated that the treaty was not self-executing, essentially making it unenforceable in U.S. courts.[40] Thus, the *Roper* decision cites the ICCPR as evidence of world opinion, rather than as law binding the Court's decision. Despite this, conservatives continue to protest that "[t]he American people have not consented to being ruled by foreign powers or tribunals."[41]

The Courts: Transjudicial Dialogue

The Supreme Court's recent references to international sources may be more accurately characterized as an interest in engaging in a dialogue with other legal systems about the contours of fundamental rights than a capitulation to international standards. For many decades, the U.S. Supreme Court had been a legal exporter and the source of inspiration for constitutional courts around the world. The increased receptivity of the Supreme Court to consider foreign and international sources suggests a new openness to a two-way "transjudicial dialogue." Justice O'Connor has stated that "American judges and lawyers can benefit from broadening our horizons." Justices Breyer and Ginsburg have made similar statements recognizing the value of looking to other jurisdictions as "offering points of comparison" and to see what they "can tell us about endeavors to eradicate bias against women, minorities, and other disadvantaged groups."[42]

The late Chief Justice William Rehnquist also endorsed judicial dialogue. In 1989 at a symposium in Germany, he stated:

For nearly a century and a half, courts in the United States exercising the power of judicial review had no precedents to look to save their own, because our courts alone exercised this sort of authority. When many new constitutional courts were created after the Second World War, these courts naturally looked to decisions of the Supreme Court of the United States, among other sources, for developing their own law. But now that constitutional law is solidly grounded in so many countries, it is time that the United States courts begin looking to the decisions of other constitutional courts to aid in their own deliberative process.[43]

Commentators on transjudicial dialogue agree that the Supreme Court's move to consider the opinions of other jurisdictions can be traced to the development and growth of strong independent judiciaries in other countries. Thus, the dearth of such references in the past can be explained by a historical lack of relevant peers rather than a conscious decision not to look outside the United States. This process has been aided by increasing interaction between judges, which has made it easier to learn of key decisions in other countries. U.S. Supreme Court justices, in particular, attend conferences with judges from the constitutional courts of other countries as well as the European Court of Justice and the European Court of Human Rights.[44] At the same time, the Internet makes international materials more easily available.

The Supreme Court's interest in international and foreign law is also reflected in and encouraged by a marked increase in attention to international law in law schools in the mid-1990s. In addition to adding new international law courses, some schools are making them mandatory, and others are integrating them into the first year curricula.[45] In 2007, *U.S. News and World Report* added an "international law" ranking to its category of specialty ratings for law schools, reflecting the increasing relevance of international law for domestic legal practitioners and the demand for international training from law schools.

In a 2000 article, law professor and civil rights litigator Martha F. Davis predicted a change in the Supreme Court's treatment of international sources "within the next five years."[46] Davis's prediction was based on pure pragmatism, linking the Court's consideration of international and foreign sources to its own legitimacy. Noting increasing globalization, she wrote, when the United States' policies on issues such as affirmative action "are now 180 degrees apart from worldwide trends, the explanation 'because this is the United States' is not sufficient." Although the Court should not "second-guess the United States' failure to ratify widely accepted treaties and abide by international norms. . . . judicial legitimacy is a separate issue, which the Court can address by consistently recognizing the persuasive value of comparative and international law, and explaining its reasoning in that context."[47] Recognizing the limitations placed on judicial reliance on human rights treaties following the Bricker era and the ratification of human rights treaties with RUDs, she added:

This change will be much less than the wholesale incorporation of international law that many internationalists have argued for. . . . [C]ourts will not override [the non-self-executing limitations on human rights treaties] by permitting private rights of action in domestic courts directly under international instruments. . . . But domestic courts, and particularly the Supreme Court, will begin to view international law in much the same way that social science data was first viewed by courts during the Progressive era—as useful and potentially persuasive authority outside of the narrow framework of precedent.[48]

In an interesting echo of executive branch policy supporting civil rights reform during the Cold War to further U.S. prestige abroad and ultimately foreign relations objectives, proponents of transjudicial dialogue are making similar foreign policy claims today. U.S. allies have become vocal critics of U.S. human rights violations. In particular, the European Union frequently intervenes and files amicus briefs in U.S. death penalty cases.[49] Reflecting this concern, briefs submitted in death penalty cases by former U.S. diplomats argue that the practice of executing juveniles and individuals with mental retardation in the United States "strains diplomatic relations, increases America's diplomatic isolation, and impairs important U.S. foreign policy interests."[50] Others argue that the Supreme Court's explicit consideration of international opinion in *Roper* will have a positive impact on U.S. foreign relations and that showing the Court takes world opinion seriously in a context where the United States is becoming increasingly isolated "is bound to help our image around the world."[51]

As we discuss the Supreme Court's new receptivity to consideration of international sources, it would be remiss to suggest that it occurred in a vacuum. In a 2003 speech to the American Society of International Law, Justice Breyer noted what he called the "chicken and egg problem": "Neither I nor my law clerks can easily find relevant comparative material on our own. The lawyers must do the basic work, finding, analyzing, and referring us to, that material. . . . The lawyers will do so only if they believe the courts are receptive. By now, however, it should be clear that the chicken has broken out of the egg. The demand is there."[52] The next section addresses the lawyers who first broke out of the egg.

The Lawyers: Supreme Court Anti–Death Penalty Litigation

As Justice Breyer notes, the Court's current references to international sources could not have occurred but for the efforts of a small but determined group of lawyers who continued to cite such material even when courts appeared uninterested and, on occasion, openly hostile. The use of international norms by progressive lawyers reemerged in the 1970s, primarily in death penalty cases.

Lawyers for the NAACP Legal Defense Fund and capital defense attorneys presented evidence of international norms in a series of death penalty cases in the 1970s and 1980s, joined on occasion by Amnesty International and the International Human Rights Law Group (IHRLG, now known as Global Rights).[53] The particular appeal of international standards in death penalty cases can be explained by several factors. First, the constitutionality of the death penalty is based on the Eighth Amendment standard of evolving decency, and in the 1950s, the Supreme Court had indicated that international practice was relevant to Eighth Amendment analysis. Second, as world consensus against the death penalty, especially as it applied to juveniles and people with mental retardation, grew, the clear disparity between international norms and U.S. practice made references to international sources more appealing to anti–death penalty advocates. Finally, as domestic avenues to challenge the death penalty dwindled, death penalty activists were increasingly willing to try new strategies. Despite these efforts, the Supreme Court took little notice, failing to reference international sources except for statements that international standards were "not irrelevant" in footnotes in two cases considering whether the death penalty was an appropriate punishment for rape and felony murder.[54]

Two death penalty cases in the late 1980s foreshadowed the current controversy within the Supreme Court over the use of international sources. In the 1988 case *Thompson v. Oklahoma*, which involved the juvenile death penalty for defendants fifteen years old or younger, Justice Stevens moved references to international norms out of a footnote, citing countries that abolished the juvenile death penalty in the text of the plurality opinion finding the execution of fifteen-year-olds unconstitutional.[55] In a footnote in his dissent, Justice Scalia characterized the "plurality's reliance upon Amnesty International's account of what it pronounces to be civilized standards of decency in other countries . . . totally inappropriate as a means of establishing the fundamental beliefs of this Nation."[56]

One year later, Justice Scalia, now in the majority, authored a decision upholding the juvenile death penalty for defendants sixteen and older. His decision emphasized that "it is American conceptions of decency that are dispositive."[57] These views were echoed in Justice Scalia's majority decision in a 1997 federalism case in which he criticized Justice Breyer's consideration of the European system, stating, "We think such a comparative analysis inappropriate to the task of interpreting a constitution."[58]

Justice Scalia's decision in *Thompson* appeared to quell the Court's reliance on international human rights standards, and lower courts followed.[59] Although international sources appeared out of favor, international law groups such as the IHRLG and Human Rights Advocates, law school human rights clinics, and international law scholars continued to file international law briefs and even expanded the subject matter beyond the death penalty to include discrimination and women's rights issues in the 1980s through 2002.[60] "Human rights" amicus briefs also continued to be filed in cases involving the rights of immigrants in immigration proceedings.[61]

Changing Judicial Attitudes

Between 2002 and 2004, legal activists' efforts to use international sources finally began to bear fruit. As discussed above, the attitude of Supreme Court justices appeared to shift, with international sources being cited in *Roper* and *Lawrence* in addition to two other death penalty cases and a case involving affirmative action.[62] In 2004, the Supreme Court also considered and rejected a challenge to cases under the Alien Tort Statute, which allows foreign nationals to sue for violation of human rights law in U.S. courts. In doing so, it affirmed that international law is part of U.S. law and in certain circumstances can be applied by U.S. courts. Finally, as cases challenging the U.S. actions in response to terrorism post-9/11, especially the treatment of detainees at Guantánamo Bay, have made their way up to the Supreme Court, the Court has begun to deal with issues of human rights and humanitarian law on a more regular basis.

Appeals to International Human Rights Forums

At the same time that U.S. courts are citing international sources with greater frequency, there is a growing engagement of U.S. lawyers in international human rights forums such as the United Nations and the Organization of American States (OAS) human rights system. The next two sections discuss the evolution of U.S. advocacy in these forums from the 1970s to the present.

U.S. Cases in the Inter-American Human Rights System

The filing of cases involving the U.S. with the Inter-American Commission on Human Rights, the only OAS body empowered to hear human rights claims from the United States, is not new. However, recent years have marked significant increases in both the number and the types of U.S. cases brought before the commission. In an article looking at U.S. cases before the commission, law professor Rick Wilson found only seven decisions in contentious cases concerning the United States in the 1970s and 1980s. Most of the cases had an international aspect to them, such as the treatment of aliens in the United States.[63] In 2006, seventy-five new U.S. cases were filed with the commission involving a wide array of domestic issues.

The increase in U.S. cases before the commission started with death penalty cases in the 1980s.[64] According to Wilson, these cases resulted from a conscious strategy choice on the part of death penalty lawyers at the NAACP Legal Defense Fund (LDF), who were looking for "new directions."[65] By the 1990s, death penalty cases constituted the majority of the commission's U.S. cases, but other types of domestic cases slowly began to appear on the commission's docket. Many of these cases reflected lawyers' frustration with the limitations of domestic law and the hope that a favorable decision from the commission would increase political pressure for change. For instance, in the 1990s, the Indian Law Resource Center brought a case challenging the seizure of tribal lands after U.S. courts had rejected their claims. Other cases filed in the 1990s argued that 1996 welfare reforms violated economic and social rights and that the lack of congressional representation for D.C. residents violated rights to equality and political participation.

Favorable rulings and publicity around several of these cases as well as a 2002 case challenging U.S. detention policies on Guantánamo Bay have increased the commission's profile among U.S. lawyers, expanding both the number and diversity of cases filed. Current cases involve a wide range of issues, including domestic violence, juvenile justice, environmental justice, and labor and worker rights issues.

U.S. Issues in UN Forums

A lack of interest in international forums among domestic lawyers and a dearth of UN forums in which to address country-specific issues combined to result in little UN advocacy in the 1970s and 1980s. In the 1970s, several American Indian tribes tried to utilize procedures that allowed the UN Human Rights Commission to examine patterns of human rights violations,[66] but the complaint failed to lead to concrete results. Other UN efforts during this period included the work of the National Conference of Black Lawyers (NCBL), which raised the issue of U.S. racism in UN forums addressing apartheid and decolonization in the 1970s,[67] and Human Rights Advocates, which included United States practices in its work before the UN Human Rights Sub-Commission on migrant workers rights in the 1980s and the juvenile death penalty in the late 1990s.[68]

Additional avenues for advocacy opened up in the late 1990s when the United States ratified three major UN human rights treaties: the ICCPR, the Torture Convention, and the Race Convention. Although RUDs preclude direct enforcement through a private right of action in U.S. courts, each treaty requires that ratifying countries participate in periodic reviews conducted by a committee of UN experts. The committees actively encourage input from civil society, creating an opportunity to expose U.S. human rights violations and engage in advocacy around treaty compliance.

In the 1990s, the ACLU collaborated with Human Rights Watch on a joint submission to the UN for the U.S.'s first review under the ICCPR in 1995.[69] Several other domestic groups contributed to a separate report. However, at the time, neither the ACLU nor the other domestic groups had prior experience submitting material to a UN treaty body or in advocacy before the United Nations. Once the review was over, little was done with the shadow reports or the "concluding observations and recommendations" issued by the UN experts.[70]

The United States would not file its next report on ICCPR compliance (which triggers the review process) until October 2005. By then, both the number and the sophistication of U.S. groups involved in the process had greatly increased. In 2006, over 140 civil society groups participated in the ICCPR review and approximately 65 of them attended the formal review in Geneva. Participants varied from international NGOs to national civil rights and liberties groups to local activists focusing on issues specific to their communities. According to UN officials, the number of participants, the quality of the intervention, and the level of coordination were unprecedented. Activists who traveled to participate in the reviews actively engaged the media, and the proceedings garnered good press coverage. Following the review, U.S. lawyers have incorporated the committees' concluding recommendations into legal briefs, op-eds, education, and training work.

Changing Domestic Legal Attitudes and the Role of Domestic International Human Rights Lawyers

As discussed above, during the 1970s, 1980s, and 1990s, a small group of U.S. activists were engaged in UN and inter-American human rights forums. However, involvement drastically increased in the twenty-first century just as arguments raising human rights law and international standards in U.S. courts started to gain some traction. The change in arguments in U.S. courts can be partly explained by indications of increased receptiveness from courts, especially the Supreme Court. Steve Shapiro, ACLU legal director, comments that in *Roper v. Simmons* international and comparative law arguments "struck a chord with the Supreme Court." Lawyers "want to make arguments the Court pays attention to and it became clear that they were paying attention."[71] Lawyers' increased engagement in international human rights forums can be partly explained as a reaction to the limitations on domestic court strategies resulting from the growing conservatism of federal courts, the changes in the advocacy environment post-9/11, and the increasing globalization of U.S. society. These factors are discussed later in this chapter.

However, characterizing the shift in advocacy strategies solely as a response to external factors ignores the impact of the growing involvement of U.S. lawyers in international human rights work. The next two sections discuss the experiences of domestic lawyers with international human rights, the crossover of human rights standards and forums into domestic work, and the conscious efforts of individual and organizational trailblazers to engage their colleagues in a larger effort to "bring human rights home."

U.S. Lawyers and International Human Rights Work

The involvement of domestic lawyers in international human rights work has played an important role in bridging the gap between human rights and civil rights. In the 1970s through the 1980s, a large number of U.S. civil rights lawyers became involved in international human rights work and cases challenging U.S. foreign policy abroad. For some, this work simply reflected a personal commitment to human rights with no immediate connection to their domestic work. For others, particularly in the black activist community, there was a greater awareness of the interconnection between struggles at home and abroad.

African Liberation and Antiapartheid Struggles

In the 1960s, Martin Luther King and Malcolm X often articulated domestic racial justice issues in human rights language that included a demand for economic and social rights. Malcolm X in particular advocated internationalizing the struggle for equality and utilizing UN and international forums. However, these calls went largely unheeded in the 1970s as "no genuine and concerted mobilization around a human rights agenda and strategy" emerged among black activists.[72] It is important to note, however, that a small but significant group continued to link the fight for international human rights and racial struggles in the United States. According to human rights and civil rights lawyer Gay McDougall, this group "identified with the politics of the African liberation struggle" and "thought we could learn something there that would be of relevance here." Included in this group was the NCBL, which promoted a U.S. social justice platform that included economic and social rights and actively linked UN antiapartheid and decolonization work to racial justice issues in the United States.[73]

Irrespective of whether they recognized a link between domestic and international issues, according to McDougall, when "the steam started to roll out of the civil rights movement . . . a lot of black Americans who were in the movement started to look at the emerging struggles in Africa and turned towards Africa."[74] For instance, in the late 1960s, personal connections between an attorney at the Lawyers Committee for Civil Rights Under Law and a South African lawyer led to the founding of the Southern Africa Project at the Lawyers Committee. The project involved domestic lawyers in supporting the defense of political prisoners and brought cases in U.S. courts challenging economic ties to South Africa. During the transition from apartheid, U.S. lawyers served as experts on civil rights issues, monitored elections, and assisted in the drafting and negotiation of the South African and Namibian Constitutions.

Antiapartheid advocacy played an important role in engaging domestic civil rights lawyers in international human rights work and issues. Gay McDougall, who started with the NCBL as a "civil rights lawyer" in the early 1970s, became director of the Lawyers Committee's Southern Africa Project in 1980. McDougall continued as a prominent activist on Southern African issues through the early 1990s and became an international human rights expert, holding many important positions at the UN.

Struggles in Latin America

Other domestic civil rights lawyers worked on international issues involving Vietnam and later Central America. The Center for Constitutional Rights (CCR) was founded in 1966 to defend civil rights activists in the South, but its docket quickly expanded to include both domestic civil rights cases and cases in U.S. courts challenging rights abuses abroad. Starting in the 1970s, CCR became involved in cases challenging U.S. foreign policy in Vietnam and later in Central and South America. These cases typically involved legal challenges to U.S. foreign policy or the defense of individuals who dissented from, or challenged, such policies.

In addition to constitutional claims, many of these cases included international law and human rights arguments. CCR's commitment to using international law arguments in these cases was heavily influenced by Peter Weiss, an attorney who began working with CCR in the 1970s and was deeply committed to international law and the Universal Declaration of Human Rights as the "ultimate setter of standards for the whole world." Weiss's family left Austria during the Holocaust, and law professor and civil rights lawyer Rhonda Copelon speculates that this experience had a powerful impact on Weiss's early orientation toward human rights.[75]

In the 1970s and 1980s, CCR attorneys and other civil rights lawyers became involved in Latin American human rights issues. CCR brought several cases that questioned U.S. involvement in human rights abuses in Central America. Copelon, who worked at CCR at the time, describes the cases as "solidarity cases" in which "we were doing something . . . to reveal and draw attention to and try to stop U.S. law-breaking under domestic and international law."[76] CCR attorneys and prominent civil rights lawyers, such as Paul Hoffman, who served as the legal director of the ACLU of Southern California and an Amnesty International USA board member in the 1980s, also represented U.S. religious organizations that granted "sanctuary" to Central American refugees who fled political repression in Guatemala and El Salvador.

Other U.S. lawyers became directly involved in challenging human rights abuses in Latin America. Rick Wilson began his career as a domestic criminal defense lawyer. Research on Nicaragua under the Sandinista government in the mid-1980s led him in 1990 to start a human rights clinic at American University Law School, where he became an expert in human rights litigation in the inter-American human rights system. In 1991, Wilson was approached by Amnesty International USA to bring a U.S. death penalty case before the Inter-American Commission for Human Rights.[77] Since then, Wilson has been actively involved in U.S. death penalty advocacy both before the IACHR and the U.S. Supreme Court.

Alien Tort Statute

In 1980, another important link was made between domestic litigators and international human rights work. That year, CCR won a significant victory in the Second Circuit in the case *Filartiga v. Pena-Irala*. *Filartiga* was brought on behalf of the family of a Paraguayan citizen who was tortured to death by a Paraguayan police officer under the Alien Tort Statute (ATS), a federal statute which dates back to 1789. In *Filartiga*, CCR established that non–U.S. citizens could use the statute to sue for damages for violations of international human rights law in U.S. federal courts. Since then, a significant number of cases have been brought under the statute concerning human rights abuses committed abroad, including claims against U.S. corporations that are complicit in human rights abuses occurring outside the United States.

In the 1980s and 1990s, a few ATS cases were filed against U.S. local and federal officials, but most concerned actions that occurred outside the United States.[78] Additional cases against U.S. officials for acts occurring both within and outside the United States have been filed post-9/11, but procedural hurdles have made it difficult for claimants to prevail in such cases. Nevertheless, ATS cases concerning human rights abuses abroad have required federal judges to apply (and thus learn about) international human rights law. The cases have played an important role in educating U.S. lawyers and judges about international human rights law and building case law on which they can rely.

Rhonda Copelon credits her work on ATS cases at CCR with making her aware of international human rights standards and precedents to incorporate into her domestic work. Although she initially worked on both international human rights cases and civil rights cases without connecting the two, in the 1980s as the Supreme Court issued decisions rejecting government obligations to assist in the exercise of fundamental rights or prevent private acts of violence, it occurred to her that international human rights law might offer a helpful alternative vision.[79] Since the 1980s she has been using international human rights law on domestic women's rights and social and economic rights issues.

Struggles for Immigrants' Rights

Another area in which U.S. lawyers historically were involved in human rights issues involves the treatment of immigrants and noncitizens. These matters typically involve domestic cases concerning individuals in the United States. In the immigration context, human rights law generally comes into play in interpreting U.S. international obligations to protect refugees and in assessing conditions in other countries to determine whether an immigrant is entitled to political asylum or withholding of deportation. These cases have engaged U.S. lawyers in exposing and identifying rights violations in other countries as well as developing U.S. law on the meaning of torture.

In the 1990s, U.S. lawyers began to use human rights law to challenge U.S. immigration policy. In 1993, a case argued that U.S. policy of interdicting and returning Haitian refugees at sea violated human rights treaties protecting refugees. Cases in 2001 and 2003 argued that certain U.S. immigration detention practices violated human rights standards prohibiting arbitrary detention.[80] Because of limited protections under U.S. law available to immigrants, U.S. lawyers also began to bring claims for human rights violations under the ATS and to international forums. In 1997, an ATS case challenged conditions and treatment in an immigration detention center in Elizabeth, New Jersey.[81] More recently, ATS cases have been brought on behalf of immigrant domestic workers who have been forced to work under slavelike conditions. Lawyers have also actively engaged the inter-American human rights system in addressing discrimination against immigrant workers.

Conscious Efforts to Bridge Civil Rights and Human Rights

By the 1990s many "domestic international human rights" lawyers began integrating human rights into their work in the United States. In addition to developing and adapting human rights strategies for the domestic context, these lawyers played a crucial role in training and engaging their peers. Their efforts were aided by an increased investment in and emphasis on international law in U.S. law schools, including the development of human rights clinics, a growing human rights consciousness in the United States, and a new generation of public interest lawyers committed to "bringing human rights home."

Organizational Change: The ACLU

Even as individual lawyers became intrigued by the possibilities of incorporating human rights strategies within their domestic work, they often faced the skepticism of their peers and internal institutional battles. By the late 1990s, several civil rights and civil liberties organizations had begun to incorporate human rights into their domestic work, including NOW Legal Defense Fund under legal director Martha F. Davis and the National Law Center for Homelessness and Poverty.[82]

Perhaps the most striking change occurred at the ACLU. With a network of affiliates in all fifty states, the ACLU is the nation's oldest, largest, and most well-known civil liberties organization. Historically, the ACLU has focused on domestic civil rights and civil liberties issues, with very limited connections to international human rights work. In 2003, the ACLU announced its commitment to human rights by hosting a three-day human rights conference in Atlanta. In 2004, the ACLU created a Human Rights Working Group at its national offices.[83] The working group quickly solidified its position within the organization, building support from ACLU board members and actively engaging its affiliates to become a full program of the ACLU national office. Although the changes at the ACLU appeared sudden, they emerged out of decades of work by internal human rights supporters such as Paul Hoffman, as well as changing attitudes among public interest lawyers about human rights.

The ACLU experience is instructive because many of the concerns about incorporating human rights initially expressed by ACLU lawyers reflected the attitudes of the larger civil rights and civil liberties communities. When Paul Hoffman began to push for integration of human rights standards into domestic legal work at the ACLU in the mid-1980s, he was a voice in the wilderness.[84] An ACLU policy dating back to 1973 permitted general references to international law in ACLU cases, but most lawyers were unconvinced that international human rights standards actually improved upon domestic law or could lead to different results in the cases they were litigating. Steve Shapiro recalls the debates, stating that at the time "I was skeptical as a matter of tactics. When you are a litigator with 50 pages in a brief, why devote 10 pages to an argument that won't succeed?" Because the United States had ratified such a limited number of treaties and international sources were not legally binding on the United States, lawyers had difficulty seeing their value.[85] A wholesale embrace of human rights also posed problems in cases where international human rights law was inconsistent with ACLU policy, such as international prohibitions on racial hate speech, and in areas such as social and economic rights, which fell outside the ACLU's historic mission.[86]

Undeterred, Hoffman continued to push a human rights agenda. In 1991, he became the National Coordinator of the ACLU's International Human Rights Task Force and created the ACLU International Civil Liberties Report. The report summarized developments in human rights law and became an important resource for domestic public interest lawyers. From the mid-1980s through the 1990s, Hoffman faithfully organized panels and spoke about the integration of human rights into the ACLU's work at its national biannual conferences.[87]

In the 1990s, Hoffman noted increased support for human rights. During the presidencies of Ronald Reagan and George H. W. Bush, ACLU members had become more knowledgeable about human rights, and many were also members of Amnesty International. According to Hoffman, there was a sense that there were "opportunities that weren't being taken advantage of."[88] Also instrumental in the changes at the ACLU were the attitudes of lawyers like Ann Beeson, who joined the ACLU in 1995 after a fellowship at Human Rights Watch and pushed for greater integration of human rights strategies at the ACLU's national office.

In 2001, just four days before the terrorist attacks of September 11, Anthony Romero, the former director of Human Rights and International Cooperation at the Ford Foundation, became the ACLU executive director, and Hoffman and Beeson had the champion they needed. Romero appointed Beeson the head of a new Human Rights Working Group, and she set out to hire a staff to bring human rights to the ACLU. Although the ACLU has yet to endorse economic and social rights and continues to oppose restrictions on hate speech, it has become a leader in domestic human rights work concerning civil and political rights. Since 2003, the ACLU has devoted significant resources and institutional support to the integration of human rights strategies into the work of its national office and local affiliates and has become an important provider of human rights training to the broader domestic legal community.

While the transformation of the ACLU provides an important insight into changing attitudes at civil rights and civil liberties organizations, institutional change at other organizations has been slower. In particular, some identity-based civil rights organizations have been more circumspect about embracing and integrating human rights strategies than organizations like the ACLU or CCR. This reticence has been linked to a deeper internalization of the post–Cold War distinction between civil rights and human rights[89] and concerns that the universality of human rights may "suggest a retreat from a deep engagement with the persistent and differential experience of discrimination."[90] Irrespective of ideological differences, the ability of civil rights and civil liberties groups to embrace new strategies not only requires the commitment of its leadership and the interest of its staff, but also depends on available resources. Post-9/11, ACLU membership expanded from 200,000 to 600,000 members with a corresponding growth of financial resources.[91] In contrast, many civil rights organizations struggle financially and are unable to devote significant resources to developing new strategies.[92]

Engaging and Training Domestic Human Rights Lawyers

Since the mid-1990s, there has been a steady growth of projects and programs to encourage and train domestic lawyers about human rights. These initiatives were both sought out by domestic lawyers looking for new strategies and encouraged by pioneers of domestic human rights work. For instance, NAACP LDF lawyers interested in human rights as a new strategy pushed to include presentations at annual death penalty litigators meetings at Airlie House, Virginia, starting in the mid-1990s. Lawyers who had already begun to use human rights in their own work began to seek out opportunities to speak about the strategies to their peers at conferences and other gatherings.[93]

In addition to these ad hoc trainings, several projects were created to engage, train, and support domestic lawyers in a more sustained and deliberate manner. One of the first projects was started by Gay McDougall at Global Rights (formerly the International Human Rights Law Group). When McDougall became the executive director of Global Rights in 1994, she changed its mission to focus on developing partnerships with local activists and building their capacity to use international human rights mechanisms. In an unusual move for an international human rights organization, Global Rights included U.S. activists in its work, creating a U.S. program in 1998.[94] In creating the program, McDougall was able to draw on her deep connections to both the international human rights and domestic civil rights communities, and she quickly formed a program advisory committee which included the heads of many of the major civil rights organizations.[95]

During the three-year period leading up to the UN World Conference on Racism in Durban (WCAR) in 2001, Global Rights worked closely with coalitions of civil rights groups such as the Leadership Conference for Human Rights and the Lawyers Committee for Civil Rights Under Law and also reached out to smaller grassroots groups. Through these efforts, U.S. civil rights lawyers became involved in setting the conference's agenda and participated in the negotiation of the conference outcome document, ensuring that it would speak to racial justice issues in the United States. Global Rights also did outreach and coordination around the United States' first review for compliance with the Race Convention. As a member of the UN expert committee that reviewed compliance with the Race Convention, McDougall organized a day-long meeting at which U.S. civil rights leaders briefed the committee about particular issues of concern.[96]

By the late 1990s, other human rights activists from diverse backgrounds began discussing building a domestic human rights movement. Domestic lawyers played an important role in these discussions, but the potential movement was much broader, seeking to bring together activist work across different issue areas and methodologies, under a unifying human rights framework. These efforts, which led to the founding of the U.S. Human Rights Network (USHRN) in 2003, are beyond the scope of this chapter. However, the USHRN, and conferences that led to its founding at Mill Valley, California, in July 1999 and Howard Law School in July 2002, provided important opportunities to bring lawyers and grassroots human rights activists together to develop common strategies.

Recognizing the need for domestic lawyers to discuss and develop human rights strategies across issues, Catherine Powell, a former lawyer with the NAACP LDF, founded the Human Rights Institute at Columbia Law School in 1998 and created the Bringing Human Rights Home Project (BHRH) soon thereafter.[97] Since 2001, the program has convened a network that brings together domestic lawyers working on civil rights and social justice issues with international human rights lawyers and law school human rights programs. Over time the network has emerged as a place for attorneys to monitor each others' cases, to get and give feedback and guidance, and to coordinate and develop joint projects. In 2006, BHRH, Global Rights and the USHRN collaborated on outreach, coordination and technical support for U.S. groups involved in the UN review of U.S. compliance with the ICCPR and Torture Convention.

BHRH, Global Rights, the USHRN, and the ACLU have also been actively involved in providing in-depth human rights training. Significant legal human rights trainings have also been provided by organizations specializing in particular issues and law school human rights programs.[98] And, perhaps a more significant indication of the mainstreaming of human rights approaches into domestic legal advocacy, international human rights panels have been included in countless legal conferences discussing issues ranging from criminal defense work and racial justice work to health law.

Human Rights Clinics

Human Rights Clinics have also emerged as a major force in training and developing domestic human rights lawyers. In 2003, law professor Deena Hurwitz wrote, "Ten years ago, only three law schools offered clinical programs in human rights. Today, there are about a dozen human rights clinics and over twenty human rights centers in law schools across the country."[99] Four years later in 2007, a list of over forty human rights clinics, existing or in formation, was compiled following a conference for human rights clinical faculty at Georgetown Law School. The new lawyers coming out of these programs are helping to change the culture of domestic public interest organizations and educating their supervisors, who as law school graduates of ten or fifteen years ago, had little training in human rights or international law.

Not only are human rights clinics training students in human rights law, unlike international human rights NGOs, which have only recently included U.S. work as part of their missions, many human rights clinics actively engage in U.S. cases and have played a significant role in developing domestic human rights strategies. When law professor Harold Koh and CCR attorney Michael Ratner founded the Lowenstein International Human Rights Clinic at Yale Law School in 1989, their initial focus was on suing foreign government officials for human rights abuses committed abroad. In 1992, the clinic became involved in a case challenging the U.S. government's repatriation of Haitian refugees.[100] The highly publicized case marked a shift in the clinic's work to include cases involving the United States. Since then the Yale clinic has emerged as a major player in developing domestic human rights legal strategies, authoring several important human rights amicus briefs to the Supreme Court.

Other pioneering clinics founded in the early 1990s by Rick Wilson at American University, Washington College of Law, and Rhonda Copelon at CUNY Law School also include U.S. cases in their docket.[101] While the AU clinic has focused on the death penalty and cases involving civil and political rights, the CUNY clinic has brought ATS cases and filed amicus briefs concerning domestic violence, abuse of immigrant domestic workers, and social and economic rights. Newer human rights clinics continue to be involved in domestic cases, including Columbia's Human Rights Clinic, which has devoted a significant part of its docket to domestic human rights work since its founding in 1998.

Changing Attitudes About Advocacy

As discussed in the preceding sections of this chapter, several factors have contributed to the current interest in human rights strategy among progressive lawyers. Lawyers and institutions committed to the development of domestic human rights strategies have emerged as key bridges, promoting and supporting domestic human rights work. Their efforts have been aided by globalization, changes in judicial attitudes toward international sources, and a new emphasis on international law in law schools. However, interest in human rights strategies has also resulted from a changed advocacy environment. As progressive lawyers face increasingly conservative courts, the wisdom of relying on traditional litigation strategies is being challenged. As U.S. lawyers look for new tactics, human rights strategies, which have been significantly developed and strengthened since the 1940s, have become much more appealing.

The Changing Advocacy Environment in the United States

As discussed above, when U.S. lawyers began to reengage with human rights law, their strategies had to shift to take into account the RUDs attached to human rights treaties, which precluded direct enforcement of the treaties in U.S. courts. In part, their willingness to reconsider human rights resulted from the narrowing of other options. In the 1980s and 1990s, the Rehnquist Court and lower federal courts were rolling back civil rights protections as Congress was cutting legal aid funding and limiting access to the courts for prisoners, immigrants, and other vulnerable groups. Changes in the composition of the federal judiciary made lawyers more open to consider nonlegal strategies. Tanya Coke, a civil rights lawyer, describes the 1990s as a difficult time. "Lots of doors were being closed as courts became more conservative. It has become much more difficult to find a case to litigate that you can win and that will have a large impact. This is driving an interest in other norms, standards and venues."[102] Even as there was a growing consensus that traditional litigation strategies were being undermined by political changes, others questioned the inherent limitations of the litigation model. Chandra Bhatnagar, a staff attorney with the ACLU's Human Rights Program, notes that historically judgments in civil rights cases have been difficult to enforce and that legal doctrines, including governmental immunities and courts' refusal to address issues that involve political questions or state secrets, often preclude U.S. courts from reaching the merits of whether a human rights violation has occurred.

The sense that there was a need to develop new strategies intensified post-9/11. The Bush administration's arguments that torture abroad and prolonged arbitrary detention were justified (or at least not illegal) under U.S. law clearly exposed the fact that the U.S. legal system might prove insufficient to protect rights that many had taken for granted. As Wendy Patten writes post-9/11, "international human rights law became a key bulwark against the erosion of fundamental rights."[103] Responses to the Bush administration's "anti-terrorism" policies was an important "teaching moment" for U.S. lawyers about human rights and humanitarian law. After 9/11, the Center for Constitutional Rights launched a program to enlist private attorneys to represent Guantánamo Bay detainees and has trained and coordinated over five hundred pro bono attorneys.

Domestically, the immigrant community was perhaps hardest hit by the Bush administration's post-9/11 antiterrorism measures. The failure of U.S. courts to protect the rights of noncitizens led Karen Narasaki, executive director of the Asian American Justice Center, to conclude that human rights standards provided "a better place to try to nail down rights for immigrant communities."[104]

Post-9/11, a second area in which U.S. legal protections have fallen short is the United States' treatment of noncitizens abroad, including suspected terrorists and "enemy combatants." As U.S. behavior increasingly became a target for international criticism, the American public gained greater exposure to international human rights and humanitarian law and the international forums that sought to uphold them. Use of human rights standards also became important to invoke international pressure on the United States. Steve Shapiro notes that post-9/11, bilateral diplomatic pressure has been a particularly effective tool in gaining the release of individual Guantánamo Bay detainees, but if U.S. lawyers hope to engage international support, they need to adopt a human rights vocabulary. "The European public doesn't respond to constitutional arguments. They respond to human rights arguments."[105]

And, it is not just Europeans who respond to human rights. Many domestic social justice activists are interested in human rights language because of its resonance with growing segments of the U.S. population. The turn to human rights is not simply a reflection that domestic courts aren't working says Narasaki. "Human rights" has more resonance for "the younger generation," who are used to thinking about problems in a global way, and the "immigrant generation," who think of fundamental rights in terms of human rights and not civil rights.[106]

The Development of International Human Rights Strategies and Forums

As legal, historical, societal, and strategic changes encourage U.S. lawyers to reconsider human rights strategies, "human rights in the twenty-first century" looks quite different from the 1940s.[107] In the intervening fifty-plus years since the UN Human Rights Commission asserted that it did not have the power to take action on the NAACP petition, much has happened on the human rights front. The UN and Organization of American States have taken great strides to build human rights institutions to enforce human rights norms. In addition to adopting procedures for examining gross or consistent patterns of human rights violations in the late 1960s and early 1970s, the UN Human Rights Commission created new mechanisms, working groups and experts (special rapporteurs) to investigate and report on human rights violations.[108] International and regional human rights forums, such as the UN treaty bodies and the Inter-American Court and Commission, were developed and strengthened. This process continued with the establishment of the UN High Commissioner for Human Rights and the creation of new procedures for civil society involvement in the 1990s.[109]

The 1970s marked the rise of a new player in the global fight for human rights with the development of international human rights nongovernmental organizations or "NGOs."[110] Designed to "globalize" struggles against human rights abuses, NGOs like Amnesty International and Human Rights Watch used public pressure and scrutiny to combat rights abuses. Often working in countries that may not have ratified human rights treaties or in which the judiciary failed to enforce fundamental rights, these international NGOs eschewed local judicial remedies. Instead, they developed a "shame and blame" strategy that was as much moral and political as legal. Rather than focusing on domestic litigation, international NGOs produced detailed "human rights reports" documenting and exposing human rights abuses. The reports used human rights standards, drawn from treaties and other international documents, to articulate a standard against which to measure a country's treatment of its citizens and residents, relying on public opinion and political pressure for change. As credible outside experts, these organizations played an important role in exposing and substantiating abuses. International human rights NGOs also became regular and repeat players in advocacy before the developing international and regional human rights bodies.

Given the different context in which they were operating, human rights lawyers and activists working for international human rights NGOs necessarily developed a different advocacy model from the domestic civil rights lawyer. Deena Hurwitz writes, "Relatively little of what human rights lawyers actually do looks like traditional legal practice. . . . [H]uman rights law . . . exists as a set of standards by which to measure state practices and seek to 'enforce' norms or hold actors accountable—often by means that are as much political as legal."[111] Even when human rights lawyers "litigate" cases or matters before international bodies, the decisions are often unenforceable or difficult to enforce in domestic courts and require the additional components of political pressure or mobilization to ensure compliance.

After international and regional human rights forums were strengthened and advocacy strategies were developed by NGOs and "human rights" lawyers in the 1970s, a further shift took place which made human rights standards and forums more relevant to U.S. issues. In the 1970s, human rights violations related to apartheid or the abuses of dictatorships—torture, political assignations, summary execution, and disappearances—took center stage for the international human rights community. Many of these issues were of great concern to people living in the United States, but the public did not perceive them to be related to domestic issues. According to Rhonda Copelon, with the exception of the European Court of Human Rights, it was largely in the 1990s, after the fall of many dictatorships and the end of the Cold War, that international human rights mechanisms were pressed to tackle "the seriousness of everyday violations apart from states of exception." The subsequent reinvigoration of the UN mechanisms protecting women's rights and economic and social rights and a reorientation of the IACHR to consider "what human rights mean for a democratic society" made human rights a more compelling strategy for U.S. social justice lawyers.[112]

A Second Look at Human Rights

At the beginning of the twenty-first century, U.S. civil rights lawyers became frustrated with the limitations of the U.S. legal system and took a second look at human rights standards and advocacy strategies. As lawyers began to look beyond domestic legal avenues, it became clear that human rights strategies could play an important role in advocacy work. Tanya Coke, who has worked both as a civil rights lawyer and funder of social justice work, emphasizes the significance of human rights as "an integrated strategy." She notes, "American rights advocates tend to work in one way or another, but single note strategies are less effective. Litigation and even legislation don't give you a long term win unless people on the ground are invested in the reform and will police and protect it."[113]

Of course, a more holistic approach to advocacy that looks beyond litigation is not limited to human rights work. "Human rights did not invent integrated advocacy, but the lawyers who understand integrated strategies are more open to human rights," says Ann Beeson. During her tenure as director of the ACLU Human Rights Program, she noted that within the organization some lawyers had a very narrow litigation focus and others naturally had a "more of a campaign style strategy. Many ACLU lawyers were already doing organizing and legislative work. The natural allies for human rights weren't necessarily those with knowledge about human rights, but those who were open to new and innovative strategies."[114]

Although many progressive U.S. lawyers have historically engaged in community education, media outreach, fact-finding, and reporting in addition to litigation, such nonlitigation work is integral to human rights advocacy precisely because human rights activists cannot rely on judicial enforcement. Coke adds that human rights strategies stress the participation of those who are most affected in a way that other advocacy work has not.[115] Another way that human rights strategies go beyond other integrated strategies is the international nature of the enterprise. Rick Wilson comments that it is not just that lawyers are looking beyond litigation strategies, but also that they "are seeing their mission in more global terms, and using broader international strategies that include an international and domestic component, as well as litigation and non-litigation aspects."[116]

Lawyers using integrated human rights strategies are just beginning to understand their potential. Such strategies often are complex and indirect, involving interaction between different legal systems and forums and transnational advocacy. Lawyers may simultaneously work in different forums or move between forums. Chandra Bhatnagar describes working with local activists in Texas concerned about a sheriff who decided to implement immigration laws by racial profiling and "pulling over people of color asking for immigration papers." In addition to local advocacy efforts that included protests and meetings with local officials, the ACLU brought concerns to the UN committee reviewing U.S. compliance with the ICCPR. When committee members began questioning U.S. officials about the situation, the headline in the local paper declared that the sheriff was being denounced at the United Nations for human rights abuse. Statements from the UN proceedings were read into the record during a state assembly meeting. The resulting pressure from state legislators and the mayor forced the sheriff to suspend the program. Bhatnagar describes the interaction between the international and local forums as an "echo chamber" in which the efforts in one forum are reflected and magnified in the other ultimately building pressure for change.[117]

Similarly, Maria Foscarinis, executive director of the National Law Center on Homelessness and Poverty, describes herself as a "do it yourself lawyer" who works on the international level to develop and expand international human rights standards and then incorporates the standards in her domestic advocacy. Rhonda Copelon describes women's rights activists as trying to "work everywhere to establish rights internationally and then bring them home."[118]

Unlike traditional litigation strategies, which take for granted that a victory or settlement will lead to an enforceable judgment, lawyers cannot assume that successful advocacy in international forums will result in a change in domestic law, policy, or conditions. Instead, they must learn to effectively leverage such victories not only in U.S. courts, but also in the media, as part of legislative strategy, as a way to exert international or diplomatic pressure or as part of an organizing or educational campaign. Successful political mobilization requires that U.S. lawyers work in coalition with organizers, activists, and those most affected. To be effective the "do it yourself lawyer" cannot be a "do it on your own lawyer." The ability of domestic lawyers to work with communities will be a major factor in the success of domestic human rights strategies.

According to Steve Shapiro, the indirect nature of integrated human rights strategies often make their effects hard to quantify. "We are still trying to learn how to use international forums effectively. We are at a preliminary stage and still struggling about how you make any of it matter. However, in another 20 years, civil rights law in the U.S. is going to be deeply engaged in international human rights issues, and it will not be possible to be a civil rights lawyer without knowing about international human rights."[119]

Notes

I am grateful to Martha Davis and Chandra Bhatnagar for their helpful comments and ideas and to Karen Lin for her skillful editing. Many thanks to the following people for sharing their experiences and perspectives: Ann Beeson, Chandra Bhatnagar, Tanya Coke, Rhonda Copelon, Connie de la Vega, Paul Hoffman, Gay McDougall, Karen Narasaki, Steve Shapiro, Peter Weiss, and Rick Wilson.

1. *Roper v. Simmons*, 543 U.S. 551 (2005); *Lawrence v. Texas*, 539 U.S. 558 (2003).
2. Available online at www.law.harvard.edu/news/2006/10/06_curriculum. php.
3. Deena R. Hurwitz, "Lawyering for Justice and the Inevitability of International Human Rights Clinics," *Yale Law Journal of International Law* 28 (2003): 505–6. However, international and comparative law courses are still not required in most other law schools. Vicki C. Jackson, "Ambivalent Resistance and Comparative Constitutionalism: Opening Up the Conversation on 'Proportionality,' Rights and Federalism," *University of Pennsylvania Journal of Constitutional Law* 1 (1999): 583, 592.
4. Paul Gordon Lauren, "A Human Rights Lens on U.S. History: Human Rights at Home and Human Rights Abroad," Chapter 1 in the current volume.
5. Sarah Cleveland, "Our International Constitution," *Yale Law Journal* 31 (2006): 1, 12, 88.
6. Catherine Albisa, "Economic and Social Rights in the United States: Six Rights, One Promise," Chapter 6 in the current volume; Hope Lewis, "'New' Human Rights? U.S. Ambivalence Toward the International Economic and Social Rights Framework," Chapter 4 in the current volume; Cass Sunstein, *The Second Bill of Rights* (New York: Basic Books, 2004).
7. Sunstein argues that U.S. Supreme Court decisions were moving toward a greater recognition of such rights until Nixon's Supreme Court nominees turned back the march toward social and economic rights in a series of decisions in the 1970s. *The Second Bill of Rights*, pp. 162–71.
8. Carol Anderson, *Eyes off the Prize* (Cambridge: Cambridge University Press, 2003), p. 2.

9. For an in-depth discussion of the petition, see Carol Anderson, "A 'Hollow Mockery': African Americans, White Supremacy, and the Development of Human Rights in the United States," Chapter 3 in the current volume.

10. Anderson, *Eyes off the Prize*, p. 150. According to Anderson, part of the reason the NAACP abandoned the petition was to preserve its ability to influence the Truman administration on the drafting of the Universal Declaration and the documents that would eventually become the International Covenant on Civil and Political Rights and the International Covenant on Economic, Social, and Cultural Rights.

11. Ibid., pp. 179–80.

12. Ibid., pp. 186–87, 192.

13. Bert B. Lockwood, Jr., "The United Nations Charter and United States Civil Rights Litigation: 1946–1955," *Iowa Law Review* 69 (1984): 901, 918; Judith Resnik, "Law's Migration: American Exceptionalism, Silent Dialogues, and Federalism's Multiple Points of Entry," *Yale Law Journal* 115 (2006): 100, 136–45.

14. Lockwood, "The United Nations Charter," pp. 932–48.

15. Thomas Borstelman, *The Cold War and the Color Line* (Cambridge, Mass.: Harvard University Press, 2001), p. 57.

16. Brief of the U.S. government at p. 60, *Henderson v. United States*, 339 U.S. 816 (1950), cited in Lockwood, "The United Nations Charter," p. 941.

17. The justices expressed their views in two separate concurring decisions. *Oyama v. California*, 332 U.S. 633 (1948), Black, J. concurring at pp. 649–50, Murphy, J., concurring at p. 673. See Lockwood, "The United Nations Charter," pp. 919–21.

18. *Sei Fuji v. State*, 217 P.2d 481, 486–88 (Cal. Dist. Ct. App. 1950).

19. Natalie Hevener Kaufman, *Human Rights and the Senate: A History of Opposition* (Chapel Hill: University of North Carolina Press, 1990), pp. 16–18.

20. Lockwood, "The United Nations Charter," p. 927.

21. *Sei Fuji v. State*, 242 P.2d 617, 622 (Cal. 1952). Interestingly, the court noted that other provisions of the charter were self-executing. Ibid., p. 621.

22. For more detailed accounts of the history of the Bricker Amendment, see Anderson, *Eyes off the Prize*, pp. 218–30; Natalie Hevener Kaufman, *Human Rights and the Senate*, pp. 9–36; Louis Henkin, "U.S. Ratification of Human Rights Conventions: The Ghost of Senator Bricker," *American Journal of International Law* 89 (1995): 341; Resnik, "Law's Migration," pp. 145–51.

23. Anderson, *Eyes off the Prize*, pp. 180, 253.

24. Kaufman, *Human Rights and the Senate*, p. 18.

25. Anderson, *Eyes off the Prize*, p. 230.

26. Mary Dudziak, *Cold War Civil Rights* (Princeton, N.J.: Princeton University Press, 2000), p. 13.

27. Henkin, "U.S. Ratification," p. 349.

28. Dudziak, *Cold War Civil Rights*, p. 29.

29. Lockwood, "The United Nations Charter," pp. 930–31.

30. Both foreign law sources (statutes and cases from other countries) and international law can be used as comparative authority by U.S. courts. International law can also be used as a tool of statutory construction. The Supreme Court has held that courts should interpret U.S. law to avoid conflicts with international law whenever possible. *Murray v. Schooner Charming Betsy*, 6 U.S. (2 Cranch) 64 (1804).

31. *Lawrence v. Texas*, 539 U.S. 558, 572–73, 576–77.

32. Prior to *Roper* and *Lawrence*, international human rights and foreign law

were increasingly cited in footnotes, concurring decisions and dissenting opinions. *Atkins v. Virginia*, 536 U.S. 304, n. 21 (2002) (footnote in majority opinion noting that the execution of mentally retarded was "overwhelmingly disapproved" within the world community); *Grutter v. Bollinger*, 539 U.S. 306, 344 (2003) (Ginsburg, J., concurring) (concurrence decision citing the Race Convention and the Convention on the Elimination of All Forms of Discrimination Against Women for the proposition that affirmative action must end when its goals are achieved); *Knight v. Florida*, 528 U.S. 990 (1999) (Breyer, J. dissenting) (dissenting opinion opposing denial of review in death penalty case citing European Court of Human Rights, British Privy Council and foreign court decisions).

33. Resnik, "Law's Migration," pp. 109, 159.

34. Cleveland, "Our International Constitution," p. 6.

35. Interestingly, Sarah Cleveland notes that historically international law has been used to expand government authority and to restrict individual rights. Ibid., p. 9.

36. H.Res. 568, S.2323, S.2082, H.3799, 108th Congress.

37. Available online at www.cnn.com/2006/LAW/03/15/scotus.threat/.

38. Attacks on the use of international sources ignored that fact that Supreme Court use of such sources was not new. As Professor Sarah Cleveland testified before Congress "reliance on international and foreign sources is fully part of the American Constitutional heritage." House Judiciary Subcommittee on the Constitution, *H. Res. 97 and the Appropriate Role of Foreign Judgments in the Interpretation of American Law: Hearing Before the Subcommittee on the Constitution of the Committee on the Judiciary*, 109th Congress, 1st sess., July 19, 2005, pp. 38–41.

39. *Roper*, 543 U.S. at p. 578.

40. For a discussion of *Roper* and U.S. death penalty cases raising the ICCPR, see Sandra Babcock, "Human Rights Advocacy in United States Capital Cases," in Cynthia Soohoo, Catherine Albisa, and Martha F. Davis (eds.), *Bringing Human Rights Home*, vol. 3 (London: Praeger, 2008), pp. 91–120.

41. Available online at www.cc.org/content.cfm?id=142.

42. Ruth Bader Ginsburg and Deborah Jones Merritt, "Affirmative Action: An International Human Rights Dialogue," *Cardozo Law Review* 21 (1999): 253, 282.

43. William Rehnquist, "Constitutional Courts—Comparative Remarks" (1989), reprinted in Paul Kirchhof and Donald P. Kommers (eds.), *Germany and Its Basic Law: Past, Present and Future—A German-American Symposium* (Baden-Baden, Germany: Nomos, 1993), pp. 411, 412.

44. Michael Dorf, "The Hidden International Influence in the Supreme Court Decision Barring Executions of the Mentally Retarded," *Findlaw*, June 26, 2002, available online at writ.news.findlaw.com/dorf/20020626.html.

45. John A. Barrett, Jr., "International Legal Education in the United States: Being Educated for Domestic Practice While Living in a Global Society," *American University Journal of International Law & Policy* 12 (1997): 975, 991–93. Both Harvard Law School and the University of Michigan require that students take courses in transnational law. Columbia and NYU law schools offer electives on international and comparative law to its first-year students, and Washington College of Law at American University recently added a first-year elective course specifically on international law in U.S. courts.

46. Martha F. Davis, "International Human Rights and the United States Law: Predictions of a Courtwatcher," *Albany Law Review* 64 (2000): 417, 420.

47. Ibid., 427.

48. Ibid., 420.

49. Available online at www.eurunion.org/legislat/deathpenalty/deathpen home.htm#ActiononUSDeathRowCases.

50. These practices were struck down by the Supreme Court in *Roper v. Simmons*, 543 U.S. 551 (2005) and *Atkins v. Virginia*, 536 U.S. 304 (2002).

51. David Fontana, *Foreign Exchange*. Available online at www.tnr.com/doc. mhtml?i=w050228&s=fontana030305.

52. Justice Stephen Breyer, "The Supreme Court and the New International Law" (remarks at the American Society of International Law 97th Annual Meeting, April 4, 2003).

53. For a further discussion of briefs submitted by lawyers for the NAACP LDF in *Furman v. Georgia*, 408 U.S. 238 (1972), *Gregg v. Georgia*, 428 U.S. 153 (1976), *Coker v. Georgia*, 433 U.S. 584 (1977), and *Enmund v. Florida*, 458 U.S. 782 (1982) and defense counsel in *Thompson v. Oklahoma*, 487 U.S. 815 (1988) and *Stanford v. Kentucky*, 492 U.S. 361 (1989), see Babcock, "Human Rights Advocacy." Amnesty International filed briefs in *Gregg v. Georgia* and *Thompson v. Oklahoma*, and *Stanford v. Kentucky* and the IHRLG filed briefs in *McClesky v. Kemp*, 481 U.S. 279 (1987), *Thompson* and *Stanford*.

54. *Coker v. Georgia*, 433 U.S. 584, 596 n. 10 (1977); *Enmund v. Florida*, 458 U.S. 782, 796–97 n. 22 (1982).

55. *Thompson v. Oklahoma*, 487 U.S. 815, 830–31 (1988).

56. Ibid., p. 869 n. 4.

57. *Stanford v. Kentucky*, 492 U.S. 361, 370 n. 1 (1989), emphasis in original.

58. *Printz v. United States*, 521 U.S. 898, 921 n. 11 (1997).

59. In a survey of cases Supreme Court cases in which human rights briefs were filed from 1995 through 2000, Silla Brush found that human rights briefs were filed in eleven cases, and the Supreme Court only cited international and comparative law in two cases involving the treatment of immigrants and refugees. Silla Brush, "Globalized Advocacy in U.S. Courts" (senior thesis, Princeton University, 2004), p. 60.

60. The IHRLG filed an amicus brief in *Bob Jones University v. United States*, 461 U.S. 574 (1983) (challenging tax exempt status for private schools with racially discriminatory admission policies). Human Rights Advocates filed an amicus brief in *California Federal Savings and Loan Ass'n v. Guerra*, 479 U.S. 272 (1987) (defending a California statute that provided leave and reinstatement provisions for pregnant employees). International Law Scholars filed an amicus brief in *Morrison v. United States*, 529 U.S. 598 (2000). The Lowenstein Human Rights Clinic at Yale Law School filed an amicus brief on behalf of U.S. diplomats in *McCarver v. North Carolina*, 531 U.S. 1205 (2002).

61. *Zadvydas v. Davis*, 533 U.S. 688 (2001); *DeMore v. Kim*, 583 U.S. 510 (2003).

62. *Grutter v. Bollinger*, 539 U.S. 306 (2003) (Ginsburg, J., concurring); *Atkins v. Virginia*, 536 U.S. 304 (2002).

63. Rick Wilson, *A Case Study: The United States in the Inter-American Human Rights System, 1971–2002*, p. 13 (on file with the author). Two cases involved the treatment of aliens. The other two involved Cuban nationalists charged with trying to overthrow the Cuban government and Spanish-speaking U.S. citizens asserting land grant and political claims. Ibid., pp. 14–15.

64. In the 1980s, the commission also issued a decision stating that the "right to life" under the American Declaration of Independence does not extend to protect an unborn fetus from abortion. *White and Potter v. United States*, Case 2141, Inter-Am. Ct. H.R. 25, OEA/Ser. L/V/II.54.doc.rev (1980).

65. Rick Wilson, in email discussion with the author, May 8, 2007.

66. Steven Tullberg, "Securing Human Rights of American Indians and Other Indigenous Peoples Under International Law," in *Bringing Human Rights Home*, vol. 3 (London: Praeger, 2008)

67. Gay McDougall, in discussion with the author, May 3, 2007.

68. Connie de la Vega, in email discussion with the author, April 16 and 25, 2007.

69. Available online at www.skepticfiles.org/aclu/12_14_93.htm.

70. Steve Shapiro, in discussion with the author, April 18, 2007.

71. Ibid.

72. Clarence Lusane, "Changing (Dis)course: Mainstreaming Human Rights in the Struggle Against U.S. Racism," *Black Scholar* (Fall 2004): 5.

73. Gay McDougall, in discussion with the author, May 3, 2007.

74. Ibid.

75. Peter Weiss and Rhonda Copelon, in discussion with the author, May 9, 2007, May 11, 2007.

76. Rhonda Copelon, in discussion with the author, May 11, 2007.

77. Rick Wilson, in email discussion with the author, May 8, 2007.

78. See *Sanchez-Espinoza v. Reagan*, 770 F.2d 202 (D.C. Cir. 1985); *Martinez v. City of Los Angeles*, 141 F.3d 1373 (9th Cir. 1998); *Jama v. United States*, 22 F. Supp.2d 353 (D. N.J. 1998).

79. Copelon was counsel in both the *Filartiga* case and *Harris v. McRae*, a Supreme Court case upholding Medicaid restrictions on abortions. 448 U.S. 297 (1980). Following the Supreme Court's decision in *Harris*, Copelon filed a motion for reconsideration citing a 1979 European Court of Human Rights case, *Airey v. Ireland*, 32 Eur. Ct. H.R. Ser A (1979), holding that meaningful access to a right may require affirmative obligations on the part of the government, as persuasive authority. The Supreme Court denied the motion. Rhonda Copelon, in discussion with the author, May 11, 2007.

80. *Sale v. Haitian Centers Council*, 509 U.S. 155 (1993) (challenging U.S. interdiction and return policy); *Zadvydas v. Davis*, 533 U.S. 678 (2001) (challenging practice of indefinitely detaining certain immigrants who could not be deported); *DeMore v. Kim*, 583 U.S. 510 (2003) (challenging mandatory detention of deportable "criminal aliens" pending deportation without an individualized determination of whether they constitute a flight risk).

81. Penny Venetis, "Jama v. United States: A Guide for Human Rights Litigation," *ACLU Civil Liberties Report*.

82. For a more in-depth discussion of the NLCHP's work, see Maria Foscarinis and Eric Tars, "Housing Rights and Wrongs: The U.S. and the Right to Housing," in *Bringing Human Rights Home*, vol. 3, pp. 149–72.

83. Scott L. Cummings, "The Internationalization of Public Interest Law" (Research paper no. 06-41, University of California, Los Angeles School of Law, 2006), p. 62, available online at ssrn.com/abstract=944552.

84. Paul Hoffman, in discussion with the author, February 7, 2007.

85. Chandra Bhatnagar, in discussion with the author, May 24–25, 2007.

86. Steve Shapiro and Chandra Bhatnagar, in discussions with the author, April 18, 2007, May 24–25, 2007.

87. Paul Hoffman, in discussion with the author.

88. Ibid.

89. Chandra Bhatnagar, in discussion with the author, May 24–25, 2007.

90. Cummings, "Internationalization," 88.

91. Chandra Bhatnagar, in discussion with the author, May 24–25, 2007.

92. Tanya Coke, in discussion with the author, April 9, 2007.

93. Rick Wilson, in email discussion with the author, May 8, 2007.

94. Cummings, "Internationalization," 64.

95. Gay McDougall, in discussion with the author, May 3, 2007.

96. Ibid.

97. In 2001, the author joined the institute to run the Bringing Human Rights Home Project. The author has also served on the planning committee for the Howard Conference and on the Coordinating Committee and Board of the U.S. Human Rights Network.

98. It is impossible to list all the organizations that have been involved in human rights training targeting or including U.S. lawyers. However, groups that have been actively involved include the National Economic and Social Rights Initiative, the National Law Center on Homelessness and Poverty, the Center for Constitutional Rights, Penal Reform International, the Center for Human Rights and Humanitarian Law, American University, Washington College of Law, and the Program on Human Rights and the Global Economy at Northeastern Law School.

99. Hurwitz, "Lawyering for Justice," p. 527.

100. Brandt Goldstein, *Storming the Court* (New York: Scribner, 2005), p. 34.

101. Hurwitz, "Lawyering for Justice," p. 549.

102. Tanya Coke, in discussion with the author, April 9, 2007.

103. Wendy Patten, "The Impact of September 11 and the Struggle Against Terrorism on the U.S. Domestic Human Rights Movement," Chapter 10 in the current volume.

104. Karen Narasaki, in discussion with the author, May 8, 2007.

105. Steve Shapiro, in discussion with the author, April 18, 2007.

106. Karen Narasaki, in discussion with the author, May 3, 2007.

107. Kenneth Cmiel, "The Emergence of Human Rights Politics in the United States," *Journal of American History* 86(3) (December 1999). "Human rights has a long intellectual pedigree, yet the contemporary human rights movement only took off in the 1970s."

108. Thomas Buergenthal, *International Human Rights* (St. Paul, Minn.: West Publishing, 1988), pp. 88–89. In 2006, the commission was replaced by the UN Human Rights Council. William Korey, *NGOs and the Universal Declaration of Human Rights* (New York: Palgrave, 1998).

109. Margaret Huang, " 'Going Global':Appeals to International and Regional Human Rights Bodies," Chapter 8 in the current volume.

110. Cmiel, "The Emergence of Human Rights Politics."

111. Hurwitz, "Lawyering for Justice," p. 513.

112. Rhonda Copelon, in discussion with the author, May 11, 2007.

113. Tanya Coke, in discussion with the author, April 9, 2007.

114. Ann Beeson, in discussion with the author, May 20, 2007.

115. Tanya Coke, in discussion with the author, April 9, 2007.

116. Rick Wilson, in email discussion with the author, May 8, 2007.

117. Chandra Bhatnagar, in discussion with the author, May 24–25, 2007.

118. Rhonda Copelon, in discussion with the author, May 11, 2007.

119. Steve Shapiro, in discussion with the author, April 18, 2007.

Chapter 8
"Going Global": Appeals to International and Regional Human Rights Bodies

Margaret Huang

> [B]efore we learned about human rights, we looked for laws in the U.S. that could provide protection for people who live, work, play and worship in places that are also sites for polluting industrial facilities and waste dumps. But we recognized that [U.S.] laws really do not support the fundamental human rights to life, health and non-discrimination.[1]

Since the early 1990s, a growing number of domestic social justice groups have turned to the international human rights system to challenge inequities and rights violations in the United States. While previous attempts had been made by civil rights leaders to engage the United Nations in the fight against racism and segregation,[2] it is only in the last decade that activists have expanded their efforts to utilize international human rights mechanisms in a range of domestic advocacy issues. Today, U.S. human rights advocates are taking their struggles to the United Nations, to the international treaty bodies, and to the regional human rights system at the Organization of American States (OAS). There are several reasons for this increasing interest in the international human rights system: a rising frustration with unresponsive domestic institutions and laws; changes within the international institutions making them more accessible to U.S. advocates; and a growing awareness among social justice advocates of what the international system has to offer coupled with increased support and resources from institutions committed to building a human rights movement in the United States.

The growing dissatisfaction with domestic institutions felt by many U.S. activists has been discussed in earlier chapters.[3] This broad frustration has given impetus to efforts to find new venues and procedures that might offer justice to victims where domestic remedies have failed. For example, when a victim has been denied the right to file a case in U.S. courts, it can be empowering for the victim to tell her or his story before an international tribunal. Or, when U.S. laws do not recognize a violation of human rights, it can be reaffirming for a victim to have her or his rights recognized under international law.

Over the last decade, international institutions have also adopted new methods of procedure to facilitate civil society participation in human rights mechanisms. For example, in 1996 the United Nations Economic and Social Council adopted a resolution governing the "consultative relationship between the United Nations and non-governmental organizations" to encourage the participation of civil society groups in UN activities, including the Commission on Human Rights.[4] Similarly, in 1999 the OAS adopted new guidelines for the participation of civil society groups in its activities.[5]

Also in the last ten years, the UN Commission on Human Rights established a number of new special procedures to monitor particular human rights problems, such as the denial of the right to housing and violations of the rights of migrants. Of the twenty-eight UN special procedures that currently exist, seventeen have been established since 1997.

Perhaps the most important impetus for increasing U.S. activists' engagement of the international human rights system has been the growing number of organizations committed to providing training, technical assistance, and other resources toward building a domestic human rights movement. Many of the organizations or programs providing training and technical assistance have been established only in the last ten years, including the U.S. Program at Global Rights, the Mississippi Workers' Center for Human Rights, the National Economic and Social Rights Initiative, the National Center for Human Rights Education, the Human Rights Project at the Urban Justice Center, and the Bringing Human Rights Home Project at Columbia Law School. These efforts were given further momentum by the 2003 launch of the U.S. Human Rights Network (USHR Network) initiative linking organizations and individuals from around the country to hold the U.S. government accountable for human rights protections. The USHR Network offers monthly training conference calls and skills-building workshops, and it also disseminates weekly announcements about activities and resources offered by organizational members around the country.

Finally, there are a number of private foundations that have committed funding to support human rights work in the United States, as reflected by the establishment of the U.S. Human Rights Fund in 2005. The fund is a collaborative effort to provide strategic support to the U.S. human rights movement, emphasizing training and education, networking, communications, and strategic advocacy. Many of the current members of the fund also provide direct grants to civil society organizations working on human rights in the United States.

What Is the International Human Rights System?

The international human rights system is a complex arena, including actors at the regional and international level. There are essentially three categories of international human rights institutions accessible to U.S. advocates: those created by the United Nations Charter and/or subsequent resolutions adopted by the UN member states (also known as the charter-based bodies); those established through the adoption and ratification of international human rights treaties (also known as the treaty-based bodies); and those established by regional institutions, such as the OAS (known as the inter-American human rights system). In this section, I provide an overview of some of the key human rights mechanisms in each of these categories, as well as a brief analysis of the relevance and importance of these mechanisms to U.S. activists. In the next section, I present specific examples where U.S. advocates have engaged these procedures.

United Nations Charter-Based Institutions

The United Nations was established with the adoption of its charter at the San Francisco Conference in June 1945. In early proposals for the international organization, the United States and the other leading Allies of World War II sought to limit references to individual rights, hoping to preserve national sovereignty and limit interventions into domestic affairs.[6] But a concerted response led by governments from smaller, often former colonial countries and nongovernmental organizations won the day.[7] Citing the failure of the Treaty of Versailles to prevent further bloodshed after World War I, and motivated by the horrors and devastation wrought by World War II, human rights advocates successfully pressed their demands that the UN Charter emphasize the protection and promotion of human rights. As Paul Gordon Lauren has noted, "The U.N. Charter explicitly drew a connection between human well-being and international peace, reiterated support for the principle of equal rights and self-determination, and committed the organization to promote universal respect for, and observance of, human rights and fundamental freedoms without discrimination—'for all.'"[8]

To carry out this important duty of protecting human rights, Article 68 of the UN Charter required the UN Economic and Social Council (ECOSOC) to "set up commissions . . . for the promotion of human rights," resulting in the creation of the UN Commission on Human Rights (UNCHR or Commission) in 1946. In its earlier years, the Commission focused on drafting and adopting international treaties to elaborate human rights standards.[9] But the UN soon began receiving formal complaints from victims of human rights violations, including representatives of the National Association for the Advancement of Colored People (NAACP) and other groups in the United States, forcing the Commission to resolve the question of whether or not it could take action in individual cases.[10] Reflecting the general reluctance of its member states to allow the international community to get involved in matters of national concern, the ECOSOC adopted a resolution in 1947 stating that the Commission had "no power to take any action in regard to any complaints concerning human rights."[11] This resolution was challenged in the 1960s by a series of petitions regarding apartheid in South Africa, and the Commission was pressured into establishing a procedure to allow public debate on specific countries' human rights records.[12] After that time, the Commission established a set of special procedures to examine particular human rights problems, submit regular reports, and offer expert advice. These procedures are examined in greater detail later in this section.

U.S. domestic advocates have been active participants in the UNCHR for many years, particularly since the late 1990s. For instance, in 1999 the National Coalition to Abolish the Death Penalty took its campaign to the Commission, calling for international pressure to end the practice of executions in the United States.[13] During that same session, advocates from Louisiana made the first formal intervention on environmental racism as a human rights violation before the Commission, highlighting the failure of the U.S. government to protect its citizens from grave violations of the right to health and other abuses.[14] In 2000, advocates fighting racism in the criminal justice system, including the National Association of Criminal Defense Lawyers and the NAACP Legal Defense and Educational Fund, participated in a delegation to the Commission.[15] Since that time, many other U.S. organizations have asked the Commission to examine issues including poverty in the United States, violence against women, the right to housing, and discrimination against migrant workers.

In 2005, UN Secretary General Kofi Annan laid out a vision of reform for the United Nations' human rights system.[16] Because of political disputes and the actions of some member states seeking to prevent the Commission from addressing critical human rights violations, Annan proposed to replace the UNCHR with a new body, the Human Rights Council (HR Council), which would serve as a subsidiary body to the General Assembly. (In UN terms, the Council is considered more important than the Commission because it reports to a higher department— the General Assembly rather than ECOSOC.) After several months of negotiation, and despite U.S. government objections, the General Assembly approved the creation of the HR Council in April 2006.[17]

The new HR Council is a significant departure from its predecessor in several ways. First, unlike the UNCHR which met for only one session per year, the HR Council meets at least three times per year for a total of ten weeks, with the option of requesting additional sessions as needed. This reform enables the Council to consider time-sensitive issues as they arise. Second, the HR Council will undertake a universal periodic review of the human rights situation in every member state of the United Nations. Unlike the Commission, whose members frequently sought to avoid scrutiny of their own records, the HR Council will start its review by examining its members first. Third, the method by which states are elected to the HR Council differs. Unlike the UNCHR, for which countries were nominated by their regional groups (Asia, Africa, and so on) and approved without question by the ECOSOC, election to the HR Council requires an affirmative vote by an absolute majority of the United Nations' 191 members.[18]

Because the HR Council is still new, U.S. activists (along with their counterparts around the world) are still exploring how best to engage this new mechanism. Because the U.S. government did not apply to be a member of the HR Council, its human rights record will not be examined among the first universal periodic reviews. But it is important to remember that the HR Council has the mandate to consider human rights violations in *any* member state. As the HR Council begins to develop a track record, U.S. advocates will be better able to assess how best to engage this mechanism to promote human rights at home.

Many of the rest of the United Nations' Charter-based institutions fall under the purview of the Office of the High Commissioner for Human Rights (OHCHR). Established by the 1994 General Assembly Resolution 48/141, the creation of the Office of the High Commissioner for Human Rights was a direct response to a recommendation emerging from the 1993 World Conference on Human Rights in Vienna, Austria. The mandate of the high commissioner is to serve as the UN official with principal responsibility for UN human rights activities, including providing advisory services and technical assistance to UN member states, engaging in a dialogue with governments to secure respect for all human rights, and coordinating all human rights activities within the UN system.[19] The high commissioner oversees a staff of more than five hundred in offices around the world, with the great majority working at the headquarters for the United Nations' human rights system in Geneva, Switzerland.

The OHCHR provides support to several special procedures, or human rights experts, which are currently divided into two categories: One group of experts holds thematic mandates, such as the use of torture or violence against women, while the second group is tasked with monitoring the human rights situation in a particular country or territory. Special procedures can have different designations, including "special rapporteur," "independent expert," or in some cases a "working group," which usually has five members representing the five regions recognized by the United Nations (Asia, Africa, Latin America, Eastern Europe, and "Western Europe and Others"—where the United States is represented). Each of the special procedures submits an annual report to the United Nations documenting violations covered by her or his mandate and making recommendations to member states and UN officials on how to remedy the violations.

In the last several years, U.S. activists have worked with several of the UN special procedures, including participating in the official visits of several experts to the United States:

- In 1997, the special rapporteur on extrajudicial, summary, or arbitrary executions undertook a mission to the United States to investigate reports of "discriminatory and arbitrary use of the death penalty and a lack of adequate defense during trial and appeal procedures."[20]
- In 1998, the special rapporteur on the question of religious intolerance visited several sites across the country and made recommendations on how the government could improve protection of religious rights, particularly for indigenous peoples.[21]
- The special rapporteur on violence against women visited the United States in 1998 and reported on violence against women in state and federal prisons.[22]
- In 2001, the special rapporteur on the right to education visited the United States in order to examine issues of discrimination in the protection and promotion of the right to education.[23]
- The special rapporteur on the adverse effects of the illicit movement and dumping of toxic and dangerous products and wastes on the enjoyment of human rights also visited the United States in 2001 to learn more about the laws, policies, and practices of the United States.[24]
- In 2005, the independent expert on the question of human rights and extreme poverty visited the United States to examine the impact of extreme poverty on the exercise of human rights in the wealthiest country in the world.[25]
- In May 2007 the special rapporteur on the human rights of migrants spent three weeks examining the situation of migrants in the United States and recommended that the government take actions to ensure that federal, state, and local authorities are all in compliance with international human rights law in the treatment and protection of migrants.[26]

For each of these official visits, U.S. activists provided information and recommendations to the UN experts. Civil society groups also arranged interviews with victims of human rights violations and encouraged official meetings with state and federal officials. More important, advocates used the experts' visits and reports to push for policy and legislative action. For example, during the visit of the independent expert on human rights and poverty in November 2005, activists from Louisiana and Mississippi used his official meetings with local and state government representatives to demand that the needs of the poorest victims of Hurricane Katrina not be forgotten during the reconstruction effort.

It is important to note that the role of the UN special procedures is currently under debate in the negotiations over the methods of work for the new Human Rights Council. While many observers have predicted that the special procedures with thematic mandates will continue under the new structure, there is some concern that the expert positions with country mandates might be eliminated and that the independence of all of the rapporteurships might be compromised.

United Nations Treaty-Based Institutions

During the last sixty years, UN member states have negotiated and adopted nine core human rights treaties to protect and promote human rights around the world:

- The International Convention on the Elimination of All Forms of Racial Discrimination (ICERD);
- The International Covenant on Civil and Political Rights (ICCPR);
- The International Covenant on Economic, Social and Cultural Rights (ICESCR);
- The Convention on the Elimination of All Forms of Discrimination against Women (CEDAW);
- The Convention Against Torture and Other Cruel, Inhuman or Degrading Treatment or Punishment (CAT);
- The Convention on the Rights of the Child (CRC);
- The International Convention on the Protection of the Rights of All Migrant Workers and Member of Their Families (ICRMW);
- The International Convention for the Protection of All Persons from Enforced Disappearance (not yet in force); and
- The Convention on the Rights of Persons with Disabilities (not yet in force).

Among these treaties, the U.S. government has ratified only three: the ICCPR in 1992, and the ICERD and the CAT in 1994. U.S. activists played a significant role in achieving the ratification of these treaties, and many continue to push for ratification of the other ones.[27]

Once a country has ratified a treaty, the government is required to submit periodic reports on its compliance with the treaty's obligations to the treaty monitoring body—a committee of independent human rights experts. For U.S. activists, the reporting process offers an important opportunity to highlight the human rights situation in the country and to demand reforms that would bring the U.S. government into compliance with its international legal obligations. Since May 2005, the U.S. government has filed periodic reports with the three UN committees responsible for the treaties it has ratified: the Committee Against Torture, the Human Rights Committee (which monitors compliance with the International Covenant on Civil and Political Rights), and the Committee on the Elimination of Racial Discrimination. As part of the official reviews of each of these reports, civil society groups have collaborated to submit "shadow reports" to the UN Committees. Shadow reports are information, analysis, and recommendations provided by nongovernmental organizations about specific human rights abuses in the country being reviewed.

For example, in May 2006, U.S. advocates presented information to the UN Committee Against Torture (CAT) about police brutality and the use of torture by law enforcement and prison guards; the conditions of incarceration in "super-max" prisons; the placing of children in long-term isolation while in detention; the sexual abuse and rape of women by law enforcement agents; and the use of electroshock weapons against unarmed individuals. Advocates also provided evidence of the use of torture and the ill treatment of those detained as part of the U.S. government's "war on terrorism" in Iraq, Afghanistan, Guantánamo Bay, and secret CIA detention centers. The members of the CAT responded to U.S. civil society activists by issuing a series of recommendations to the U.S. government addressing all of these concerns.

In July 2006, sixty-five U.S. activists participated in the formal review of the U.S. government's report to the UN Human Rights Committee (HRC). More than twenty issue-based, collaborative shadow reports were submitted to committee members on a broad range of issues including the rights of American Indians; the rights of lesbian, gay, bisexual, transgender, and intersex people; the criminalization of dissent; the failure to prohibit propaganda for war; the human rights of migrants; the failure of government to protect the victims of Hurricane Katrina; and violations of the right to vote and participate in democratic processes of governance. Similar to the response of the Committee Against Torture, the expert members of the HRC incorporated the information from U.S. advocates into their recommendations to the U.S. government.

Once the treaty bodies released their recommendations to the U.S.

government, activists immediately incorporated them into their respective domestic advocacy campaigns. For instance, organizations seeking to end the practice of felon disenfranchisement publicized the Human Rights Committee's recommendation on that issue in ballot initiatives in the 2006 election cycle. The authority of the treaty bodies to interpret U.S. legal obligations under the international human rights treaties lends credibility to advocacy efforts with both legislators and the general public. Activists conducted a similar shadow-reporting process for the Committee on the Elimination of Racial Discrimination, which conducted a review of the U.S. government in 2008.

The Inter-American Human Rights System

Founded in 1948, the OAS is a regional forum to facilitate multilateral cooperation and discussion among the countries of the Western Hemisphere. With thirty-five member states, the OAS works to promote democracy, protect human rights, and confront problems such as terrorism, poverty, corruption, and the illegal trade in drugs.[28] The OAS has two primary mechanisms for protecting human rights: the Inter-American Commission on Human Rights (the Inter-American Commission) and the Inter-American Court of Human Rights (Inter-American Court). The Inter-American Commission is based in Washington, D.C., and the Inter-American Court is housed in San Jose, Costa Rica. Under the OAS Charter, all member countries are bound by the provisions of the American Declaration of the Rights and Duties of Man, placing them under the jurisdiction of the Inter-American Commission. Because the U.S. government has not ratified the American Convention on Human Rights and has therefore not accepted the jurisdiction of the Inter-American Court, U.S. advocates have primarily focused their advocacy efforts at the Inter-American Commission.

The Inter-American Commission is composed of seven independent human rights experts, elected to serve by the General Assembly of the OAS.[29] Commission members carry out fact-finding missions to OAS member states, investigate individual complaints of human rights violations, and monitor the general human rights situation in the countries of the Americas. Similar to the UN system, the Inter-American Commission has the authority to appoint special procedures, each with a mandate to examine a particular human rights problem such as the Special Rapporteurship on the Rights of Persons Deprived of their Liberty and the Special Rapporteurship on the Rights of Afro-Descendants. Civil society advocates from across the region, including the United States, work with the special procedures to bring attention to rights violations in their country and to pressure governments to take action.

Over the last several decades, U.S. activists have brought a number of petitions to the Inter-American Commission, many of them focused on death penalty sentences. But since the 1990s, cases have been reviewed on a much wider range of issues, including the indefinite detention of Cubans sent to the United States in the Mariel boatlift of 1980; the interdiction of Haitians seeking asylum in the United States; the U.S. military invasions of Grenada and Panama; the rights of indigenous peoples to their tribal lands; the voting rights of the residents of the District of Columbia; violations of the rights of the poor through welfare reform initiatives; the rights of undocumented migrant workers; and the practice of sentencing juveniles to life without parole.[30]

Additionally, the Inter-American Commission has adopted a new procedure of holding "thematic hearings," not for individual cases but rather to educate the commission members about a pattern or increasing trend in human rights violations. U.S. activists have used this procedure to request a number of hearings on issues specific to the United States, including racial disparities caused by mandatory minimum sentencing practices, the failure of the government to protect victims of Hurricanes Katrina and Rita, and the gross exploitation of migrant workers in the reconstruction efforts after the hurricanes in the Gulf region; and increasing racial segregation in the public education system.

The Challenges and Advantages of the International Mechanisms

In considering the three categories of international human rights institutions discussed in the proceeding section, it is useful to consider the advantages—and disadvantages—offered by each to U.S. advocates. On the one hand, the UN Human Rights Council offers U.S. activists the opportunity to network with human rights organizations around the world in one time and place. The council also facilitates advocacy with foreign governments, as representatives of forty-seven countries are simultaneously accessible to U.S. activists. On the other hand, the council has an enormous agenda with many issues and countries competing for the attention of the member states. Additionally, the fact that the council meets three times each year in Geneva poses a financial challenge for U.S. activists (as well as advocates from other parts of the world). Travel to and accommodations in Geneva are quite expensive, and without staff on the ground, many organizations are unable to effectively participate in the council's deliberations.

The UN treaty bodies offer a different set of advantages and disadvantages. The committees generally welcome substantive input from civil society groups, and in some cases they actively seek information on particular issues of interest. Because the committees are mandated to focus on the compliance of an individual country, they give more attention to specific issues and devote more time to the discussion of the situation in that country. A challenge to activists' effective use of the treaty reporting process, however, is the reporting record of the U.S. government. Since ratification of three treaties in the early 1990s, the U.S. has filed only two reports with each treaty body, precluding activists from using the shadow-reporting process more than once each decade. Also, the treaty bodies tend to issue their recommendations to governments in "UN-speak"—diplomatic language that may not arouse the public's attention to a serious human rights violation.

The Inter-American Commission offers individuals petitioners who have been denied access to U.S. courts the opportunity to have their case heard by an official body. For many victims of human rights violations, the Inter-American Commission process offers the only formal acknowledgment of their experience. The thematic hearings before the commission also offer the opportunity to raise interest in a particular human rights violation, which can be used in education and media outreach efforts. But it is important to note that the U.S. government usually does not accept the jurisdiction of the commission and refuses to comply with any decisions taken against it. Because of the government's refusal to accept the legal authority of the commission, advocates must have clear and limited expectations about what a commission decision can actually accomplish.

There are also some general advantages and disadvantages that all of the international institutions offer to U.S. activists. On the positive side, unlike the legal institutions in the domestic judicial system, advocates do not have to be lawyers to engage the international procedures. For instance, several of the activists participating in the shadow-reporting processes with the treaty bodies were grassroots organizers and community-based leaders, working on issues such as racial profiling and prison conditions. Their information was vital to the committee members, who consistently requested the views of local activists on specific issues. The result was a democratization of the advocacy process, with national and local organizations sharing information and working collaboratively to influence the reporting process.

Another advantage of the international human rights mechanisms is that they provide access to the international community, which can add pressure to demands for domestic policy changes. The National Campaign to Abolish the Death Penalty, an organization dedicated to ending capital punishment in the United States, began campaigning at the UN Commission on Human Rights in the late 1990s, seeking to win the support of other countries for efforts to ban the death penalty in the United States.[31] Later, anti–death penalty advocates expanded their advocacy to the European Union and the OAS, particularly the Inter-American Commission on Human Rights. This outreach through various international institutions was successful in attracting attention from several countries—particularly in Europe and Latin America—to the U.S. practice of sentencing the mentally disabled and juveniles to death. Widespread censure of these practices was demonstrated by diplomatic interventions, public petitions, and even intercessions by the pope of the Roman Catholic Church.[32] The campaign to end this practice was successfully concluded in 2002 with the Supreme Court decision in *Atkins v. Virginia* and in 2005 with the Supreme Court decision in *Roper v. Simmons*.[33] Although international condemnation alone would likely not have achieved these victories, the Supreme Court decisions did make reference to international legal standards and the practices of other governments around the world.[34]

U.S. advocates have also gained from participating in international human rights meetings by connecting to the broader international human rights movement. Whether in Geneva at the UN Human Rights Council, or in Washington before the Inter-American Commission, U.S. groups have learned from the experience of activists from other parts of the world. By hearing about the similar struggles and successes of human rights advocates in other countries, U.S. activists gain a new arsenal of tools and strategies for combating human rights violations at home. Equally important, U.S. advocates have the opportunity to build solidarity with their counterparts across the globe.

Finally, one other advantage of the international human rights mechanisms is the opportunity that they offer survivors of human rights violations to tell their own stories. When victims are denied the chance to see their cases prosecuted or to seek legal remedy in domestic courts, submitting a petition to an international mechanism gives them a platform to demand accountability and to be heard. International institutions may provide victims with the opportunity to testify, to share their experiences in their own voices, and to gain recognition from the international community of the violation of their rights. Such opportunities demonstrate to victims that they are not alone in their struggle and inspire them (and others) to continue the struggle for justice at home.

On the negative side, U.S. advocates are generally unfamiliar with the international human rights system, and they often require training and technical assistance on how to engage the international mechanisms. Organizations may have to commit significant resources to international human rights work including staff time, the costs of training, the costs of participating in international meetings, translation or interpretation costs, and other expenses. Another disadvantage for U.S. civil society groups is the skepticism of members, boards of directors, and other key constituencies who are also unfamiliar with the international human rights system. Activists may have to commit additional time and energies to persuading their primary stakeholders of the value of this work. Finally, U.S. advocates must confront a significant obstacle in the attitude of the U.S. government, which frequently considers itself unbound by international legal obligations. This challenge is discussed in more detail in a later section.

Case Studies: U.S. Activism in the International Human Rights Institutions

During the last decade, U.S. advocates have engaged a range of international organizations and procedures in their efforts to hold the government accountable for human rights violations. These efforts have usually been undertaken in support of existing campaigns for social justice, complementing other activities and contributing new forms of pressure for policy or legal change. Activists consider international advocacy strategies for different purposes—to change the discourse (and therefore public sentiment) about a particular problem; to seek a remedy for a victim who cannot or has not received justice under domestic laws; or to bring international pressure to bear on government officials who are unresponsive to community demands. This section explores the experiences of U.S. advocates working on different issues and campaigns, and how they have utilized the international human rights mechanisms to promote their causes.

Environmental Racism at the UN Commission on Human Rights

During the 1990s, a group of activists from "Cancer Alley" in Louisiana struggled to end the pollution produced by corporations operating petrochemical facilities and oil refineries in their communities. Calling for an end to "environmental racism," these advocates emphasized that the people who suffered disproportionately from this corporate pollution were African American, Latino, and other poor minority communities.[35] After years of attacking the problem through lawsuits and community organizing demanding action from the Environmental Protection Agency and other regulatory bodies, the activists became frustrated by the lack of response from governmental institutions. In 1998 they started to look toward the international human rights system for inspiration.[36]

In 1999, a delegation of community activists from Louisiana traveled to Geneva to testify before the UN Commission on Human Rights about environmental racism. This was the first time that the issue of environmental racism was addressed in the commission.[37] In addition to formal written and oral interventions, the activists also met with UN human rights experts and conducted a briefing for member states of the commission on the problems of environmental racism in the United States. A key objective of the delegation's participation in the commission was to invite the UN special rapporteur on the adverse effects of the illicit movement and dumping of toxic and dangerous products and wastes on the enjoyment of human rights to visit the United States. This effort was successful, and the special rapporteur visited the United States in December 2001, including a stop in the affected Louisiana communities.[38] Although her report did not focus on the issue of environmental racism in great detail, advocates used the special rapporteur's visit to raise the visibility of their struggle, winning attention from both the media and members of the U.S. Congress.[39]

After the visit by the UN special rapporteur, activists stepped up their campaigns targeting the corporations responsible for the pollution. Having linked up with activists fighting similar battles in Nigeria and Ecuador through their international advocacy efforts, Louisiana advocates went after corporate parent companies in the United Kingdom and the Netherlands. After years of struggle, U.S. activists finally won a major settlement with a petroleum company, which agreed to purchase homes from community members affected by its operations in Cancer Alley.[40] While the victory was not achieved through international advocacy alone, using the international human rights mechanisms did change the terms of the debate between community members and corporate representatives. By using international activism and publicity to call attention to environmental racism as a human rights violation, activists succeeded in shaming the corporations to do the right thing. Advocates were also able to link their struggle with similar battles taking place in other parts of the world, reinforcing the message that human rights must be protected for all people.

International Treaty Compliance: Chicago Police Torture

From 1972 to 1991, approximately 135 African American men were tortured by former Police Commander Jon Burge and detectives under his command at police headquarters in Chicago, Illinois.[41] A veteran of the Vietnam War, Burge used similar techniques to the ones he had employed against enemy combatants in the war—electric shock, suffocation with a plastic bag, mock executions, and beatings with telephone books and rubber hoses. The torture was systemic and racist in nature, inflicted to extract confessions from the suspects, many of whom remain incarcerated.[42] At least eleven decisions in both federal and state courts have acknowledged the practice of torture by Burge and his men, and officials of the City of Chicago have also admitted to widespread knowledge of the torture during and after this period.[43] Despite this overwhelming evidence, not a single officer or member of the chain of command has been prosecuted for torture or for conspiracy to obstruct justice by covering up these crimes. Many of the officers responsible for the torture have subsequently been promoted and allowed to retire with their full pensions.[44]

Activists in Chicago formed an ad hoc coalition to push for justice in the Burge cases. While they achieved some victories in the campaign (the firing of Jon Burge, the pardoning of some innocent victims of the torture, the settlement of a few civil cases brought by victims, and the appointment of a special prosecutor to investigate the matter), advocates were not able to achieve justice on behalf of all the victims nor were they able to win official recognition of the systemic and racist nature of the torture.[45] After waiting more than three years for special prosecutors appointed in April 2002 to finish their investigation of the Burge cases, the coalition decided to take their campaign to the UN treaty bodies. In May 2006, they presented evidence and recommendations to the UN Committee Against Torture, and in July of the same year, they made the same case before the UN Human Rights Committee. In response to this advocacy, the Committee Against Torture in its *Concluding Observations* cited its concerns about the lack of investigation and prosecution in regard to allegations against the Chicago Police Department and called for an immediate and thorough investigation into all allegations of torture by law enforcement personnel.[46] The committee also requested that the U.S. government provide further information about prosecutions related to the Burge cases.

The recognition by an international human rights institution was incredibly empowering for the victims of Jon Burge. Not only was it an acknowledgment of the violations that they had suffered, but it lent further authority to their demands for action by the government. Equally important, there was substantial media coverage of the UN committee's concern about the Burge cases in the Chicago area. Newspapers, radio programs, and the major television stations all carried stories reporting on the UN committee's recommendations. Advocates in Chicago credit this media attention with the decision by the special prosecutors to finally release their report on the Burge cases. In July 2006 after a four-year investigation, the special prosecutors concluded that torture had indeed taken place and that Burge and his men committed criminal acts in violation of Illinois laws "beyond a reasonable doubt."[47] However, the prosecutors declined to issue indictments against any of the individuals involved on the grounds that the statute of limitations for these crimes had run out. Outraged, the coalition of advocates in Chicago responded with *A Report on the Failure of Special Prosecutors Edward J. Egan and Robert D. Boyle to Fairly Investigate Police Torture in Chicago,* issued in April 2007. The group also filed a supplemental report to the UN Committee Against Torture, calling for a federal investigation and prosecution of all those responsible for the torture and its cover-up.[48]

Petitioning the Inter-American Commission on Domestic Violence

One of the most fundamental human rights is a right to a remedy for those whose rights have been violated. Whether a person is a victim of police brutality, of corporate malfeasance, of medical malpractice, or of discriminatory treatment or harassment, that person should be able to get a remedy through criminal prosecution, civil litigation, or mediation and settlement. If a person is denied a remedy for a rights violation, then her or his rights are violated again. Advocates for human rights victims in the United States are increasingly turning to international human rights mechanisms when domestic institutions fail to recognize their claims. While the international procedures are generally unable to provide a direct remedy for the human rights violations, they do offer activists an opportunity to highlight the lack of remedy within the domestic legal system. These mechanisms can also provide a forum to create a public record of the violation and give the victim her or his "day in court."

On June 22, 1999, Simon Gonzales abducted his three daughters from their mother's home in Castle Rock, Colorado, directly violating a court-issued temporary restraining order.[49] Jessica Gonzalez (now Jessica Lenahan), who had filed for divorce earlier that year, quickly called the local police department and requested the immediate enforcement of the restraining order against her estranged husband. Despite Colorado's mandatory arrest law, which requires police officers to "use every reasonable means to enforce a protection order," the police department ignored Ms. Lenahan's repeated calls and never took any steps to locate Mr. Gonzalez or to enforce the order.[50] At 3:20 A.M., Mr. Gonzalez arrived at the police station and opened fire with a handgun. Police responded by shooting him dead, after which they discovered the bodies of his three children in his truck, killed that same evening.

Following this tragedy, Jessica Lenahan filed a lawsuit against the City of Castle Rock for failing to enforce her protective order. The case was heard by the Supreme Court, which ruled against her in June 2005, stating that Ms. Lenahan had "no personal entitlement to police enforcement of the order."[51] Having lost her case in the highest domestic court, Ms. Lenahan was left without any remedy in the domestic judicial system. She decided to turn to the international human rights system, hoping to keep her case alive and to prevent other victims of domestic violence from suffering the same violation of their rights. She and her lawyers filed a petition with the Inter-American Commission on Human Rights (Inter-American Commission). In her petition, she requested monetary compensation for the violations of her rights, as well as the adoption by the U.S. government, and particularly the State of Colorado, of necessary measures to deter future domestic violence crimes. Ms. Lenahan also requested an advisory opinion from the Inter-American Court of Human Rights regarding the nature and scope of U.S. government obligations under the American Declaration of the Rights and Duties of Man to prevent and prosecute domestic violence.

In March 2007, Ms. Lenahan told her story in a formal hearing before the Inter-American Commission. It was the first time that she was allowed to personally testify in an official proceeding, as U.S. courts had rejected her claims on procedural grounds and prevented any consideration of the merits of her case. For Ms. Lenahan, the acknowledgment of her suffering and the recognition of the violation of her rights were a form of remedy that she had been denied by domestic courts. Although Ms. Lenahan may not win her individual case before the Inter-American Commission, the petition also serves to advance the advocacy efforts of those fighting domestic violence. These advocates hope to use the publicity around her petition—and the final decision of the Inter-American Commission—to pressure government officials to pass legislation that requires enforcement of protective orders. Thus, the role of the Inter-American Commission is to complement ongoing domestic advocacy and to enhance efforts to enact meaningful reforms.

U.S. Government Engagement with the International Bodies

Despite its claims to leadership of the international human rights system, the U.S. government works very hard to avoid accountability for its international legal obligations. This position of U.S. "exceptionalism"—claiming that the rules and laws that apply to everyone else do not apply to the United States—is well documented within the international human rights institutions. Such exceptionalism is reflected in the U.S. government's refusal to ratify other human rights treaties, such as the Convention on the Rights of the Child which has been nearly universally accepted by governments around the world.[52] It is also demonstrated by the U.S. government's decisions to withdraw as a signatory to the International Criminal Court Treaty in 2002[53] and to reject international consensus around the Kyoto Protocol in 2001.[54] In 2005 the U.S. government also withdrew from an international legal protocol that grants the International Court of Justice (ICJ) oversight of U.S. protection of foreign nationals' consular rights.[55] The withdrawal took place after the

ICJ ruled in 2004 that the cases of fifty-one Mexican nationals sentenced to execution in the United States should be reopened because U.S. authorities failed to notify the Mexican government about their cases. Perhaps the clearest example of U.S. exceptionalism is the failure of the U.S. government to publicize its reports to UN treaty bodies or even to educate the public about its human rights treaty obligations. By keeping quiet about these obligations, the United States seeks to avoid accountability for the same rights it demands be protected in other countries of the world.

The U.S. government is usually represented by the State Department in activities at the international human rights institutions, though other federal agencies have also played a role in reporting on U.S. compliance with international legal standards. This odd arrangement makes the foreign affairs agency responsible for providing information about domestic policies and state laws. Such a practice is not unusual—most countries are represented before international institutions by their foreign ministry officials. But in the United States, it has created serious challenges for the federal government to meet its obligations efficiently and effectively. For example, the Office of the Legal Advisor at the State Department is responsible for drafting compliance reports to the various treaty bodies. But much of the information on how the United States is meeting its obligations actually originates with the Departments of Justice, Defense, Health and Human Services, and Homeland Security, as well as the governments of the fifty states.

Recognizing the need to coordinate among the federal agencies to gather information and report to the UN treaty bodies, in 1998 the Clinton administration issued Executive Order 13107 on the *Implementation of Human Rights Treaties.*[56] The order established an Inter-Agency Working Group on Human Rights Treaties, which was tasked with coordinating reporting efforts as well as with developing plans for public education about the treaties. These efforts have not resulted in widespread understanding of U.S. obligations under the treaty. In fact, in a series of meetings with U.S. government officials in early 2007, civil society advocates learned that representatives of the Department of Justice, the Department of Homeland Security, and the Federal Emergency Management Agency had never heard of the human rights treaties and were unaware of any obligations that these treaties placed on their departments.[57] Even more disturbing, a number of state attorneys general responded to U.S. Department of State requests for information by asking "which state" the department was representing.[58] The government's failure to educate even public officials about their international legal obligations is itself a violation of the human rights treaties.

In addition to its responses to the UN treaty bodies, the United States has also been ambivalent in its engagement with other international human rights mechanisms. In litigation at the Inter-American Commission, for example, the government is usually very active in responding to petitions brought against the United States. However, it also consistently denies the legitimacy of any decision taken against it by the commission and posits that the American Declaration of the Rights and Duties of Man is not binding.[59] When UN special procedures have requested to conduct fact-finding missions to the United States, the government has usually accommodated these requests but has rejected any subsequent criticism documented in the mission reports.[60]

Beyond the executive branch, Congress and the judiciary also have roles to play in upholding U.S. human rights obligations. First and foremost, the Senate is responsible for ratifying human rights treaties signed by the president, and the ratification process is assigned to the Foreign Relations Committee. However, there has been no committee assigned to monitoring treaty implementation. In early 2007, a new subcommittee on Human Rights and the Law was formed under the Senate Judiciary Committee. It is not clear whether the leadership of this new subcommittee will undertake to examine issues of treaty compliance as part of its jurisdiction, though activists are working hard to persuade committee members to take on this important task. There is also a Congressional Human Rights Caucus with members in both the Senate and the House of Representatives, but its work has focused almost exclusively on the human rights situation in other countries, not in the United States.

In the judicial branch, there is an increasing awareness of international legal obligations, particularly reflected in recent decisions by the Supreme Court.[61] While the references to international human rights law are usually considered persuasive rather than authoritative in court decisions, the trend does offer hope to activists that international human rights might someday be enforceable in U.S. courts. On the other hand, international law references have also spurred a highly negative reaction from conservative activists and some members of Congress, who have called for the impeachment of any judge who cites "foreign law" in an opinion.[62] The backlash against the citing of international law could easily produce a "chilling effect" that would deter judges and lawyers from using international human rights laws when appropriate.

The common theme through all of these points is that the U.S. government adamantly rejects international criticism of its own human rights record, even while it is publicly condemning other governments for their human rights violations. Because human rights objectives are often cited as primary factors in the making of U.S. foreign policy (consider Sudan or North Korea or the justifications for the war in Iraq), the United States cannot completely abandon the international human rights regime. But it works hard to limit its engagement with the international human rights institutions, a position that U.S. activists must confront as part of their international advocacy strategies.

Conclusion

As the number of U.S. activists using international human rights mechanisms grows, there are more and more opportunities to impact domestic policy with these strategies. The more that government officials—whether legislators or judges—are exposed to international human rights treaty obligations, the more open they might become to applying these standards in their work. This possibility highlights the need for more resources—both personnel and financial—dedicated to supporting activists' engagement of the international human rights mechanisms. More education of the general public and the media is also needed to build and support the constituencies demanding human rights protection in this country. Human rights strategies alone may not accomplish the objectives of the social justice movement, but they can certainly lend strategic value to ongoing efforts while also bringing some form of remedy to the victims of human rights violations.

Notes

1. Monique Harden, quoted in *Close to Home: Case Studies of Human Rights Work in the United States* (New York: Ford Foundation, 2004), p. 94.
2. Carol Anderson, "A 'Hollow Mockery': African Americans, White Supremacy, and the Development of Human Rights in the United States," Chapter 3 in the current volume.
3. Dorothy Q. Thomas, "Against American Supremacy: ReBuilding Human Rights Culture in the United States," Chapter 5 in the current volume.
4. UN Economic and Social Council, E.S.C. Res. 1996/31, UN ESCOR, 1996 Sess., supp. no. 1, at p. 53, UN Doc. E/1996/96 (1996), available online at www.un.org/documents/ecosoc/res/1996/eres1996-31.htm.
5. Organization of American States, *CP/RES. 759 (1217/99): Guidelines for the Participation of Civil Society Organizations in OAS Activities,* adopted by the Permanent Council in December 1999, OEA/Ser.G/ CP/Res.759(1217/99) (1999), available online at www.oas.org/consejo/resoluciones/res759.asp.
6. Paul Gordon Lauren, *The Evolution of International Human Rights: Visions Seen* (Philadelphia: University of Pennsylvania Press, 2003), p. 167.
7. Ibid., pp. 180–86.
8. Ibid., p. 189.
9. *Seventeen Frequently Asked Questions about United Nations Special Rapporteurs (Including Information on the Commission on Human Rights),* United Nations Fact Sheet No. 27 (Geneva: United Nations High Commissioner for Human Rights, 2001), p. 3, available online at www.ohchr.org/english/about/publications/docs/factsheet27.pdf.

10. Carol Anderson, *Eyes off the Prize: The United Nations and the African American Struggle for Human Rights, 1944–1955* (New York: Cambridge University Press, 2003), pp. 78–98.

11. United Nations Economic and Social Council, *Resolution 75(V)*, adopted by the United Nations in January 1947, as cited in United Nations Fact Sheet No. 27, p. 3.

12. United Nations Fact Sheet No. 27, p. 3.

13. Brian Roberts, executive director of the National Campaign to Abolish the Death Penalty, in discussion with the author, January 21, 2004.

14. Global Rights (formerly the International Human Rights Law Group), *Report on the 1999 Advocacy Bridge Program* (Washington, D.C.: Global Rights, 1999), p. 10.

15. Global Rights (formerly the International Human Rights Law Group), *Report on the 2000 Advocacy Bridge Program* (Washington, D.C.: Global Rights, 2000), p. 10.

16. Kofi Annan, *In Larger Freedom: Towards Development, Security and Human Rights for All* (New York: United Nations, 2005), pp. 45–46.

17. UN General Assembly Resolution 60/251, UN GAOR, 60th Sess., UN Doc. A/Res/60/251 (April 2006), para 5(e).

18. Ibid., para 7.

19. UN General Assembly Resolution 48/141, UN GAOR, 48th Sess., UN Doc. A/Res/48/141 (1994), para 4.

20. UN Commission on Human Rights, 54th Session, *Report of the Special Rapporteur on Extrajudicial, Summary or Arbitrary Executions, Mr. Bacre Waly Ndiaye, Submitted Pursuant to Commission Resolution 1997/61*, UN Doc. E/CN.4/1998/68 (December 23, 1997), at p. 3, available online at daccessdds.un.org/doc/UNDOC/GEN/G98/102/37/PDF/G9810237.pdf?OpenElement.

21. UN Commission on Human Rights, 55th Session, *Report Submitted by Mr. Abdelfattah Amor, Special Rapporteur, in Accordance with Commission on Human Rights Resolution 1998/18*, UN Doc. E/CN.4/1999/58/Add.2 (December 29, 1998), available online at www.unhchr.ch/Huridocda/Huridoca.nsf/TestFrame/3129ccf9f586f71680256739003494e4?Opendocument.

22. UN Commission on Human Rights, 55th Session, *Report of the Special Rapporteur on Violence Against Women, Its Causes and Consequences, Ms. Radhika Coomaraswamy, in Accordance with Commission on Human Rights Resolution 1997/44*, UN Doc. E/CN.4/1999/1999/68/Add.2 (January 4, 1999), available online at daccessdds.un.org/doc/UNDOC/GEN/G99/100/12/PDF/G9910012.pdf?OpenElement.

23. UN Commission on Human Rights, 58th Session, *Report Submitted by Katarina Tomaševski, Special Rapporteur on the Right to Education, Mission to the United States of America 24 September–10 October 2001*, UN Doc. E/CN.4/2002/60/Add.1 (January 17, 2002), available online at daccessdds.un.org/doc/UNDOC/GEN/G02/101/52/PDF/G0210152.pdf?OpenElement.

24. UN Commission on Human Rights, 59th Session, *Adverse Effects of the Illicit Movement and Dumping of Toxic and Dangerous Products and Wastes on the Enjoyment of Human Rights, Report of the Special Rapporteur, Ms. Fatma-Zohra Ouhachi-Vesely*, UN Doc. E/CN.4/2003/56/Add.1 (January 10, 2003), available online at www.unhchr.ch/Huridocda/Huridoca.nsf/0/857e2f721fbc3a8ec1256ccc00366e78/$FILE/G0310229.pdf.

25. UN Commission on Human Rights, 62nd Session, *Human Rights and Extreme Poverty, Report Submitted by the Independent Expert on the Question of Human Rights and Extreme Poverty, Arjun Sengupta*, UN Doc. E/CN.4/2006/43/Add.1

(March 27, 2006), available online at daccessdds.un.org/doc/UNDOC/GEN/G06/122/70/PDF/G0612270.pdf?OpenElement.

26. United Nations Press Release, *Special Rapporteur on Human Rights of Migrants Ends Visit to the United States*, available online at www.unhchr.ch/huricane/huricane.nsf/view01/BA409950651325ECC12572E2002845A5?opendocument.

27. Office of the High Commissioner for Human Rights, "Ratifications and Reservations," United Nations, available online at www.ohchr.org/english/countries/ratification/index.htm.

28. Organization of American States, "The OAS at a Glance," available online at www.oas.org/key_issues/eng/KeyIssue_Detail.asp?kis_sec=20.

29. Inter-American Commission on Human Rights, "What Is the IACHR?," Organization of American States, available online at www.cidh.oas.org/what.htm.

30. Rick Wilson, "A Case Study: The United States in the Inter-American Human Rights System, 1971–2002" (unpublished paper, January 16, 2003), p. 2; "Petition Alleging Violations of the Human Rights of Undocumented Workers by the United States of America" (petition submitted to the Inter-American Commission on Human Rights, Washington, D.C., November 1, 2006); "Petition Alleging Violations of the Human Rights of Juveniles Sentenced to Life Without Parole in the United States of America" (petition submitted to the Inter-American Commission on Human Rights, Washington, D.C., February 21, 2006).

31. Brian Roberts, executive director of the National Campaign to Abolish the Death Penalty, in discussion with the author, January 21, 2004.

32. See, for example, Office of Media Relations, "Papal Appeals for Clemency Sent to Governors in Three States," United States Conference of Catholic Bishops, available online at www.usccb.org/comm/archives/1999/99-142.shtml; Delegation of the European Commission to the United States, "EU Statement on Death Penalty in the USA," European Union, available online at www.eurunion.org/legislat/DeathPenalty/OSCEPattersonTorresLe.htm; Walter Schwimmer, "Death Penalty in U.S. Must Be Rethought," *International Herald Tribune,* January 25, 2001, available online at www.iht.com/articles/2001/01/25/edwalt.t.php.

33. *Atkins v. Virginia,* 536 U.S. 304 (2002); *Roper v. Simmons,* 543 U.S. 551 (2005).

34. See, for example, *Atkins,* 536 U.S. 304, 325; *Roper,* 543 U.S. 551, 567.

35. Ford Foundation, *Close to Home: Case Studies of Human Rights Work in the United States,* pp. 92–94.

36. Ibid.

37. Global Rights, *Report on the 1999 Advocacy Bridge Program,* pp. 15–16.

38. UN Commission on Human Rights, 59th Session, *Adverse Effects of the Illicit Movement and Dumping of Toxic and Dangerous Products and Wastes.*

39. Ford Foundation, *Close to Home,* p. 96.

40. Ibid.

41. Tonya D. McClary and Andrea J. Ritchie, *In the Shadows of the War on Terror: Persistent Police Brutality and Abuse in the United States* (report prepared for the United Nations Human Rights Committee, Geneva, Switzerland, May 2006), p. 19.

42. Locke E. Bowman et al., *A Report on the Failure of Special Prosecutors Edward J. Egan and Robert D. Boyle to Fairly Investigate Police Torture in Chicago* (Chicago, Ill., April 2007), pp. 14–35.

43. McClary and Ritchie, *In the Shadows,* p. 19.

44. Ibid., pp. 19–20.

45. Joey Mogul, "Racial Disparities in Law Enforcement" (speech, conference

on Racial Discrimination in the U.S. Criminal Justice System and International Human Rights Standards, Washington, D.C., May 18, 2007).

46. UN Committee Against Torture, *Consideration of Reports Submitted by States Parties Under Article 19 of the Convention, Conclusions and Recommendations of the Committee against Torture on the United States of America*, UN Doc. CAT/C/USA/CO/2 (July 25, 2006), p. 7, available online at daccessdds.un.org/doc/UNDOC/GEN/G06/432/25/PDF/G0643225.pdf?OpenElement.

47. Bowman et al., *A Report on the Failure of Special Prosecutors*, p. 3.

48. Joey Mogul, letter submitted to the United Nations Committee Against Torture, May 1, 2007.

49. "Petition Alleging Violations of the Human Rights of Jessica Gonzalez by the United States of America and the State of Colorado, with Request for an Investigation and Hearing on the Merits" (petition submitted to the Inter-American Commission on Human Rights, Washington, D.C., December 23, 2005), pp. 9–13, available online at www.aclu.org/pdfs/apetitionallegingviolationsofthehumanrightsofjessicagonzales.pdf.

50. Ibid.

51. Ibid., pp. 16–17.

52. Office of the High Commissioner for Human Rights, "Ratifications and Reservations," United Nations, available online at www.ohchr.org/english/countries/ratification/index.htm.

53. U.S. Department of State, "Letter to UN Secretary General Kofi Annan" (submitted to the United Nations, New York, N.Y., May 6, 2002), available online at www.state.gov/r/pa/prs/ps/2002/9968.htm.

54. See, for example, George W. Bush, "Text of a Letter from the President to Senators Hagel, Helms, Craig, and Roberts" (Washington, D.C.: White House Office of the Press Secretary, March 13, 2001), available online at www.whitehouse.gov/news/releases/2001/03/20010314.html.

55. Jennifer Yau, "US Withdraws from International Court of Justice Oversight on Consular Rights," *Policy Beat*, April 1, 2005, available online at www.migrationinformation.org/USfocus/display.cfm?id=298.

56. Executive Order no. 13107, "Implementation of Human Rights Treaties," *Code of Federal Regulations*, title 3, sec 234 (December 10, 1998), available online at www.fas.org/irp/offdocs/eo13107.htm.

57. Nongovernmental organizations' meeting with State Department officials, January 19, 2007; nongovernmental organizations' meeting with Department of Justice officials, March 29, 2007.

58. Nongovernmental organizations' meeting with State Department officials, January 19, 2007.

59. Rick Wilson, "A Case Study: The United States in the Inter-American Human Rights System, 1971–2002," pp. 11–12.

60. See, for example, Reed Brody, "American's Problem with Human Rights," *Third World Network* (May 1999), available online at www.twnside.org.sg/title/1893-cn.htm.

61. See, for example, the Supreme Court decisions in *Atkins v. Virginia*, 536 U.S. 304 (2002); *Roper v. Simmons*, 543 U.S. 551 (2005).

62. See, for example, "The Constitution Restoration Act of 2005" (introduced in the U.S. House of Representatives and the U.S. Senate, March 2005), available online at www.thomas.gov/cgi-bin/bdquery/z?d109:SN00520:@@@L&summ2=m&.

Chapter 9
Thinking Globally, Acting Locally: States, Municipalities, and International Human Rights

Martha F. Davis

Mayors, governors, city councils, and state legislators are not usually associated with foreign affairs. The United States Constitution states that the federal government has the power to make treaties, and it has been widely accepted that this authority encompasses a more general "foreign affairs power." A large share of that power rests with the executive branch. While the Constitution also reserves some residual powers to be exercised by the states or "the people," the argument that the nation must speak with one voice on issues of international concern has reinforced the idea that there is little role for the divergent perspectives of individual states and cities in the world of international relations.

This constitutional bedrock, however, is not impervious to cracks, fissures, and even earthquakes. History provides many examples of state and local involvement in foreign affairs as notions of states' rights ebb and flow, and as activists pressure their local governments to stake out positions on the important global issues of the day. The relationship between the subnational and national governments in the United States is dynamic, as it must be to preserve such a complex union. Catherine Powell has called this give and take between locally and federally driven international policy perspectives a "dialogue" between different levels of government.[1] Alternatively, states and localities might be viewed as laboratories of foreign affairs, testing policies before initiating full-blown national programs. Such approaches may, at the very least, "trickle up" to the federal level over time. Or in some instances, states and localities may be simply exercising their own sovereignty, without concern about how their constituent-driven local policies might play on the national or international stage.

Whatever characterization is most apt, in the area of international human rights, many states and localities in recent years have used their position within the federal system to promote human rights approaches both abroad and at home. Their actions (for example, in addressing global warming or divesting from South Africa) often make a practical difference in their own right, while also pushing the nation toward greater involvement in both the informal and formal mechanisms of international human rights. Despite some significant setbacks, particularly in the courts, grassroots activists as well as states and localities themselves continue these efforts, creatively taking advantage of the gray areas of federalism that leave some space for local involvement in foreign affairs.

A Brief History of State and Local Foreign Affairs

Historically, state and local engagement in foreign affairs has fallen into three general categories: (1) direct engagement with foreign governments on issues of mutual concern; (2) symbolic statements, such as resolutions, intended to influence national and international policies; and (3) local adoption and implementation of international standards, including human rights standards, that may or may not have been endorsed by the federal government. State and local activity is explicitly circumscribed by constitutional requirements that prevent states from entering into treaties. But subnational governments continue to test their boundaries in areas where the respective responsibilities of federal and state governments are less clearly delineated.

In terms of direct engagement, since the beginning of the republic, states and cities have responded to the expectations and demands of their citizens by interacting directly with foreign governments, with or without federal support and approval, and often with profound effects on federal policy. There are many examples. As early as 1793, when President Washington proclaimed the United States' neutrality in the Franco-British War, the governor of South Carolina took sides and allowed a British ship to be prepared in Charlestown. A few years later, residents of Boston raised $125,000 to build two frigates for the British forces.[2]

In the twentieth century, subnational governments continued their direct involvement in international affairs, driven initially by efforts to improve their international trading positions. In 1959, for example, the governor of North Carolina headed a business delegation to Europe, hoping to yield more direct investment in the state. In the early 1960s, states began opening their own offices abroad. (By 2006, thirty-eight states operated more than two hundred offices around the world.)[3] Pursuing a more bilateral approach, the state of Louisiana reached out to Quebec in 1965 in an effort to establish a closer cultural relationship between the two former French colonies. U.S. cities have also pursued economic and trade measures across international boundaries. For example, the City of Denver's Mayor's Office of Economic Development and International Trade maintains offices in Shanghai and London. And since the late 1950s, cultural and technical exchanges have been the norm in hundreds of U.S. cities that have sister-city relationships around the world.[4]

Regional relationships between state and local governments and foreign nations are also common. For example, as early as 1966, representatives of states along the southern United States border met with their Mexican counterparts to establish a cooperative arrangement to promote education, commerce, and tourism. By 2006, one of the most sophisticated transnational regional alliances in North America was the Pacific Northwest Economic Region (PNWER). Its members—British Columbia, Alberta, Yukon, and the states of Alaska, Idaho, Montana, Oregon, and Washington—cooperate on issues relating to the environment as well as common economic concerns.

In addition, shared concerns about a variety of global issues are leading states to play a greater role on the international stage more generally, transcending regional groupings. For example, in July 2006, the state of California entered into a historic agreement with the United Kingdom to collaborate on climate change and promote energy diversity. Frustrated by federal foot-dragging, California Governor Arnold Schwarzenegger announced that "California will not wait for our federal government to take strong action on global warming." While careful not to call the agreement with the United Kingdom a treaty (since only the federal government can bind the United States in that particular way), Governor Schwarzenegger opined that "California has a responsibility and a profound role to play to protect not only our environment, but to be a world leader on this issue as well."[5]

In addition to this direct engagement, state and local governments have often engaged in more symbolic actions directed at influencing foreign affairs at home and abroad. For example, spurred by grassroots activists exercising influence on the local level, in the 1960s city governments began to directly and formally challenge U.S. foreign policy in Vietnam. From 1966 to 1968, seven U.S. cities—San Francisco, California; Beverly Hills, California; Dearborn, Michigan; Cambridge, Massachusetts; Lincoln, Massachusetts; Madison, Wisconsin; and Mill Valley, California—held local referenda condemning the Vietnam War.

Though clearly symbolic, these municipal forays into foreign affairs were not without controversy. The Cambridge resolution, on the ballot in the 1967 municipal elections, asked residents to vote on whether they favored a "prompt return home" of U.S. troops. Before election day, however, the city solicitor refused to let the referendum proceed, arguing that it was "not a fit matter for city business." The Cambridge Neighborhood Committee on Vietnam sued to keep the referendum on the ballot and the Middlesex Superior Court ruled that it could proceed, in part because the city council had already passed three pro-war resolutions, setting a precedent for city activity on the issue.[6]

Like most of the other municipal referenda on Vietnam during this period, the antiwar forces lost the vote in Cambridge, with only 39 percent of the voters favoring withdrawal. However, this multicity referendum campaign did serve as an early endorsement of such municipal engagement in foreign affairs. Indeed, in the Dearborn, Michigan, referendum, nearly 78 percent of the people voting in the midterm election weighed in on the Vietnam issue, suggesting broad acceptance of the idea of submitting these issues for local consideration.[7]

By the 1970s, the attention of many activists had turned to South Africa and the scourge of apartheid. Not satisfied with the more symbolic actions of the Vietnam era, these activists sought to implement human rights standards opposing apartheid in corporations, municipalities, and states. Initially, concerned individuals focused on curtailing private investment in South Africa, mounting an apartheid divestment campaign. Many believe that the movement began in 1970 when Caroline Hunter and her husband, Ken Williams, started the Polaroid Revolutionary Workers Movement, a ragtag band of Polaroid employees who risked their jobs by protesting when they found that the Polaroid Company's equipment was used to create the passbooks and identification cards necessary to apartheid's enforcement. The Polaroid group was, according to Willard Johnson, a political science professor at the Massachusetts Institute of Technology, the "first case in which someone actually challenged their own employer and organized workers around the divestment issue."[8]

By 1978, the divestment movement—framed as an issue of international human rights—had spread to other U.S.-based companies and $40 million had been withdrawn from the South African economy. Students took up the call as well, and private universities across the country slowly began to divest. By the early 1980s, local governments had joined in. Continuing to operate on the level of rhetoric and symbolism, many state and local resolutions condemned apartheid and urged the federal government to take decisive action against it, including trade sanctions.

But other state and local proposals went further, seeking to adopt and implement international human rights standards as a matter of local law and policy. For instance, building on the foreign trade expertise and infrastructure that states and localities had established over the past decades, twenty-three states, fourteen counties, and eighty cities in the United States enacted either divestment or procurement legislation to limit their own investment and procurement from companies doing business with South Africa's apartheid regime. Under these laws, local governments were required to divest public holdings of stocks in firms that did business with South Africa or to restrict procurement opportunities when the bidder for a government contract did business with South Africa. When the apartheid regime finally toppled in 1991, most viewed the cumulative effect of such local laws and their impact on U.S. federal policies and on South Africa itself as a significant factor, though at least one report—by the South African de Klerk Foundation—argued that the economic burdens caused by sanctions actually slowed the pace of progressive reform.[9]

Within the United States, however, activists cheered the South African divestment and procurement laws as a successful intervention by both grassroots groups and local policymakers to influence national priorities and to advance human rights in the international arena. The campaign's apparent success was not lost on others who were looking to use the United States' huge commercial and financial interests to leverage an expansion of human rights in other parts of the world. At the same time, many activists knew that there was another shoe waiting to drop.

Though states and localities had historically, and frequently, engaged in activities that might be characterized as foreign affairs, there was little clarity about how far they might go. The antiapartheid movement brought this issue into clear focus. From the beginning of cities' and states' involvement with the antiapartheid campaign, scholars had been writing about the constitutional limitations on this expression of "municipal foreign affairs." Views were divided. In the *Virginia Law Review* and the op-ed pages of the *Wall Street Journal*, then–law student Peter Spiro called for immediate judicial and legislative action to curb municipal human rights activism. Cautioned Spiro, "Allowed to act untrammeled for the time being, cities and states may grow accustomed to their new-found role and resort to it more frequently on a broader range of issues."[10] Georgetown Professor John M. Kline responded in a letter to the editor that "Mr. Spiro's narrow and legalistic discussion misses the fact that, since the mid-1970s, international forces have penetrated the domestic U.S. economy so deeply that they overlap traditional and legitimate state economic power." Kline concluded, "these activities give states a direct stake in foreign-policy matters and a potential influence on them."[11]

Clearly, as Spiro argued, there was a case to be made that the local antiprocurement laws were unconstitutional based on the federal government's supremacy in controlling the nation's foreign affairs. Yet only a single legal challenge was brought against an antiapartheid divestment ordinance. The case, filed against Baltimore, Maryland's ordinance by the trustees of the city's pension funds and two employee beneficiaries, was unsuccessful. Maryland's Court of Appeals, that state's highest court, ultimately upheld the ordinances in September 1989, concluding that the divestment requirements did not violate the city's fiduciary duty to invest the pension funds prudently.[12]

With only one case generated against the antiapartheid policies sweeping the country, the real-world impact of the heated scholarly debate was virtually nonexistent. There was little to no interest by the Reagan administration in interfering with "states rights" on this issue. Attorney General Edwin Meese even issued an opinion concluding that state and local South African laws were constitutional exercises of states' rights to spend and invest their own funds as "guardian and trustee of [their] people."[13] So, as Professor David Caron writes, "Although the literature tended to be quite confident of the law (one way or the other), [the absence of litigation] . . . made the extensive analysis seem oddly irrelevant. No cases . . . were brought, although industry and the federal government were most certainly aware of the arguments to be made. Everyone conceded that Congress could explicitly preempt local action, but that did not occur either. . . . Given this separation of law from practice, the literature seemingly had nowhere to go. For the most part, it was set off in a circle referencing itself and piling on to one side or the other."[14]

Instead of becoming embroiled in these tail-chasing theoretical debates, activists and other engaged citizens were eager to build on the success of the antiapartheid movement. Likewise, local governments were apparently willing to see what how far they could go in responding to international human rights initiatives. New human rights campaigns moved in to fill the void when apartheid ended. One of the most prominent and successful of these campaigns was the effort to influence events in Burma, also known as Myanmar.

Activists Looking Outward: The Burma Law

In 1994, Simon Billenness of Boston, Massachusetts, a coordinator for the New England Burma Roundtable and analyst with the socially responsible investment firm Trillium Asset Management, approached State Representative Byron Rushing of Boston about the situation in Burma. In a prodemocracy uprising in 1988, the Burmese government had slaughtered three thousand civilians. Since then, human rights organizations like the Roundtable and other allied Free Burma organizations and activists continued to document human rights violations, including restrictions on speech and the extended house arrest of Nobel Laureate and political leader Aung San Suu Kyi. Rushing, who represents several diverse Boston neighborhoods, had been a key supporter of the Massachusetts laws sanctioning South Africa for apartheid. Would he, Billenness asked, be willing to adapt the South African antiapartheid law to Burma?

Rushing agreed and the two "dusted off the state's earlier South African selective purchasing law and replaced every South Africa mention with 'Burma.'"[15] The new bill generally barred state entities from buying goods or services from any business organization identified on a "restricted purchase list" of those doing business with Burma. It was introduced in spring 1994. During the next two years before the Massachusetts legislation was signed into law, a growing list of progressive municipalities of increasing size and significance enacted selective purchasing laws targeting Burma, including Berkeley, Madison, Santa Monica, Ann Arbor, San Francisco, and Oakland. Massachusetts was the first state to join the list when Governor William Weld, a Republican who wanted to burnish his progressive credentials in a Senate race against incumbent Democrat John Kerry, signed the Burma legislation into state law in June 1996.

The Free Burma movement continued to grow. Los Angeles, Portland (Ore.), Vermont, and New York City joined the list of states and municipalities with Burma selective purchasing laws. State legislation was also introduced in California, Connecticut, and Texas, though none of these bills became law. In September 1996, even the federal government joined in when Congress passed a statute barring all new investment by U.S. companies in Burma and authorizing the president to impose further sanctions in the event of continued violence and abuses in the country.[16] In May 1997, President Clinton invoked his authority under the law, issuing an executive order that banned new investments in Burma because of the country's repression of human rights and democracy.[17] While it differed in many respects and did not go as far as the Massachusetts law, activists hailed the presidential order as a significant breakthrough. As Byron Rushing told the *Boston Globe*, "Suddenly, putting pressure on companies to get out of Burma is not a harebrained idea. It is an idea that has been discussed seriously by people doing foreign policy on the federal level. They have agreed with Massachusetts that this makes sense."[18]

Still, without a groundswell of deep popular support nationwide—and the traction that the South African divestment campaign had among civil rights activists in the United States—the Burma laws were vulnerable to political and legal attack. The international business community showed little reluctance to undermine the law. The Japanese government and the European Commission, representing many multinational corporations in their countries doing business with Burma, openly threatened to challenge the Massachusetts law before the World Trade Organization (WTO); the European Union also asked for a WTO consultation on the law, a precursor to filing a complaint. Similarly, whereas domestic business and trade groups had not wanted to risk the appearance of sup-porting apartheid, they were less concerned about political fallout from opposing the Burma laws. In April 1998, the National Foreign Trade Council, a consortium of more than five hundred U.S. transnational corporations, initiated a test case challenging the constitutionality of the Massachusetts law in federal district court. The district court struck down the law, and that decision was upheld on appeal by the First Cir-cuit Court of Appeals. The Massachusetts attorney general, defending the law, then requested Supreme Court review, and the Court agreed to hear the case.

The case, *Crosby v. National Foreign Trade Council*, became a forum for fighting out the constitutional question that had long been simmering just beneath the surface of the myriad campaigns to enact municipal and state human rights laws, that is, did state and municipal governments impinge on federal authority when they used government procurement restrictions to put economic muscle behind their views of international human rights? Amicus briefs supporting the Massachusetts Burma law were filed by dozens of organizations, as well as seventy-eight members of Congress and twenty-two state attorneys general. They argued that the states and municipalities could properly enter the arena of foreign affairs so long as they did not directly contradict official U.S. foreign pol-icy. In this instance, they pointed out, the Massachusetts law was entirely consistent with the anti-Burma thrust of the federal executive order. Fur-ther, in a classic states' rights argument, Massachusetts argued that it had a right to apply the moral standards of its own state citizens to the state's spending decisions.

Appearing before a conservative Supreme Court that often found favor with states' independence from federal constraints, defenders of the Massachusetts law expected to find some support among the justices. Instead, the Court unanimously ruled to strike down the state law. Inter-estingly, it was the Free Burma movement's own success that sealed the Massachusetts law's demise. Noting President Clinton's 1997 executive order, the Supreme Court ruled that the federal government had pre-empted the state's sanctions law. Justice David Souter, himself a former state attorney general for New Hampshire, wrote for the Court that "The state act is at odds with the president's intended authority to speak for the United States among the world's nations in developing a compre-hensive, multilateral strategy to bring democracy to and improve human rights practices and the quality of life in Burma."[19] Even though both the Massachusetts law and the federal law took similar steps to impose eco-nomic pressure and condemn the Burma government's human rights abuses, once the federal government had articulated the national posi-tion on the matter, Massachusetts could go no further.

Simon Billenness and the other activists who had crafted the Massachusetts Burma law, along with Representative Rushing, put a brave face on the loss. Even before the decision came down, Billenness anticipated the outcome and told the press, "We will come out with a new generation of selective purchasing bills which conform to the court's ruling, while making sure they have as much teeth as possible and put as much pressure as possible on those who want to do business in Burma."[20] State Representative Rushing was similarly combative, saying that he was "now ready to push the House and Senate to pass a bill that would ban the investment of state pension funds in firms that do business with Burma."[21] Such funds were solely within the purview of the state and arguably beyond the reach of the federal authority.

Indeed, after the Supreme Court's decision, Minneapolis passed a new measure focused solely on municipal investments in companies doing business with Burma. Byron Rushing also introduced a new Burma bill in Massachusetts that focused restrictions on the Commonwealth's investments instead of its procurement. But even the most progressive communities were now newly concerned with the legal risks involved with their foreign affairs activism.

Even before the Supreme Court issued its opinion, the lower court decisions had an immediate effect on the similar measures being considered by state and local governments. As early as 1997, activists in both Amherst, Massachusetts, and the state of Maryland backed away from proposed selective purchasing laws aimed at Nigeria, concerned that such measures would leave them open to a lawsuit.[22] After the decision, new municipal and state legislation slowed to a trickle and then virtually ceased. Representative Rushing wryly observed that "[i]f selective purchasing had been banned 10 years ago, Nelson Mandela might still be in prison today."[23] In *Crosby*, Justice Souter acknowledged the issue, but sidestepped it, writing that "[s]ince we never ruled on whether state and local sanctions against South Africa in the 1980s were preempted or otherwise invalid, arguable parallels between the two sets of federal and state Acts do not tell us much."[24]

Nevertheless, the Burma selective purchasing laws undoubtedly had a major impact on national policies. Dozens of companies withdrew from Burma, several citing state and local Burma laws as the reason. And significantly, in a dramatic example of the potential for policies to trickle up from states and municipalities to the federal level, in 2003, Congress enacted the Burmese Freedom and Democracy Act, which banned all U.S. imports from Burma.

Human Rights Activism Close to Home:
San Francisco CEDAW and Its Progeny

While activists intent on using U.S. economic power to improve human rights in faraway places struggled to go beyond symbolism and find a new wedge in the face of constitutional limitations and economic opposition, another group of human rights activists in San Francisco was simultaneously looking for ways to "bring human rights home." Their goal was to use international human rights standards to reduce the gender-based discrimination that they saw in their own communities.

In September 1995, Krishanti Dharmaraj and Wenny Kusuma of San Francisco joined more than twenty thousand other country representatives and activists from around the world at the Fourth United Nations World Conference on Women: Action for Equality, Development, and Peace, convened in Beijing, China. Attending the unofficial forum for nongovernmental organizations, Dharmaraj and Kusuma began to consider how they could "bring Beijing home," using their experiences at the conference to begin changing policies in the United States.

Within a year of their return to the United States, they founded a new organization, Women's Institute for Leadership Development for Human Rights—known as WILD for Human Rights. Then, working with the local Amnesty International staff and the San Francisco Women's Foundation, they hit upon a strategy: They would launch a campaign to enact the International Convention on the Elimination of All Forms of Discrimination Against Women (CEDAW) in their hometown, San Francisco. Sixteen states and dozens of cities and counties had passed resolutions calling on the United States to ratify CEDAW—largely symbolic actions. But no state or local government had actually adopted CEDAW as its own law.

There were good reasons why prior local and state government actions had taken the form of resolutions. Treaty ratification is an activity reserved to the federal government, not available to the states. State and local resolutions typically urged federal action consistent with these constitutional parameters. In contrast, adopting CEDAW as municipal law would move toward implementation of the treaty. Such local implementation might be necessary if an international treaty had been previously ratified by the federal government; some areas of government activity such as welfare and family are left to the states, and treaty obligations touching on those areas must be implemented by the states in order to be effective. But when a treaty is unratified, there is no such obligation to implement. In that instance, state and local activity to implement the treaty begins to look more like a renegade action to circumvent federal prerogatives and to set foreign policy in the face of federal opposition.

Of course, unratified treaties may be the ones most in need of domestic implementation. It was no accident that WILD's focus turned to CEDAW, one of the international human rights treaties that the United States has not ratified despite the convention's acceptance by 170 other nations of all stripes. The opportunity to fill that gap and send a strong message to Washington, D.C., was one of the things that attracted both the activists and members of San Francisco's city government.[25] Indeed, at the time he signed the ordinance, San Francisco Mayor Willie Brown, Jr., commented, "[T]he United States is the only industrialized country in the world that has yet to ratify CEDAW. . . . We want to set an example for the rest of the nation because it is long overdue."[26] But while the activists were well aware of the federal government's posture, they were also directly responding to developments in their own state and local community. As Dharmaraj recalls, "At the time of WILD's founding, there were many bad propositions in California, including the erosion of minimum standards for welfare. In contrast, human rights principles had minimum standards for what people were entitled to, what they must have."[27]

WILD began its work on a local CEDAW in late 1996, starting with an intensive coalition-building effort. Few local activists were familiar with international human rights principles, and even fewer people in city government had considered a human rights agenda. For more than a year leading up to the local CEDAW's passage, WILD and its coalition partners focused on training and information sessions. "We trained economic justice groups, violence against women groups, reproductive rights groups, disability groups, and not just the grassroots, but people working on every level of the community," recalls Dharmaraj. "We had to show why they needed to use a human rights framework to address gender discrimination. It was slow, because people were just 'not there' in their thinking about this kind of proactive legislation."[28]

After enlisting the San Francisco Commission on the Status of Women, a municipal agency, as part of their coalition, the CEDAW activists were ready to begin contacting the Board of Supervisors, the city officials who would ultimately vote on the proposal. As Sonia Melara, former head of the Women's Commission, recalls, "We did not go first to the most liberal Supervisor. Instead, we went to the most conservative, Barbara Kaufman, who was also the President of the Board of Supervisors. She felt strongly that for the legislation to be viable, the primary issue to address was economic."[29] The coalition responded to that suggestion, focusing on economic issues along with violence and health when they staged a large public hearing on the CEDAW proposal. Similarly, the CEDAW ordinance itself, drafted by the Commission on the Status of Women, the office of Supervisor Kaufman, and the San Francisco city attorney, focused on nuts-and-bolts economic issues facing women.

In April 1998, the nearly two years of groundwork paid off. The Board of Supervisors passed the CEDAW ordinance in a unanimous vote, and it was signed into law by Mayor Brown. Tracing CEDAW's language exactly, the enacted legislation broadly defines discrimination against women and girls as any "distinction, exclusion or restriction made on the basis of sex that has the effect or purpose or impairing or nullifying the recognition, enjoyment or exercise by women, irrespective of their marital status, on a basis of equality of men and women, of human rights and fundamental freedoms in the political, economic, social, cultural, civil or any other field."[30] By incorporating distinctions with a discriminatory effect, this definition goes further than the definitions of equality recognized under the U.S. Constitution or most state constitutions.

In other respects, however, the San Francisco CEDAW ordinance is tailored to municipal goals in ways that reflect the spirit, but not the precise text, of CEDAW. For example, under the ordinance, selected city departments are required to undergo an extensive gender analysis to identify areas of gender discrimination in their internal practices and service delivery. All city departments must participate in periodic human rights trainings. Notably, the new ordinance did not give individuals the right to sue the city for CEDAW violations, but rather it put the onus on city government to affirmatively assess its compliance with human rights standards and to proactively address problems.

Further, in 2000, the ordinance was amended to incorporate principles of the International Convention on the Elimination of All Forms of Racial Discrimination (ICERD). Unlike CEDAW, ICERD has been ratified by the United States. As discussed above, as a ratified treaty, subnational governments have an obligation to implement ICERD.

Implementation of San Francisco's CEDAW has at times been rocky, and the results have not always been dramatic. With an initial budget of only $100,000, the task force set up to implement the CEDAW ordinance could not possibly hope to evaluate the entire city's practices. Instead, the task force focused in on a handful of city agencies, with the intention of gradually phasing in gender analyses at all of the agencies over time. After the task force was legislatively dissolved in 2002, ongoing monitoring is now handled by a committee of the Women's Commission with a budget allocation from the city to support staffing.

To date, six city agencies have completed a gender analysis. Despite San Francisco's progressive reputation, it has often been slow going. Just because the Board of Supervisors approved the legislation did not mean that the San Francisco CEDAW had the unequivocal support of city agencies. Ann Lehman, the analyst at the Women's Commission who staffed the implementation effort, reports that the initial reaction from city departments was "you've got to be kidding." As she recalls, there was even some hostility, particularly from the city's Department of Public Works, and many of the agencies "saw it as just one more group looking over their shoulders and telling them what to do."[31]

However, once the agencies began conducting gender analyses—that is, breaking down the sex, parental status, age, and so on of the people they served, and then analyzing their internal and external practices in light of that information—there were some gradual changes in perspective. Lehman notes, for example, that the Art Commission was initially resistant to the idea that there were gender issues in the administration of its program. "Though primarily male artists were funded for large public art projects," Lehman says, "the Commission said it was due to societal imbalances rather than their own practices."[32] The CEDAW gender-analysis process provided the commission with the means to conduct strategic planning in a way that they never had before, with a gender perspective. Once they went through the process, says Lehman, "they found that the street artist program, which was a lottery to get spots to sell wares, was set up in a way that made it difficult for people with children to get in. So they changed the program."[33]

In fact, many of the changes generated by the CEDAW ordinance are so small and limited that, according to one report, "few residents are even aware that the city adopted the treaty."[34] For the individuals relying on specific city services, however, the changes could make a significant difference. For example, the Juvenile Probation department was initially very resistant to the gender-analysis approach. Says Lehman, "they already had a Task Force on Girls in the Juvenile Justice System, and they didn't see the need for more attention. But their own process of beginning to look at gender issues was pushed along by CEDAW."[35] Using the gender analysis, the task force found that the Juvenile Probation department was not providing services that young women needed, such as sexual assault counseling and pregnancy prevention services. According to Patricia Chang, president and CEO of the San Francisco Women's Foundation, "girls' needs were considered something extra." San Francisco's CEDAW shifted its orientation. "By changing the agency's standard from boys to both boys and girls," says Chang, "we were able to move to more of a true notion of equity in city services."[36] And the process happened more quickly, adds Lehman, because of the city's CEDAW ordinance.

Similar issues were identified by other agencies. The Department of Public Works found that women often felt unsafe in the city at night because city lights were spaced too far apart. The department changed the spacing between lights in certain areas of the city. The city's rent-control board now gathers data on women minorities who use affordable housing, rather than misleadingly categorizing its constituents as either women or minorities. Further, the board found that many of the landlords it served were elderly women, leading it to reassess some of its own practices.

In the area of economics that was so important to the ordinance's initial passage, the law has provided a framework for evaluating the city's hiring practices, among other things. Sonia Melara reports that during the gender-analysis phase, "family issues kept coming up in every department."[37] In each instance, agencies found that workers faced hard choices between providing child care or caring for an elderly relative, and obligations to their job. Sometimes, the task force found, city policies unnecessarily exacerbated these problems. For example, some employees at the Department of Public Works punch in at 6 A.M., but day care rarely starts before 8 A.M., putting these jobs beyond the reach of most single parents. It is no surprise, then, that data collected from the department also showed that 98 percent of the skilled craftsmen were men; aside from societal pressures that keep women from these jobs, the department's own policies discouraged their participation. In response to this finding, according to the department's personnel manager Jim Horan, the agency has been open to more flexible schedules for employees with children and has increased job-training courses intended to support women's entry into nontraditional positions.[38]

San Francisco's innovative approach to incorporating human rights laws into domestic legislation has spawned similar efforts in other U.S. states and cities. Most of these remain "works in progress." For example, on December 19, 2003, the Los Angeles City Council unanimously passed an ordinance to provide for local implementation of CEDAW. The ordinance designated the Los Angeles Commission on the Status of Women as the implementing agency. After a slow start, the commission staff is now going forward to develop agency-level gender analyses inspired by San Francisco's approach. In 2004, a state-level CEDAW modeled on the San Francisco law was also passed by the California Assembly but was vetoed by Governor Schwarzenegger.[39] In his veto statement, the governor cited a range of antidiscrimination laws already on the books and asserted that a state CEDAW "is duplicative of existing policy and unnecessary,"[40] despite the clear evidence that San Francisco's law led to new changes in city policies that existing laws had not achieved.

A few municipalities, such as Chicago, have enacted CEDAW ordinances but have made little headway toward actual implementation. Several others, including Santa Clara, California, Eugene, Oregon, and New York City, are still in the throes of the legislative and organizing process.

As home to the United Nations and as America's most cosmopolitan city, New York would seem to be a natural place for local implementation of international human rights standards. Yet activists in New York have faced more bumps in the road than their counterparts in San Francisco. The New York City effort—called the Human Rights in Government Operations Audit Law (Human Rights GOAL)—began in 2002, when representatives of New York–based advocacy groups including the Urban Justice Center, Amnesty International, and the American Civil Liberties Union met in the offices of the NOW Legal Defense and Education Fund to discuss the possibility of "bringing human rights home" to New York. Unlike the West Coast campaign, the proposed New York City ordinance from its outset addressed local implementation of both CERD and CEDAW. In other respects, however, the New York campaign drew directly on the San Francisco model. One of the group's first initiatives was to invite Krishanti Dharmaraj to speak to the New York City coalition. Following her advice, the New York activists then engaged in the same kind of extensive public education initiative that preceded the successful adoption of the ordinance in San Francisco, ultimately lining up more than ninety coalition members in the community to endorse the proposed ordinance.

Like the San Francisco initiative, the New York City proposal draws on international human rights law for inspiration and basic standards, while tailoring the provisions to local implementation needs. For example, the Human Rights GOAL, as introduced before the New York City Council in 2005, called for creation of a Human Rights Advisory Committee comprised of both public and private citizens. Interestingly, advocates report that this was the first time that a city council bill had mandated such a public/private partnership, with community members included alongside public administrators in the oversight of city agencies' compliance. The proposed ordinance further mandated that city agencies take a proactive approach to monitoring inequities and preventing discrimination by, among other things, conducting compliance audits similar to those utilized in San Francisco. The bill did not create any new cause of action to enforce its provisions, but instead provided various avenues for public pressure and transparency to ensure agency accountability.

At the end of the city council's 2005 legislative session, the proposal had thirty-five cosponsors in the fifty-one-member council. Proponents of Human Rights GOAL, such as former New York City Mayor David Dinkins, argued that the law could prevent discrimination and save tax dollars by "identifying potentially harmful policies in advance."[41] The city's existing human rights law is reactive, said Dinkins providing redress for discrimination only after a lawsuit is filed and the damage is done.[42] Further, advocates pointed out, the proactive approach might be the only way to address the cumulative effects of unintentional biases in city decision making—effects that are often beyond the reach of litigation but that have a significant effect on the participation of women and minorities in the life of the city.

Yet New York City Mayor Bloomberg has suggested that he will veto the bill should it ever be approved by the city council. His objections, delivered during a city council hearing, are apparently not based on concern about New York City's potential encroachment on federal foreign affairs. Instead, like his West Coast counterpart Governor Schwarzenegger, Bloomberg objects to the breadth of the proposal's mandates and its overlap with existing civil rights enforcement mechanisms. In general, the mayor's office called for a more "realistic approach to governing," ignoring the real-world lessons from San Francisco.[43]

In the face of this standoff, local organizing to promote the Human Rights GOAL continues as activists try to solidify and expand support among city council members. After failing to gain approval during its initial consideration, the bill was reintroduced before the city council in 2007. Using an approach particularly suited to New York City, advocates have made efforts to enlist support from the many international human rights leaders who pass through the city. For example, when the city council held a hearing on the proposed law, Mary Robinson, former UN high commissioner for human rights, submitted a written statement supporting the bill. An announcement on a UN Web site also urged international visitors to attend in person and, in doing so, connected the dots between this local effort and human rights initiatives around the world: "The hearing will provide an exciting opportunity to witness democracy in action, learn why good governance is contingent upon core human rights and anti-discrimination principles, and hear some of our city's most eloquent scholars, politicians and social justice advocates make the case for why human rights are as important, relevant and necessary in New York City as they are in Baghdad, Kabul and Beijing."[44]

The Opposition from Within: California's Short-Lived CERD

Opposition to local human rights implementation can arise from substantive disagreements as well as disputes over turf and political viability. The short-lived California CERD is a case in point.

On August 9, 2003, California Governor Gray Davis signed Assembly Bill 703, "An act to add Section 8315 to the Government Code, relating to racial discrimination." This modest provision, which had passed through the legislature with little attention or debate, effectively overturned Proposition 209, the controversial provision adopted through a 1996 state referendum that barred state-sponsored affirmative action programs. AB 703 provided that for purposes of construing California law, the relevant definition of the term "racial discrimination" is the definition set out in

CERD. Proposition 209 did not include a specific definition of discrimination, but its clear intent was to outlaw affirmative action. In contrast, the CERD definition specifically permits the use of "special measures securing adequate advancement of certain racial or ethnic groups or individuals requiring such protection," and indicates that these affirmative measures shall not be considered racial discrimination.

AB 703 was itself part of the backlash to Proposition 209. Among the state institutions most affected by Proposition 209 are California schools, particularly the state's flagship university system. Dr. J. Owens Smith, a member of the faculty at California State University and head of the Black Faculty Association of the California University system, did the background research and drafting for AB 703. He was keenly aware that there was a David-and-Goliath quality to his effort. On the one hand, he notes, opponents of affirmative action had "an obscene amount of money to fight civil rights." On the other side—on his side—he felt, was "nothing."[45] So he turned to international human rights law.

State Assemblyman Mervyn Dymally, a progressive African American representing the city of Compton, introduced the bill in the California legislature.[46] According to Smith, it was Dymally's legislative skills that got the bill through the process with little to no opposition. One critical factor was clearly the element of surprise. State legislators simply didn't expect to see references to CERD appearing in state legislation and didn't take the time to educate themselves about its significance. Says Smith, "International law is complicated and not a lot of people understood it, so they just said 'we are not going to vote either way.' "[47] With no organized opposition, and with strong support from the NAACP and the Mexican American Legal Defense Fund as well as some state agencies and unions, the bill passed handily.

Once it was on the books, however, AB 703 started to get attention. Upon the bill's passage, Dymally's office notified the heads of state agencies and state universities that affirmative action was now permissible. Eager to defend their long-standing affirmative action programs and maintain diversity in their agencies, progressive city governments soon started using the new provision in court. Notably, the initial reliance on AB 703 came in a suit filed by the conservative Pacific Legal Foundation attacking the Berkeley, California, school district's racial diversity policy. Berkeley defended its program by citing AB 703. In dismissing the Pacific Legal Foundation's charges and upholding the school district's affirmative action policy, the Alameda County Superior Court cited AB 703's definition of racial discrimination.[48]

The forces that had backed Proposition 209 so effectively did not stay in the background for long. Ward Connerly, the wealthy developer and activist who had spearheaded the Proposition 209 campaign, began by filing a lawsuit challenging AB 703's constitutionality. He pointed out that the new law attempted to use a statute to override the constitutional changes made by Proposition 209; the judge ruled that Connerly did not have standing to bring the suit.[49] Another lawsuit, however, was ripe for resolving the question of AB 703's constitutionality.

Beginning in 1988, years before the campaign that ended affirmative action in California, the Sacramento Metropolitan Utility District (SMUD) declared that it intended to provide national leadership in affirmative action programs.[50] Responding to intervening U.S. Supreme Court opinions narrowing the permissible scope of such programs, in 1993 SMUD conducted disparity studies to justify its continued use of race-based goals to be utilized by minority businesses. After Proposition 209's passage in 1996, SMUD conducted another study and revised its affirmative action program, but it did not abandon affirmative action altogether.

The Pacific Legal Foundation represented C&C Construction, a company which did not meet the definition of a minority-owned business and therefore did not benefit from SMUD's affirmative action program. C&C sued to challenge SMUD's continued use of affirmative action criteria in awarding contracts.

In considering the case, the court began by examining the threshold question: Does SMUD's minority preference program constitute racial discrimination? Under Proposition 209, any racial classification is discriminatory, even if the classification is made with the intention of ameliorating the effects of discrimination. But under AB 703, an affirmative action measure such as SMUD's program would be covered by the CERD definition that permits affirmative measures.

The court, however, never reached the merits of this issue. Instead, in an opinion issued just thirteen months after AB 703 was enacted, the court concluded that the legislature had overstepped its bounds by enacting legislation to define a term—"discrimination"—in the California Constitution. Instead, the court determined, the California Supreme Court "is the final authority on interpretation of the state Constitution"—not the legislature.[51] According to the court, "Assembly Bill No. 703 amounted to an attempt by the Legislature and the Governor to amend the California Constitution without complying with the procedures for amendment. This attempt was manifestly beyond their constitutional authority."[52] The Sacramento authorities sought review by the California Supreme Court, but the court turned down their appeal.

California's routine use of propositions to amend its state constitution is not the norm in other states. Substantively similar legislation in another state jurisdiction might have been able to overcome the legal hurdles that scuttled AB 703. But legal hurdles are not always separable from political hurdles. The anti–affirmative action forces have amassed considerable financial and political support. Reliance on international law alone will not be enough to change that dynamic, as the California CERD experience teaches.

Professor Smith, however, still has ambitions to use international law in defending affirmative action in the long run. The problem, he argues, is that that the California court got it wrong because it focused narrowly on the status of the state legislation instead of its international origins. "The state constitution should be subordinate to the human rights treaty," says Smith, and not the other way around. "The CERD definition, the Supreme Law of the Land, should have trumped the state law."[53]

Do States and Municipalities Have a Role to Play in Bringing Human Rights Home?

Despite its singular status as the only major U.S. state or local government that has both adopted and implemented an international human rights treaty, San Francisco is not alone. Around the world, subnational governments are flexing their muscles in the international human rights arena. Canadian provinces regularly submit reports to augment the national reports that Canada presents to United Nations monitoring bodies.[54] Indeed, the United Nations Human Rights Committee expressed regret that the United States' 2006 report on its compliance with the International Covenant on Civil and Political Rights (ICCPR) provided "only limited information . . . on the implementation of the Covenant at the state level."[55]

Representing local governments, a new organization, United Cities and Local Governments (UCLG), was created in 2004 to serve as the "voice of local government before the international community."[56] A successor to the venerable International Union of Local Authorities, founded in 1913, the UCLG's priority areas include developing close links with the United Nations. Toward that end, the UCLG established the United Nations Advisory Committee of Local Authorities (UNACLA), the first formal advisory body of local authorities to be attached to the United Nations.[57] Further, following a meeting between a UCLG delegation and then–UN Secretary General Kofi Annan, the secretary general expressed interest in expanding cities' role in the United Nations. It is a direction that the United Nations has already begun to pursue with its sponsorship of a series of World Urban Forums addressing issues facing cities worldwide.

Some countries, particularly those in Europe, are well represented in the UCLG, which boasts membership of over one thousand cities representing half of the world's population. However, U.S. cities are notably missing. On the list of eleven U.S. cities, the only major population centers are Washington, D.C., Santa Fe, New Mexico, and Indianapolis, Indiana. No other major U.S. cities or states participate in the UCLG; indeed, the U.S. list is rounded out by cities like Northglenn, Colorado (pop. 36,000), a self-proclaimed "city of the future," and towns such as Gulf Breeze, Florida, population 6,129.

U.S. municipalities have been more active in organizations focused on particular substantive issues, such as the International Council for Local Environmental Initiatives (ICLEI), established in 1990 to help local governments "think globally, act locally."[58] Of the organization's 500 members worldwide, 109 are U.S. municipalities, including Chicago, New York City, and Los Angeles. The ICLEI began working on the issue of global climate change in 1991, when it launched urban carbon dioxide reduction initiatives in fourteen cities worldwide, including Dade County, Florida, Denver, Colorado, Minneapolis and St. Paul, Minnesota, and Portland, Oregon. More recently, in 1999 the ICLEI spearheaded a "Mayors and Local Officials Statement on Global Warming," signed by more than 570 municipal officials in the United States.[59] Led by Mayor Greg Nickels of Seattle, Washington, 132 U.S. mayors pledged to have their cities meet the standards set out in the Kyoto Protocol on global warming, openly embracing an international agreement rejected by the Bush administration.[60] California's agreement to collaborate on international environmental issues with the United Kingdom continues down this path of local leadership in the global environmental movement.

Significantly, the international focus of these state and local initiatives is not necessarily in tension with the accepted notion that foreign affairs power rests with the federal government. Even within the United States, the federal government has recognized a role for states and cities in implementing the United States' international obligations. The starting point is the U.S. Constitution, which provides that ratified treaties such as ICERD are not just relevant to the federal government, but constitute the "Supreme Law of the Land" binding on the "Judges in every State."[61] Further, the U.S. government has repeatedly observed that state and local authorities have an independent role in implementation of ratified treaties. According to the statements made by the U.S. Senate in ratifying ICERD (1994), the ICCPR (1992), and the Convention Against Torture and Other Cruel, Inhuman, or Degrading Treatment or Punishment (1994), "the United States understands that this Covenant shall be implemented by the Federal Government to the extent that it exercises legislative and judicial jurisdiction over the matters covered therein, and otherwise by the state and local governments; to the extent that state and local governments exercise jurisdiction over such matters, the Federal Government shall take measures appropriate to the Federal system to the end that the competent authorities of the state or local governments may take appropriate measures for the fulfillment of the Covenant."[62]

In short, the federal government takes responsibility for implementing human rights treaties only so far, and leaves the rest to state and local authorities.

But what, then, are the areas over which state and local governments properly exercise jurisdiction? The United States offered its view in 1994 when it submitted its first report to the UN Human Rights Committee detailing its compliance with the ICCPR. According to the federal government, its authority did not extend to those areas where state and local governments exercised significant responsibilities, including "matters such as education, public health, business organization, work conditions, marriage and divorce, the care of children, and exercise of the ordinary police power."[63] Again, the United States reiterated that it would "remove any federal inhibitions to the abilities of the constituent states to meet their obligations" under the ICCPR.[64] Nevertheless, the United States' reports to the UN Human Rights Committee describing implementation of the ICCPR were virtually silent on the issue of state implementation.[65] However, the United States' 2007 report to the ICERD Committee does address state implementation more directly, a development which may signal that the government is finally heeding the appeals from international bodies for more comprehensive reporting.

Even within the parameters set by the federal government, jealous of its foreign affairs power, there would seem to be ample room for states and localities to adopt policies designed to effectuate their own and the nation's international human rights obligations. In the area of education, state courts and legislators might read the United States' obligations under ICERD to, as Professor Smith has suggested, trump state-based limitations on affirmative action—at least to the extent that those restrictions (such as Proposition 209) go further than is required under the U.S. Constitution. Exercising their authority over public health, state and local actors might also adopt comprehensive sex education programs in recognition of both international public health and education obligations under the Beijing Platform of Action, despite federal grant programs favoring abstinence only until marriage. Implementing their primary responsibility for marriage and divorce, states and municipalities might permit same-sex marriage in order to fulfill U.S. obligations to provide basic equality under the ICCPR. Certainly, it would seem that city agencies could conduct gender audits, adjust work schedules, and shift the distances between lampposts—all under the rubric of the state's regulation of work conditions—in the name of international human rights without running afoul of federal principles.

Whether states' positions on politically controversial issues like same-sex marriage and sex education might cause the federal government to reassess the respective legislative responsibilities of federal versus subnational governments is a different matter. When political concerns are paramount, the federal government has not shied away from redrawing the lines between federal and state responsibilities. Meanwhile, there is certainly no federal preemption issue in those areas where the federal government has not acted or where its actions are intended to simply create incentives rather than set standards—such as the abstinence grants.

The Future of State and Local Human Rights Implementation

Local activists are understandably not wholly satisfied by encouraging local governments to shift lamppost placements. "Bringing human rights home" should, many believe, lead to more profound and comprehensive changes in the relationship between the individual and his or her representative government.

Yet "bringing human rights home" is a process like any other legislative effort that must build over a period of time. Several states have enacted legislation that takes tentative steps in this direction but still stops short of providing the teeth necessary for real changes. For example, the Massachusetts Commission on the Status of Women is statutorily charged with conducting "an ongoing study of all matters pertaining to women," guided by the tenets of the Beijing Platform for Action.[66] But reflecting the exigencies of real-world politics, the Massachusetts Commission has reworked its mission statement to omit any reference to the Beijing Platform.[67] In Pennsylvania, a human rights–minded legislator succeeded in creating a statewide commission to review state law's compliance with the Universal Declaration of Human Rights.[68] The resulting hearings contributed to public education and organizing around issues facing the poor, but without any additional state funding the ultimate recommendations are all too likely to gather dust at the Pennsylvania Statehouse.[69]

Having already achieved some modest results under CEDAW, however, San Francisco is in a position to go further. Building on their earlier successes, San Francisco activists are now mounting a campaign to secure adoption of the principles of the ICCPR and the International Covenant on Economic, Social and Cultural Rights (ICESCR) as municipal law.

The United States ratified the ICCPR in 1992, subject to a number of reservations on issues such as the death penalty, and it has participated in the treaty-monitoring process by filing a series of compliance reports with the UN Human Rights Committee. However, the ICESCR, concluded in 1966, has not been ratified by the United States. Among other things, the ICESCR outlines rights to shelter, food, and education. These economic and social rights are not foreign to the United States. In fact, they were anticipated in President Roosevelt's famous Four Freedoms speech to Congress in 1941. Sandwiched between the first two freedoms of speech and of religion, and the fourth, freedom from fear, was "freedom from want—which, translated into world terms, means economic understandings which will secure to every nation a healthy peacetime life for its inhabitants—everywhere in the world."[70] Rights to education and welfare appear in the majority of state constitutions, though the U.S. Supreme Court has repeatedly found that such rights are beyond the scope of the federal constitution. Nevertheless, the economic, social, and cultural rights protected by the ICESCR are often subject to vague questions about their "American-ness" as well as the capacity of United States judges to enforce these rights since their realization often involves courts in reviewing legislative allocations and priorities.

Undaunted by the apparent difficulty of its task, WILD for Human Rights launched its latest local human rights campaign in 2004 with a series of community-based briefings.[71] While the law has not yet been formally introduced, it is being circulated far and wide in draft form. The sticking points between WILD and the San Francisco city attorney principally concern the implementation mechanisms in the law. Stung by the erratic process for CEDAW implementation at the city agency level, WILD's Maria Catoline explains that this time, "we want community-based monitoring and accountability, with a formal implementation body."[72]

One of the implementation processes that WILD proposed is a "human rights impact screen" (HRIS), modeled on the environmental impact statements required before a government takes action that might have environmental repercussions. Human rights impact statements are not a new idea; the UN secretary general proposed the preparation of such statements in 1979 in conjunction with new development projects that might affect human rights. The United Nations Committee on Economic, Social, and Cultural Rights subsequently endorsed the suggestion in its General Comment 2 on International Technical Assistance Measures.[73] Since then, it has been bandied around in places as far-flung as the United Kingdom, Australia, and Seattle, Washington, as a possible approach to quantifying human rights impacts of governmental policies.

WILD's proposal is, however, not merely a sunshine law designed to reveal human rights impacts to the wider public. Instead, the proposed human rights impact assessment document would be implemented by the city comptroller's office. It would apply to city agencies as well as independent contractors. For the agencies, their budgets would be contingent on meeting certain human rights performance measures. For contractors, their continued financial relationship with the city might be jeopardized by an unfavorable human rights assessment.

The Burma laws used similar mechanisms for screening potential contractors, with criteria focused on external trade practices, that is, the extent of a corporation's business in Burma. To clearly fall within permissible boundaries of local human rights implementation, San Francisco's screening questionnaire would presumably focus on issues such as domestic partnership benefits, health insurance, and wages—issues of family, welfare, and work—rather than foreign trade. Yet the impact on the companies could well be the same. And like the South Africa and Burma divestment laws, if dozens of states and hundreds of localities imposed similar human rights criteria, it would certainly have an impact on the practices of both private and public institutions nationwide. Perhaps, as the U.S.-focused activists envision, a human rights culture would begin to trickle up to the federal government.

Among activists looking outward, seeking to use the United States' influence to curb human rights abuses abroad, the work also continues. The *Crosby* decision in 2000 was just the first bump in the road. In 2003, the U.S. Supreme Court decided the case of *American Insurance Association v. Garamendi*, striking down a California law that required any insurer doing business in California to disclose information about all policies sold in Europe between 1920 and 1945, setting up a scheme of regulatory sanctions. Several other states had passed similar measures.[74] The goal of these laws was to facilitate identification of misappropriated Holocaust-era assets. However, by applying sanctions to companies that failed to comply, California and the other states acting in this arena went further than the voluntary measures adopted by the federal government.

Writing for the Supreme Court, but this time with only a bare majority of justices in agreement, Justice Souter's opinion echoed his conclusions in the *Crosby* case. "There is, of course, no question," he wrote, "that at some point an exercise of state power that touches on foreign relations must yield to the National Government's policy."[75] Resolving Holocaust-era insurance claims is within the executive's foreign affairs responsibility, Souter opined, and the federal government's actions in this area preempt any state authority.

If even state disclosure laws like California's Holocaust assets law interfere with foreign affairs, activists wondered what was left. In the wake of the Supreme Court's decision in *Crosby*, Georgetown Law School Professor Robert Stumberg outlined five areas in which he believed state and municipal governments could still act. Now only four remain: (1) municipal and state pension funds could divest stocks of companies that violate human rights; (2) local pension funds could use their stock to engage in shareholder advocacy; (3) cities and states could engage in political speech, passing resolutions that urge Congress or the administration to take action; or (4) local governments could continue to explore restrictions on their own procurement.[76]

But while the number of viable state and local approaches appears to be dwindling, the next wave of campus activists focused on deterring and redressing human rights abuses is fully engaged and forging ahead. Divestment remains a powerful human rights tool, and a growing student movement is urging both public and private campus divestment from Sudan, which has engaged in a series of massive genocidal campaigns and human rights abuses in sub-Saharan Africa.[77]

Shareholder advocacy and municipal resolutions continue to be popular and viable ways of organizing and speaking out on these issues, though the results of those approaches are harder to quantify. For example, for many years the New York City comptroller sponsored resolutions calling for shareholder votes on human rights issues.[78] Vermont's Burma law explicitly encourages the Vermont state treasurer to support shareholder resolutions at companies that focus on trade with Burma.[79]

More than a dozen states have gone even farther and enacted laws to limit their state pension funds' investment in Sudan, with additional states considering similar measures.[80] And just as states' human rights procurement policies were challenged in the past, the actions to limit pension fund investment are being challenged in court as exceeding state authority, with some initial success.[81]

Meanwhile, with their proposals for municipal adoption of international treaties and implementation of human rights impact screens as a part of city contracting, San Francisco activists are aggressively pushing the boundaries that the Supreme Court has erected between the foreign and the domestic. There may be many questions. Does the United States' failure to ratify the ICESCR constitute a preemptive action, or does it leave economic, social, and cultural rights open for subnational engagement? Does the United States' ratification of the ICCPR, but without specific federal implementation, preempt local implementation as well? Is domestic implementation of international treaties an aspect of foreign affairs that is properly under the federal government's control, or is it—as the United States has previously stated—a domestic activity open to subnational governments' leadership?

If businesses begin to feel the sting of having to comply with human rights standards in their domestic business practices, history suggests that some group or other will come forward to challenge the approach, arguing that the state or municipality has overstepped its bounds. While the outcome of such a challenge is not entirely clear, past statements from the federal government and the courts continue to suggest that there is an important leadership role that states and municipalities should play, by virtue of the federal system itself, in certain substantive areas such as family, economic, and health issues addressed in international human rights treaties. Some also argue that state and municipal procurement restrictions that rest on moral grounds are protected First Amendment speech. While Justice Souter is undoubtedly correct that "at some point an exercise of state power that touches on foreign relations must yield to the National Government's policy," that point is a moving target in an era in which states and cities have starring roles on the international stage.

It is risky to predict the ultimate outcome of San Francisco's next stage of human rights implementation, but it seems clear when one traces the story from the American Revolutionary War to the Franco-British War, to the Vietnam War, to the South Africa divestment campaign, to the Free Burma movement, to San Francisco, that grassroots activists as well as states and municipalities will not back down when they feel that the federal government's approach fails to adequately implement human rights principles. Rather, activists as well as state and municipal actors will continue to look for the cracks and fissures in the edifice of federalism that will allow a human rights culture to grow in small places close to home.

Notes

Many thanks to research assistants Jessica White, Carol Jun, and Kirsten Patzer, who contributed a great deal to this article. Kyle Courtney of the Northeastern Law School library also provided exceptional research guidance and assistance, while Richard Doyon contributed well-honed administrative skill. Simon Billenness, Scott Cummings, and Cindy Soohoo provided insightful editorial suggestions that improved this chapter immeasurably.

1. Catherine Powell, "Dialogic Federalism: Constitutional Possibilities for Incorporation of Human Rights Law in the United States," *University of Pennsylvania Law Review* 150 (2001): 245.
2. Michael H. Shuman, "Dateline Main Street: Courts v. Local Foreign Policies," *Foreign Policy* no. 86 (Spring 1992): 158–77.
3. See list at National Export Directory, available online at www.export.gov/salesandmarketing/ext_int_db_resources.asp.
4. See Trenton, "Getting Down to the Business of Cultural Exchange," *Bulletin of Municipal Foreign Policy* 3(2) (Spring 1989): 28–29; Sister Cities International, available online at www.sister-cities.org/sci/aboutsci/faqs.
5. Press release, "Gov. Schwarzenegger, British Prime Minister Tony Blair Sign Historic Agreement to Collaborate on Climate Change, Clean Energy," Office of the Governor, State of California, July 31, 2006.
6. Victoria Bonnell and Chester Hartman, "Cambridge Votes on the Vietnam War," *Dissent* 15 (March–April 1968): 103–6.
7. Harlan Hahn and Albert Sugarman, "A Referendum on Vietnam," *War/Peace Report* 11 (May 1967): 14–15.
8. Diane E. Lewis, "Pioneers Recall Divestment Batter," *Boston Globe*, February 16, 1980, p. B-1.
9. See "The Effect of Sanctions on Constitutional Change in SA," speech de-

livered by Dave Steward on behalf of former President F. W. de Klerk to the Institute Choiseul, Paris, June 14, 2004, available online at www.fwdklerk.org. za/download_speech/04_06_14_DWS_Institut_Choiseul_S_PDF.pdf.

10. Peter Spiro, *Wall Street Journal*, September 24, 1986, p. 28.

11. Professor John M. Kline, Letter to the Editor, *Wall Street Journal*, October 13, 1986.

12. Michael Shuman, "A Tale of Two Courts," *Bulletin of Municipal Foreign Policy* 4(3) (Summer 1990): 4.

13. Constitutionality of South African Divestment Statutes Enacted by State and Local Governments, 10 Op. Off. Legal Counsel 49, 54–55 (April 9, 1986).

14. David D. Caron, "Cities, States and Foreign Affairs: The Massachusetts Burma Case and Beyond: The Structure and Pathologies of Local Selective Procurement Ordinances: A Study of the Apartheid-Era South Africa Ordinances," *Berkeley Journal of International Law* 21 (2003): 159, 161.

15. Kevin Danaher and Jason Mark, *Insurrection: Citizen Challenges to Corporate Power* (New York: Routledge, 2003), p. 204.

16. Foreign Operations, Export Financing, and Related Programs Appropriations Act, 1997, s. 570, 110 Stat. 3009-166 to 3009-167.

17. Exec. Order No. 13047, 3 C.F.R. 202 (1997 Comp.).

18. Frank Phillips, "State Was in Lead on Burma; Backers of Mass. Law Welcome US Sanctions," *Boston Globe*, April 23, 1997, p. B-1.

19. 530 U.S. 363, 380 (2000).

20. "Reaching out to Refugees/Myanmar Purchasing Law Is Before Supreme Court," *Worcester Telegram & Gazette*, April 25, 2000.

21. Frank Phillips, "Mass. Law on Burma Struck Down," *Boston Globe*, June 20, 2000, p. A-1.

22. William Sweet, "Amherst to Address World Issues," *Union-News* (Springfield, Mass.), April 14, 1999.

23. "Defending the Massachusetts Burma Law: A Moral Standard for Avoiding Businesses That Support Repression," Harris Institute for Public Law, Georgetown University Law Center, March 7, 2000, p. 3.

24. *Crosby*, 530 U.S. at 388.

25. Sonia Melara, former executive director, Commission on the Status of Women, in discussion with the author, San Francisco, California, July 17, 2003.

26. Gretchen Sidhu, "San Francisco Plunges Ahead in Adopting a CEDAW Treaty of Its Own," *Chicago Tribune*, August 2, 1998, p. 8.

27. Krishanti Dharmaraj, in discussion with the author July 7, 2003.

28. Ibid.

29. Sonia Melara, in discussion with the author, July 17, 2003.

30. S.F. Cal., Admin. Code chap. 12K (2001).

31. Ann Lehman, in discussion with the author, July 17, 2003.

32. Ibid.

33. Ibid.

34. Rebecca Vesely, "U.N. Women's Treaty Molds San Francisco Government," *Women's e-news*, July 25, 2002, available online at www.womensenews. org/article/cfm/dyn/aid/983.

35. Ann Lehman, in discussion with the author, July 17, 2003.

36. Ibid.

37. Ibid.

38. Mark Sappenfield, "In One US City, Life Under UN Treaty on Women," *Christian Science Monitor*, January 20, 2003.

39. "California's CEDAW Bill (Vetoed)," *Minerva* 28 (February 2005): 31.

40. See Governor's Veto Statement, available online at leginfo.ca.gov/pub/03-04/bill/asm/ab_0351-0400/ab_358_vt_20040929.html.

41. Testimony of Mayor David Dinkins, New York City Council, Committee on Government Operations, Human Rights Government Operations Audit Law, Intro. 512, April 8, 2005, p. 2, available online at nychri.org/document/Dinkins.pdf.

42. Andy Humm, "Proposed Law Aims to Prevent Discrimination," *Gotham Gazette*, November 2005.

43. Ibid.

44. Council of Ethics-Based Organizations Associated with the Department of Public Information of the United Nations, available online at cebo.org/2005_03_01_index.archive.html.

45. Dr. J. Owens Smith, in discussion with the author, June 26, 2006.

46. Applied Research Center [ARC], "Defining Racial Discrimination: Assembly Bill 703, State of California 2003."

47. Dr. J. Owens Smith, in discussion with the author, June 26, 2006.

48. ARC Report, p. 2

49. Ibid., p. 3.

50. *C&C Construction, Inc. v. Sacramento Municipal Utility District*, 122 Cal. App. 4th 284 (2004).

51. Ibid., p. 302.

52. Ibid.

53. Dr. J. Owens Smith, in discussion with the author, June 26, 2006.

54. See, e.g., Fifth Report of Canada, CEDAW, pp. 83–228 ("Measures Adopted by the Governments of the Provinces").

55. UN Human Rights Committee, 87th Session, July 10–28, 2006, Consideration of Reports Submitted by States Parties Under Article 40 of the Covenant, United States of America, para. 4.

56. Available online at www.cities-localgovernments.org.

57. Ibid.

58. Michele M. Betsill, "Acting Locally, Does It Matter Globally? Contributions of U.S. Cities to Global Climate Change Mitigation," Paper prepared for the Open Meeting of the Human Dimensions of Global Environmental Change Research Community, Rio de Janeiro, Brazil, October 6–8, 2001.

59. Ibid., p. 7.

60. Eli Sanders, "Rebuffing Bush, 132 Mayors Embrace Kyoto Rules," *New York Times*, May 14, 2005.

61. U.S. Const. art. VI, cl. 2.

62. 138 Cong. Rec. 8068, 8071 (1992) (understanding for the ICCPR).

63. U.S., Initial Report of the United States of America, delivered to the U.S. Human Rights Comm. (HRC), para. 3, U.S. Doc. CCPR/C/81/Add.4 (August 24, 1994).

64. Ibid., para. 4.

65. UN Human Rights Committee, Consideration of Reports Submitted by States Parties Under Article 40 of the Covenant, Concluding Observations, 87th Sess., July 10–28, 2006, paras. 4, 39.

66. Mass. Gen. L. ch. 3, s. 66(3).

67. See Massachusetts Commission on the Status of Women, available online at www.mass.gov/women/aboutus/mission.htm.

68. Gen. Assembly of Pennsylvania, House Res. 144 (2002).

69. See Report of the Select Committee on House Resolution 144 Investigating the Integration of Human Rights Standards in Pennsylvania Laws and Policies, November 30, 2004, available online at www.nasw-pa.org.

70. President Franklin D. Roosevelt, "Four Freedoms Speech," January 6, 1941.

71. Maria Catoline, WILD for Human Rights, in discussion with the author, June 28, 2006.

72. Ibid.

73. CESCR General Comment 2, para. 8(b).

74. *American Insurance Association v. Garamendi*, 539 U.S. 396 (2003).

75. *American Insurance*, 539 U.S. at 413.

76. Simon Billenness, "Narrow Supreme Court Ruling Leaves Room for New Burma Laws," available online at www.trilliuminvest.com/pages/news/news_detail.aspx?ArticleID=14&Status=Archive.

77. Available online at sudandivestment.org.

78. Press release, "New York Pension Funds Call for Shareholder Votes on Human Rights Issues," NYC Comptroller William C. Thompson, Jr., February 8, 2006.

79. 1999 Vt. Acts & Resolves 13 (requiring state pension funds to support certain shareholder resolutions concerning business done in Burma).

80. See, e.g., www.prnewswire.com/cgi-bin/stories.pl?ACCT=104&STORY=/www/story/04-05-2007/0004560826&EDATE= (reporting that Iowa became eighth state to adopt divestment legislation on April 5, 2007).

81. See *NFTC v. Giannoulias*, Case No. 06C 4251 (N.D. Ill. February 23, 2007) (striking down Illinois law limiting pension investments). See also www.nasra.org/resources/Illinois%20court%20ruling.pdf.

Chapter 10

The Impact of September 11 and the Struggle Against Terrorism on the U.S. Domestic Human Rights Movement

Wendy Patten

The terrorist attacks of September 11, 2001 and the government policies implemented in their aftermath had an important impact on the way in which U.S.-based social justice groups used international human rights in their advocacy in the United States. As the Bush administration put in place new measures to fight terrorism, basic rights to liberty, due process, nondiscrimination, and humane treatment were put under a new kind of pressure. The public debate framed the issues as a tradeoff between rights and security in a post-9/11 world, with the administration justifying its actions as necessary to prevent future terrorist attacks and protect American lives.

The Bush administration's war on terror created an urgent need for new strategies to defend the rights of people in the United States. Many U.S. social justice groups—civil rights, civil liberties, immigrant rights, and other legal advocacy organizations—found that traditional forms of advocacy, such as appeals to U.S. courts and the Congress, were not sufficient in the new post-9/11 climate. As social justice groups looked for ways to protect and promote rights placed at risk in the name of fighting terrorism, they increasingly began to use international human rights strategies in their domestic advocacy in the United States. Thus they expanded the framework of rights advocacy to include international human rights alongside civil and constitutional rights.

This chapter explores why and how U.S.-based social justice groups used international human rights to address certain key U.S. policies that violated basic rights in the fight against terrorism after September 11, 2001. It argues that these policies shifted the nascent U.S. domestic human rights movement away from its focus on economic and social rights and toward civil and political rights. Whether this shift is a temporary exigency in response to the Bush administration's counterterrorism policies, or whether it will work a lasting change on the direction of the movement, is difficult to predict. What is clear, however, is that the advocacy movement's response to post-9/11 counterterrorism policies has helped to bridge the gap between international human rights and civil or constitutional rights as a way of framing and defending rights in the United States.

Post-9/11 counterterrorism policies have had a catalyzing effect on the process of bringing human rights home to the United States, even as they sometimes complicated the process. International human rights law became a key bulwark against the erosion of fundamental rights, such as the prohibition on torture and detention without charge, which were put into play by the Bush administration's conduct and its new legal theories. In this climate, many U.S. social justice groups became more open to using international human rights language, standards, and mechanisms as a component of their advocacy work in the United States. Still, efforts to mount a broad-based movement to counter these policies were not without their challenges. Even as the counterterrorism policies brought an unprecedented level of attention to the human rights practices of the U.S. government, they sometimes reinforced the domestic-international divide among U.S. social justice groups. Many of the Bush administration's counterterrorism policies targeted noncitizens held outside the United States, whether at Guantánamo,[1] in secret detention sites abroad, or in Afghanistan and Iraq. With some important exceptions, international human rights groups generally took the lead on these issues, which tended to reinforce the long-held view that human rights were principally about people in other countries, while civil rights dealt with the rights of people in the United States. Despite this challenge, international human rights and domestic social justice groups increasingly collaborated across the divide of geography and citizenship. They began to find ways to build links between efforts to challenge U.S. conduct abroad and rights abuses at home.

These issues could be discussed by examining responses to many different counterterrorism policies with important implications for human rights. This chapter focuses on two sets of issues: First, the detention of noncitizens in the United States on immigration grounds in the weeks and months after the September 11 attacks, and, second, U.S. detention and interrogation policies for terrorist suspects held outside the United States.

A Shift in Focus to Civil and Political Rights

The aftermath of the September 11 attacks ushered in a renewed focus on civil and political rights for U.S. social justice groups. This focus stemmed not so much from a conscious decision among domestic rights groups to favor civil and political rights over economic, social, and cultural rights, but rather was driven by the actions of the Bush administration. The administration's policies on investigation, surveillance, detention, and interrogation called into question fundamental rights that had been largely considered "won" in the United States. U.S. constitutional law prohibits detention without charge and inhumane treatment and ensures equal protection of the laws. While there were persistent and often serious problems in ensuring these rights were respected in practice prior to September 11, 2001, there was no serious debate over whether torture was legal, or whether people could be imprisoned without charge. Because U.S. constitutional law guaranteed these rights, there was little impetus to invoke international human rights law to protect these rights in the United States.

In the aftermath of the September 11 attacks, however, government policies began to undercut long-standing civil and political rights protections under U.S. law. Both U.S.-based international human rights groups and domestic social justice groups were concerned that U.S. constitutional and statutory law, long seen as largely adequate to protect civil and political rights, might be fundamentally altered by the government's counterterrorism policies and the legal battles over them. They feared that Congress and the Supreme Court might redraw the basic lines of rights under U.S. law, putting rights at risk in a new way. U.S. law and practice was falling below international human rights baselines, as the Bush administration began to pursue policies that looked more like those of governments that historically have been far less protective of basic rights.

U.S. social justice advocates needed new legal and advocacy strategies to protect rights. Much like human rights advocates elsewhere, they began to draw on international human rights language, standards, and mechanisms. They began asking themselves the same questions that lawyers from other countries sometimes asked U.S. advocates. Why is it that many U.S. lawyers view human rights as principally concerned with other people's suffering in far away places? Why don't U.S. lawyers look to international human rights standards to understand and defend the rights of people in the United States? Do people in the United States see themselves as having human rights as well as civil rights?

These questions lurked beneath efforts to protect the rights of persons targeted by counterterrorism measures. The constitutional versus international human rights debate sat on shifting terrain. The erosion of certain core civil and political rights after September 11 brought those fault lines into sharper relief. Confronted with a pressing need to defend rights that were suddenly called into question, U.S. social justice advocates mounted efforts to bridge the divide between the two ways of framing and protecting rights for people living in the United States. They talked about civil *and* human rights, looked to international human rights law as a source of obligation for U.S. conduct, and undertook more concerted efforts to use international human rights strategies and mechanisms alongside their traditional forms of advocacy to effect change in U.S. policy and practice.

U.S. Counterterrorism Policies: A Post-9/11 Overview

The terrorist attacks of September 11 created a climate of fear of another impending attack and a sense of vulnerability that required urgent action. As the U.S. public sought to understand why these attacks had occurred and what could be done to prevent future acts of terrorism against the United States, the Bush administration moved swiftly to remake laws and policies to enhance its ability to detect, investigate, detain, and interrogate suspected terrorists. The administration undertook measures that targeted Arabs and Muslims in the United States based principally, if not wholly, on religion and national origin. It implemented policies that permitted prolonged detention without charge or due process in the immigration context and for U.S. citizens and noncitizens whom it deemed "enemy combatants." In the fall of 2001, Congress passed the USA PATRIOT Act, which authorized new investigative powers that created widespread concern regarding an unchecked executive sifting through the private lives of ordinary people. In January 2002, the U.S. government opened a detention camp at Guantánamo Bay, Cuba, and insisted it could hold detainees there without charge beyond the reach of U.S. law and U.S. courts. By year's end, allegations of torture and inhumane treatment of detainees in Afghanistan had begun to surface.

As debates ensued about how to protect rights in the struggle against terrorism, social justice groups began looking not only to U.S. constitutional law but also to international human rights standards. In the early stages, advocates focused on the roundup of immigrants as well as the detentions at Guantánamo Bay. Over time, other Bush administration policies with serious human rights implications came to light, including secret detention sites for high-level terrorist suspects, the rendition (extralegal apprehension and transfer) of persons suspected of links to terrorists to countries where they were at risk of torture, the effort to reshape the rules of interrogation to skirt absolute legal prohibitions on torture and on cruel, inhuman, or degrading treatment, and warrantless domestic surveillance. The torture question took center stage after the revelation of the horrific photos from Abu Ghraib prison in Iraq in April 2004.

This chapter focuses on two major sets of issues that were especially important in encouraging domestic social justice groups to consider using international human rights as a frame of reference and action in defending rights in the United States. Noncitizens comprised the first major group to be subjected to new, harsh policies in the wake of the September 11 attacks. The Justice Department, which then included the Immigration and Naturalization Service (INS), rounded up noncitizens, primarily Arab and Muslim men, detained them on immigration charges, and subjected them to a set of new, harsh policies that violated their rights. Advocacy to vindicate the rights of these detainees came to include greater use of international human rights language, standards, and methods alongside traditional strategies, long employed by civil and immigrants rights groups, that focused on defending and extending constitutional rights and other protections found in U.S. law. A second major development was the detention and treatment of terrorist suspects at Guantánamo Bay and locations abroad. Because these policies principally involved U.S. conduct outside the United States, they posed new legal and practical challenges that further galvanized efforts to bridge the gap between the human rights and civil rights frameworks, while at times also reinforcing that divide as well.

Detention of Noncitizens in the United States

In the weeks and months after September 11, 2001, noncitizens quickly became the primary target of measures taken by the Bush administration both to investigate the terrorist attacks and to prevent future incidents. The reasoning was simple: Al Qaeda had orchestrated the attacks and the nineteen hijackers were Muslim men from Middle Eastern or North African countries. The Justice Department, led by Attorney General John Ashcroft, embarked on a strategy to search through the haystack of immigrants fitting this extremely broad description in an effort to find the proverbial needle.[2] The Bush Justice Department used its substantial discretionary powers over immigration enforcement, combined with the public perception that immigrants had fewer rights, to eviscerate the basic human rights of noncitizens. Senior Bush administration officials helped foster this perception of two levels of rights through comments such as those by Vice President Cheney, who defended the newly authorized military commissions by arguing that noncitizens accused of terrorism "don't deserve the same guarantees and safeguards" that the

U.S. justice system affords U.S. citizens.[3] Still fearful of another al Qaeda attack, the U.S. public generally did not question the government's approach or raise concerns about the rights of noncitizens who were subject to these new policies.

The targeting of noncitizens in the campaign against terrorism posed serious challenges for immigrant rights groups, which included both national policy advocacy organizations and local organizations with deep ties in their communities. With immigrant communities feeling under siege, immigrants rights groups were at the forefront of the advocacy response. So too were U.S.-based international human rights groups, such as Human Rights Watch, Amnesty International USA, and Human Rights First. As the detentions grew in number, these groups explored a variety of advocacy strategies to contest them, both individually and collaboratively.

Use of Immigration Law to Detain Noncitizens

In the aftermath of the September 11 terrorist attacks, the Bush administration began to detain noncitizens under U.S. immigration law. The "special interest" detainees—so called because they were considered to be of special interest to the investigation into the September 11 attacks— were men largely of Arab or Muslim backgrounds. Indeed, a 2003 report by the Justice Department's inspector general found that nearly half of the detainees were from two countries: Egypt and Pakistan.[4] Often, the men who became special interest detainees were targeted for questioning or detention based on little more than their religion or national origin. Some detainees were arrested after neighbors or members of the public reported an "Arab" who seemed suspicious. In November 2001, for example, an Indian man was detained along with three Pakistani men in Torrington, Connecticut, after a resident reported that he had heard two "Arabs" talking about anthrax. Although the man was legally in the United States, the INS detained him for eighteen days. The person who called the police later failed a polygraph test.[5] Others were detained following a random encounter with law enforcement, such as one man who asked a police officer for directions at the Newark train station. The police officer asked him where he was from and he replied, "Egypt." After questioning him about his immigration status, the police officer took him into custody and he was later deported.[6] In assessing the classification process for the special interest detainees, the Justice Department's inspector general would later conclude that the FBI and INS made little attempt to distinguish between those noncitizens who were the subject of a lead in the investigation and those who had no connection to terrorism but were encountered coincidentally.[7] In the end, no special interest detainee was ever charged with involvement in the September 11 attacks. By late 2002, only 6 of the 765 special interest detainees remained in detention, as the FBI had cleared the rest of any links to terrorist activity and they had been either released or deported.

Throughout fall 2001, the Justice Department released to the public the number of persons, including noncitizens, whom it had detained inside the United States. Once the number reached 1,182 in early November, the department announced it would no longer give a running total. It also closed all immigration hearings involving special interest detainees to the public, the press, and even family members. The secrecy that surrounded these detentions hindered public accountability and contributed to the abuses suffered by those who were detained and designated as special interest detainees.

While it is routine to apprehend noncitizens who are out of immigration status, the treatment of the special interest detainees was anything but routine. The Justice Department used the immigration laws to detain noncitizens and keep them detained while it investigated them—without probable cause—for possible involvement in criminal activity. The government's strategy was to use the more permissive immigrant enforcement regime to investigate and detain noncitizens whom it suspected, often with little or no basis, of terrorist involvement. It then changed the rules governing immigration procedures, using its considerable discretion in implementing immigration laws to give itself vastly expanded powers to hold noncitizens in detention and even block their deportation from the United States in order to continue to investigate them after the immigration proceedings were completed. In short, the Justice Department used the immigration laws to facilitate an end run around the due process requirements of the criminal justice system that apply to the government's powers of arrest and detention.

The Justice Department violated the rights of detainees in five principal ways. First, it subjected them to prolonged detention without charge, in some cases up to four months. Second, it interfered with their right to counsel, including through a several-week communications blackout at the Metropolitan Detention Center (MDC) in Brooklyn, where the majority of special interest detainees were held. More generally, the lack of information about who was being detained and where made it difficult for lawyers to assist detainees and their families. Third, the Justice Department promulgated regulations that permitted its attorneys to override judicial decisions to release detainees on bond after a hearing. Fourth, the department kept detainees in U.S. custody for months after they had been ordered deported, continuing to investigate them for ties to criminal activity despite the lack of probable cause needed for detention on criminal grounds. Finally, detainees were subjected to extremely harsh conditions of confinement, including excessive use of solitary confinement and, in some cases, physical and verbal abuse. For example, detainees at the MDC in Brooklyn reported that correctional officers slammed their faces into walls, in one case loosening a detainee's front teeth.[8]

The government's handling of the right to counsel is a prime example of the blurring of the lines between criminal and immigration enforcement in ways that compromised rights guaranteed to defendants in criminal matters. In a criminal case, all defendants—regardless of citizenship or immigration status—have a right to counsel to assist them in mounting a legal defense to the charges against them. If they cannot afford a lawyer, the government will provide one for them. If they are in custody and are being questioned about a criminal matter, they have a right to have counsel present and must be informed of that right.[9] Under immigration law, because the proceedings are not criminal, noncitizens do not have a right to court-appointed counsel. Instead, they have a more limited right to the assistance of counsel if they are able to secure legal representation through their own efforts. U.S. immigration authorities are required by law to provide immigrants with a list of attorneys who are available to provide pro bono legal assistance. If noncitizens are able to retain counsel, their attorney will be allowed to represent them in their immigration case. If, however, they are not able to retain counsel, the case may proceed against them without representation.[10]

The Justice Department interfered with the right to counsel in two ways. First, it prevented immigration attorneys from meeting or talking to their clients, most prominently at the MDC in Brooklyn. There it instituted a total communications blackout that prevented attorneys from counseling their clients for approximately three weeks, and even prevented family members from learning the whereabouts of their loved ones who had been detained by the government. This blackout policy, which was criticized by the Justice Department's inspector general in his report on the special interest detainees, infringed upon the right to access to counsel in immigration matters.

The department also circumvented the right to counsel in criminal matters through its misuse of immigration laws to engage in conduct that is not permitted in a criminal investigation. FBI agents questioned special interest detainees, who were being held on immigration charges, about crimes related to the September 11 attacks without affording the detainees their right to counsel. In some cases, detainees were informed about their right to counsel only after the FBI interrogated them. For example, four Mauritanians were told of their right to counsel and given telephone access only after they had been in detention for four days and had been questioned by the FBI about the September 11 attacks.[11] In other cases, detainees were given Miranda warnings but their requests for a lawyer went unheeded. An Egyptian man, for example, was detained by the FBI and interrogated about the terrorist attacks. When he requested a lawyer, he was told one would be appointed later. They continued to question him for seven or eight hours and then sent him to INS for further interrogation. He was never assigned an attorney and was subsequently ordered deported.[12] The government thus violated the right to counsel during custodial interrogations on criminal matters, a right which is enshrined in the U.S. Constitution. In this way, the Justice Department blurred the lines between immigration and criminal enforcement in order to circumvent key rights protections for persons suspected of involvement in a crime.

Enemy Aliens

The public perception of the enemy alien in our midst, who must be dealt with harshly and who has fewer rights than citizens, took on new life in the aftermath of the September 11 attacks. Longtime anti-immigrant politicians found common ground with Bush administration officials seeking new powers to detect and deter terrorist activity. They justified expansive immigration enforcement and control measures, as well as other policies that focused on Arab and Muslim immigrants, as necessary to fight terrorism. The targeting of noncitizens was more politically palatable than targeting U.S. citizens, so public concern about these policies was muted at best. Even in cases in which particular policies could have been applied to citizens and noncitizens alike—such as the establishment of military commissions to try terrorist suspects—the Bush administration chose only to subject noncitizens to these new measures. While perhaps partly based on a legal calculus as to how the Supreme Court would ultimately judge the constitutionality of such action, it seems highly likely that the decision to subject only noncitizens to these new policies was also based on a political judgment about what the U.S. public would find acceptable.

The citizen-versus-noncitizen divide became a major fault line in the debate over rights in a post-9/11 world. The struggle against terrorism was framed in terms of "us/citizens" versus "them/enemy aliens" almost from the start, with profound consequences for rights protections.[13] Noncitizens in general, and Arab and Muslim noncitizens in particular, were portrayed as "other" and as outside the realm of rights protections that the United States sought to defend against foreign terrorists. By placing Arabs and Muslims on the other side of the rights divide, the violation of "their" rights was not seen as jeopardizing "our" rights, the rights of the vast majority of the U.S. public.

The dichotomy between "us/citizens" and "them/enemy aliens" in the post–September 11 world posed a serious challenge to social justice groups in mobilizing a broad-based constituency to contest detention policies that targeted noncitizens of Arab and Muslim backgrounds. The Bill of Rights Defense Committees that formed to challenge the PATRIOT Act provide an instructive example. The public outcry over expanded government powers to obtain individuals' medical or library records—powers that could directly affect the rights of U.S. citizens—stood in sharp contrast to the relative lack of protest against detention of noncitizens in U.S. jails and detention centers, or rendition of suspects to governments widely known to engage in torture, or even to inhumane treatment of detainees held abroad. While there were various factors at work in shaping the public response to each of these policies, a key difference was the perception on the part of many U.S. citizens that their rights were not likely to be affected by these latter policies. Where they could readily see how certain new powers could compromise their rights, such as the right to privacy and Fourth Amendment protections against warrantless searches, citizens were more likely to mobilize against the administration's policies. Where, however, government policies principally affected the rights of those perceived as "other" or as "enemy aliens," public concern was largely muted or fleeting.[14]

The Limits of Traditional Litigation Strategies

To protect the rights of immigrants, advocacy groups looked to mount legal challenges to new policies undertaken by the Bush administration. They hoped that by filing lawsuits in U.S. courts, they could win rulings that would invalidate the government's new measures and force a change in policy. Such litigation strategies were very familiar to the civil rights and civil liberties movement in the United States, which had successfully challenged many policies over several decades on the grounds that they violated constitutional or statutory rights.[15]

Several groups tackled the secrecy surrounding the special interest detentions in the weeks after September 11, filing three Freedom of Information Act (FOIA) requests seeking the names of those detained, along with related information such as dates of arrest and any charges against them. The Justice Department refused to disclose any information. On December 6, 2001, nearly two dozen civil rights, civil liberties, and human rights organizations brought suit in *Center for National Security Studies v. Ashcroft* to force the Justice Department to release the names.[16] In mid-2002, under the pressure of the lawsuit as well as a Senate Judiciary Committee hearing, the Justice Department released the names of 129 people detained and charged with criminal offenses, which were all unrelated to terrorism. It also revealed that it had detained 751 people on immigration charges, but refused to provide their names or any other information about them. Although the federal court rebuked the Justice Department and ordered it to release the names, the court of appeals overturned the decision, ruling that the government did not have to release the names or the other information requested. The Supreme Court declined to hear the case.[17]

In early 2002, two separate lawsuits filed by media organizations challenged the government's September 2001 decision to bar press and public access to immigration hearings for special interest detainees, yielding mixed results and leaving the issue unsettled.[18] The Third Circuit Court of Appeals ruled that the government's policy of blanket closure of hearings in special interest cases was lawful. In the Sixth Circuit, however, the appeals court struck down the blanket closure of hearings for special interest detainees, holding that the public has a First Amendment right of access to immigration hearings and that the government cannot close the hearings without providing justification in each individual case. When the government then stated that it was reconsidering its closure policy, the Supreme Court declined to hear an appeal of the Third Circuit's decision.

Litigation was also used to counter the special interest detentions themselves. In April 2002, the Center for Constitutional Rights brought a civil rights challenge to the detentions on behalf of a class of those who were detained. The action, *Turkmen v. Ashcroft*, alleged that the detainees were subjected to prolonged detention without charge in violation of the Fourth Amendment's ban on unreasonable seizure and the Fifth Amendment prohibition on deprivation of liberty without due process of law, subjected to discrimination based on their race, religion, and national origin in violation of the Fifth Amendment's guarantee of equal protection of the laws, and denied the right to counsel and subjected to inhumane conditions of confinement, including instances of physical and verbal abuse, in violation of their Fifth Amendment due process rights.

The results have been mixed thus far in this ongoing case. While the district court allowed the challenges to conditions of confinement to proceed, it was unconcerned about the government's pretextual use of the immigration laws to detain noncitizens while investigating them for criminal activity without probable cause. As long as their eventual deportation was "reasonably foreseeable," the court found no due process or Fourth Amendment violation in their continued detention for months after they had been ordered deported. It also rejected their equal protection claim with respect to their prolonged detention, reading Supreme Court precedent to permit the government to single out nationals of particular countries and focus immigration enforcement efforts on them. Notably, the court asserted that such an "extraordinarily rough and overbroad" distinction would meet with great judicial skepticism if it were applied to U.S. citizens.[19] The case is on appeal before the Second Circuit.

A key limitation that these lawsuits confronted was the lack of robust rights protections for noncitizens in important areas of U.S. immigration law, particularly the substantive law and procedure governing deportation proceedings. As many legal scholars have described, the differences between the rights of citizens and noncitizens in the United States are not as great as is generally thought. Still, the Supreme Court's rulings on noncitizens' rights cut in two different directions, thus contributing to the widespread belief that the government can legitimately accord lesser rights to noncitizens. While the Supreme Court has generally affirmed that the Constitution protects the rights of noncitizens in the United States on equal footing with citizens (except for the right to vote and to run for federal elective office), it has taken a less rights-protective approach to the treatment of noncitizens in immigration matters, including detention. Although noncitizens can be deprived of their liberty and placed in detention centers much like jails or prison—indeed they are sometimes held in local jails alongside criminal suspects—these detentions are considered administrative rather than criminal. Thus, immigrant detainees who are being held for violation of the immigration laws while the government seeks to deport them do not have the rights and protections that the U.S. Constitution guarantees all persons charged with a crime, whether citizen or noncitizen.

The decisions in these lawsuits challenging the special immigrant detention policies reflect the limits of U.S. law in securing the rights of noncitizens in immigration proceedings. In *Center for National Security Studies*, the advocacy groups prevailed in the trial court, but the decision was overturned by the court of appeals and the Supreme Court then refused to hear the case, letting the government's refusal to reveal the names of the detainees stand. In the media cases challenging secret hearings, the government's indication of a possible shift in policy averted Supreme Court review but left in place conflicting circuit court opinions, one of which permits blanket closure of immigration hearings to the press and public in the three states that comprise the Third Circuit. In *Turkmen*, the trial court dismissed the challenges to prolonged detention and racial profiling, although it allowed claims regarding conditions of confinement to proceed.

Another limit of litigation strategies is time. The *Turkmen* case took too long to have a direct impact on those in detention, nearly all of whom had been released or deported by the end of 2002, well before the trial court issued its decision in June 2006. As with the Guantánamo detentions, however, the mere fact of a lawsuit prompted the government to rethink its policies. Faced with justifying its actions before a court of law and hoping to improve its position in the litigation, the Justice Department altered its policy on secret hearings (for example, affording the detainee at issue in the Sixth Circuit case an open deportation hearing) and released more complete information about at least some of the detainees—those held on criminal charges. Judicial scrutiny of executive branch conduct thus served to mitigate some aspects of the detention policies.

Human Rights Strategies

As advocacy groups sought effective means to defend the rights of the special immigrant detainees, they began to use international human rights language, standards, and mechanisms in their work in various ways.

Litigation Involving Human Rights Claims

International human rights language and standards factored into legal challenges to the special interest detentions not as central arguments but as complementary arguments that helped buttress claims under U.S. law. Legal advocacy groups maintained their primary focus on U.S. law both because of questions regarding whether U.S. treaty obligations created a right on the part of individuals to bring claims in U.S. courts for violation of their treaty rights and because of the controversy over whether and to what extent international and foreign law could be used by U.S. courts. Still, lawyers used international human rights standards to reinforce a U.S. legal norm under attack. Whether the international standard was broader than or coextensive with the domestic standard, it served as a useful additional argument about the importance of the rights at stake, as well as another source of legal obligation. Lawyers also hoped that, over time, U.S. courts would become more accustomed to considering questions of U.S. obligations under international law.

In *Turkmen*, the legal advocacy groups argued that the special interest detainees were denied their right to seek assistance from their consulates under the Vienna Convention on Consular Relations. They also asserted a claim under the Alien Tort Statute that the government had violated international legal prohibitions against arbitrary detention and cruel, inhuman, and degrading treatment. The court dismissed the international law claims for lack of jurisdiction, reasoning that these claims must proceed under the Federal Tort Claims Act, which recognizes claims that arise under state law rather than international law.

In *Center for National Security Studies,* several human rights groups joined the litigation as co-plaintiffs, bringing a human rights frame to public advocacy surrounding the case. While the legal arguments in the lawsuit were based on U.S. law, groups such as Human Rights Watch articulated international human rights principles related to secret arrests and public hearings that supported the release of the names of the special interest detainees.

Documentation of Abuses

Documentation has long been central to the work of many international human rights groups. They conduct careful research to document human rights abuses and then present the factual information in widely disseminated reports. Documentation work enables human rights groups to bring abuses to light, convey their scope and impact in a compelling way, contest government denials and obfuscation, and create public pressure on governments to change their conduct.

Many domestic groups used the media to denounce rights abuses long before September 11, 2001. In the months and years thereafter, some groups began to integrate documentation work with public advocacy in a more focused way, making in-depth field research on rights violations the basis for denouncing government policy. For example, the Arab American Institute issued a report on the first anniversary of the September 11 attacks that contained a mix of policy analysis, individual perspectives, and factual information regarding Arab Americans who were affected by the backlash against their community.[20] Similarly, the ACLU collaborated with Human Rights Watch on a project to document the misuse of material witness warrants. Although the warrant was designed to secure the testimony of witnesses, the Justice Department began to use it as a way to detain terrorist suspects and deprive them of their rights. In 2005, the two organizations published a report entitled "Witness to Abuse," which documented the use of the material witness statute against more than seventy-five people in the United States. The project combined research and reporting with subsequent litigation to challenge the Justice Department's novel and troubling use of this type of warrant as part of its counterterrorism policies.

Documentation work played a particularly important role in the efforts of U.S.-based advocates to respond to the special interest immigrant detentions. Human Rights Watch issued an in-depth report on the special interest detainees in August 2002, based principally on interviews with lawyers for detainees and with those detainees to whom it was allowed access by the Justice Department.[21] Through its report, Human Rights Watch was able to paint a powerful picture of the human rights abuses suffered by the detainees. Other groups, including Amnesty International USA and the ACLU, also engaged in research and documentation work that underscored the severity of the problems with the government's handling of special interest detentions.[22]

While human rights documentation was not a new strategy in the United States, having been used notably by Human Rights Watch and Amnesty International, documentation work took on greater importance in light of the lack of access to information about the detainees and the government's treatment of them after September 11. The Bush administration's efforts to shield its policies from scrutiny through secret hearings, the refusal to release the names of those detained and resistance to judicial oversight made traditional avenues for protecting rights, such as litigation and in-depth press reporting, more difficult. In this climate, human rights strategies of documenting abuses and naming and shaming became critical to effective advocacy.

Indeed, the documentation work helped shape the government's own understanding of what happened to the special interest detainees. The report of an investigation by the Justice Department's inspector general issued in June 2003 largely corroborates the findings of the Human Rights Watch report from the previous year. The Inspector General's Office could make use of information and leads contained in the reports by human rights groups in conducting its own independent investigation. When the inspector general issued his report in June, the Justice Department's leadership was placed on the defensive. It could not dismiss a highly critical 198-page report containing twenty-one specific recommendations for reform by its own internal watchdog. Extensive press coverage followed, along with congressional hearings and a well-attended congressional staff briefing organized by a group of civil rights, immigrant rights, and human rights groups. Congress and the press then sought more information about the special interest detentions, while the inspector general carried out his mandate to monitor the department's response to his findings and recommendations.

Advocacy on special interest detainees led to a particularly important outcome in the cases of detainee abuse at the MDC in Brooklyn. In a supplemental report issued in December 2003, the Justice Department's inspector general determined that officers slammed detainees into walls, subjected them to other forms of physical and verbal abuse, and punished them by keeping them restrained for long periods of time.[23] The inspector general's findings on strip searches provide an illuminating example: "[M]any of the strip searches appeared to be unnecessary, and a few appeared to be intended to punish the detainees. For example, many detainees were strip searched after attorney and social visits, even though these visits were in no-contact rooms separated by thick glass, the detainees were restrained, and the visits were filmed."[24] The inspector general found the detainees' allegations of abuse to be credible and largely consistent, while many officers at MDC gave blanket denials of mistreatment that the inspector general did not find credible. Some officers, for example, denied taking actions that had been captured on videotape.[25]

The inspector general recommended further investigation into these incidents of abuse and appropriate disciplinary action against those officials responsible for the mistreatment. Finally, in February 2006, the Federal Bureau of Prisons, which runs the facility, took various disciplinary actions against eleven officers at MDC. Two officers were terminated, two received thirty days without pay, four received two or four days without pay, and three were demoted.[26] While many social justice groups maintained that more severe punishment was warranted, it seems clear that human rights documentation strategies called attention to the abuse of detainees at MDC and helped set in motion the inspector general's thorough investigation of these abuses, resulting in corrective action by the Bureau of Prisons.

In sum, the use of human rights documentation strategies helped gather and analyze isolated facts and individual stories into a coherent whole, painting a compelling picture of systemic abuses that facilitated press coverage and public understanding. Reports by Human Rights Watch and other groups contributed to a substantial public record, which gave impetus to more robust congressional oversight, supported litigation efforts, and brought information to light on which the Justice Department's inspector general could draw in its own investigation. As a result, the Bush administration took some corrective action and modified certain policies it had applied to the special interest detainees. For example, in 2004, the Department of Homeland Security, which is now responsible for immigration enforcement, issued guidance to improve the timeliness of decisions to charge a noncitizen with an immigration violation and to notify the noncitizen of the charges. This guidance, while still containing a troubling loophole in cases of a broadly defined emergency or extraordinary circumstance, represented an effort to set clearer default rules in order to prevent detainees from languishing in detention without charge.[27] While the special interest detention policies largely remain in place for use in another time of threat,[28] careful documentation of the abuses that occurred will likely make it harder for the government to abuse its authority to the same extent that it did in the wake of the September 11 attacks.

Use of International Human Rights Mechanisms

U.S. social justice advocates also began to use international human rights mechanisms to protect and promote the rights of noncitizens who were detained after September 11. This work was led largely by U.S.-based international human rights groups, which had experience in working with the machinery of international human rights institutions. A few domestic advocacy groups became involved in this work directly, while others were exposed to these efforts in ways that increased their knowledge of these mechanisms and their ability to consider using them in their own advocacy.

In June 2002, Global Rights, the Center for Justice and International Law, and the Center for Constitutional Rights (CCR) filed a petition before the Inter-American Commission on Human Rights, a regional human rights body that hears petitions alleging human rights violations by member states of the Organization of American States. The groups challenged the Bush administration's policy of detaining noncitizens on immigration grounds after they had been ordered deported by an immigration judge or had agreed to leave the United States. They argued that once a person has been ordered deported, the government must move expeditiously to deport the noncitizen, and in any event within the ninety days required by a U.S. statute. Instead, they claimed, the government was unlawfully keeping these noncitizens in detention in order to investigate whether they had any links to terrorism.[29]

In September 2002, the Inter-American Commission on Human Rights granted the petition and issued precautionary measures, requesting that the U.S. government take urgent steps to protect the fundamental rights of the detainees, including the right to liberty and personal security, the right to humane treatment, and the right of access to a court.

The decision of the Inter-American Commission against the United States did not garner much attention nor did it spur a public outcry against the treatment of the special interest detainees, which is likely attributable to three factors. First, lack of familiarity in the United States with the machinery of the Inter-American human rights system created a significant hurdle to communicating the import of this decision to the public at large. A critical ruling from the Inter-American Commission on Human Rights did not resonate with most people in the United States as a major setback for the Bush administration's policies in the way, for example, that a ruling from the Supreme Court did. Second, the commission issued its decision after the vast majority of the special interest detainees had been deported or released, and therefore the decision received less media coverage than it might have when the detainees numbered over seven hundred. Third, the public was less troubled by the abuse of the rights of noncitizens who had committed immigration violations than by other counterterrorism policies that infringed on basic rights.

Still, the petition to the Inter-American Commission resulted in increased scrutiny of U.S. conduct at a time when it was difficult to challenge the treatment of special interest detainees both in courts of law and in the court of public opinion. The petition pushed the U.S. government to respond publicly and formally to questions about its human rights record in the struggle against terrorism. In addition, legal advocacy groups such as the CCR cited language from the commission's rulings in its litigation to challenge government treatment of detainees in U.S. courts.

Moreover, the petition was significant because it helped further awareness of possible international human rights remedies among domestic social justice groups. A number of these groups met with the UN Special Rapporteur on Contemporary Forms of Racism, Racial Discrimination, Xenophobia, and Related Intolerance, raising the special interest immigrant detentions among a range of issues. Similarly, the UN Working Group on Arbitrary Detention reviewed the cases of a group of twenty special interest detainees. In all but one case, the detainees had already been released or deported by the time the Working Group considered their detention in 2004. In the one case, however, the UN Working Group found Benamar Benatta's detention arbitrary and asked the United States to remedy the situation.[30] The Working Group's opinion contributed to Benatta's eventual release from detention. His immigration attorney referenced the opinion in her submissions to the immigration court and in her negotiations with the government, which eventually decided to release him.

U.S. social justice groups used international human rights mechanisms to call attention to the plight of detainees. The ACLU filed a petition with the Working Group on Arbitrary Detention on behalf of thirteen detainees. Media was a key part of the group's strategy. The ACLU conducted simultaneous press conferences in Geneva and New York on the day it filed the petitions and published an accompanying report. Part of its media strategy was to highlight the effect of these detentions not only on the men detained but also on their families, dramatizing this impact through the participation of a family split apart on two continents at the press conferences. The use of this international human rights mechanism was a significant new development for domestic rights groups. The ACLU characterized its advocacy efforts as a fight on two fronts: domestic and international. In a report on these detainees, the ACLU wrote that "[t]oday, nations are linked more tightly than ever—through immigration and commerce. They should also, we believe, be encouraged to measure their democratic institutions against an internationally accepted standard of human rights."[31]

The momentum for using international human rights mechanisms to address U.S. counterterrorism measures continued to build. In 2006, over 140 U.S. social justice groups participated in sending information to the UN Human Rights Committee during its review of U.S. compliance with the International Covenant on Civil and Political Rights (ICCPR). In its concluding observations, the Committee expressed its concern regarding the special interest detainees, directing the United States to review its policies and practices to ensure that "immigration laws are not used so as to detain persons suspected of terrorism or any other criminal offences with fewer guarantees than in criminal proceedings."[32] It further directed the U.S. government to provide reparations to those who were improperly detained.

Reframing the Issue

Even more important, however, was the use of human rights language in public advocacy in order to reframe the debate about proper treatment of noncitizens held in U.S. jails and detention centers. There was a prevailing sense among many advocacy groups that it was strategically important to frame challenges to the administration's counterterrorism policies in terms of a collective American identity. Such language was intended to deflect charges that criticisms of counterterrorism policies were unpatriotic—a frequent tactic of the administration's defenders. Press statements, letters, and other public messages were often drafted using language that referred to the rights of "citizens," the protection of "Americans," or safeguarding "our" national security.

Despite the political judgment that such language would make the defense of basic rights more palatable, some advocacy groups insisted that this kind of language actually reinforced the us-versus-them divide by excluding noncitizens. To protect the rights of everyone in the United States, they argued, advocacy groups should speak not in terms of the rights of citizens but of the rights of all human beings. They argued that, notwithstanding the rhetorical use of "citizens" to dampen criticism of their message, rights language could not be limited to citizens because language so often shapes public understanding of an issue. Speaking in terms of U.S. citizens would reinforce the idea that noncitizens had fewer rights, which would make it more difficult to challenge policies such as the treatment of noncitizens detained by the Justice Department. International human rights language often became the common ground among immigrant rights, Arab and Muslim groups, human rights groups, and civil rights and civil liberties groups as they collaborated to develop public messages on specific issues.

The challenge of defending the rights of noncitizens in this climate was enormous. Long before September 11, noncitizens were typically perceived as having fewer rights than U.S. citizens. In the aftermath of the September 11 attacks, fierce anti-immigrant rhetoric on the airwaves often exaggerated the difference between the rights of citizens and noncitizens under U.S. law. As advocates struggled to find new ways to defend immigrants' rights, they found that international human rights standards could serve both as a way of emphasizing U.S. legal obligations and as a way of reframing the debate. Referencing due process rights under international treaties ratified by the United States, such as the ICCPR, gave immigrant advocacy groups a new way of talking about the rights of noncitizens in a difficult climate.

International human rights language also helped to reframe the debate about rights in order to make the case that the United States could not and should not compromise the rights of noncitizens in order to address the threat posed by international terrorism. Those who defended the detention of noncitizens often justified the administration's policies by arguing that the Constitution afforded lesser protection to noncitizens than to citizens. Advocates turned to international human rights language and standards to emphasize that all human beings, regardless of immigration status, have certain basic human rights. Framing the questions in terms of human rights, rather than constitutional rights, helped to emphasize the human dignity of all persons and to neutralize the power of the "enemy alien" narrative.

Similarly, advocates also used human rights language to convey the seriousness of the abuses suffered by the special interest detainees. Here they borrowed from some of the effective work done by other domestic advocates, such as those working on LGBT rights and workers' rights,[33] who used the message that the violence and discrimination against LGBT students in U.S. schools and impediments to workers' rights to form unions had risen to the level of human rights abuses. Indeed, advocates across these varied issues have felt that framing the problems in human rights terms gave them a new and powerful way of helping U.S. audiences understand the nature and scope of the rights abuses at issue.

In sum, human rights strategies advanced advocacy efforts to defend the rights of noncitizen detainees. Contesting government policies that targeted Arab and Muslim immigrants was difficult given the widely held view that they were the "other"—enemy aliens entitled to fewer rights than U.S. citizens. The language of human rights was helpful in shifting the debate away from the differences in rights afforded to citizens and noncitizens under the U.S. Constitution. International human rights served as a way of leveling the playing field between citizen and non-citizen by emphasizing the common humanity and human dignity of all persons, regardless of their citizenship. Advocates began to include arguments based on U.S. obligations under international human rights law in their litigation efforts. They also expanded their use of international human rights mechanisms, both at the Inter-American and UN levels, to challenge the policies of the Bush administration, with modest results. Human rights documentation work helped to bring a pattern of abuses to light, which shamed the government into taking action against the worst of the abuses, including the incidents of physical abuse of detainees at the MDC in Brooklyn. Only time will tell, however, whether these advocacy efforts will result in a significantly different policy toward noncitizens should there be another emergency that causes the government to use its immigration powers to detain noncitizens suspected of involvement in terrorism.

Treatment of Terrorist Suspects Abroad: Guantánamo, Rendition, and Torture

The detention of more than 750 noncitizens inside the United States using special measures under immigration law was only a first step in the erosion of basic rights in the aftermath of the September 11 attacks. The Bush administration's lack of respect for rights guaranteed under U.S. law—protections against torture and cruel, inhuman, or degrading treatment and against indefinite detention without charge—continued and expanded with the opening of the Guantánamo detention camp in January 2002, the detention of high-level terrorist suspects in secret locations abroad, the use of torture and cruel treatment in the interrogation, and the rendition of individuals to countries where they were at risk of being subjected to torture.

The Bush administration justified its policies in national security terms, claiming they were necessary to gather intelligence, disrupt terrorist networks, and prevent another terrorist attack. A nervous public largely accepted such arguments. The secrecy that surrounded government conduct made it difficult to evaluate the administration's claims that its controversial policies were critical to the struggle against terrorism. To prevent the erosion of basic rights and to regain lost ground, social justice groups had to devise new strategies to contest the treatment of noncitizens detained abroad in a context that was either perceived literally as a war or accepted as being sufficiently like a war to justify extraordinary measures.

The handling of foreign terrorist suspects—at Guantánamo, in secret locations abroad, and at Abu Ghraib prison in Iraq—became perhaps the most prominent symbols of the U.S. government's failure to uphold human rights in the struggle against terrorism. The detention and treatment of noncitizens abroad had a catalyzing impact on nascent efforts by U.S. domestic social justice groups to apply international human rights standards to U.S. conduct. The fact that these policies implicated fundamental human rights violations galvanized U.S. advocates and encouraged them to press the Bush administration to uphold international legal standards. The CCR, the ACLU, and many pro bono attorneys challenged U.S. conduct abroad in court, represented Guantánamo detainees, and pressed the administration to release information about its policies and decisions. Their efforts complemented the work of international human rights groups, such as Human Rights Watch, Amnesty International USA, and Human Rights First. At the same time, because these policies involved treatment of noncitizens suspected of links to terrorism who were held outside the United States, the policies also tended to reinforce the domestic-international divide within the social justice movement in the United States. Many domestic advocates felt that these policies involved foreign issues that went beyond their mandate, thus leaving it to international human rights groups and a relatively small number of other groups to contest them.

Detentions at Guantánamo Bay

In January 2002, the U.S. government opened the detention camp at the U.S. Naval Base at Guantánamo Bay, Cuba. The camp quickly became a prominent global symbol of the Bush administration's excesses in the struggle against terrorism. The number of detainees reached approximately 775 at its height. Many were captured in the conflict in Afghanistan, while many others were apprehended in places far from any battlefield. Despite the secrecy that surrounded the detainees, press reports and human rights documentation slowly yielded information about the nationality of the detainees and the circumstances of their capture. A dozen children under age eighteen were held at Guantánamo, the three youngest of whom were separated from the adult detainees and eventually released in January 2004. Plans for military commission trials of the detainees, first announced in fall 2001, were put on hold as the U.S. government focused on interrogating detainees. The detentions wore on. The Bush administration dug in its heels, constructing more permanent prison facilities at the base and initiating proceedings before military commissions for six detainees in 2004. As of January 2009, seven years after the camp opened and despite extensive international pressure, the U.S. government still held some 245 detainees at Guantánamo Bay.

The core of the Bush administration's detention policy at Guantánamo was its effort to place detainees beyond the reach of the law. Detainees were held largely incommunicado and without access to counsel or to the courts. The Bush administration's position was that detainees did not have a right to challenge their detention by the United States in U.S. courts. As lawyers filed initial habeas corpus petitions on behalf of detainees, the administration countered by arguing that U.S. courts lacked jurisdiction over claims filed by non-Americans held at the U.S. Naval Base at Guantánamo Bay, Cuba, which it claimed was outside U.S. territory. Although ultimately litigation in U.S. courts became pivotal in protecting the due process rights of detainees, initially the prospects for using traditional litigation approaches to challenge the Guantánamo detentions seemed very limited. It was far from clear how the Supreme Court ultimately would rule on a case, and litigation was fraught with practical as well as legal challenges.

Early on, the total isolation of the detainees made it extremely difficult for them to communicate their interest in serving as plaintiffs in any lawsuit challenging their detention. Shortly after the U.S. government brought the first detainees to Guantánamo in early 2002, a group of clergy, lawyers, and professors filed suit in federal court in California, asserting the habeas rights of the detainees on their behalf because they "appear to be held incommunicado and have been denied access to legal counsel."[34] The court dismissed the case for lack of standing, finding that the petitioners could not represent the interests of the detainees without their assent. Advocates then turned to various international human rights bodies to make their case, including the Inter-American Commission on Human Rights (IACHR) and several of the UN special rapporteurs and the Working Group on Arbitrary Detention.

In February 2002, the CCR, the Columbia Law School Human Rights Clinic, and the Center for Justice and International Law filed a petition with the IACHR seeking to protect the rights of the approximately three hundred persons then detained at Guantánamo. Given the lack of access to detainees, an IACHR petition was a logical choice because under IACHR rules, nongovernmental organizations have standing to assert claims on behalf of persons whose rights have allegedly been violated. In March, the IACHR issued the first of a series of decisions and requests for information that would continue over the next four years. The IACHR urged the United States to comply with the due process and humane treatment requirements of the American Declaration of the Rights and Duties of Man, as the U.S. government undertook to do when it joined the Organization of American States. This petition to the IACHR was significant because it was brought at a time when it was unclear whether U.S. courts would take up the issue of prolonged, arbitrary detention at Guantánamo. Even if a case did make its way to the Supreme Court, there was a risk the Court would rule that U.S. courts had no jurisdiction over claims by Guantánamo detainees. The more permissive standing rules of the IACHR helped legal advocacy groups who, in the prevailing climate of secrecy surrounding the detention camp, lacked access to the detainees as well as information about who they were.

Human rights groups and a small number of domestic groups also appealed to UN bodies. Numerous groups provided detailed information to the UN Committee Against Torture and the UN Human Rights Committee, which in 2006 reviewed U.S. reports on its compliance with the Convention Against Torture and the International Covenant on Civil and Political Rights respectively. The committees found the U.S. government in violation of its human rights treaty obligations at Guantánamo, particularly with regard to the lack of judicial review and legal safeguards, and urged prompt action to remedy the situation. The Committee Against Torture was especially strong in its criticism, urging the U.S. government to "cease to detain any person at Guantánamo Bay and close this detention facility, permit access by the detainees to judicial process or release them as soon as possible, ensuring that they are not returned to any State where they could face a real risk of being tortured, in order to comply with its obligations under the [Torture] Convention."[35] Similarly, advocates engaged in dialogue with several UN special rapporteurs with human rights mandates, who continually raised concerns about Guantánamo with the U.S. government.

In June 2004, four UN human rights officials—the special rapporteurs on torture, the independence of judges and lawyers, and the right to the highest attainable standard of health, along with the chairperson of the Working Group on Arbitrary Detention—jointly sought permission to visit the Guantánamo detention camp. Although it was willing to discuss the possibility and terms of such a visit, the Bush administration, in a much-publicized response, would only grant them restricted access to the detainees. In October 2005, the U.S. government extended an invitation to only three special rapporteurs—those dealing with torture, freedom of religion, and arbitrary detention—for just a one-day visit. The UN human rights officials declined the offer to visit Guantánamo because they would not be allowed to meet with detainees privately. Despite this setback, they continued to press the Bush administration on this issue. In a report issued in February 2006, they urged the U.S. government either to "expeditiously bring all Guantánamo Bay detainees to trial, in compliance with articles 9(3) and 14 of ICCPR, or release them without further delay."[36] They also called on the Bush administration to close the detention camp at Guantánamo.[37]

Even as they pursued these international human rights strategies, social justice groups continued to seek ways to mount legal challenges in

U.S. courts, filing numerous habeas cases that eventually led to the Supreme Court's decision in *Rasul v. Bush* in June 2004, in which the Court held that U.S. courts had jurisdiction over habeas claims by Guantánamo detainees under the federal habeas statute.[38] The *Rasul* decision opened the courthouse door to detainees, granting them access to U.S. courts to determine whether their continued detention was lawful. Congress sought to overturn this ruling when, in 2005 and 2006, it amended the habeas statute to strip U.S. courts of jurisdiction over claims by detainees at Guantanamo. Lawyers challenged the constitutionality of these enactments, winning a landmark victory in the Supreme Court in *Boumediene v. Bush* in June 2008. The Court held that detainees at Guantanamo had a constitutional right to habeas corpus to challenge their detention in U.S. courts and struck down Congress's attempt to deprive them of that right.[39] These pivotal Supreme Court decisions ensured that the government could not hold people beyond the reach of the law and arrogate to itself the exclusive power to determine whether its own conduct was lawful. Courts would play their time-honored role in the U.S. constitutional scheme as the ultimate arbiter as to whether the executive branch was operating within the bounds of the law.

International legal issues played an important role in domestic litigation over detentions at Guantánamo Bay. While the cases turned on issues of U.S. constitutional and statutory law, the Geneva Conventions and international human rights standards formed part of the body of law that the Supreme Court considered in determining the rights of detainees. Numerous amicus curiae briefs filed in the *Rasul* case addressed international human rights and humanitarian law issues. While the case was decided principally on the basis of the federal habeas statute, the international legal standards pertaining to prolonged detention without charge and the due process rights of detainees under the laws of war loomed in the background. In the *Hamdan v. Rumsfeld* decision handed down in 2006,[40] international human rights and humanitarian law factored more centrally in the Court's ruling. The Supreme Court held that the military commissions established by the Bush administration to try detainees at Guantánamo Bay were illegal under both the U.S. Uniform Code of Military Justice and the Geneva Conventions. The Court found that Common Article 3 to the Geneva Conventions, which sets the baseline of fair and humane treatment for all persons regardless of status under the laws of war, applied to the armed conflict with al Qaeda. In a stunning reversal after four years of staunch resistance, the Pentagon acceded to the Court's command and reversed its position, declaring that it would apply this core international legal protection to all persons in Defense Department custody, which includes those detained at Guantánamo.

Rendition to Torture

In a *Washington Post* article in December 2002, reporters Dana Priest and Barton Gellman wrote about abuse of detainees held at a secret CIA interrogation center at Bagram Air Base in Afghanistan. Some detainees who do not cooperate, they reported, were handed over to foreign intelligence services whose use of torture is widely known. The article quoted one U.S. official with direct involvement in transferring detainees to third countries, who explained the understanding behind renditions: "We don't kick the [expletive] out of them. We send them to other countries so *they* can kick the [expletive] out of them."[41]

While the term "rendition" can signify a range of transfer practices, it is used here to refer to the transfer of persons suspected of links to terrorism to countries where they are at risk of being tortured. Sometimes called extraordinary rendition, these transfers most often occur without any legal process. Persons are simply apprehended and transferred in secret from one country to another, entirely outside of the legal system. Under international human rights law, the absolute prohibition on torture entails an equally absolute prohibition on transferring a person to a country where he or she is at risk of being subjected to torture. When the United States ratified the Convention Against Torture and Other Cruel, Inhuman, and Degrading Treatment or Punishment in 1994, it accepted without reservation the ban on such transfers contained in Article 3. Although the U.S. government had engaged in rendition prior to 2001, the suspects were typically transferred *to* justice—apprehended and brought to the United States to face criminal charges—whereas after the September 11 attacks the Bush administration used rendition to whisk suspects *away from* justice.[42]

To carry out secretive, extralegal transfers of suspects to countries with well-documented records of torture, such as Syria, Jordan, Morocco, and Egypt, the Bush administration developed a legal theory to evade the absolute prohibition on transferring persons to risk of torture. It argued that rendition did not violate Article 3 of the Convention Against Torture if the United States had obtained diplomatic assurances from the government of the country to which the person was transferred. Diplomatic assurances are unenforceable promises, either oral or written, from governments that they will not subject a particular detainee to torture. To transfer certain suspects for detention and interrogation, the Bush administration claimed that governments that routinely flout their binding legal obligation not to torture could be trusted to honor unenforceable promises not to engage in the very same conduct. These assurances are simply a fig leaf on transfers that violate a fundamental human rights guarantee against torture.

Litigation to challenge renditions faced serious hurdles. It was difficult to uncover specific cases of rendition, owing to the extreme secrecy
that surrounded both the transfers and the detentions. Most often, an
individual had to be released and returned to a country where he could
safely challenge the rendition in public, such as Maher Arar, who was
rendered to Syria and released back to Canada, or Khaled el Masri, who
was rendered to Afghanistan, released, and then returned home to Germany. Moreover, the Bush administration blocked legal challenges to its
rendition policy, in part by using a state secrets defense. In response to
a lawsuit filed by Maher Arar, the U.S. government asked the court not
to allow the case to proceed because doing so would require the government to reveal state secrets, thereby harming national security. The
federal district court dismissed Arar's lawsuit in early 2006. Although it
did not reach the state secrets claim, the court found no cause of action
against U.S. officials for his rendition to Syria and his treatment in a Syrian prison, relying on national security and foreign policy considerations
in reaching this conclusion.[43] Arar's lawyers appealed the ruling to the
Second Circuit. El Masri's case was dismissed on state secrets grounds by
the Fourth Circuit in March 2007[44] and in the fall the Supreme Court
declined to hear the case, letting the dismissal stand.

In such a secretive context, documentation of abuses became crucial.
Human Rights Watch took up the issue, focusing not just on the United
States but on comparative practices through its research and reporting
on Sweden's rendition of two Egyptian asylum seekers to Egypt (a Swedish television program eventually uncovered that the CIA flew the plane
from Stockholm to Cairo) and on efforts by the British government to use
diplomatic assurances to send terrorist suspects in Britain to countries
where they were at risk of torture. This research helped demonstrate the
breadth of the problem and the commonalities in approach used by numerous governments in dealing with persons suspected of terrorist ties.
Documentation strategies helped bring these cases to light and built a
body of knowledge about how renditions worked, how they violated fundamental human rights, and how governments were using diplomatic
assurances to circumvent their absolute legal obligation not to transfer
people to torture. Research and documentation on the Sweden-Egypt
cases, for example, enabled policymakers, legal advocacy groups, and
the public to learn about the flimsy promises made by Egypt in regard to
the treatment of the two men, the serious problems with Swedish monitoring of their treatment in prison in Egypt, and the due process flaws in
the trial of one of the detainees in Egypt after his rendition.

Documentation and reporting on rendition led to three concrete advocacy outcomes that have helped increase pressure on the United States
and other governments to change their policies. First, the Canadian gov-

ernment established an official commission of inquiry into the handling of Maher Arar's case, focusing on Canadian law enforcement and other officials and their interaction with U.S. officials. After extensive public and private hearings, the commission issued a lengthy report in September 2006 that exonerated Arar, finding no evidence of any connection between Arar and terrorist activity. The Canadian government then issued a public apology to Maher Arar and offered him $9 million (10.5 million Canadian dollars) in compensation for his ordeal. The Canadian commission's work put pressure the U.S. government to justify its rendition of Arar to Syria, whose human rights record is perhaps most difficult of all rendition destination countries to defend. The subsequent decision by the Bush administration to maintain Arar on a U.S. terrorism watch list despite his exoneration by the Canadian commission of inquiry created a public disagreement between the two countries.

Second, documentation work and advocacy led to the introduction of legislation in the U.S. Congress in 2005 to ban rendition to torture. Led by Senator Patrick Leahy (D-Vt.) and Representative Ed Markey (D-Mass.), these bills sought to rein in the Bush administration's rendition policy largely by prohibiting the use of diplomatic assurances from countries with records of torture. While they were not enacted, the bills helped call public attention to the problem, and the surrounding advocacy put the administration further on the defensive regarding its practice of rendering suspects to countries that use torture. In March 2007, Rep. Markey reintroduced his bill, the Torture Outsourcing Prevention Act (H.R. 1352). Advocates continued to press for legislative action to ban rendition.

Third, U.S.-based human rights groups engaged in direct advocacy with the UN special rapporteur on torture, raising the issue of use of diplomatic assurances to circumvent Article 3 of the Convention Against Torture based on their careful documentation of rendition cases. The special rapporteur reexamined the previous positions of his office on diplomatic assurances in light of this new information and determined that diplomatic assurances are unreliable and ineffective in the protection against torture and ill treatment and therefore may not be used in cases where there are substantial grounds for believing the person would be at risk of torture if transferred.[45]

Torture and Cruel Treatment of Detainees

The question about whether detainees in U.S. custody were being subjected to torture or ill treatment during interrogation first surfaced in Afghanistan in late 2002. These reports were followed by the horrific photographs of abuse at Abu Ghraib prison in Iraq in April 2004, as well as allegations of abusive treatment at Guantánamo and of waterboarding of high-level al Qaeda suspects in secret CIA detention centers. As more details emerged, they began to paint a picture of interrogation techniques involving the use of stress positions, prolonged exposure to extremes of heat and cold, sleep deprivation, and use of dogs.

The detainees who were subjected to abuse were not U.S. citizens and were being held outside the United States, so the Bush administration took the position that they had no constitutional rights. The U.S. government still had to grapple with its obligations under international human rights law. In an August 2002 legal memorandum by the Justice Department's Office of Legal Counsel, the Bush administration twisted the international definition of torture beyond recognition, attempting to limit it only to acts that cause the severity of pain associated with, for example, death or organ failure.[46] The memorandum also asserted that the president could lawfully order torture by using his authority as commander in chief to override laws prohibiting torture.[47] Government lawyers also reinterpreted Article 16 of the Convention Against Torture, which prohibits cruel, inhuman, or degrading treatment. They invented a new exception to Article 16, asserting that it did not apply to noncitizens held outside the United States. Because certain federal statutes prohibiting torture governed the conduct of the U.S. military anywhere in the world, the principal effect of this reinterpretation of U.S. human rights treaty obligations was to give the CIA a free hand in its interrogation of noncitizens detained abroad.

The classic human rights strategy of naming and shaming governments through the media was effective in putting the administration on the defensive on torture, in no small part because the Abu Ghraib photos themselves generated such intense media and public interest. U.S. social justice groups used a variety of media and public campaigning strategies to press the administration to change its policies, repudiate the Office of Legal Counsel torture memo, and reverse its reinterpretation of its obligation under Article 16 of the Convention Against Torture. At the end of 2004, the government rescinded the torture memo, replacing it with a less radically narrow definition of torture and withdrawing, but not repudiating, the previous memo's assertion of the commander in chief's power to override laws prohibiting torture. The media scrutiny created great diplomatic pressure on the U.S. government as well as significant domestic public concern. Reflecting this concern and spurred by targeted advocacy from social justice groups, Senator John McCain led the movement in the Senate to pass legislation to prevent the use of cruel, inhuman, or degrading treatment on anyone in the custody or effective control of the U.S. government, resulting in the enactment of the Detainee Treatment Act of 2005. While this law contained a harmful provision that attempted to strip the federal courts of jurisdiction over habeas petitions from Guantánamo detainees, the act is important for its strong statement against inhumane treatment of noncitizen detainees abroad and its refutation of the loophole devised by Bush administration lawyers in U.S. obligations under the Convention Against Torture.

Litigation proved to be a helpful tactic in contesting the government's policies on torture and interrogation. In *Hamdan v. Rumsfeld,* the Supreme Court held that the laws of war, specifically Common Article 3 to the Geneva Conventions, governed the treatment of detainees captured as part of the armed conflict with al Qaeda. Common Article 3 mandates humane treatment for all detainees, regardless of whether they are prisoners of war or unlawful combatants. Faced with this clear rejection of its position by the Supreme Court, the Bush administration relented and declared that Common Article 3 applied to all detainees in Defense Department custody. Although the July 7, 2006 directive by the Pentagon did not extend to detainees in CIA custody, it was still an extremely important acknowledgment by the Bush administration that detainees in military custody are entitled to humane treatment as a matter of law and not simply as a matter of policy that can be altered at will.

Similarly, the ACLU filed a FOIA lawsuit that had a profound impact on efforts to challenge the abuse of detainees. The lawsuit was successful in forcing the Bush administration to disclose information regarding its interrogation policies and practices. The disclosures were critical in the public advocacy strategies used by a wide variety of international human rights organizations and domestic social justice groups. The FOIA action and the resultant disclosure of information also facilitated media coverage of detainee abuse, monitoring by international human rights mechanisms, and the filing of international law claims against the government by torture victims in U.S. courts. On the issue of torture and abuse, there was a symbiotic relationship between more traditional litigation strategies and the documentation and denunciation strategies that are central to human rights advocacy.

A Catalyzing Effect on the Use of Human Rights Strategies

The Bush administration's treatment of terrorist suspects abroad had a catalyzing effect on the movement to apply international human rights to U.S. government conduct. At perhaps the most basic level, the Guantánamo detentions, rendition, and abusive interrogation policies were widely understood to implicate fundamental human rights—the prohibition on torture and cruel treatment, the right not to be imprisoned indefinitely without charge or, even worse, in secret and without access to the outside world. The use of international human rights language, standards, and mechanisms seemed a natural fit for these issues, which the U.S. public largely associated with repressive regimes elsewhere in the world. The fact that the U.S. government had put in place policies similar to that of governments known for their human rights abuses further encouraged the use of international human rights advocacy strategies to challenge these new policies.

The first contested issue was the law itself. When the Bush administration made various arguments under U.S. law to claim that its policies were lawful, such as the commander-in-chief authority to set aside criminal statutes, advocates pointed to international human rights standards as a way to reject these arguments. International human rights law became a vital source of both legal obligation and moral authority in defending the prohibition on torture and cruel treatment and on prolonged, arbitrary detention. Advocates used the international standards to expose the Bush administration's effort to circumvent its treaty obligations by reinterpreting international legal standards in ways that twisted the law and undermined core rights protections.

Human rights language was also helpful because these policies involved individuals who were widely considered unsympathetic by the U.S. public. Perhaps the most glaring example involved the detainees held in secret prisons operated by the CIA. Those detained included senior al Qaeda operatives such as Khaled Sheikh Mohamed and Ramsi Binalshib. Reports of their abuse during interrogation, including the waterboarding of Mohamed, often were met with only fleeting public concern. On the contrary, advocacy groups that defended their right not to be tortured received strident responses from members of the public decrying their defense of individuals who, in their view, deserved the treatment they received because of their alleged role in the September 11 attacks. Given the challenge of defending the rights of these detainees, the use of human rights standards enabled advocates to emphasize basic human dignity for all, even those who may have committed heinous crimes.

Using the language of human rights to frame the debate over U.S. treatment of terrorist suspects abroad also lent itself to a comparative analysis of U.S. practices on a global scale. This advocacy strategy proved useful in contextualizing U.S. practices in order to persuade policy makers and the public of the severity of the abuses and the importance of the rights at stake. Human rights groups drew on the State Department's Country Reports on Human Rights Practices to compare the Bush administration's conduct to that of other governments the administration itself had condemned for human rights violations, such as Burma, North Korea, and Saudi Arabia. This approach was quite effective in painting a clear picture of just how far the U.S. government had moved in the direction of policies that violated basic rights. At the same time, this strategy held the U.S. government up to the light of its own expectations as a global champion of human rights. As such, it was in some ways an internationalized version of the strategy employed by civil rights advocates in the 1950s, when they worked to end racial segregation by forcing the courts, the government, and ultimately the country to confront the contradiction between core U.S. values of freedom and equality before the law and the reality of racial discrimination.

A useful example of comparative rights advocacy involved the response to Maher Arar's rendition to Syria. Arar, a dual Canadian-Syrian national, was transiting New York on his way home to Canada when he was apprehended by U.S. immigration officials and sent by the U.S. government to Syria, where he spent nine months in a tiny prison cell. After Canadian officials pressed for his release and he returned to Canada, Arar provided a detailed and credible account of his torture and abuse at the hands of his Syrian captors, including beatings with an electrical cord. The government of Syria has been widely condemned for its human rights abuses, including by the U.S. government. Advocates undercut the credibility of diplomatic assurances, the linchpin of the Bush administration's rendition policy, by emphasizing that the administration had accepted Syria's word that it would not subject Arar to torture. Yet this was a regime that the U.S. government had itself criticized for its use of torture. Because Arar's case involved rendition to Syria, it demonstrated only too well that diplomatic assurances from governments that engage in torture could not be trusted.

International advocacy was another strategy used by U.S. groups to contest the Bush administration's detention policies. They engaged in direct advocacy with foreign governments and in public advocacy designed to create pressure on other governments to press the U.S. government on its human rights record. Some of this work was bilateral, such as efforts to engage the British government on the issue of military commissions at Guantánamo. Other times, U.S. social justice groups focused on multilateral advocacy efforts, such as the annual UN Commission on Human Rights (for example, the ACLU sent representatives to the commission's session in 2005, joining traditional attendees such as Human Rights Watch and Amnesty International), work with UN special rapporteurs and working groups to strengthen international human rights standards and pressure the U.S. government to change its policies, and successful advocacy to urge the UN to create a special mechanism on counterterrorism and human rights. Similarly, U.S. advocacy groups provided information on renditions to the European Parliament in its investigation into CIA renditions and secret detentions in and through Europe.

Challenges Posed by Detainees Abroad to Bringing Human Rights Home

Even as the handling of detainees abroad helped galvanize the use of international human rights strategies by U.S. social justice groups, it also complicated these efforts at the same time. The extraterritorial nature of U.S. conduct tended to reinforce the domestic-international divide not only on the part of the general public, but also on the part of the social justice movement in the United States, albeit with some important exceptions. Because the policies concerned noncitizens held abroad, either in a war zone or in connection with the September 11 attacks, international human rights groups largely took the lead in contesting these policies. While the treatment of detainees was considered unlawful and deeply troubling, it seemed to many domestic social justice advocates far afield from their missions and the communities they served.

When the government implemented a counterterrorism policy inside the United States (such as the PATRIOT Act, detention of noncitizens on immigration grounds, and domestic surveillance), social justice groups could often make the connection between the human rights and civil rights agendas. When the abuses took place against non-U.S. citizens on foreign soil, however, the connection often became too attenuated for many advocates. They would of course condemn the practices, but would continue to focus on the rights of persons in the United States as part of their long-standing agendas. In this way, the advocacy community's response to the U.S. government's treatment of noncitizens abroad largely tracked the constitutional law–international law divide and reinforced the notion that civil rights are for U.S. citizens and human rights are for others.

The challenge of connecting the human rights and civil rights perspectives on these issues was perhaps most evident in the debate over the nomination of Alberto Gonzales to serve as attorney general in late 2004 and early 2005. The positions taken or not taken on the Gonzales nomination, and the reasons why, shed light on the this domestic-international divide, even as some progress was made in drawing links between U.S. conduct abroad and rights protection at home.

A few voices from both international human rights groups and domestic civil liberties and civil rights groups attempted to make the connection. They argued forcefully in coalition meetings that the powers claimed and the rationale offered by the Bush administration for its treatment of foreign terrorist suspects could easily justify significant incursions on the rights of U.S. citizens in the United States, not only in areas related to counterterrorism, but also in areas traditionally of concern to the civil rights community. For example, the Mexican American Legal Defense and Educational Fund, a Latino civil rights organization, emphasized the link between international human rights and domestic rights in explaining why it could not support Gonzales's confirmation: "[Gonzales's] association with memoranda setting aside the application of international war conventions . . . raises concerns about whether he may set aside constitutionally guaranteed due process protections in various domestic circumstances."[48] Months later, after Gonzales was confirmed as attorney general, this point was driven home by the revelation of the NSA's warrantless domestic surveillance of U.S. citizens, justified by the same notion of a commander-in-chief exception to the Constitution that had been used to cast aside laws against torture and inhumane treatment.

Moreover, these few advocates argued, the administration's radical expansion of executive power entailed a concomitant reduction in the power of the judiciary. Its assault on judicial review should be of great concern to the domestic civil rights movement, which had long relied on the courts as guarantors of minority rights. Courts are central to rights enforcement and to ensuring that rights not only exist on paper but also have real meaning in people's lives. The administration's efforts to weaken judicial review of government conduct and its expansive claims of executive power should be seen as a threat to rights guarantees, not only for detainees held abroad, but also for its easy transformation into a justification for eroding "traditional" civil rights at home.

In an effort spearheaded by the Leadership Conference on Civil Rights, eighteen domestic advocacy groups, together with nine human rights organizations, sent a joint letter to the Senate Judiciary Committee in November 2004 expressing concerns about Gonzales and urging careful scrutiny of his nomination. In the end, however, only a small number of domestic social justice groups joined the international human rights groups in opposing the confirmation of Alberto Gonzales to serve as attorney general.

The social justice community's response to the Gonzales nomination suggests both the possibilities and the challenges of overcoming the domestic-international rights dichotomy. To be sure, there are many factors that account for an organization's decision to express concerns about a cabinet-level nominee, and especially to oppose his or her confirmation. However, the discussion within the advocacy community on the Gonzales nomination suggests that it was easier to link a policy or practice to the domestic rights agenda when the victims of the abuses were U.S. citizens or the abuses occurred in the United States. Still, social justice advocates began to find common ground in contesting the Bush administration's radical expansion of executive authority to act without meaningful judicial review, legislative oversight, or public scrutiny. This issue may hold great potential for building links between international human rights and civil rights frameworks for rights advocacy in the United States. Defending checks and balances, and in particular the vital role of courts in ensuring that the government operates within the bounds of the law, may help connect U.S. conduct abroad in the struggle against terrorism with domestic policies and practices that infringe on basic rights. In so doing, it may help further the development of a U.S. human rights movement that contests U.S. conduct at home and abroad using both constitutional and international human rights frames.

Looking Ahead: 2009 and Beyond

U.S. social justice advocates expanded their use of international human rights language, standards, and mechanisms in the months and years following the attacks of September 11, 2001 as a way of challenging U.S. counterterrorism policies that infringed on basic rights. These policies implicated rights—such as detention without charge and the prohibition on torture and cruel, inhuman, or degrading treatment—that were considered firmly established in U.S. law. The Bush administration misused immigration laws to violate the rights of "special interest" immigrant detainees and crafted novel legal theories to circumvent its legal obligations not to engage in torture, inhumane treatment, or prolonged detention without charge. The need for effective strategies to combat the erosion of rights in the struggle against terrorism was acute. As a result, U.S. social justice advocates focused their efforts to apply international human rights standards in the United States on civil and political rights, such as detention, due process, and torture. Only time will tell whether the post–September 11 years will mark a permanent shift in emphasis toward civil and political rights, or rather a temporary exigency that will give way to a more balanced focus on both civil and political rights and economic, social and cultural rights in the U.S. domestic human rights movement.

Even as the Bush administration's counterterrorism policies helped catalyze efforts by domestic groups to hold the United States to its commitments under international human rights law, important challenges remained in bringing human rights home. The domestic-international and us-other divides influenced the way many domestic social justice groups responded to the treatment of noncitizen detainees held abroad. The remoteness of the abuses reinforced the tendency to see such matters, however troubling, as international issues to be addressed by international human rights groups. This tendency had the effect of reinforcing the old fault lines in U.S. rights advocacy—civil rights were for people in the United States and human rights were for those in other countries.

Still, more than seven years later, social justice groups have begun to look at issues in new ways and to link abuses by the U.S. government at home and abroad in a human rights frame. U.S.-based international human rights groups and a growing number of domestic social justice groups have found common cause, using human rights language, mechanisms, and strategies in their domestic rights advocacy in varied and increasing ways. This trend will likely continue even after the end of the Bush administration and the anticipated shift away from its counterterrorism policies that raised the most serious human rights concerns. The skills and strategies that social justice advocates have developed to respond to the erosion of basic rights in the struggle against terrorism will leave a lasting mark on rights advocacy in the United States.

Advocates hailed a major human rights victory at the start of the Obama administration. On January 22, 2009, President Obama issued a series of executive orders that reaffirmed the ban on torture and set a firm one-year deadline for closure of the Guantánamo detention camp. Coming on just his third day in office, these actions signaled a deep commitment by the new administration to reclaiming U.S. credibility in the world as a champion of human rights. The centrality of human rights to the new president's initial narrative may portend a unique opportunity to bring human rights home. The executive orders send a clear message to Americans and to the world: the U.S. government will respect human rights. To honor that commitment, the new administration must not only implement its newly declared policies on interrogation and detention; it must also uphold human rights here at home, every day, in the way it governs on matters large and small. Social justice advocates will hopefully succeed in using this breakthrough moment to make great strides in advancing the cause of human rights at home.

Notes

The views expressed in this chapter are the author's and do not necessarily reflect the views of the Open Society Institute.

1. The Bush administration maintained that the U.S. Naval Base at Guantánamo Bay was outside U.S. territory in order to justify its policy of seeking to deny detainees access to U.S. courts and the protection of the U.S. Constitution. The Supreme Court rejected the administration's argument regarding access to the courts under the federal habeas statute in *Rasul v. Bush* in 2004 and ruled against the administration again in *Boumediene v. Bush* four years later, holding that detainees at Guantánamo had a constitutional right to challenge their detention in habeas proceedings.

2. A federal court described the Justice Department's strategy as a "crude" approach to unearthing information to prevent another attack, even as it found the approach sufficiently rational to warrant judicial deference to the government's choice to target noncitizens in this way. *Turkmen v. Ashcroft*, no. 02-CV-2307 (2006), p. 79. Available online at http://ccrjustice.org/files/Turkmen_Opinion_06_06.pdf.

3. CNN.com, "Bush Officials Defend Military Trials in Terror Cases," November 15, 2001, available online at http://www.cnn.com/SPECIALS/2001/trade. center/invest.stories.11.html.

4. U.S. Department of Justice, Office of the Inspector General, "The September 11 Detainees: A Review of the Treatment of Aliens Held on Immigration Charges in Connection with the Investigation of the September 11 Attacks" (April 2003), pp. 20–21.

5. Human Rights Watch, "Presumption of Guilt: Abuses of Post September 11 Detainees" (August 2002), p. 13 (citing Human Rights Watch telephone interview with attorney Neil Weinrib, New York, N.Y., January 28, 2002).

6. Ibid, p. 14 (citing Human Rights Watch interviews with Osama Sewilam, Hudson County Correctional Center, Kearny, N.J., February 6, 2002; and his attorney, Sohail Mohammed, Clifton, N.J., November 5 and 19, 2001).

7. Office of the Inspector General, "The September 11 Detainees," p. 196.

8. *Turkmen v. Ashcroft*, Class Action Complaint and Demand for Jury Trial, April 17, 2002, pp. 25, 30.

9. See *Miranda v. Arizona*, 384 U.S. 436 (1966).

10. See 8 USC 1229 (a)(1)(E) and (b).

11. Human Right Watch, "Presumption of Guilt," p. 35 (citing Human Rights Watch telephone interviews with Bah Isselou, Fla., November 6, 2001; and his attorney, Dennis Clare, Louisville, Ky., October 23 and 31, 2001).

12. Ibid, p. 40 (citing Human Rights Watch interview with Osama Salem, Hudson County Correctional Center, Kearny, N.J., February 6, 2002).

13. See generally David Cole, *Enemy Aliens: Double Standards and Constitutional Freedoms in the War on Terrorism* (New York: New Press, 2003) and Leti Volpp, "The Citizen and the Terrorist," *UCLA Law Review* 49 (June 2002).

14. The United States is not alone is facing this dichotomy between the rights of citizens and noncitizens. In the United Kingdom, the public outcry over detention without charge of British citizens at Guantánamo Bay stood in sharp contrast to the lack of widespread concern over detention of noncitizens of Arab and Muslim background held primarily at a British prison called Belmarsh. Similarly, Canadians protested the U.S. rendition of Maher Arar, a Canadian citizen, to Syria but did not express a similar level of concern about efforts by Canadian immigration authorities to deport Arab and Muslim noncitizens to countries where they faced a risk of torture.

15. See, for example, *Brown v. Board of Education*, 347 U.S. 483 (1954).

16. *Center for National Security Studies v. Department of Justice*, Complaint for Injunctive Relief, December 6, 2001.

17. The district court decision can be found at *Center for National Security Studies v. Department of Justice*, 215 F. Supp.2d 94 (D.D.C. 2002). The court of appeals ruling can be found at 331 F.3d 918 (D.C. Cir. 2003), and the denial of certiorari by the Supreme Court at 124 S.Ct. 1041 (2004).

18. *Detroit Free Press v. Ashcroft*, 303 F.3d 681 (6th Cir. 2002) (secret hearings unconstitutional); *North Jersey Media Group v. Ashcroft*, 308 F.3d 198 (3rd Cir. 2002) (secret hearings not unconstitutional), *cert. denied*, 123 S.Ct. 2215 (2003).

19. *Turkmen v. Ashcroft*, no. 02-CV-2307 (2006), p. 78, available online at http://ccrjustice.org/files/Turkmen_Opinion_06_06.pdf.

20. Arab American Institute, "Healing the Nation: The Arab American Experience After September 11" (2002).

21. Human Rights Watch, "Presumption of Guilt: Abuses of Post September 11 Detainees" (August 2002).

22. Amnesty International USA, "Amnesty International's Concerns Regarding Post-September 11 Detentions in the USA," AI Index: AMR 51/044/2002, pp. 14–16 (March 2002), available online at www.aiusa.org/usacrisis/9.11.detentions2.pdf; ACLU, "America's Disappeared: Seeking International Justice for Immigrants Detained After September 11" (January 2004); ACLU, "Worlds Apart: How Deporting Immigrants After 9/11 Tore Families Apart and Shattered Communities" (December 2004).

23. U.S. Department of Justice, Office of the Inspector General, "Supplemental Report on September 11 Detainees' Allegations of Abuse at the Metropolitan Detention Center in Brooklyn, New York," December 2003, p. 28.

24. Ibid, p. 45.

25. Ibid, p. 46.

26. U.S. Department of Justice, Office of the Inspector General, "Report to Congress on Implementation of Section 1001 of the USA PATRIOT Act," March 8, 2006, p. 14.

27. U.S. Department of Homeland Security, Memorandum for Michael J. Garcia, Assistant Secretary, U.S. Immigration and Customs Enforcement, and Robert Bonner, Commissioner, U.S. Customs and Border Protection, "Guidance on ICE Implementation of Policy and Practice Changes Recommended by the Department of Justice Inspector General," March 30, 2004.

28. By the end of December 2003, only a handful of special interest detainees remained in detention. Nearly all had either been deported or released. Yet when Michael Chertoff, former head of the Criminal Division at the Justice Department during the September 11 investigation, came before the Senate as the nominee for secretary of homeland security in February 2005, he vigorously defended the government's use of immigration laws to detain noncitizens and investigate them without probable cause of involvement in a crime. While he criticized the mistreatment of detainees, he defended the overarching policy, testifying that all detentions were in accordance with the law and that the problems identified by the inspector general were ones of implementation that could be addressed through better training and improved databases.

29. The request for precautionary measures is available online at www.globalrights.org/site/DocServer/IACHRPrecautionaryMeasures.pdf?docID=125. At the time of the filing, Global Rights was known as the International Human Rights Law Group.

30. Commission on Human Rights, 61st Session, *Civil and Political Rights, Including the Question of Torture and Detention—Opinions Adopted by the Working Group on Arbitrary Detention*, E/CN.4/2005/6/Add.1, November 2004, pp. 67–70.

31. ACLU, "America's Disappeared," p. 4.

32. Human Rights Committee, 87th Session, *Consideration of Reports Submitted by States Parties Under Article 40 of the Covenant—Concluding Observations of the Human Rights Committee: United States of America*, CCPR/C/USA/CO/3/Rev.1 December 2006, p. 6, para. 19.

33. See Human Rights Watch, "Hatred in the Hallways: Violence Against Lesbian, Gay, Bisexual and Transgender Students in U.S. Schools" (2001); and Human Rights Watch, "Unfair Advantage: Workers' Freedom of Association in the United States under International Human Rights Standards" (2000).

34. Order Dismissing Petition for Writ of Habeas Corpus and First Amended Petition for Writ of Habeas Corpus, *Coalition of Clergy v. Bush* (February 2002) (citing Petitioners' Memorandum 7:20–23), available online at www.cacd.uscourts.gov, accessed February 11, 2007.

35. UN Committee Against Torture, 36th Session, *Conclusions and Recommendations of the Committee Against Torture: United States of America,* CAT/C/USA/CO/2, June 25, 2006, p. 6.

36. UN Commission on Human Rights, 62nd Session, *Situation of Detainees at Guantánamo Bay,* E/CN.4/2006/120, February 15, 2006, p. 38.

37. Ibid.

38. *Rasul v. Bush,* 542 U.S. 466 (2004).

39. *Boumediene v. Bush,* 553 U.S. ___ (2008).

40. *Hamdam v. Rumseld,* 126 S.Ct. 2749 (2006).

41. Dana Priest and Barton Gellman, "U.S. Decries Abuse but Defends Interrogations: 'Stress and Duress' Tactics Used on Terrorism Suspects Held in Secret Overseas Facilities," *Washington Post,* December 26, 2002, p. A-1.

42. For more information, see Wendy Patten, Human Rights Watch Report to the Canadian Commission of Inquiry into the Actions of Canadian Officials in Relation to Maher Arar, May 17, 2005, available online at www.hrw.org/legacy/backgrounder/eca/canada/arar/arar_testimony.pdf.

43. *Arar v. Ashcroft,* 414 F. Supp. 2d 250 (E.D.N.Y. 2006).

44. *El-Masri v. United States,* 479 F.3d 296 (4th Cir. 2007).

45. UNGA, 60th Sess., *Report of the Special Rapporteur on Torture and Other Cruel, Inhuman, or Degrading Treatment or Punishment,* A/60/316, August 2005, p. 13.

46. Memorandum from Jay S. Bybee, Assistant Attorney General, Office of Legal Counsel, Department of Justice, to Alberto R. Gonzales, Counsel to the President, Re: Standards of Conduct for Interrogation under 18 U.S.C. §§ 2340–2340A, August 1, 2002, p. 13.

47. Ibid., pp. 31–39.

48. Mexican American Legal Defense and Educational Fund, "MALDEF Statement on the Likely Confirmation of White House Counsel Alberto Gonzales to the Position of United States Attorney General," January 19, 2005, available online at www.maldef.org/news/press.cfm?ID=249.

Chapter 11

Bush Administration Noncompliance with the Prohibition on Torture and Cruel and Degrading Treatment

Kathryn Sikkink

Introduction

In recent years, U.S. executive branch actions have led to the perception that it is particularly hostile to international law, especially in the area of human rights and humanitarian law. A series of high-profile U.S. decisions to try to withdraw its signature from the International Criminal Court (ICC) Statute and make side agreements to undermine its application and to declare that the Geneva Conventions do not apply to the case of the conflict in Afghanistan, and thus to detainees in Guantánamo, have given the impression of a country not committed to the application of international law.[1]

On some other human rights issues, U.S. policy continues to adhere to international legal standards and the United States has provided leadership on global human rights. Bush administration policy makers have been at the forefront of pressures for world attention and action to the crisis in Darfur, Sudan. Some scholars have argued that the United States was careful to adhere to the norms of noncombatant immunity in the major combat phase of the 2003 war in the Iraq and that the number of civilian casualties was as a result relatively low, given the ambitious nature of the war which required coalition forces to take Iraqi cities.[2] At the same time, the Supreme Court has brought U.S. practice more in line with international law on the death penalty by prohibiting the death penalty for juveniles and for mentally retarded individuals. Finally, on a whole series of issues, including women's rights and children's rights, the United States is generally in compliance with international law, even in cases where the Senate has failed to ratify the relevant treaties. So, for example, the United States has not ratified the Convention on the Elimination of All Forms of Discrimination Against Women, even though it is substantially in compliance with most of its provisions.[3]

These are the mixed signals that the United States is sending to the world on human rights. But of the signals we send to the world, none are as important as our own human rights practices. And of the recent signals we have sent, none is as grave as U.S. practice of torture and cruel and degrading treatment in Abu Ghraib, Guantánamo, and Afghanistan. The United States was substantially in compliance with the prohibition of torture until late summer 2002, when the first known cases of ill treatment of detainees at Guantánamo occurred.[4] Starting in 2002 the United States has been in violation of the prohibition on torture and cruel and degrading treatment. In a 2004 memo, however, the Justice Department signaled a retreat from the most egregious forms of noncompliance. The McCain Amendment to the Detainee Treatment Act of 2005 prohibited cruel, inhuman, and degrading treatment of any individual in custody of the U.S. government. Finally, after the Supreme Court's decision in the *Hamdan v. Rumsfeld* case, in July 2006 the Department of Defense mandated that its policies and practice comply with Common Article 3 of the Geneva Convention, which calls for humane treatment of all detainees. The executive, however, still claims the right to engage in "extraordinary rendition" that is, the practice of turning U.S. detainees over to other states known to use torture, a practice in violation of international legal obligations. This chapter will explore why the United States first violated international law on torture and then eventually brought policy back in greater compliance with international practice and law.

Scholars of international relations and global civil society have long said that the real test of international law and the power of transnational human rights advocates will be their ability to limit the action of the most powerful states. In the short term, this case illustrates a central point of realist theory of international politics: Powerful states are able to disregard international rules at will. In the longer term, however, this case shows that even the United States is not above the reach of international human rights law that it itself helped build.

The individuals who instigated the policy of noncompliance with the prohibition on torture made some grave errors in perception and judgment. They have misread the political realities of the current world and in doing so have put themselves, the victims of their policies, and the legitimacy of the U.S. government at risk. Most tragically, their misjudgment had dire human consequences, not only for the victims of torture, but also for the young soldiers who were its direct perpetrators.

One of the basic tenets of the neoconservatives in the Bush administration is a disdain and skepticism for international institutions and international law.[5] But their ideological bias against the United Nations and international law led them to misunderstand the very nature of modern human rights law and particularly the law prohibiting torture. They believed it was voluntary and malleable. Second, they also discounted the possibility of significant international and domestic opposition to their policy, resistance that eventually made the policy so politically costly that it had to be altered.

International law prohibits torture absolutely. Under no circumstances may states engage in torture. In 1980, a U.S. federal court judge summed up the customary international law prohibition against torture, declaring that the "the torturer has become—like the pirate and slave trader before him—*hostis humani generic,* an enemy of all mankind."[6] The Torture Convention also grants universal jurisdiction in the case of torture. That is, under the treaty any state has jurisdiction over a case of torture if the alleged torturer is present on its territory. Universal jurisdiction provides for a system of decentralized enforcement in any national judicial system against individuals who commit or instigate torture.[7] In other words, any country that has ratified the Torture Convention could in principle indict and try U.S. individuals reputed to be responsible for torture in Iraq or Guantánamo Bay. The British House of Lords recognized the universal jurisdiction in the case of torture when it allowed extradition proceedings against General Augusto Pinochet to go forward for torture that occurred in Chile during the Pinochet regime (1973–90).[8] Universal jurisdiction for torture and the high-profile use of the universal jurisdiction in a handful of cases (such as the Pinochet case) have made it clear that some enforcement of the prohibition on torture is possible. U.S. policy makers have disregarded this possibility of decentralized international enforcement for the violation on the prohibition on torture.

By misunderstanding these political realities, the Bush administration gave the wrong advice and signals to operatives in the field. It led them to believe that they were operating under the cover of law when they were not. It led them to believe that the power of the U.S. government could protect them from retribution. The U.S. government can and will certainly try to protect individuals involved in torture from retribution, and it will succeed in many cases. But it is unlikely to succeed in all cases. In other words, the realists engaged in wishful thinking. They described a world as they thought it ought to be, not as it actually is, and in doing so, they put themselves, their victims, and the very legitimacy of the U.S. government in harm's way.

Realists, Neoconservatives, and International Law

The foreign policy agenda of the Bush administration was guided by neoconservative intellectuals, often in reaction to what they perceived to be the failings of the realists such as Henry Kissinger. Neoconservatives critiqued realists for being inattentive to the internal politics of states, and in particular, for failing to be concerned with democracy and human rights. Also, contrary to the realists, neoconservatives believed that U.S. power could and should be used for moral purposes.[9] Realists on the other hand, believe that a "prudent" understanding of self-interest rather than morality should drive foreign policy.[10]

What these differences between the realists and the neoconservatives has tended to obscure, however, is that both realists and neoconservatives shared a common view about international law and international institutions. Both believe that international law is not an effective legal system and cannot be enforced against the wishes of a hegemon. Realists argue that because there is no central authority in the international system to enforce international law, enforcement will depend on political considerations and the actual distribution of power in the international system. Thus, they conclude, international law exists and is complied with only when it is in the interests of the most powerful states to do so. Neoconservatives basically share these beliefs, and add to them an even stronger ideological bias against the United Nations, international law, and international institutions such as the ICC. Realists and neoconservatives believe that a great power can violate international legal obligations without significant cost. Realism leads its adherents to believe that while international law may be useful in dealing with other weaker countries, it does not bind hegemons, especially when their security is at stake. Thus, after 9/11, the United States believed that it did not need to heed international law and limit its discretion in interrogations. This position was recognized by an official involved in formulating Bush administration policy on detainees. "The essence of the argument was, the official said, 'it applies to them, but it doesn't apply to us.' "[11] A former CIA lawyer said, "There are hardly any rules for illegal enemy combatants. It's the law of the jungle. And right now, we happen to be the strongest animal."[12]

Neoconservatives in particular also believe in American exceptionalism, "the idea that America could use its power in instances where others could not because it was more virtuous than other countries."[13] Because neoconservatives see the United States as exceptional and benevolent, they did not believe that international law and international institutions could or should be used to constrain the United States. These ideas held by neoconservatives are an important part of the explanation for why the Bush administration felt able to violate international law on this issue.

In contrast to this realist and neoconservative view of international law, constructivist theories explore the role of ideas and norms in effecting political change. Constructivists believe that in today's world international norms and law, international institutions, and global civil society are part of the political realities of the modern world. Modern constructivists know that not all law is equal—some law is stronger than others. The prohibition against torture, however, is a clear example of strong law. Even for this strong law to be effective—it has to be backed up by some form of sanctions and implementation. Sanctions sometimes come from international bodies, but there are also more decentralized forms of sanctions, through domestic courts, for example. Global civil society has been very active in searching out tactics that will impose some form of sanctions on violators of international human rights standards. Constructivists pay attention to key developments in the political realities of the world that the realists and neoconservatives miss because they believe that power only resides with wealthy and militarily strong states.

Constructivism also reminds us that the key concept in the realist analysis—"national interest" isn't as obvious as the realists would have us believe. Our very understandings of national interest are about highly contested beliefs about who we are as a nation and what constitutes our interests. Many of the arguments in the debate over torture in the United States revolve around contested notions of what constitutes the national interest. The realists acted as though the national interest was clear, but they encountered significant resistance, not just from civil society but from within the security apparatus of the U.S. government itself.

U.S. Compliance with the Prohibition on Torture and Cruel, Inhuman, and Degrading Treatment

A definition of compliance needs to include both what states do (behavior) but also what they say (are they aware of the norm and use it as justification for behavior).[14] Thus the examination of U.S. compliance with the prohibition on torture needs to look at both U.S. behavior and U.S. explanations for and justifications of its behavior. What has made U.S. practice so unsettling is the *explicit* quality to its noncompliance. Not only was U.S. behavior not in conformity with the rules, but the justification of state officials made it clear that they didn't believe they were bound by international law. This explicit policy noncompliance takes either the form of direct repudiation of the law or the form of justifying actions with such weak legal arguments that they must be considered "cheap talk," a rhetorical fig leaf of a sort to justify noncompliance with the law. In the case of the U.S. decision not to apply the Geneva Conventions to the conflict in Afghanistan, for example, even the legal advisor in the

Bush State Department immediately signaled that the position was "untenable," "incorrect," and "confused."[15]

There are many reasons why we might expect a powerful state like the United States not to be in compliance with international law. As the only hegemon in the international system, it is difficult for other states to sanction the United States for flouting the law. The United States also has particularly difficult treaty ratification rules and an ideological tradition of isolationism and skepticism about international institutions. As a federal system and a common law system, the United States may face additional difficulties with ratifying and implementing international law.[16]

But there are also reasons to believe that the United States might willingly comply with international human rights law. The United States also has a long liberal tradition of concern with human rights, a democratic regime that allows for checks and balances by the judicial and legislative branch on excesses of executive power, and a strong civil society, including many nongovernmental organizations (NGOs) working on human rights and civil rights. Oona Hathaway has argued democracies with these characteristics are more likely to face internal pressure to abide by their international treaty commitments, including lobbying, media exposure, and litigation. If these countries fail to comply, they are more likely to face sanctions from their domestic constituencies rather than from the international community. Thus these internal processes should lead democracies to have higher levels of compliance with their commitments.[17]

First, it is important to note that human rights change never comes easily or quickly in any country. Previous studies of human rights change in a wide range of countries around the world found that virtually all countries initially resist and reject international and domestic criticism and pressure for change in their human rights violations.[18] For those who believe in "American exceptionalism," part of the story here is that the United States was not exceptional in its early reactions to international and domestic criticism and pressures. Similar to other cases in the world, the Bush administration first denied that any human rights violations were occurring and tried to discredit those individuals and groups that brought attention to the issue of torture.

Both international and internal pressures were brought to bear on the Bush administration and eventually did play a role in leading to some changes in policy. Internal pressures were particularly important, especially pressures from the judicial branch and, belatedly, from the U.S. Congress. Opposition also came from within the U.S. military itself, especially the legal professionals within the military. This kind of opposition from within the military is unprecedented and unique. No studies of human rights change in countries around the world have previously identified the military itself as a force for compliance with human rights law.

Any evaluation of compliance with the Torture Convention must look at state policies with regard to torture, the actual occurrence of torture, and state responses to reported incidents of torture. Policy change with regard to torture and cruel and degrading treatment did not occur voluntarily within the Bush administration or as a result of confidential internal critiques. Rather it changed its policy as a result of relatively high-profile domestic opposition, particularly from the U.S. Supreme Court.

While there is evidence that the United States condoned torture in U.S. training programs in the past, there are important differences between the past and present practices and justifications.[19] Prior to 2002, high-level policy makers did not explicitly justify practices that can be considered torture and cruel, inhuman, and degrading treatment. In the 1970s, when members of Congress learned of accusations that U.S. personnel were complicit with torture in Brazil and Uruguay through an Agency for International Development (AID) program called the Public Safety Program the executive agreed to close down the program.[20] In the 1990s, when critics found training manuals used at the Army School of the Americas that advocated the use of the torture, the Pentagon decided to discontinue use of the manuals.[21] But the army did not discipline any of the individuals responsible for writing or teaching the lesson plans, nor were any students retrained.

Although the main pressure on the United States began after the publication of the photos of Abu Ghraib prison in April 2004, the use of torture and cruel and degrading treatment began in the detention center in Guantánamo Bay in 2002. Many official reports and secondary literature document the widespread practices of torture and cruel and degrading treatment directly by U.S. troops and personnel.[22] Perhaps never before in the history of debates over torture and cruel and degrading treatment has so much information been available about the different techniques used by specific individuals and units. Much of this information comes from sources within the U.S. government, but there are also numerous reports from international NGOs.

When the photos were first released from Abu Ghraib prison, officials characterized it as isolated aberrant acts by a few low-level soldiers during a short time period. However, since that time, reports from the Red Cross and a barrage of leaked reports from within the U.S. government reveal that the U.S. practice of torture and inhuman and degrading treatment is far more widespread and long-standing, occurring not only in Abu Ghraib, but also in other detention centers in Iraq, in Afghanistan, and in Guantánamo. A widespread practice in multiple locations implies an institutional policy, not human error.[23] The International Committee of the Red Cross (ICRC) visited Guantánamo in June 2004, and reported in a confidential report later made public that the military there had used coercion techniques that were "tantamount to torture." Specifically, the ICRC said its investigators found a system of "humiliating acts, solitary confinement, temperature extremes, use of forced positions." "The construction of such a system, whose stated purpose is the production of intelligence, cannot be considered other than an intentional system of cruel, unusual and degrading treatment and a form of torture."[24] Continuing revelations of reports by FBI agents reveal ongoing use of practices that the FBI deems unacceptable, such as keeping detainees chained in uncomfortable positions for up to twenty-four hours.[25] There are still debates about exactly which techniques constitute torture and which constitute inhuman and degrading treatment and about what the Geneva Conventions mean when they refer to humane treatment. But there is no doubt that the United States was not in compliance with its international legal obligations with regard to humane treatment at least from 2002 to 2006.

Bush administration officials began offering explicit justifications and authorization for torture to military and intelligence agencies in a series of now-public legal memos and reports prepared by the Department of Justice and the Department of Defense between August 2002 and September 2003. These memos offered general signals about the need for and acceptability of harsher interrogation techniques sent from high levels of the administration. These general signals were then "translated" on the ground into a wide range of techniques, some explicitly approved from above and many not explicitly approved from above. By circulating the memos and reports but not issuing executive orders, the top level of the administration was able to set policy while still retaining legal deniability about accountability for the effects of that policy.

In these memos and documents, the Bush administration made three main arguments that helped justify and authorize torture and cruel and degrading treatment. The first was the argument that the Geneva Conventions did not apply to the conflict in Afghanistan, and thus the detainees from that conflict would not be considered prisoners of war, but rather illegal combatants. This decision is problematic with regard to the laws of war, but it carried with it implications that opened the door to torture. The Geneva Conventions absolutely protect any detainee from torture. Thus, a decision that the Geneva Conventions don't apply to a conflict could be understood as saying that torture is therefore permitted. That some U.S. soldiers read these as signals is clear from some of their comments and testimony. "One member of the 377th Company said that the fact that prisoners in Afghanistan had been labeled 'enemy combatants' not subject to the Geneva Conventions had contributed to an unhealthy attitude in the detention center." "We were pretty much told that they were nobodies, that they were just enemy combatants," he said. "I think that giving them the distinction of soldier would have changed our attitude toward them."[26] Military intelligence officials and interrogators at Guantánamo said that "when new interrogators arrived they were told they had great flexibility in extracting information from detainees because the Geneva Conventions did not apply at the base."[27]

The second argument Bush administration officials made was about the definition of torture. Rather than actually say that they supported the use of torture, they made strenuous efforts to reinterpret the definitions of torture and to redefine our obligations under the Geneva Conventions and the Torture Convention so that the United States could use the interrogation techniques it wanted. The Bybee memorandum of August 1, 2002, written at the request of Alberto Gonzales, attempts to use a definition of torture that is outside any standard definition. First, it suggested that "physical pain amounting to torture must be the equivalent in intensity to the pain accompanying serious physical injury, such as organ failure, impairment of body function, or even death." Nowhere in the history of the drafting of the Torture Convention or in U.S. legislation implementing the convention does the idea appear that to be counted as torture, the pain must be equivalent to death or organ failure. Second, the Bybee memorandum said that in order to qualify for the definition of torture, "the infliction of such pain must be the defendant's precise objective."[28] The Bybee memorandum attempts to create such a narrow definition of torture that only the sadist (i.e., one for whom pain is the "precise objective") that engages in a practice resulting in pain equivalent to death or organ failure is a torturer. In other words, the memo creates an absurd and unsustainable definition, a definition contrary to the language of the law and common sense.

The third argument was about the president's ability to order torture in certain circumstances. The memos relied on a controversial constitutional position about the president's role as commander in chief of the armed forces to argue that the president had the authority to supersede international and domestic law and to authorize torture. Again, this runs contrary to the plain language of the Torture Convention, which says that "No exceptional circumstances whatsoever, whether a state of war or a threat of war, internal political instability or any other public emergency, may be invoked as a justification of torture," and "[a]n order from a superior officer or public authority may not be invoked as a justification for torture."

Because these three arguments were so central to the government's case, one way to trace progress (or lack thereof) on U.S. compliance with the prohibition on torture is to trace the history of these three arguments or justifications: (1) nonapplicability of the Geneva Conventions; (2) unconventional definitions of torture; and (3) the president's authority to authorize torture.

Bush administration policy makers decided to ignore the fact that the United States had clearly accepted a strong international legal obligation not to torture and had implemented that obligation in our domestic law. The United States had ratified two treaties that clearly state its international legal obligation not to engage in torture and inhuman and degrading treatment under any circumstances. Not only that, but the United States was deeply involved in the process of drafting these treaties. U.S. delegates worked to make the treaty more precise and enforceable and clearly supported treaty provisions on universal jurisdiction with regard to torture.[29] The administration of George H. Bush submitted the treaty to the Senate in 1990 and supported ratification. A bipartisan coalition in the Senate, including conservative Senator Jesse Helms, worked to ensure that the Senate gave its advice and consent for ratification. The Senate Foreign Relations Committee voted 10-0 to report the convention favorably to the full Senate. When she spoke in support of ratification, Senator Nancy Kassebaum (R-Kans.) said, "I believe we have nothing to fear about our compliance with the terms of the treaty. Torture is simply not accepted in this country, and never will be."[30]

Despite this history, the memos written by Bush administration lawyers justifying the use of harsh interrogation techniques reveal no principled commitment to the prohibition on torture. The concern throughout is with how to protect U.S. officials from possible future prosecution, not about how to adhere to the principles of the law. The memos read like the defense attorney briefs for a client accused of torture, rather than expert advice on the generally accepted understandings about international law. Not until twenty-nine months after the first memo, in a memo prepared explicitly for public consumption just before the confirmation hearing for Alberto Gonzales as attorney general, does the government state, "Torture is abhorrent both to American Law and values and to international norms."[31]

Opposition to Bush Administration Noncompliance with International and Domestic Law

Opposition Within the Executive Branch

The Bush administration could not persuade key legal advisors in its own State Department nor many legal experts within the branches of the U.S. military of its interpretations. Opposition to the decision that the Geneva Conventions didn't apply in Afghanistan and to the revision of interrogation techniques surfaced early. One day after the memorandum by Gonzales recommending that the administration not apply POW status under the Geneva Conventions to captured al Qaeda or Taliban fighters, Secretary of State Colin Powell wrote to Gonzales urging in the strongest terms that the policy be reconsidered. Powell argued that "It will reverse over a century of U.S. policy and practice in supporting the Geneva Conventions and undermine the protections of the rule of law for our troops, both in this specific conflict and in general. It has a high cost in terms of negative international reaction, with immediate adverse consequences for our conduct of foreign policy. It will undermine public support among critical allies, making military cooperation more difficult to sustain."[32]

Despite Powell's misgivings, the Bush administration determined to move ahead with the policy on the Geneva Conventions in the face of the opposition of the State Department. The State Department legal counsel made another effort to oppose it, in which he again echoes Powell's protest. In clear and firm language, he says that a decision to apply the Geneva Conventions to the conflict in Afghanistan would have been consistent with the "plain language of the Conventions and the unvaried practice of the United States in introducing its forces into conflict over fifty years . . . [and] the positions of every other party to the Conventions."[33]

Lawyers within the Bush administration did not only oppose the policy but also warned of the possible legal consequences that administration officials could face if they insisted on these policies. In a memo dated January 11, 2002, State Department legal counsel William Taft IV wrote that "if the U.S. took the war on terrorism outside the Geneva Conventions, not only could U.S. soldiers be denied the protections of the Conventions—and therefore be prosecuted for crimes, including murder—but President Bush could be accused of a 'grave breach' by other countries, and prosecuted for war crimes." Taft also sent a copy of the memo to Gonzales, hoping it would reach Bush.[34] Alberto Mora, general counsel of the navy, also warned his superiors of the possibilities of trials if they continued to disregard the prohibition on torture and cruel and degrading treatment, but his warnings were disregarded.[35] The Bush administration did not use these warnings as a reason to reconsider its policies. But this may explain why the following memos read more like a defense lawyer's briefs already defending their client against the charge of torture.

Other individuals associated with the military accused members of the Bush administration of "endangering troops," "undermining the war effort," "encouraging reprisals," or "lowering morale," not to mention "losing the high moral ground." Military sources criticized the administration for failing to ask the advice of the military's highest legal authorities, the judge advocates general (JAGs) of the various services.[36] Some retired military generals and admirals were so concerned about the positions taken by Gonzales that they wrote an open letter to the Judiciary Committee considering the nomination of Gonzales for attorney general. In it, they argued that military law has been ignored:

The August 1, 2002 Justice Department memo analyzing the law on interrogation references health care administration law more than five times, but never once cites the U.S. Army Field Manual on interrogation. . . . The Army Field Manual was the product of decades of experience—experience that had shown, among other things that such interrogation methods produce unreliable results and often impede further intelligence collection. Discounting the Manual's wisdom on this central point shows a disturbing disregard for the decades of hard-won knowledge of the professional American military.[37]

According to retired Brigadier General Cullen, the White House and Justice Department memos created the policy which in turn "spawned" torture and abuse. The Army Field Manual has sixteen approved methods of interrogation.

Mr. Gonzales embarked on a campaign to justify expanding those approved methods into areas that at least anyone would say are "inhuman and degrading treatment. . . . when you are on that level and you speak you're carrying a lot more weight, you are sending signals to the field that have enormous implications. It is development of policy by winks and nods, and that is the last thing you want to do at that level."[38]

In the minds of some military legal experts, the problem was exactly that "political lawyers," not military lawyers, were in charge of this policy, and they cut military lawyers with operational experience, as well as a central understanding of what they call "complex security interests," out of the policy formulation process. Retired Brigadier General Cullen argued that the decision-making process was "clearly stacked and the military lawyers were outvoted."[39]

Members of the military also argued that torture is ineffective. General Hoar argued that torture may be effective in the short term, but in the long term it undermines the war effort. "Nowhere was this more graphic than the French counter-insurgency operations in Algeria, where torture was used in extracting timely intelligence from recently captured insurgents. This practice may have helped the French in winning the Battle of Algiers, but in the process, the French army lost its honor and ultimately lost the war."[40] People within the FBI also argued that torture was ineffective. Investigative journalist Jane Mayer said that "the fiercest internal resistance to this thinking has come from people who have been directly involved in interrogation, including veteran F.B.I. and

C.I.A. agents. Their concerns are practical as well as ideological. Years of experience in interrogation have led them to doubt the effectiveness of physical coercion as a means of extracting reliable information."[41] The FBI complaints about harsh interrogation practices began in December 2002, according to released internal documents. In late 2003, an agent complained that "these tactics have produced no intelligence of threat neutralization nature to date."[42]

Opposition from International and Domestic Human Rights Groups

International and domestic human rights organizations responded almost immediately to evidence of U.S. noncompliance with the prohibition of torture and cruel and degrading treatment, and their positions were well reflected in key print media outlets. Transnational advocacy networks in the area of human rights emerged and became especially significant in the 1970s and 1980s.[43] They have continued to grow since that time. Initially the transnational advocacy networks did not work extensively on human right practices within the United States. One exception was Amnesty International, which had long adopted prisoners of conscience in the United States and had been especially active working on the issue of the death penalty. Although many groups like Human Rights Watch or Human Rights First are based in the United States, in the past they focused their efforts on international human rights issues and left the domestic human rights scene to civil rights organizations such as the American Civil Liberties Union (ACLU) or the NAACP. By the 1990s, however, this had become an untenable political position, as other NGO allies within the networks frequently asked why U.S.-based groups did not work on the human rights practices of their own government. In the 1990s, Human Rights Watch significantly increased its work on U.S. human rights and humanitarian law violations and in 2001 created its U.S. program, and many other human rights organization followed suit.

Nevertheless, U.S. violations of human rights in the wake of the 9/11 attacks led to a dramatic increase in the activities of the transnational human rights networks with regard to the United States. The emerging revelations of torture and degrading treatment at Abu Ghraib and elsewhere created more consternation and effort. Never before have transnational human rights advocacy organizations and networks turned their spotlight on U.S. practices as they have today. As with advocacy network work in the past, these efforts have been supported by private foundations and individual funders.

Human rights advocacy groups for the most part have not organized major mobilization in the streets, nor have they been able to persuade large number of U.S. voters to care enough about their issues. They have been very active in producing reports, publicizing their reports, lobbying Congress, and in some cases, filing lawsuits against Bush administration officials and requesting documents through the Freedom of Information Act (FOIA) to document their charges. As with all campaigns by networks, their potential for effectiveness comes in the long term, not the short term. It is also enhanced to the degree that they are able to build coalitions outside and inside of governments. In the United States, the traditional international human rights groups have formed coalitions with the civil liberties groups such as the ACLU, social justice groups, or the scores of immigration law activists to carry forward their work. As Wendy Patten points out in her chapter in this volume, these domestic groups working alongside U.S.-based international human rights groups became more open to using the "language, standards, and mechanisms" of international human rights in their work.[44] They have also worked with people in government and the media. So, for example, the many leaks and releases of documents related to torture have been the result of dissatisfaction of individuals within government and the concerted efforts of groups outside of government. Most documents have been made available as a result of FOIA requests that the ACLU has made in reference to their lawsuits against the government. When retired military lawyers became increasingly disenchanted with the Bush administration policy on interrogations and the laws of war, it is interesting that they reached out to colleagues in the human rights organization in the United States, and collaborated on some joint activities.

Organizations including the ACLU, Human Rights First, and the Center for Constitutional Rights have filed lawsuits against Bush administration officials for human rights violations in the war against terror. Although the lawsuits filed by national and international human rights organizations against Bush administration officials have not yet achieved any judicial victories, they have communicated the importance of holding state officials even in powerful countries accountable for past human rights violations. In the past twenty years, there has been a dramatic increase in the world of domestic, foreign, and international trials for human rights violations.[45] It seems likely that this is not a passing trend but a deep structural shift toward accountability for past human rights. Many of these trials, perhaps the majority of them, are not of the actual soldiers who pulled the trigger or applied the electric shocks, but of one of their superior officers in the chain of command for bearing responsibility for the actions of his subordinates. As a result, while in the past most perpetrators of gross human rights violations could expect never to face any consequences for their actions, today it is more likely that some perpetrators may face some kind of judicial process.

Foreign lawsuits against Bush administration officials for torture could prosper eventually because universal jurisdiction is written into the language of the Torture Convention. The United States ratified the treaty, and despite numerous reservations, understandings, and declarations, it did not reserve against universal jurisdiction. The abuses happened well after U.S. ratification. Thus the criteria used by the Law Lords in the Pinochet case are satisfied. In principle, any ratifying country could exercise universal jurisdiction over U.S. citizens in the case of torture. Some judicial proceedings against Bush administration officials have already been initiated in Germany. While many of these judicial processes will eventually stall or lead to dismissals or acquittals for political or legal reasons, at a minimum, they can endanger the peace of mind, financial security, or reputation of suspected perpetrators. In the next few decades, former Secretary of Defense Donald Rumsfeld and others who advocated the policy of explicit noncompliance with the Geneva Conventions and the Torture Convention at a minimum may find themselves in a difficult position when they travel abroad. Before they initiate any international trip they may need to make inquires about the state of trials in any country where they intend to travel.

Other International Pressures

International pressure in opposition to Bush administration policy on torture and cruel and degrading treatment has presented an inconvenience, at a minimum, to the fulfillment of other Bush administration policy goals. A *Washington Post* article in November 2005 reporting that the CIA was holding detainees in secret prisons in Eastern Europe led to an uproar in Europe and to an investigation by the EU of secret detention centers in Europe and cooperation of European governments with the U.S. policy of extraordinary rendition. Despite such criticisms, Condoleezza Rice, traveling in Europe in December 2005, maintained a tone of denial by chastising European leaders for their criticisms and claiming that interrogation of these suspects helped "save European lives."[46] Rice simultaneously argued that "at no time did the United States agree to inhumane acts or torture" and continued to state that "terrorists are not covered by the Geneva Conventions."[47]

In February 2006, a UN-appointed independent panel released a report calling on the United States to close the prison in Guantánamo, where it claimed that U.S. personnel engaged in torture, detained people arbitrarily, and denied fair trials. In May 2006, the UN Committee Against Torture was critical of U.S. policy and urged the United States to close down the Guantánamo Bay prison and to end the use of secret overseas detention centers. The United States was not totally indifferent to this body, as witnessed by the size of its delegation to the meeting and the size of its supplemental report. While this suggests that the Bush administration was prepared to engage with its international critics, in the meeting, the U.S. government did not move away from its most controversial positions on torture and cruel and degrading treatment.

Opposition from the U.S. Judicial Branch

The most effective opposition to Bush administration policies has come from within the U.S. judicial branch, and in particular from the U.S. Supreme Court. In a series of path-breaking decisions, the Supreme Court has upheld the rights of detainees to humane treatment and to the protections offered by the rule of law, both domestic and international. In June 2006, in the case *Hamdan v. Rumsfeld*, the Supreme Court gave a major rebuke to the Bush administration policy and legal interpretations. The Court ruled that the military commission system set up to try accused war criminals in Guantánamo Bay violated both U.S. laws and the Geneva Conventions. In what is now considered a landmark decision about the limits of executive power, the Court said that even during war, the president must comply not only with U.S. laws as established by Congress but also with international law.[48] In this sense, the Court directly contradicted the legal theories put forward by President Bush's legal advisors that the president has broad discretion to make decisions on war-related issues, which in turn they used to claim the president could authorize torture. In this sense, although *Hamdan* did not directly address torture, it addressed the legal claims of executive authority upon which the torture arguments had been based.

The development and evolution of the *Hamdan* case reveal the internal pressures that governments in democracies face to comply with international law. First, the Supreme Court acted as a true check on executive power. Second, both the military and civil society were actively involved in the case: Hamdan was successfully defended by his military-appointed defense lawyer, in cooperation with volunteer lawyers from both the academic world and private law firms, and some forty amicus curiae briefs were filed in support of the Hamdan brief by human rights organizations, retired military officers, diplomats, and legal scholars.[49]

Bush Administration Responses to Internal and External Pressures

Initially the Bush administration did not respond to the internal or international opposition to its policies. The worldview of the neoconservative was initially confirmed. There were apparently few domestic or international political costs to this position. The large negative publicity in the release of the Abu Ghraib photos was not sufficient to end the practices. The American public did not demand more accountability for the use of torture. Despite the fact that the graphic revelations of torture came in an election year, torture did not become a campaign issue.

Not only was the administration not deterred by domestic and international criticism of its practices, but it promoted many of the individuals most associated with noncompliance of the prohibition on torture. Mr. Bybee, who wrote the first controversial "torture" memo, was named to the Ninth Circuit Court of Appeals; White House Legal Counsel Alberto Gonzales, who solicited and approved the Bybee memorandum, was nominated and confirmed for the attorney general; and Michael Chertoff, who as head of the Criminal Division of the Justice Department advised the CIA on the legality of coercive interrogation methods, was selected by Bush to be the new secretary of homeland security.[50] John C. Yoo, one of the authors of controversial Bush administration memos on the Geneva Conventions, said that President Bush's victory in the 2004 election, along with the lack of strong opposition to the Gonzales confirmation, was "proof that the debate is over." He claimed, "The issue is dying out. The public has had its referendum."[51]

But, contrary to Yoo's prediction, the issue did not die out. In anticipation of the confirmation hearings of Gonzales, the Justice Department issued a memo that began to retreat from the Bush administration's most egregious position on torture. Some members of Congress have criticized Gonzales for his position on torture, and the administration wished to defuse any issue that might interfere with his confirmation, and avoid a possible public embarrassment or reversal.

The Justice Department memo of December 30, 2004, "withdraws" and supersedes the August 2002 memorandum and modifies important aspects of its legal analysis. The new memo says "we disagree with statements in the August 2002 Memorandum limiting 'severe' pain under the statute to 'excruciating and agonizing' pain, 'equivalent in intensity to the pain accompanying serious physical injury, such as organ failure, impairment of bodily function, or even death.'" The new memo rejects the earlier assertion that torture only occurs if the interrogator had the specific intent to cause pain. "We do not believe it is useful to try to define the precise meaning of 'specific intent' . . . In light of the President's directive that the United States not engage in torture, it would not be appropriate to rely on parsing the specific intent element of the statute to approve as lawful conduct that might otherwise amount to torture." And finally, though the new memo does not reject the president's authority to order torture, it says it is "unnecessary" to consider that issue because it would be "inconsistent with the President's unequivocal directive that United States personnel not engage in torture."[52] This is still problematic because it continues to ignore the legal obligation of the United States not to engage in torture under any conditions. Nevertheless, this new memo on torture was recognition that the administration had not been able to unilaterally redefine torture. The definitional attempts had been costly, or were going to be costly, to the confirmation of the attorney general, and thus some had to be put to rest. As retired Rear Admiral John Hutson recognized during the Gonzales hearing, the Justice Department memo was not an exoneration of Judge Gonzales, but an indictment. "It's an acknowledgment of error." Thus, by late 2004, U.S. policy had been moderated on one of the three issues discussed above. The administration backed down from the most egregious efforts to redefine torture in ways utterly inconsistent with international law.

During his confirmation hearings, Gonzales faced criticism from NGOs and legal academics, including those associated with the military. Retired Rear Admiral John Hutson, who testified against the confirmation of Gonzales for attorney general, said, "Abrogating the Geneva Conventions imperils our troops and undermines the war effort. It encourages reprisals. It lowers morale. . . . Government lawyers, including Judge Gonzales, let down the U.S. troops in a significant way by their ill-conceived advice. They increased the dangers that they'd face. At the top of the chain of command, to coin a phrase that we've heard in the past, they set the conditions so that many of those troops would commit serious crimes."

Although Gonzales was confirmed without problems, the criticisms he faced signaled the beginnings of more assertive congressional actions on torture. William J. Haynes II, the Department of Defense chief legal officer who helped oversee Pentagon studies on the interrogation of detainees, faced opposition when he was twice nominated to the Fourth Circuit Court of Appeals, and President Bush eventually chose not to resubmit the nomination in the face of political opposition.[53]

In 2005, Senator John McCain introduced an amendment to the Department of Defense Appropriation Act that prohibited cruel and degrading treatment and confined all interrogation techniques to those authorized by the U.S. Army Field Manual on Intelligence and Interrogation. Once again, the Bush administration continued to oppose these efforts to prohibit the use of abusive interrogation techniques. The Senate passed the amendment by a 90 to 9 margin, and the House by 308 to 122, and the amendment was incorporated into the Detainee Treatment Act of 2005.

Throughout the debate over the McCain Amendment the White House sought to exclude the CIA from complying with the antitorture legislation.[54] Even after President Bush was obliged to withdraw his veto threat and reached an agreement with McCain, the language of the signing statement still was couched in ways that implied that the president could override the ban if necessary. In other words, in early 2006, the administration continued to hold firmly to the third argument discussed above—that the president, facing a clear and present danger to national security, was not bound by the obligation to prohibit torture. It was not until the Supreme Court explicitly opposed this doctrine in the *Hamdan v. Rumsfeld* case in September 2006 that the Bush administration backed off its claim that the president could authorize the use of torture and cruel and degrading treatment.

Other provisions of this Detainee Treatment Act, however, undermine some of the protections offered by the McCain Amendment, by stripping federal courts of jurisdiction over detainees in Guantánamo and implicitly permitting the Department of Defense to consider evidence obtained through torture. In addition, the Army Field Manual, previously publicly available, has now been rewritten to include ten classified pages on interrogation techniques.

In response to the Supreme Court's decision in *Hamdan v. Rumsfeld*, the Department of Defense finally issued a memo on July 7, 2006 that instructs recipients to ensure that all DOD policies comply with Common Article 3 of the Geneva Conventions. In an important reversal of its earlier policy, the memo helped bring administration policy in line with the Supreme Court decision. But even as the administration appeared to accept Common Article 3, it asked Congress to pass legislation governing military commissions that would redefine Common Article 3, replacing its requirement that all detainees captured during armed conflict be treated humanely with a new "flexible" standard. The president sought to determine on a case-by-case basis whether treatment was cruel, inhuman, and degrading. Even after the failure of its repeated efforts to redefine the meaning of torture, the administration still persisted in its belief that it could redefine international law to suit its purposes. Fortunately, Congress rejected this proposal; the final Military Commission Act of 2006 (MCA) preserved the meaning of humane treatment under Common Article 3. But the MCA had other worrisome aspects as regards laws about torture and abuse. First, it makes it harder to prosecute those who commit war crimes, including torture, and it permits some evidence obtained under coercion to be used in military commissions. In summary, since 2005, the Congress has moved to limit executive noncompliance with the prohibition on torture and cruel and degrading treatment, but congressional action has fallen short of a full endorsement of international law on the subject.

Meanwhile, the Pentagon created a new Office of Detainee Affairs, "charged with correcting basic problems in the handling and treatment of detainees, and with helping to ensure that senior Defense Department Officials are alerted to concerns about detention operations raised by the Red Cross." A Human Rights First report concludes that "while the effect of this new structure is unclear, it has the potential to help bring U.S. detention policy more in line with U.S. and international legal obligations."[55] The Pentagon has also completed a series of investigations into abuses in detention centers and identified some of the possible causes of such abuses, including the failure to give meaningful guidance to soldiers in the field about rules that governed the treatment of detainees.

Since Abu Ghraib, the U.S. military has also moved to hold some soldiers accountable for abuse of detainees. First, the military has initiated a series of investigations and courts-martial. A comprehensive summary of a project on detainee abuse and accountability found that at least 600 U.S. personnel are implicated in approximately 330 cases of detainee abuse in Iraq, Afghanistan, and Guantánamo Bay. Authorities have opened investigations into about 65 percent of these cases. Of seventy-nine courts-martial, fifty-four resulted in convictions or guilty pleas. Another fifty-seven people faced nonjudicial proceedings involving punishments of no or minimal prison time.[56] Although many cases were not investigated and no senior officers have been held accountable, this is not an insignificant amount of accountability and punishment. This reaffirms the fact that the U.S. government officials who asserted that certain practices were legal or desirable misunderstood the law and misguided personnel in the field. There is reason to believe that investigations into torture and cruel and unusual punishment have not yet ended and that higher-level officials may someday also face accountability, if not in the United States, then perhaps abroad.

The definition of torture in the Torture Convention focuses on pain or suffering "inflicted by or at the instigation of or with the consent or acquiescence of a public officials or a person acting in an official capacity." In the drafting of the treaty, the United States itself proposed the language "or with the consent or acquiescence of a public official," which appears in the convention.[57] To date, U.S. sanctions have focused only on torture committed "by" public officials, and have disregarded the issues of instigation, consent, or acquiescence of other higher-level public officials. Almost all (95 percent) of the military personnel who have been investigated are enlisted soldiers, not officers. Three officers were convicted by court-martial for directly participating in detainee abuse, but no U.S. military officer has been held accountable for criminal acts committed by subordinates.[58]

Conclusion

After 9/11 in the United States, there were deep disputes about the nature of the security threats and the proper response to them. What made torture possible was not the national security situation per se, but the neoconservative ideas held by a small group of individuals in power about the nature of the crisis and the appropriate response to it. If another group (for example, those associated with the position of Colin Powell) had prevailed in internal policy debates, it is plausible that the United States would currently be in compliance with the prohibition on torture.

Because this is an area of international law that is highly legalized and where the United States has ratified the relevant treaties and implemented them in corresponding national legislation, it is quite clear that the United States is in breach of existing legal obligations that it and the world community have long accepted. On this particular issue human rights advocacy groups and most legal scholars around the world are in agreement.

In the short term, this group of mainly political (not military) advisors closely associated with the president won the debate and prevailed with an argument that noncompliance with aspects of the Geneva Conventions and the Torture Convention was appropriate in the new circumstances. They justified their position with questionable international legal arguments that met opposition from the legal department of the State Department and the JAGs of the various military branches, not to mention human rights organizations, academics, and much of foreign legal opinion.

But although this group of neoconservative individuals won out in internal policy debates in the short term, their position was eroded in the longer term. In particular, the U.S. judicial system, both military and civilian, has provided some effective checks to the executive power. In addition, civil society organizations and some print media have denounced and worked against U.S. government abuse of detainees. Some international actors have also challenged U.S. practices of noncompliance. It would appear that domestic pressures have been more effective than international pressures in changing Bush administration practices. The Bush administration made changes in its policy on the treatment of detainees only as a result of concerted and public opposition. The lesson we can take from this is common to most studies of compliance with human rights law around the world. Governments are usually unwilling to recognize that they have committed human rights violations and to make changes in policy necessary to bring their practices in accordance with international law. Only concerted, public, and costly pressures from a wide variety of both domestic and international actors lead to improvements in human rights practices. But despite the similarities between the U.S. case and other cases of human rights violations in the world, there are also some interesting differences. Human rights organizations responded very rapidly to the evidence of torture and abuse. Those charges were echoed by segments of the print media, including the *New York Times*, the *Washington Post*, the *New Yorker*, and the *New York Review of Books*, whose reporters also produced crucial investigative articles that gave impetus and evidence for the internal and international opposition. Perhaps most unique to the U.S. case was the fact that there was significant and sustained opposition within the military itself to the policy of noncompliance with the Geneva Conventions and the Torture Convention. Finally, the U.S. judicial branch, and particularly the Supreme Court, played a crucial role in restraining the worst excesses of executive power. As is common in the world of human rights, these responses and changes did not happen rapidly and are still underway. As of mid-2007, it is not clear if the United States is now in compliance with domestic and international law on torture.

But the issue of U.S. noncompliance with the prohibition on torture has not gone away and has started to pose significant costs on the individuals associated with the policy as well as for the U.S. government. The policy has already been costly for U.S. soft power and claims to leadership in the area of democracy and human rights. In the future it is very likely that the policy of noncompliance will be costly in more concrete terms, such as lawyers' fees, compensation paid to victims, and in some cases, imprisonment.

The people whose positions carried the day within the administration misunderstood and misjudged the current nature of the international system on the issue of torture and mistreatment of detainees. They believe it to be a realist world where international law and institutions are quite malleable to exercises of hegemonic power. In the short term, their beliefs were confirmed. In the longer term, they will find that this misreading of the nature of the international system is personally and professionally costly to them, not to mention costly to the reputation and soft power of the U.S. government.

Notes

1. Harold Hongju Koh, "On American Exceptionalism," *Stanford Law Review* 55 (May 2003): 5.

2. See Colin H. Kahl, "In the Crossfire or the Crosshairs? Norms, Civilian Casualties, and U.S. Conduct in Iraq," *International Security* 32(1) (Summer 2007): 7–46, 11.

3. The United States, for example, uniformly ranks high among countries for

its level of "gender development" and "gender empowerment," as measured by the UN Development Program in its annual *Human Development Report*. Both are composite measures that reflect the enjoyment of many aspects of the rights enumerated in the CEDAW Convention.

4. The exception to this argument is that by sending detainees to Egypt in the "exceptional rendition" program, initiated in 1995, the United States has been in violation of Article 3 of the Torture Convention, which says state parties can not return detainees to states where there are substantial grounds to believe they will be subjected to torture. See Jane Mayer, "Outsourcing Torture," *New Yorker*, February 14 and 21, 2005.

5. See Francis Fukuyama, *America at the Crossroads: Democracy, Power, and the Neoconservative Legacy* (New Haven, Conn.: Yale University Press, 2006).

6. *Filartiga v. Pena-Irala*, 630 F.2d 876 (2nd Cir. 1980).

7. Herman Burgers and Hans Danelius, *The United Nations Convention Against Torture: A Handbook on the Convention Against Torture and Other Cruel, Inhuman or Degrading Treatment or Punishment* (Dordrecht, Netherlands: Martinus Nijhoff Publishers, 1988).

8. *5 R v. Bartle and Commissioner of Police for the Metropolis and others, ex parte Pinochet*, House of Lords, March 24, 1999.

9. Fukuyama, *America at the Crossroads*.

10. George F. Kennan, "Morality and Foreign Policy," *Foreign Affairs* 64 (1985–86): 205–18.

11. As quoted in Michael Isikoff, "A Justice Department Memo Proposes that the United States Hold Others Accountable for International Laws on Detainees; but That Washington Did Not Have to Follow Them Itself," *Newsweek*, May 21, 2004.

12. Quoted in Mayer, "Outsourcing Torture," p. 123.

13. Francis Fukuyama, "After Neoconservatism," *New York Times*, February 19, 2006.

14. Benedict Kingsbury, "The Concept of Compliance as a Function of Competing Conceptions of International Law," *Michigan Journal of International Law* 19 (1998): 2.

15. As cited in Mayer, "Outsourcing Torture," p. 82.

16. Beth Simmons, "Why Commit? Explaining State Acceptance of International Human Rights Obligations," forthcoming.

17. Oona Hathaway, "The Cost of Commitment," *Stanford Law Review* 55 (May 2003): 5.

18. See, for example, Thomas Risse, Stephen Ropp, and Kathryn Sikkink (eds.), *The Power of Human Rights* (New York: Cambridge University Press, 1999), which includes chapters on international and domestic pressures to bring about human rights changes in Chile, Guatemala, Kenya, Uganda, South Africa, Tunisia, Morocco, Indonesia, the Philippines, Poland, and Czechoslovakia.

19. Kathryn Sikkink, *Mixed Signals: U.S. Human Rights Policy and Latin America* (Ithaca, N.Y.: Cornell University Press, 2004).

20. United States, Congress, House, *The Status of Human Rights in Selected Countries and the United States Response; Report Prepared for the Subcommittee on International Organization of the Committee on International Relations of the United States House of Representatives by the Library of Congress*, Ninety-fifth Congress, 1st sess., July 25, 1977 (Washington, D.C.: G.P.O., 1977), p. 2.

21. United States, Department of Defense, "Memorandum for the Secretary of Defense," "Improper Material in Spanish Language Intelligence Training Manuals" (March 10, 1992).

22. See "Article 15-6 Investigation of the 800th Military Police Brigade" (The Taguba Report); "Final Report of the Independent Panel to Review DOD Detention Operations" (The Schlesinger Report), August 2004; "AR 15-6 Investigation of the Abu Ghraib Prison and 205th Military Intelligence Brigade," LTG Anthony R. Jones; "AR 15-6 Investigation of the Abu Ghraib Detention Facility and 205th Military Intelligence Brigade," MG George R. Fay; "Report of the International Committee of the Red Cross (ICRC) on the Treatment by the Coalition Forces of Prisoners of War and Other Protected Persons by the Geneva Convention in Iraq During Arrest, Internment and Interrogation," February 2004. All of these reports are available in the appendices to Mark Danner, *Torture and Truth: America, Abu Ghraib, and the War on Terror* (New York: New York Review of Books, 2004).

23. See Human Rights and Global Justice, Human Rights First, and Human Rights Watch, *By the Numbers: Findings of the Detainee Abuse and Accountability Project*, 2006.

24. Neil A. Lewis, "Red Cross Finds Detainee Abuse in Guantánamo: U.S. Rejects Accusations: Confidential Report Calls Practices Tantamount to Torture," *New York Times*, November 30, 2004, pp. A1, A14.

25. Kate Zernike, "New Released Reports Show Early Concern on Prison Abuse," *New York Times*, January 6, 2004, p. A18.

26. "Cuba Base Sent Its Interrogators to Iraqi Prison," *New York Times*, May 29, 2004.

27. Neil A. Lewis, "Fresh Details Emerge on Harsh Methods at Guantánamo," *New York Times*, January 1, 2005.

28. United States, Department of Justice, Office of Legal Counsel, Office of the Assistant Attorney General, "Memorandum for Alberto R. Gonzales, Re: Standards of Conduct for Interrogation under 18 U.S.C. 2340–2340A," August 1, 2002,

29. Burgers and Danilius, *The United Nations Convention Against Torture*, pp. 78–79, 58, 62–63.

30. *Congressional Record, Senate*, October 27, 1990, p. S17491.

31. United States, Department of Justice, Office of Legal Counsel, Office of the Assistant Attorney General, "Memorandum for James B. Comey, Deputy Attorney General, Re: Legal Standards Applicable Under 18 U.S.C. 2340–2340A," December 30, 2004.

32. "Memorandum from Secretary of State Colin Powell to Counsel to the President re Draft Decision Memorandum for the President on the applicability of the Geneva Convention to the Conflict in Afghanistan," available online at www.humanrightsfirst.org/us_law/etn/gonzales/index.asp#memos.

33. "To: Gonzales, from William H. Taft, IV, re: Comments on Your Paper on the Geneva Convention," February 2, 2002.

34. Mayer, "Outsourcing Torture," p. 82.

35. Jane Mayer, "The Memo," *New Yorker*, February 27, 2006.

36. Statement by Brigadier General James Cullen, press conference by Human Rights First and Retired Military Leaders, January 4, 2005, audio available online at www.humanrightsfirst.org, transcription of remarks by author.

37. "An Open Letter to the Senate Judiciary Committee," January 4, 2005, signed by Brigadier General David M. Brahms (Ret. USMC), Brigadier General James Cullen (Ret. USA), Brigadier General Evelyn P. Foote (Ret. USA), Lieutenant General Robert Gard (Ret. USA), Vice Admiral Lee F. Gun (Ret. USN), Rear Admiral Don Guter (Ret. USN), General Joseph Hoar (Ret. USMC), Lieutenant General Claudia Kennedy (Ret. USA), General Merrill McPeak (Ret.

USAF), Major General Melvyn Montano (Ret. USAF Nat. Guard), and General John Shalikashvili (Ret. USA).

38. Response by Brigadier General James Cullen during the question-and-answer session, press conference by Human Rights First and retired military leaders, January 4, 2005, audio available online at www.humanrightsfirst.org, transcription of remarks by author.

39. Ibid.

40. Statement by Hoar, Press Conference, January 4, 2004.

41. Mayer, "Outsourcing Torture," p. 108.

42. FBI, Criminal Justice Information Services, "E-mail from REDACTED to Gary Bald, Frankie Battle, Arthur Cummings Re: FWD: Impersonating FBI Agents at GITMO," December 5, 2003, available online at www.aclu.org/torturefoia/released/122004.html.

43. See Margaret Keck and Kathryn Sikkink, *Activists Beyond Borders: Advocacy Networks in International Politics* (Ithaca, N.Y.: Cornell University Press, 1998); and Risse et al. (eds.), *The Power of Human Rights*.

44. Wendy Patten, "The Impact of September 11 and the Struggle Against Terrorism on the U.S. Domestic Human Rights Movement," Chapter 10 in the current volume.

45. See Ellen Lutz and Kathryn Sikkink, "The Justice Cascade: The Evolution and Impact of Foreign Human Rights Trials in Latin America," *Chicago Journal of International Law* 2 (Spring 2001): 1; and Kathryn Sikkink and Carrie Booth Walling, "The Impact of Human Rights Trials in Latin America," *Journal of Peace Research* 44(4) (2007): 427–45.

46. Joel Brinkley, " 'U.S. Interrogations Are Saving European Lives,' Rice Says," *New York Times*, December 6, 2005, p. A3.

47. Richard Bernstein, "Rice's Visit: Official Praise, Public Doubts," *New York Times* (online), December 11, 2005, p. 22.

48. U.S. Supreme Court, *Hamdan v. Rumsfeld*, available online at www.supreme courtus.gov/opinions/05pdf/05-184.pdf.

49. Nina Totenberg, "Hamdan v. Rumsfeld: Path to a Landmark Ruling," NPR, June 29, 2006, available online at www.npr.org/templates/story/story.php?storyId5751355.

50. "Following the Paper Trail to the Roots of Torture," *New York Times*, February 8, 2005, p. B1.

51. Mayer, "Outsourcing Torture," p. 82.

52. United States, Department of Justice, Office of Legal Counsel, Office of the Assistant Attorney General, "Memorandum for James B. Comey, Deputy Attorney General, Re: Legal Standards Applicable Under 18 U.S.C. 2340–2340A," December 30, 2004.

53. "Bush Drops Plans to Resubmit Three Judicial Nominations," *New York Times*, January 10, 2007.

54. Eric Schmitt, "Exception Sought in Detainee Abuse Ban: White House Wants More Leeway for C.I.A. on Interrogations," *New York Times*, October 25, 2005, p. A17.

55. Deborah Pearlstein and Priti Patel, *Behind the Wire: An Update to Ending Secret Detentions* (New York: Human Rights First, 2005).

56. *By the Numbers*, pp. 3, 7.

57. Burger and Danilus, *The United Nations Convention Against Torture*, p. 41.

58. *By the Numbers*, p. 7.

Chapter 12
Trade Unions and Human Rights

Lance Compa

Trade unionists and human rights advocates in the United States pursued separate agendas in the last half of the twentieth century. Labor leaders focused their demands on recognition from employers, collective bargaining, and a greater share for workers of growing national wealth. Tough organizing and hard bargaining were workers' immediate challenges. Trade unionists had little time for learning, invoking, and using international human rights standards to advance their cause. Besides, the United States for many years was such a dominant economic power that a purely domestic agenda sufficed to meet labor's needs.

Where trade union leaders took up international questions, it was mostly part of a Cold War dynamic. The Congress of Industrial Organizations (CIO) purged its left-wing unions in the late 1940s and went on to merge with the more conservative American Federation of Labor (AFL) in 1955.[1] The new AFL-CIO's international advocacy focused on building anticommunist unions in other countries.[2] Trade unionists' invocations of human rights were usually aimed at violations in the Soviet Union, not at home.

Earlier generations of trade unionists and their supporters developed notions of workers' rights linked to home-grown notions of "industrial democracy" and "Americanism," even among many immigrants who helped to build the labor movement.[3] In the 1930s, Senator Robert Wagner and other champions of collective bargaining argued that it would bring industrial democracy and civil rights into the workplace. Union leaders claimed that organizing and bargaining "was the only road to civil rights, civil liberties, and real citizenship."[4] Wagner's National Labor Relations Act (NLRA) contains a ringing declaration of workers' "right" to organize and to bargain collectively. But once the 1935 Wagner Act became law and the labor movement tripled its membership in ten years, pointing to basic rights as a foundation for trade unionism faded in importance.

For its part, the modern human rights movement that emerged from the wreckage of World War II rarely took up labor struggles. Although workers' freedom of association and the right to decent wages—even the right to paid vacations—are part of the 1948 Universal Declaration of Human Rights and other international human rights instruments, many advocates saw union organizing and collective bargaining as strictly economic endeavors, not really human rights.

To be fair, human rights advocates had their hands full with genocide, death squads, political prisoners, repressive dictatorships, and other horrific violations around the world. Compared with these, American workers' problems with organizing and collective bargaining were not human rights priorities. Rights groups' leaders and activists might personally sympathize with workers and trade unions, but they did not see labor advocacy as part of their mission.[5]

In the 1990s the parallel but separate tracks of the labor movement and the human rights movement began to converge. This chapter examines how trade union advocates adopted human rights analyses and arguments in their work and human rights organizations began including workers' rights in their mandates.

The first section, "Looking In," reviews the U.S. labor movement's traditional domestic focus and the historical absence of a rights-based foundation for American workers' collective action. The second section, "Looking Out," covers a corresponding deficit in labor's international perspective and action. The third section, "Labor Rights Through the Side Door," deals with the emergence of international human rights standards and their application in *other* countries as a key labor concern in trade regimes and in corporate social responsibility schemes. The fourth section, "Opening the Front Door to Workers' Rights," relates trade unionists' new turn to human rights and international solidarity and the reciprocal opening among human rights advocates to labor concerns. The conclusion of the chapter discusses criticisms by some analysts about possible overreliance on human rights arguments and offers thoughts for strengthening and advancing the new labor–human rights alliance.

Looking In

The Commerce Clause Foundation

Adopted by a progressive New Deal Congress in 1935 at a time of widespread industrial conflict, the NLRA affirmed American workers' right to organize and bargain collectively. But the rights proclaimed in Section 7 were not really based on a foundation of fundamental rights. Senator Wagner and his legislative drafters thought (perhaps rightly for the historical moment in which they found themselves, without viewing longer-term consequences) that a still-conservative Supreme Court would strike down the act if they based it on First Amendment freedoms or Thirteenth Amendment free-labor guarantees. Instead, they fixed the law's rationale on the Constitution's Commerce Clause giving Congress the power to regulate interstate commerce.[6]

The act's Section 1, *Findings and Policies*, pointed to "strikes and other forms of industrial strife or unrest, which have the intent or the necessary effect of burdening or obstructing commerce." Section 1 mentions "commerce" thirteen times and contains many other references to the "free flow of goods" and equivalents. There are three references to "rights" of workers. In short, the NLRA was based on the need to remove "burdens on commerce," not the need to protect workers' fundamental rights.

Business forces indeed challenged the NLRA's constitutionality. The Supreme Court upheld the law in its 1937 *Jones & Laughlin Steel* decision (301 U.S. 1). The Court mentioned in passing that employees' self-organization is a "fundamental right," saying that "employees have as clear a right to organize and select their representatives for lawful purposes as the respondent has to organize its business and select its own officers and agents." But the Court based its constitutional analysis on the Commerce Clause:

It is a familiar principle that acts which directly burden or obstruct interstate or foreign commerce, or its free flow, are within the reach of the congressional power. . . . When industries organize themselves on a national scale, making their relation to interstate commerce the dominant factor in their activities, how can it be maintained that their industrial labor relations constitute a forbidden field into which Congress may not enter when it is necessary to protect interstate commerce from the paralyzing consequences of industrial war?

Trade union organizing and bargaining was now protected by law. Workers' struggles had brought passage of the NLRA; workers' organizing surged under protection of the NLRA. But their protection was rooted in unstable soil of economic policy, not solid ground of fundamental rights. As the Supreme Court said in its 1975 *Emporium Capwell* decision (420 U.S. 50), "These [rights] are protected not for their own sake but as an instrument of the national labor policy of minimizing industrial strife."

Workers' rights depended on economic policy choices, and the economic system enshrined private ownership and control of property, including the workplace. The Wagner Act itself contained a painful policy choice contrary to basic rights: excluding agricultural workers from its protection, a price for Southern Democrats' support.

Employers' Long March

After passage of the act and the *Jones & Laughlin* decision, employers mounted a long march through courts, Congresses, and administrations to claw back workers' organizing and bargaining space. Their counter-thrust began with an early but little-noticed prize. In the 1938 *Mackay Radio* decision (304 U.S. 333), the Supreme Court said that employers can permanently replace workers who exercise the right to strike.

Striker replacement was not the issue in the case. In fact, the union won the case, because Mackay Radio only replaced union leaders who led the strike, a clear act of unlawful discrimination for union activity. However, in what is called dicta—tangential asides in a court opinion not bearing on the legal issue—the Supreme Court said, "Although section 13 of the act provides, 'Nothing in this Act shall be construed so as to interfere with or impede or diminish in any way the right to strike,' it does not follow that an employer, guilty of no act denounced by the statute, has lost the right to protect and continue his business by supplying places left vacant by strikers. And he is not bound to discharge those hired to fill the places of strikers, upon the election of the latter to resume their employment, in order to create places for them."

For many years afterward, the *Mackay Radio* decision had little effect. Labor advocates did not seek a legislative "fix" of the judge-made striker-replacement rule. New organizing continued apace, and employers rarely tried the permanent replacement option when unions were strong and growing. Getting replacements was not easy when respect for picket lines was an article of faith among workers. Employers knew they had to live with their unions after a strike and did not want to poison the relationship by replacing union members.

The permanent striker-replacement doctrine remained a relatively obscure feature of U.S. law until employers began wielding it more aggressively in the late 1970s and early 1980s. Many analysts attribute this development to President Ronald Reagan's firing and permanent replacement of ten thousand air traffic controllers in 1981 even though, as federal employees, controllers did not come under coverage of the NLRA and the MacKay rule. In fact, the use of permanent replacements had begun trending upward before Reagan's action.[7] But the air traffic controllers' example served as a signal to employers to use the permanent-replacement option in several high-profile strikes in the 1980s and afterward, with intimidating effects on workers and unions.[8]

The permanent-replacement doctrine is not used only against workers' exercise of the right to strike. In almost every trade union–organizing drive, management raises the prospect of permanent replacement in written materials, in captive-audience meetings, and in one-on-one meetings where supervisors speak with workers under their authority. The permanent-replacement threat appears at the bargaining table, too. An industrial relations researcher found that management threatens permanent replacement during collective bargaining negotiations more often than unions threaten to strike.[9]

In the 1990s, trade unions tried to get Congress to prohibit permanent replacements. A majority of the House and Senate supported such a move in the 1993–94 Congress, when Bill Clinton was president. But a Republican filibuster in the Senate blocked the needed sixty votes for passage.[10] When Republicans took control of Congress in 1995, hopes for reform faded.

Employer Free Speech

Another court-launched counterthrust to union organizing came with the 1941 *Virginia Electric Power* decision (314 U.S. 469) granting First Amendment protection to employers' anti-union broadsides. After passage of the Wagner Act, the National Labor Relations Board (NLRB) closely scrutinized and limited employers' ability to campaign openly and aggressively against workers' organizing efforts. The board reasoned that such fierce campaigning was inherently coercive, given the imbalance of power in the employment relationship. The Court said:

> The [National Labor Relations] Board specifically found that the [company's anti-union bulletin and speeches] "interfered with, restrained and coerced" the Company's employees in the exercise of their rights guaranteed by section 7 of the Act. The Company strongly urges that such a finding is repugnant to the First Amendment. . . .
> The Board specifically found that those utterances were unfair labor practices, and it does not appear that the Board raised them to the stature of coercion by reliance on the surrounding circumstances. If the utterances are thus to be separated from their background, we find it difficult to sustain a finding of coercion with respect to them alone. . . . It appears that the Board rested heavily upon findings with regard to the bulletin and the speeches the adequacy of which we regard as doubtful.

The *Virginia Electric Power* decision set the stage for the conservative 1947 Congress to add a new Section 8 (c) to the NLRA, the so-called employer free speech clause insulating employers against any liability for anti-union "views, argument, or opinion, or the dissemination thereof, whether in written, printed, graphic, or visual form . . . if such expression contains no threat of reprisal or force or promise of benefit." Since then, employers and consultants who specialize in combating unions have perfected a science of using captive-audience meetings, videos, props, letters, leaflets, one-on-one "counseling" by supervisors, and other tactics to break up organizing efforts.

To take one example among thousands, at an Illinois restaurant where workers launched an organizing drive, the employer guaranteed that if the union came in he would be out of business within a year. In a tape-recorded speech in a captive-audience meeting, the owner stated, "If the union exists . . . [the company] will fail. The cancer will eat us up and we will fall by the wayside. . . . I am not making a threat. I am stating a fact. . . . I only know from my mind, from my pocketbook, how I stand on this." In the 1983 *NLRB v. Village X* decision (723 F. 2d 1360), the federal appeals court found this to be a lawful prediction that did not interfere with, restrain, or coerce employees.

Other Taft-Hartley Thrusts

The employer free speech clause only began the anti-union assault in the 1947 amendments known as the Taft-Hartley Act. In a brilliant market-ing ploy, a new clause called "right-to-work" allowed states to prohibit employers and unions from including in their collective bargaining agreement a requirement of dues payments (or a like sum from non-members, who can obtain a rebate for amounts not related to collective bargaining) from all represented employees receiving benefits under the contract. More than twenty states have adopted such "right-to-work" laws, which have nothing to do with rights or with work, but much to do with weakening workers' collective bargaining strength.[11]

In other provisions, the Taft-Hartley Act prohibited employees at sup-plier or customer firms from giving any solidarity support to workers on strike against a "primary" employer. This "secondary boycott" ban means that workers can never countervail employers' mutual support in the form of suppliers and customers continuing business as usual with a primary employer.

The Taft-Hartley Act added supervisors and independent contractors to the list of workers, like agricultural employees, "excluded" from pro-tection of the NLRA. Excluded workers can be fired with impunity for trying to form unions. Since then, Supreme Court and NLRB decisions have amplified the "exclusion" clause, leaving taxi drivers, college pro-fessors, delivery truck drivers, engineers, sales and distribution employ-ees, doctors, nurses, newspaper employees, Indian casino employees, "managers" with minimal managerial responsibility, graduate teaching assistants at universities, disabled workers, temporary employees, and others stripped of any protection for exercising rights of association. A 2002 government study found that more than thirty million U.S. workers are excluded from protection of freedom of association rights.[12]

Tectonic Shifts

As decades passed, the economic foundation of workers' organizing and bargaining rights became vulnerable to the shifting economic landscape. The implicit "social contract" and social cohesion of the New Deal and post–World War II era gave way to the "risk society" and winner-take-all inequality. In the 1930s, the lack of trade union organizing and collective bargaining was defined as a "burden on commerce" justifying the Wagner Act. But by the 1980s trade unions and collective bargaining had become burdens on a market-driven economy. Without a human rights foundation, workers' freedom of association was vulnerable to market imperatives.

New court decisions reflected the change. In 1981, a time of massive corporate "downsizing" and restructuring, the Supreme Court ruled in the *First National Maintenance* case (452 U.S. 666) that workers cannot bargain over their livelihoods. Instead, employers can refuse to bargain over decisions to close the workplace because their right to entrepreneurial "speed" and "secrecy" outweighs workers' bargaining rights. Here is what the Court said:

Congress had no expectation that the elected union representative would become an equal partner in the running of the business enterprise in which the union's members are employed. . . . Management must be free from the constraints of the bargaining process to the extent essential for the running of a profitable business. . . . Management may have great need for speed, flexibility, and secrecy in meeting business opportunities and exigencies. . . . [Bargaining] could afford a union a powerful tool for achieving delay, a power that might be used to thwart management's intentions. . . . We conclude that the harm likely to be done to an employer's need to operate freely in deciding whether to shut down part of its business purely for economic reasons outweighs the incremental benefit that might be gained through the union's participation in making the decision.

The Supreme Court could hardly have been more frank in asserting that the smooth functioning of capitalism is more important than workers' rights. In a similar vein, the Court ruled in the 1992 *Lechmere* decision (502 U.S. 527) that workers have no right to receive written information from trade union organizers in a publicly accessible shopping mall parking lot because the employer's private property rights outweigh workers' freedom of association rights. Except where employees are otherwise unreachable, as in a remote logging camp, employers can have union representatives arrested for trespassing if they set foot on even publicly accessible company property to communicate with employees.

In both *First National Maintenance* and *Lechmere*, the Supreme Court overruled NLRB decisions that favored workers and unions. Doctrinally, courts should defer to the administrative expertise of the NLRB. In practice, however, federal courts often make their own judgment on the merits of a case to overrule the NLRB. Professor Julius Getman has described the dynamic thus:

> The notion that courts would simultaneously defer and enforce was unrealistic. So long as the courts had the power to refuse enforcement, it was inevitable that they would use this power to require the Board to interpret the NLRA in accordance with their views of desirable policy. . . . The judicial attitude towards collective bargaining has increasingly become one of suspicion, hostility, and indifference. . . .
>
> The reason for the courts' retreat from collective bargaining is difficult to identify, but it seems to rest on a shift in contemporary judicial thinking about economic issues. The NLRA, when originally passed, had a Keynesian justification. Collective bargaining, it was believed, would increase the wealth of employees, thereby stimulating the economy and reducing the likelihood of depression and recession. Today, courts are more likely to see collective bargaining as an interference with the benevolent working of the market, and, thus, inconsistent with economic efficiency most likely to be achieved by unencumbered management decision making.[13]

State Judiciaries and Workers' Rights

Some state courts have shown more sympathy to fundamental rights arguments in defense of workers' interests. For example, the New Jersey Supreme Court found fundamental rights in the 1989 *Molinelli Farms* case (552 A.2d 1003) involving farm workers, who are not protected by the federal NLRA. The court said, "Article I, paragraph 19 of the New Jersey Constitution of 1947 provides in part that 'persons in private employment shall have the right to organize and bargain collectively.' . . . The constitutional provision is self-executing and that the courts have both the power and obligation to enforce rights and remedies under this constitutional provision. . . . Backpay and reinstatement are appropriate remedies to enforce the constitutional guarantee of Article I, paragraph 19 of the New Jersey Constitution."

California's Supreme Court championed workers' right to strike in its 1985 *County Sanitation District No. 2* decision (699 P.2d 835), saying:

> The right to strike, as an important symbol of a free society, should not be denied unless such a strike would substantially injure paramount interests of the larger community. . . .
>
> The right to form and be represented by unions is a fundamental right of American workers that has been extended to public employees through constitutional adjudication as well as by statute . . . whenever a labor organization undertakes a concerted activity, its members exercise their right to assemble, and organizational activity has been held to be a lawful exercise of that right. . . .
>
> If the right to strike is afforded some constitutional protection as derivative

of the fundamental right of freedom of association, then this right cannot be abridged absent a substantial or compelling justification.

But the California court's decision is far outweighed at the federal level by Supreme Court decisions insisting that there is no fundamental right to strike and that strikes can be regulated based on economic policy choices. In its 1926 *Dorchy v. Kansas* decision (272 U.S. 306), the Supreme Court said (in a decision written by Justice Brandeis, generally considered a progressive):

The right to carry on business—be it called liberty or property—has value. To interfere with this right without just cause is unlawful. The fact that the injury was inflicted by a strike is sometimes a justification. But a strike may be illegal because of its purpose, however orderly the manner in which it is conducted. . . .

Neither the common law, nor the Fourteenth Amendment, confers the absolute right to strike.

In a decision affirmed by the Supreme Court, a federal district judge ruled in the 1971 *Postal Clerks v. Blount* case (325 F. Supp. 879, aff'd. 404 U.S. 802):

Plaintiff contends that the right to strike is a fundamental right protected by the Constitution, and that the absolute prohibition of such activity . . . constitutes an infringement of the employees' First Amendment rights of association and free speech and operates to deny them equal protection of the law. . . .

At common law no employee, whether public or private, had a constitutional right to strike in concert with his fellow workers. Indeed, such collective action on the part of employees was often held to be a conspiracy. When the right of private employees to strike finally received full protection, it was by statute, Section 7 of the National Labor Relations Act, which "took this conspiracy weapon away from the employer in employment relations which affect interstate commerce" and guaranteed to employees in the private sector the right to engage in concerted activities for the purpose of collective bargaining. It seems clear that public employees stand on no stronger footing in this regard than private employees and that in the absence of a statute, they too do not possess the right to strike.

Devil's Bargain?

In retrospect, setting the National Labor Relations Act on a commercial foundation rather than a foundation of fundamental rights was a bargain with the Devil. Perhaps it was strategically necessary at the time to evade a constitutional trap. But in the more than seventy years since passage of the Act, Congress, the courts, and successive administrations and labor boards based their rulings on the Act's economic premises, not on concepts of workers' basic rights. This meant that they made decisions reflecting views about what furthers the free flow of commerce.

The 1935 Congress had seen *denial* of workers' organizing and bargaining rights as obstructing commerce. Fast-forward to the twenty-first century, in which legislative, judicial, and administrative rollbacks of workers' rights have brought the opposite view: organizing and collective bargaining are market-distorting and commerce-burdening activities that must yield to employers' property rights and unilateral control of the workplace.

Can we now rethink and refound American labor law on a human rights foundation, including what can be learned from international human rights and labor rights principles? This is the challenge for advocates of workers' rights as human rights. U.S. trade unionists and their allies are starting to take up this call. Their efforts are discussed later in this chapter. First, however, a review is offered of how and to what extent U.S. labor law and practice have been influenced by international labor and human rights concerns.

Looking Out

American Exceptionalism

"American exceptionalism" to international law is deeply rooted in American legal discourse and culture.[14] Indeed, this section could be subtitled "with blinders," because until recently U.S. labor law and practice rarely drew on international sources and counterparts. As in other legal fields, labor and employment law practitioners and jurists rarely invoke human rights instruments and standards.

Outside a small cadre of specialists interested in comparative and international labor law, most actors in the U.S. labor law system have no familiarity with labor provisions in the Universal Declaration of Human Rights; the International Covenant on Civil and Political Rights (ICCPR); the International Covenant on Economic, Social, and Cultural Rights; International Labor Organization (ILO) Conventions and Declarations; Organisation for Economic Cooperation and Development (OECD)guidelines; trade agreements; and other international instruments. The United States has ratified only 14 of the ILO's 186 conventions, and among these only 2 of the 8 "core" conventions.[15]

"Who needs it?" is a reflexive American response to suggestions that we can learn something about workers' rights from foreign sources. When the United States ratified the ICCPR in 1992, the then-Bush administration insisted that "ratification of the Covenant has no bearing on and does not, and will not, require any alteration or amendment to existing Federal and State labor law" and that "ratification of the Covenant would not obligate us in any way to ratify ILO Convention 87 or any other international agreement."[16] In its most recent report on the ICCPR, the State Department supplied nothing more than a few desultory paragraphs suggesting "general" compliance with Article 22, the ICCPR provision on workers' freedom of association.[17]

As Professor Cynthia Estlund noted:

> The official American view is that international human rights are endangered elsewhere, and that American labor law is a model for the rest of the world. The rest of the world may not be convinced that American labor law, old and flawed as it is, is a model for the modern world. But more to the present point, American legal institutions and decision makers have thus far been deaf to the claim that international labor law provides a potential model for American labor law, or even a critical vantage point from which to view American labor law.[18]

The United States and the International Labor Organization

American ambivalence toward the ILO throughout the twentieth century signaled American aversion to international labor influences. The government of Woodrow Wilson and the American Federation of Labor under Samuel Gompers actually played key roles in creating the League of Nations and the ILO after World War I. Gompers chaired the ILO's founding conference. But the U.S. Senate killed U.S. participation in the League, and the United States remained outside the ILO in its formative years. It finally joined in 1934 in the early months of the Roosevelt administration. Samuel Gompers is much better known today for his famous reply to the query "What does labor want?"—"More"—than his chairing the ILO conference.

The ILO was a forum for Cold War rivalry from the late 1940s to the 1980s. Labor movements from West and East saw each other as linked to capitalist exploiters and communist oppressors. The United States quit the ILO from 1977 to 1980 over ILO stands on the Arab-Israeli conflict and conditions of workers in occupied territories.

The Clinton administration brought a blip of prominence to the ILO in the 1990s. In 1998, Bill Clinton was the first American president ever to address the ILO's annual conference, and the United States was a strong supporter of the ILO's 1998 "core labor standards" declaration on freedom of association, nondiscrimination, and abolition of forced labor and child labor. The Clinton administration also pumped millions of dollars into ILO child labor programs.

Under Clinton, the United States for the first time acknowledged serious problems with U.S. labor law and practice on workers' organizing and bargaining rights under ILO standards. In its 1999 follow-up report to the core standards declaration, the U.S. government acknowledged that "there are aspects of this system that fail to fully protect the rights to organize and bargain collectively of all employees in all circumstances." The government report specifically identified unfair discrimination "for exercising legal rights under the NLRA," inadequate deterrence for unfair labor practices, the "lack of NLRA coverage of agriculture employees, domestic service employees, independent contractors, and supervisors," and uneven protections for public sector workers. Further, as the report stated, "Under United States labor law an employer may hire replacement workers in an attempt to continue operations during a strike. . . . This provision of United States labor law has been criticized as detrimental to the exercise of fundamental rights to freedom of association and to meaningful collective bargaining."[19]

The Clinton administration's movement toward more openness to the ILO and willingness to engage in self-criticism under ILO standards ended with the Bush government. The Bush administration missed several obligatory self-reporting deadlines. The reports it finally sent reverted to an old formula, declaring that U.S. law and practice are "generally in compliance" with ILO norms and conceding no difficulties.

In 2005, the AFL-CIO filed a complaint with the ILO charging the administration with violating Convention No. 144 on tripartite consultation, one of the few ILO conventions ratified by the United States. Under the convention, the United States commits to regular consultations with employers' and workers' representatives on ILO matters. The AFL-CIO's complaint charged that functioning of the Tripartite Advisory Committee on International Labor Standards (TAPILS), a long-standing government-business-labor group that reviews ILO conventions for potential U.S. ratification, "has virtually ground to a halt during the last three years." The complaint pointed out that "For the first time since 1991 the U.S. Government did not convene a full meeting of the Consultative Group in preparation for the International Labor Conference."[20]

Labor Rights Through the Side Door

Workers' Rights in the Generalized System of Preferences

The United States has resisted external influence of international labor rights standards, but it has insisted on including "internationally recognized worker rights" (the statutory language) in trade laws and trade agreements affecting commercial partners. Labor rights clauses first appeared in the mid-1980s in trade laws governing developing countries' preferential access for their products exported to the United States, beginning with the Generalized System of Preferences (GSP). This program allows developing countries to send products into the United States free of tariffs and duties applied to the same products from more developed countries. The goal of the GSP program is to give poorer countries a commercial advantage to boost their economies. The European Union, Japan, and other industrial powers maintain similar GSP programs.

A 1984 amendment to the U.S. GSP plan requires countries to be "taking steps" to implement "internationally recognized worker rights" defined as

1. the right of association;
2. the right to organize and bargain collectively;
3. a prohibition on the use of any form of forced or compulsory labor;
4. a minimum age for the employment of children; and
5. acceptable conditions of work with respect to minimum wages, hours of work, and occupational safety and health.

In fact, this is a mishmash of international standards. They are not based on UN human rights instruments, ILO norms, or any other consensus international authority.[21] Conspicuous by its absence is the right to nondiscrimination at work, one of the ILO's defined "core" labor standards. There is no definition of "acceptable," nor of what constitutes "taking steps" for purposes of administering the statute. In fact, one court said exasperatedly:

There is no definition of what constitutes "has not taken . . . steps" or "is not taking steps" to afford internationally recognized rights. Indeed, there is no requirement that the President make findings of fact or any indication that Congress directed or instructed the President as to how he should implement his general withdrawal or suspension authority.

Given this apparent total lack of standards, coupled with the discretion preserved by the terms of the GSP statute itself and implicit in the President's special and separate authority in the areas of foreign policy there is obviously no statutory direction which provides any basis for the Court to act. The Court cannot interfere with the President's discretionary judgment because there is no law to apply.[22]

In spite of such flaws, labor rights provisions in the GSP clause had serious consequences for labor rights violators. In 1986 labor rights advocates filed petitions under the GSP labor rights clause challenging Chile's beneficiary status because of the military government's abuses against workers.[23] They worked closely with Chilean unionists and human rights monitors to amass the information supporting the charges of systematic labor right violations. The United States suspended Chile from GSP beneficiary status in February 1988.

The GSP cutoff jolted Chilean economic and political elites. Business interests formerly comfortable with military rule and suppressed labor movements now faced economic sanctions just when they hoped to expand their exports to the United States. Some joined calls by labor, human rights, and other democratic forces for an end to the dictatorship and a return to more democratic rule.[24] In a plebiscite in October 1988 the Chilean people voted to do just that, supporting a "no" vote when asked if they wanted General Pinochet to continue as the head of government.[25] In 1991, with a new, democratically elected government in place, the most abusive features of the labor code removed, and an end to physical violence against trade union activists, Chile's GSP benefits were restored.[26]

A dramatic turn of events in Guatemala made the GSP labor rights petition a pivotal issue for the future of constitutional order in that Central American country. On May 25, 1993, President Jorge Serrano dissolved the Guatemalan parliament and Supreme Court and suspended constitutional rights.[27] He warned against "destabilizing" protest activity by trade unionists and grassroots organizations.

An impending decision on Guatemala's GSP status proved to be a critically important policy tool for the United States in pressing for the restoration of constitutional governance. The State Department issued a statement that "unless democracy is restored in Guatemala, GSP benefits are likely to be withdrawn."[28]

U.S. press analysis pointed out the leverage in the GSP decision: "But perhaps more damaging to the local economy and Mr. Serrano's cause could be the call by US labor rights groups to revoke Guatemalan industry's tariff-free access to the US market for certain products. . . . Guatemala's labor practices are already under review by the US Trade Representative's office. . . . Given Serrano's suspension of the right of public protest and strikes, analysts expect US Trade Representative Mickey Kantor to consider terminating Guatemala's trade benefits."[29]

The *New York Times* also cited the impending labor rights decision as critical to Serrano's fate. It reported on the day before his abdication that "businessmen have panicked at a threat by the United States to withdraw Guatemala's trade benefits" under the GSP.[30]

Serrano's autogolpe collapsed. On June 5, the reconvened Guatemalan Congress elected Ramiro Deleon Carpio, a leading human rights advocate in Guatemala, as the new president of the country.[31] The following day, after Serrano's flight into exile, a *New York Times* analysis concluded:

Why Mr. Serrano launched his palace coup in the first place . . . was never entirely clear. But the reasons for his downfall were clearer. Most important, it seems, was the concern of business leaders that Guatemala's rising exports to the United States and Europe could be devastated if threatened sanctions were imposed. Within hours of an American threat to cut Guatemala's trade benefits, business leaders who in the past had supported authoritarian rule began pressing government and military officials to reverse Mr. Serrano's action.[32]

Post-GSP Labor Rights Clauses in U.S. Trade Laws

The labor rights amendment in the GSP fixed into U.S. law and policy both the principle of a labor rights–trade linkage and the practice of applying it. Passage of the GSP labor rights amendment in 1984 was followed by over a half-dozen other amendments where the United States injected labor rights conditionality into trade relationships with other countries:

- In 1985, Congress added a labor rights provision to legislation governing the Overseas Private Investment Corporation (OPIC), which provides political risk insurance for U.S. companies investing overseas. Under the new labor rights clause, such insurance can only be provided in countries "taking steps to adopt and implement laws that extend" internationally recognized workers' rights, using the five-part definition from the GSP law. Determinations made in the GSP petition and review process are also applied to OPIC beneficiaries.
- In 1988, Congress made the labor rights–trade linkage a principal U.S. negotiating objective in "fast track" legislation authorizing the president to undertake multilateral trade negotiations.
- In the same Omnibus Trade Act of 1988, a labor rights amendment to Section 301 used the five-part GSP definition to make systematic workers' rights violations by *any* trading partner an unfair trade practice against which the United States could retaliate with economic sanctions.
- In 1990, a Caribbean Basin Initiative renewal bill adopted the GSP labor rights formulation. The same clause was applied to the Andean Trade Preference Act of 1991.
- In 1992, Congress swiftly enacted a bill barring the Agency for International Development (AID) from expending funds to help developing countries lure U.S. businesses to countries where workers' right are violated. Passage of the AID labor rights bill followed hard-hitting exposés on TV newsmagazines shortly before the 1992 elections, in which producers posing as businessmen recorded U.S. AID officials touting anti-union blacklists and anti-labor repression as attractive features of the Central American *maquila* zones.
- In 1994, Congress turned labor rights attention to the World Bank, the International Monetary Fund (IMF), and other international financial institutions. Congressmen Bernard Sanders of Vermont and Barney Frank of Massachusetts secured an amendment to the law governing

U.S. participation in those bodies that requires American directors to use their "voice and vote" to screen loan proposals for their effects on workers' rights.

• In 1997, Congress amended the Tariff Act of 1930, which already prohibited imports produced by prison labor, by adding a provision declaring that the same ban applies to products made by forced or indentured child labor.

• In 2000, Congress passed the African Growth and Opportunity Act (AGOA), authorizing the president to designate a sub-Saharan African country as eligible for trade preferences if he determines that the country has established or is making continual progress toward the protection of internationally recognized worker rights, using the GSP's five-part definition.

Trade Agreements

In 2002, Congress passed the Trade Act of 2002 specifying that provisions on "internationally recognized worker rights"—the five-part definition in the GSP labor rights clause and other U.S. statutes—are a "principal negotiating objective" of the United States in trade agreements with commercial partners. Congress tweaked the GSP formula, adding elimination of the "worst forms of child labor" to the child labor clause. However, Congress again failed to include nondiscrimination among the "internationally recognized worker rights."

Recent trade agreements with Jordan, Chile, Singapore, Morocco, Australia, and Central American nations require signatories, including the United States, to "effectively enforce" national laws protecting what the United States calls "internationally recognized workers rights." Beyond that, though, they also incorporate the ILO core labor standards declaration with a "strive to ensure" obligation stating that "[t]he Parties shall strive to ensure that such labor principles and the internationally recognized labor rights . . . are recognized and protected by domestic law."[33]

The most extensive subject matter treatment of workers' rights in trade agreements is contained in the North American Agreement on Labor Cooperation (NAALC), the supplemental labor accord to the North American Free Trade Agreement (NAFTA). Going beyond the GSP formula and beyond the ILO's core standards formulation, the NAALC sets forth eleven "Labor Principles" that the three signatory countries commit themselves to promote. The NAALC Labor Principles include:[34]

• freedom of association and the right to organize,
• the right to bargain collectively,

- the right to strike,
- prohibition of forced labor,
- prohibition of child labor,
- equal pay for men and women,
- nondiscrimination,
- minimum wage and hour standards,
- occupational safety and health,
- workers' compensation, and
- migrant worker protection.

The NAALC signers pledged to effectively enforce their national labor laws in these subject areas and adopted six "Obligations" for effective labor law enforcement to fulfill the principles. These obligations include:[35]

- a general duty to provide high labor standards;
- effective enforcement of labor laws;
- access to administrative and judicial forums for workers whose rights are violated;
- due process, transparency, speed, and effective remedies in labor law proceedings;
- public availability of labor laws and regulations, and opportunity for "interested persons" to comment on proposed changes;
- promoting public awareness of labor law and workers' rights.

In all these initiatives, the United States' implicit assumption is that labor rights violations are a problem in *other* countries. They are a form of "social dumping" by foreign countries and firms gaining cost advantage by abusing workers, thus gaining a commercial edge against U.S.-based producers.

American firms reacted with shock and anger when trade unions and NGOs began filing complaints against them under the NAALC—against General Electric and Honeywell for violating workers' organizing rights in Mexico, against Sprint for violating the same rights of workers in the United States, against the Northwest U.S. apple industry for violating rights of migrant Mexican workers in Washington state, and many more.

U.S. corporate executives and attorneys think the Agreement has been hijacked by trade union radicals to attack company conduct throughout North America and demand an end to contentious complaint procedures where unions and their allies brand companies as workers' rights violators. An executive of the Washington state apple industry said "unions on both sides of the border are abusing the NAFTA process in an effort to expand their power. . . . NAFTA's labor side agreement is an open invitation for specific labor disputes to be raised into an international question . . . and could open the door to a host of costly and frivolous complaints against US employers."[36]

Corporate Social Responsibility and Codes of Conduct

Workers' rights as human rights also penetrated labor discourse in the United States in the 1990s through initiatives on corporate social responsibility and codes of conduct. As with trade-labor linkage, the focus was outward, on conditions for workers in supply chain factories abroad producing for U.S.-based multinational companies. But growing concern for workers' rights abroad inevitably prompted closer scrutiny of workers' rights at home.

Beginning in the mid-1980s, journalists and NGOs delivered conscience-shocking accounts of child labor, forced overtime, hazardous conditions, beatings and firings of worker activists, and other abuses in factories supplying Nike, Reebok, Levi's, Wal-Mart, and other iconic American retail brands. Such exposés shook executives away from their earlier, arrogant position that these problems were not their business because they occurred among subcontractors.

First, many brand-name companies developed their own "internal" codes of conduct. Reebok, Levi's, Nike, J.C. Penney, and others announced that supplier firms in their global production chain would have to abide by their internal company codes or face loss of orders. The brands said they would take responsibility themselves for monitoring and enforcing their codes.

Levi Strauss & Co. and Reebok Corp. were in the forefront of this movement for internal, corporate-sponsored codes of conduct. They reviewed the United Nations' Universal Declaration of Human Rights, ILO conventions, and other international human rights instruments in formulating their codes. They established monitoring and enforcement systems with detailed questionnaires on practices in foreign supplier plants, surprise visits by auditors, and reviews by company officials charged with enforcing the code.[37]

Most of these company-sponsored codes refer to UN human rights instruments and ILO core conventions in defining their standards. Reebok, for example, calls its code "The Reebok Human Rights Production Standards" and features the Universal Declaration of Human Rights on its Web site.

Internal company codes have inherent weaknesses. Sourcing from hundreds, even thousands, of factories around the globe, even the most diligent corporate socially responsible–conscious company could not guard against labor abuses in every one of its supplier factories. Critics could always find supplier plants with terrible problems. They argued that management would sooner cover up abuses than expose them to public scrutiny. The demand for independent monitoring and verification, independent of corporate control, became irresistible.[38]

A new generation of codes called "multi-stakeholder" initiatives emerged. Companies, unions, human rights groups, community and development organizations, and other NGOs participate in formulating a code of conduct. These multi-stakeholder codes of conduct on workers' rights contain provisions on monitoring, verification, certification of supplier factories, enforcement mechanisms, and transparency. Among the most prominent U.S.-based groups are the Fair Labor Association (FLA), Social Accountability International (SAI), and the Worker Rights Consortium (WRC).[39]

The FLA combines major U.S. apparel companies, many universities, and some NGO participants in its code of conduct, monitoring, and certification system. The FLA accredits external monitors and certifies companies that meet its standards, using a statistical sampling methodology. SAI administers a code called Social Accountability 8000 (SA8000), with standards and a system for auditing and certifying corporate responsibility in supplier chain facilities.

The WRC grew out of the anti-sweatshop campaigns of U.S. students concerned about conditions of workers producing apparel and other products bearing their universities' logo. The consortium verifies that university-licensed apparel is manufactured according to its code of conduct. The WRC operates a complaints-based monitoring system, responding to reports of workers' rights abuses in factories supplying the university-logo market.

Most of these stakeholder codes assert "rights" as their foundation. SAI, for example, went so far as to trademark a brand of its own: *Human Rights @ Work*™. Its declared goal is "Making Workplace Human Rights a Vital Part of the Business Agenda." SAI states as its mission "to promote human rights for workers around the world . . . to help ensure that workers of the world are treated according to basic human rights principles."

Sharp differences have arisen among these groups and their codes, including rivalries, jealousies, and criticisms aimed at one another. Under some plans, monitoring, verification, and certification are carried out by "social auditing" firms, some of them new divisions of traditional financial auditing companies like Price Waterhouse. In others, NGOs are involved in monitoring. The codes have different degrees of transparency and public reporting of their findings. Some contain "living wage" provisions, while others do not. To overcome such problems, these and other stakeholder groups organized a unified program called the Joint Initiative for Corporate Accountability and Workers Rights (Jo-In), with a pilot project in Turkey.[40]

The Hypocrisy Gap

Labor rights in trade agreements and codes of conduct have had mixed results, reflecting serious problems of monitoring and enforcement. Analyzing these problems is not the point here. The point is, rather, that the focus on workers' human rights in labor clauses of trade agreements and in corporate codes of conduct injected more rights-consciousness into American labor discourse throughout the 1990s. The penetration was perhaps less in the labor movement itself. Many union activists condemn NAFTA and other trade agreements' lack of "teeth" to enforce workers' rights. Most unions also maintain an ambivalent attitude toward corporate social responsibility and corporate codes of conduct. They are concerned that these initiatives are meant to replace strong trade unions and effective government enforcement of labor laws.[41] But the codes of conduct movement awakened new sensibilities to workers' rights in many other segments of civil society that rallied to the labor rights banner.

In their "side door" campaigns for workers' rights in other nations, American trade unionists and their allies became more conversant and more comfortable talking about, and acting upon, workers' rights as human rights. The focus was on workers' rights overseas. But as the lens sharpened, it reflected back. What about workers' rights at home? Growing awareness and concern for labor rights in trade arrangements and in corporate codes of conduct inexorably widened a "hypocrisy gap" between official positions, both of the U.S. government and of U.S. business, and the reality of workers' rights violations in the United States. In turn, this gap created ample new space for human rights and labor rights advocates to put U.S. law and practice under a spotlight of international standards.

Opening the Front Door to Workers' Rights

Some Frame-Setting Cases

The most significant injection of international human rights principles into U.S. law came outside the labor context, in the Supreme Court's 2005 decision in *Roper v. Simmons* (543 U.S. 551). The Court ruled that the execution of minors (that is, those who committed capital crimes when they were below age eighteen) is unconstitutional under the "cruel and unusual punishment" clause of the Eighth Amendment. The Court specifically noted "the overwhelming weight of international opinion against the juvenile death penalty," observing that "[t]he opinion of the world community, while not controlling our outcome, does provide respected and significant confirmation for our own conclusions."

The challenge now is to bring a similar openness to international human rights standards to labor law and practice in the United States. Without trying to overstate the case, it is fair to say that international human rights law appears to be having a nascent "climate-changing" effect on American labor law, practice, and discourse, bringing them closer to a human rights framework.

A growing cadre of scholars and practitioners familiar with comparative and international labor law are bringing into U.S. discourse labor provisions in the Universal Declaration of Human Rights; the ICCPR; the International Covenant on Economic, Social, and Cultural Rights; ILO Conventions and Declarations; and other international instruments.

Human rights law started making inroads in U.S. labor-related jurisprudence first in litigation on behalf of workers in countries outside the United States. Human rights strictures against forced labor and ILO findings on forced labor in Burma were central elements of a lawsuit brought against the California-based Unocal Corporation in federal court. The case ultimately was settled before going to trial with millions of dollars in recompense to victims of forced labor violations.[42]

Once plaintiffs overcame procedural hurdles and the case moved toward trial before a jury, Burma was an easy case substantively. The Burmese military junta committed beatings, rapes, torture, and murder to force villagers to work on the pipeline project. Even for a U.S. court that rarely takes up international human rights law issues, defining these abuses as violations of universal human rights standards on torture and forced labor was no problem.

Whether workers' freedom of association in trade union activity rises to the same level is not so clear in U.S. law. This was the issue facing the court at the motions stage in a 2003 decision in the case of *Rodriguez v. Drummond Coal Co.* (256 F. Supp. 1250). The case involved wrongful death claims by families of murdered Colombian mineworker union leaders under the Alien Tort Claims Act.

Called as an expert witness, Professor Virginia Leary, a long-time advisor to the ILO, supported the view that workers' freedom of association achieved the level of a jus cogens norm in international law. Her testimony helped convince a federal judge to move the case toward trial. The judge denied the U.S.-based coal company's motion to dismiss the case, saying:[43]

Although this court recognizes that the United States has not ratified ILO Conventions 87 and 98, the ratification of these conventions is not necessary to make the rights to associate and organize norms of customary international law.

... After analyzing "international conventions, international customs, treatises, and judicial decisions rendered in this and other countries" to ascertain whether the rights to associate and organize are part of customary international law, this court finds, at this preliminary stage in the proceedings, that the rights to associate and organize are generally recognized as principles of international law sufficient to defeat defendants' motion to dismiss.

A jury acquitted the company, and plaintiffs' appeal was rejected by the Eleventh Circuit Court of Appeals in December 2008.[44] But the appellate court did not upset the district judge's ruling that workers' rights in international human rights instruments are justiciable in U.S. courts.

The same principle arose in a mirror-image case making *American* workers' rights justiciable in a *foreign* court under international labor standards. In 2002, the Norwegian oil workers union (NOPEF) sought judicial permission under Norwegian law to boycott the North Sea operations of Trico Corp., a Louisiana company that allegedly violated American workers' rights in an organizing campaign in the Gulf Coast region. Trico's North Sea arm was the company's most profitable venture, and a boycott could have devastating economic effects.

A key issue in the case was whether U.S. labor law and practice conform to ILO norms. Under Norwegian law, compliance with ILO Conventions 87 and 98 was the hinge on which the boycott's legality turned. The Norwegian court's finding that U.S. law failed to meet international standards would let the NOPEF boycott proceed.

NOPEF and Trico's Norwegian counsel each called expert witnesses from the United States to testify whether U.S. law and practice violate ILO core standards on freedom of association. Just before the U.S. experts' testimony, NOPEF settled the case with Trico's promise to respect workers' organizing rights in Louisiana.[45] The boycott trigger was deactivated. Still, the Trico case signaled a remarkable impact of ILO core standards within the United States. Similar cases could arise in the future as trade unions increase their cross-border solidarity work.[46]

Human Rights Organizations Make the Turn

Human rights organizations took the first step toward convergence with trade union advocates on an international labor rights agenda for American workers. For example, Amnesty International USA created a Business and Human Rights division with extensive focus on workers' rights. Oxfam International has broadened its development agenda to include labor rights and standards, and its Oxfam America group created a Workers' Rights program to take up these causes inside the United States. In 2003, Oxfam launched a "national workers' rights campaign" on conditions in the U.S. agricultural sector. In 2004 the group published a major report, *Like Machines in the Fields: Workers Without Rights in American Agriculture.*[47]

Perhaps most notably, Human Rights Watch (HRW) published three pathbreaking reports in 2000–2001 on workers' rights in the United States under international human rights standards. The reports covered child labor in American agriculture, conditions of immigrant household domestic workers, and U.S. workers' freedom of association.[48]

Fingers to the Bone declared:

United States law and practice contravene various international law prohibitions on exploitative and harmful work by children, including standards set by the Convention on the Rights of the Child. The United States appears to be headed toward noncompliance with the 1999 ILO Worst Forms of Child Labor Convention as well, which will enter into force for the U.S. in December 2000. It requires that member governments prohibit and eliminate "the worst forms of child labor."

Hidden in the Home said:

Because changing employers is difficult if not impossible, workers often must choose between respect for their own human rights and maintaining their legal immigration status. . . . Many workers choose to endure human rights violations temporarily rather than face deportation. . . .

The special visa programs for domestic workers are conducive to and facilitate the violation of the workers' human rights. The U.S. government has not removed the impediments that deter domestic workers with special visas from challenging, leaving, or filing legal complaints against abusive employers; has failed to monitor the workers' employment relationships; and has failed to include live-in domestic workers in key labor and employment legislation protecting workers' rights.

Unfair Advantage: Workers' Freedom of Association in the United States Under International Human Rights Standards forged new links with the American labor movement. This book-length HRW report garnered significant attention upon its release in August 2000. International, national, and local commentary featured the report's findings, based on exhaustive case studies, showing that the United States fails to meet international standards on workers' organizing and bargaining rights.[49] Most often cited were these passages:

Workers' freedom of association is under sustained attack in the United States, and the government is often failing its responsibility under international human rights standards to deter such attacks and protect workers' rights. . . .

Researching workers' exercise of these rights in different industries, occupations, and regions of the United States to prepare this report, Human Rights Watch found that . . . . [m]any workers who try to form and join trade unions to bargain with their employers are spied on, harassed, pressured, threatened, suspended, fired, deported or otherwise victimized in reprisal for their exercise of the right to freedom of association.

Private employers are the main agents of abuse. But international human rights law makes governments responsible for protecting vulnerable persons and groups from patterns of abuse by private actors. In the United States, labor law enforcement efforts often fail to deter unlawful conduct. When the law is applied, enervating delays and weak remedies invite continued violations. . . . As a result, a culture of near-impunity has taken shape in much of U.S. labor law and practice.

After that initial response, *Unfair Advantage* took its place as an authoritative reference point in U.S. labor law and human rights discourse, becoming the standard source for labor advocates reaching out to new constituencies in a language of human rights, not just labor-management relations.[50] For example, *Scientific American* published a feature on *Unfair Advantage* for its million-plus readership one year after the report came out.[51] At its National Convention in June 2002, Americans for Democratic Action (ADA) presented the first annual Reuther-Chavez Award to Human Rights Watch for its U.S. labor report.[52]

Unfair Advantage has also become a point of reference in the scholarly community. Many U.S. labor law teachers have added the book as a supplemental text. So have professors in human rights, political science, sociology, government, industrial relations, and other academic fields. The American Political Science Association gave a "best paper" award at its 2001 APSA Annual Meeting to "From the Wagner Act to the Human Rights Watch Report: Labor and Freedom of Expression and Association, 1935–2000."[53]

In 2005, HRW continued its program on workers' rights in the United States with a major report on violations in the U.S. meat and poultry industry. In 2007, a new report titled *Discounting Rights: Wal-Mart's Violation of US Workers' Right to Freedom of Association* on workplace rights violations of Wal-Mart employees in the United States put that company under a human rights spotlight.[54]

Blood, Sweat and Fear made these findings on workers' human rights in the meat and poultry industry:

Workers in this industry face more than hard work in tough settings. They contend with conditions, vulnerabilities, and abuses which violate human rights. Employers put workers at predictable risk of serious physical injury even though the means to avoid such injury are known and feasible. They frustrate workers' efforts to obtain compensation for workplace injuries when they occur. They crush workers' self-organizing efforts and rights of association. They exploit the perceived vulnerability of a predominantly immigrant labor force in many of

their work sites. These are not occasional lapses by employers paying insufficient attention to modern human resources management policies. These are
systematic human rights violations embedded in meat and poultry industry
employment. . . .

Health and safety laws and regulations fail to address critical hazards in the
meat and poultry industry. Laws and agencies that are supposed to protect workers' freedom of association are instead manipulated by employers to frustrate
worker organizing. Federal laws and policies on immigrant workers are a mass
of contradictions and incentives to violate their rights. In sum, the United States
is failing to meet its obligations under international human rights standards to
protect the human rights of meat and poultry industry workers.

In both meatpacking and Wal-Mart, trade unions and activist communities seized on the reports as major resources in their campaigns to reform practices in those industries and companies. The United Food and
Commercial Workers' Justice@Smithfield campaign for workers at the
Smithfield Foods hog-slaughtering plant in Tar Heel, North Carolina,
makes extensive use of the report and features it in a campaign video
and on its Web site. Smithfield's violations of workers rights, including
firings, beatings, and false arrests of union supporters, were a central
case study in the HRW report.

New Initiatives and New Organizations

The new convergence of labor and human rights communities is reflected in a variety of new campaigns and organizations with a labor-
human rights mission. The AFL-CIO has launched a broad-based Voice@
Work project, which it characterizes as a "campaign to help U.S. workers
regain the basic human right to form unions to improve their lives."
Voice@Work stresses international human rights in workers' organizing campaigns around the country. In 2005, the labor federation held
more than one hundred demonstrations in cities throughout the United
States and enlisted signatures from eleven Nobel Peace Prize winners,
including the Dalai Lama, Lech Walesa, Jimmy Carter, and Archbishop
Desmond Tutu of South Africa supporting workers' human rights in full-
page advertisements in national newspapers.[55]

In December 2006, the AFL-CIO marked International Human Rights
Day with a two-day Strategic Organizing Summit meeting for trade
union organizers. Materials for participants declared that "International
Human Rights Day is the anniversary of the ratification of the United
Nations Universal Declaration of Human Rights, which recognizes as a
basic human right the freedom of all workers to form unions and bargain
together." The conference launched a campaign for passage of the Employee Free Choice Act (EFCA) in the Congress following Democratic
gains in the 2006 midterm elections.

The EFCA would incorporate international labor rights principles into U.S. law on union organizing.[56] A key Senate sponsor said, "The right to organize and join a union is a fundamental right recognized in the United Nations Declaration of Human Rights. Yet, the United States violates this fundamental principle every day because our current laws don't adequately protect employee rights."[57]

Labor and community organizations created Jobs with Justice (JwJ) "with the vision of lifting up workers' rights struggles as part of a larger campaign for economic and social justice," as JwJ describes its mission. JwJ focuses on building local coalitions to protect workers' organizing efforts when local employers engage in union-busting tactics that violate workers' rights. A signature JwJ initiative is the creation of local Workers Rights Boards, usually composed of elected officials, religious leaders, civil rights leaders, and other respected figures who conduct public hearings exposing employers' aggressive interference with workers' organizing efforts. In recent years JwJ has broadened its work to campaign for national health care, local government accountability for economic development, and global workers' rights.[58]

In 2004, trade unions and allied labor support groups created a new NGO called American Rights at Work (ARAW). ARAW launched an ambitious program to make human rights the centerpiece of a new civil society movement for U.S. workers' organizing and bargaining rights. ARAW's twenty-member board of directors includes prominent civil rights leaders, former elected officials, environmentalists, religious leaders, business leaders, writers, scholars, an actor, and one labor leader (AFL-CIO President John Sweeney). The group's "International Advisor" is Mary Robinson, former United Nations High Commissioner for Human Rights.[59]

Less directly connected to organized labor, but with rights at work an important part of its agenda, the National Economic and Social Rights Initiative (NESRI) took shape the same year with the mission of incorporating principles of the UN Covenant on Economic, Social, and Cultural rights into U.S. law and practice.[60]

Along with NESRI, the RFK Center for Human Rights has helped the Coalition of Immokalee Workers in campaigns stressing human rights for agricultural workers in Florida. The Coalition's efforts brought a series of successful slavery prosecutions against labor traffickers in the state and won improvements in wages and working conditions for field workers in a sustained campaign against Taco Bell and its parent, Yum Brands, Inc.[61] In general, many organizations are turning to international human rights arguments in defense of immigrant workers in the United States.[62]

The National Employment Law Project (NELP) includes an immigrant worker project under the rubric "workers rights are human rights—advancing the human rights of immigrant workers in the United States." NELP has been a leader in filing complaints on immigrant workers' rights violations in the United States to the Inter-American Commission and Inter-American Court of Human Rights.[64]

Working with Mexican colleagues, NELP sought an Inter-American Court Advisory Opinion on U.S. treatment of immigrant workers. The petition was prompted by the Supreme Court's 2002 *Hoffman Plastic* decision stripping undocumented workers illegally fired for union organizing from access to back-pay remedies. In its opinion, the Inter-American Court said that undocumented workers are entitled to the same labor rights, including wages owed, protection from discrimination, protection for health and safety on the job, and back pay, as are citizens and those working lawfully in a country.

The Court said that despite their irregular status, "If undocumented workers are contracted to work, they immediately are entitled to the same rights as all workers. . . . This is of maximum importance, since one of the major problems that come from lack of immigration status is that workers without work permits are hired in unfavorable conditions, compared to other workers."

The Court specifically mentioned several workplace rights that it held must be guaranteed to migrant workers, regardless of their immigration status:

In the case of migrant workers, there are certain rights that assume a fundamental importance and that nevertheless are frequently violated, including: the prohibition against forced labor, the prohibition and abolition of child labor, special attentions for women who work, rights that correspond to association and union freedom, collective bargaining, a just salary for work performed, social security, administrative and judicial guarantees, a reasonable workday length and adequate labor conditions (safety and hygiene), rest, and back pay.

Finally, the Court declared that its consultative decision should be binding on all members of the Organization of American States, whether or not they have ratified certain conventions that formed the basis of the opinion. It based its decision on the nondiscrimination and equal protection provisions of the OAS Charter, the American Declaration, the International Covenant on Civil and Political Rights, the American Convention on Human Rights and the Universal Declaration of Human Rights. The United States has not acted on the Court's advisory opinion.[64]

Also advocating for rights of immigrant workers are nearly two hundred "workers' centers" throughout the United States. These are private, locally based service and education centers, often housed in or supported by churches. They assist immigrants with problems of discrimination, nonpayment of wages, and other violations. Many stress the human rights nature of their efforts.[65]

This section could be amplified with yet more examples of new organizations, or new projects within long-established groups, taking up U.S. workers' rights as human rights. The point here is to affirm that the human rights and labor communities no longer run on separate, parallel, never-meeting tracks. They have joined in a common mission with enhanced traction to advance workers' rights.

Trade Union Human Rights Reports

The new human rights mission in the labor movement is reflected in the use unions are making of human rights reports in specific organizing campaigns. Trade unionists find that charging employers with violations of international human rights, not just violations of the National Labor Relations Act or the Fair Labor Standards Act, gives more force to their claims for support in the court of public opinion. The Teamsters union, for example, launched a human rights campaign against Maersk-Sealand, the giant Denmark-based international shipping company, for violating rights of association among truck drivers who carry cargo containers from ports to inland distribution centers. The company fired workers who protested low pay and dangerous conditions and threatened retaliation against others if they continued their organizing effort. The union's report said that

The responsibility of multinational corporations to recognize international human rights is becoming an important facet of international law. . . . A review and analysis of recent actions by Maersk's U.S. divisions reveal a systematic pattern of reprisals against owner-drivers who seek to exercise basic rights of association. . . . Specific circumstances differ, but the underlying pattern is similar. Truck drivers dependent on Maersk's U.S. divisions . . . sought collective dialogue with Maersk companies. Company officials responded not with dialogue but with threats, harassment and dismissal of workers and leaders. These actions violate international human rights and labor rights norms for workers.[66]

This was not just a report that sat on shelves. The union printed thousands of copies for distribution to affiliates of the International Transport Federation (ITF), the global trade union for workers in the transport sector. In 2004, workers protested at the Danish embassy and at consulates around the United States, distributing copies of the report.[68] In 2005, union leaders went to the corporation's annual shareholders meeting in Copenhagen giving copies to investors and to the Danish media, with significant attention.[68] In 2006, the union introduced a shareholders resolution, common at American companies' annual meetings but a novelty for Maersk, calling on the company to adopt international labor rights standards as official company policy.[69]

Similar violations by a large Catholic hospital chain in Chicago prompted a human rights report by the American Federation of State, County, and Municipal Employees (AFSCME) on how the employer's actions violated both international human rights standards and principles of Catholic social doctrine. This report said:

> The actions of RHC management demonstrate a systematic pattern of interference with workers' organizing rights and reflect a failure to meet human rights principles and obligations. . . .
> RHC workers have the right under international human rights law to freedom of association and organization by forming and joining a trade union to seek collective representation before management. RHC has a corresponding obligation to honor this right and respect its exercise. Instead, RHC has responded with an aggressive campaign against workers' organizing rights in violation of rights recognized under international human rights law.[70]

This report too served as a tool for union organizing in the workplace and for organizing support in local political, religious, and human rights communities.[71]

Using International Mechanisms

In addition to relying on human rights arguments, unions have also begun to use international human rights complaint mechanisms to put domestic labor disputes under international scrutiny, mainly before the ILO Committee on Freedom of Association (CFA). Although these mechanisms do not have authority to compel compliance with decisions, they can provide authoritative vindication of workers' rights as human rights.

Challenging the Supreme Court on Immigrant Workers' Rights

In 2002, the AFL-CIO filed a complaint to CFA challenging the Supreme Court's *Hoffman Plastic* decision.[72] In *Hoffman*, the Supreme Court had held, in a 5–4 decision, that because of his immigration status, an undocumented worker was not entitled to back pay for lost wages after he was illegally fired for union organizing. The five-justice majority said that enforcing immigration law takes precedence over enforcing labor law.[73]

The union argued that eliminating the back pay remedy for undocumented workers annuls protection of workers' right to organize, contrary to the requirement in Convention 87 to provide adequate protection against acts of anti-union discrimination.[74]

The AFL-CIO's complaint was successful: in November 2003, the CFA announced that the *Hoffman* doctrine violates international legal obligations to protect workers' organizing rights. The Committee concluded that "the remedial measures left to the NLRB in cases of illegal dismissals of undocumented workers are inadequate to ensure effective protection against acts of anti-union discrimination."[75]

In an example of how international mechanisms can provide leverage for vindicating workers rights at home, the ILO Committee recommended congressional action to bring U.S. law "into conformity with freedom of association principles, in full consultation with the social partners concerned, with the aim of ensuring effective protection for all workers against acts of anti-union discrimination in the wake of the Hoffman decision."[76]

Challenging an Embassy's Refusal to Recognize a Union Representative

A similar reliance on international mechanisms is evident in a decision by the International Federation of Professional Technical Employees (IPFTE), together with the AFL-CIO and the global union federation Public Services International (PSI), to file a CFA complaint on behalf of locally engaged staff at the British Embassy in Washington, D.C., after embassy officials refused to bargain with employees' choice of IFPTE as their union representative.[77] The embassy said that it need not recognize the employees' choice because locally hired workers were "engaged in the administration of the state," taking them outside the protection of ILO standards based on earlier Committee decisions. IFPTE argued that locally engaged staff have the right to form and join a trade union for the defense of their interests under application of ILO principles and standards reflected in Conventions Nos. 87 and 98 as well as in the Declaration on Fundamental Principles and Rights at Work.

In March 2007, the CFA issued an opinion fully supporting the unions' position. The Committee said that "all public service workers other than those engaged in the administration of the State should enjoy collective bargaining rights" and that "the Embassy should negotiate with the [union] in respect of the terms and conditions of employment of the locally engaged staff."[78] And in this instance, the international decision had a direct impact on domestic affairs: the UK government accepted the ruling and entered into bargaining with the employees' chosen union.[79]

Challenging the NLRB on Scope of Exclusion

In October 2006, the AFL-CIO filed another CFA complaint, this time against the NLRB's decision in the so-called *Oakwood Trilogy*. In *Oakwood*, the NLRB announced an expanded interpretation of the definition of "supervisor" under the National Labor Relations Act.[80] Under the new ruling, employers can classify as "supervisors" employees with incidental oversight over coworkers even when such oversight is far short of genuine managerial or supervisory authority.

In its complaint to the ILO, the AFL-CIO relied on the ILO conventions, arguing that the NRLB's decision contravened No. 87's affirmation that "Workers and employers, without distinction whatsoever, shall have the right to establish and . . . to join organizations of their own choosing without previous authorization." The AFL-CIO further argued that the NLRB's *Oakwood* trilogy "strips employees in the new 'supervisor' status of any and all protection" in violation of Convention No. 98.[81]

In its March 2008 decision, the Committee found that the criteria for supervisory status laid out in the *Oakwood* trilogy "appear to give rise to an overly wide definition of supervisory staff that would go beyond freedom of association principles" and urged the U.S. government "to take all necessary steps, in consultation with the social partners, to ensure that the exclusion that may be made of supervisory staff under the NLRA is limited to those workers genuinely representing the interests of employers."[82]

Challenging the Executive's Denial of Collective Bargaining Rights

In November 2006, the CFA issued a decision in a complaint filed by the AFL-CIO and the American Federation of Government Employees (AFGE) against the Bush administration's denial of collective bargaining rights to airport screeners. The administration argued that the events of September 11, 2001, and concomitant security concerns made it necessary to strip Transportation Security Administration employees of trade union rights accorded to other federal employees.

The Committee said that the government's de-recognition violated employees' rights and urged it to bargain over terms and conditions of employment "which are not directly related to national security issues" with the screeners' freely chosen representative."[83]

Challenging a State's Ban on Public Employee Bargaining

In 2006, the United Electrical, Radio and Machine Workers of America (UE), an independent union known for its progressive politics and internal democracy,[84] filed a complaint with the CFA charging that North Carolina's ban on public worker bargaining violated Convention No. 87's principle that "all workers, without distinction" should enjoy organizing and bargaining rights. The complaint also argued that the North Carolina law violated Convention No. 98's rule that only public employees who are high-level policy makers, not rank-and-file workers, can be excluded from the right to bargain collectively.

In April 2007, the Committee ruled in the union's favor and urged the U.S. government "to promote the establishment of a collective bargaining framework in the public sector in North Carolina . . . and to take steps aimed at bringing the state legislation, in particular through the repeal of NCGS §95–98 [the statute prohibiting collective bargaining by public employees], into conformity with the freedom of association principles."[85]

This decision prompted North Carolina state legislators to introduce, for the first time in decades, legislation that would grant collective bargaining rights to state and local employees.[86] Although the legislation is pending and advocates recognize that achieving it will be difficult, they count getting such a bill onto the legislative agenda as an important policy advance and credit the international attention through the ILO case and other international mechanisms for reaching this point.[87]

Alongside the ILO complaint, the UE turned to the International Commission for Labor Rights, a new NGO composed of labor lawyers and professors from around the world, with a request for a "thematic hearing" under IACHR procedures on the conflict between North Carolina's prohibition on collective bargaining and freedom of association protections in the American Declaration of the Rights and Duties of Man, the American Convention on Human Rights, and the Inter-American Democratic Charter.[88] Labor experts from Canada, Mexico, Nigeria, India, and South Africa joined the hearing. The ICLR issued a report finding "significant violations of internationally recognized labor standards in the public sector in North Carolina, which were strongly correlated to the absence of collective bargaining rights."[89]

Joined by twenty-four other unions in the United States, Mexico, and Canada, the UE also filed a complaint under NAFTA's labor side agreement in October 2006. The coalition argued that North Carolina's ban on public employee bargaining violated NAALC labor principles on freedom of association.

The UE was not the first to invoke NAFTA's labor accord as a means of defending workers' rights in the United States. In 2001, supported by the NYU Law School immigration law clinic, the Chinese Staff and Workers' Association (CSWA), the National Mobilization Against SweatShops

(NMASS), local worker support groups Workers' Awaaz and Asociación Tepeyac, and several individual workers filed a NAALC complaint on the breakdown of New York State's workers' compensation system. The complaint led to consultations among the U.S. and Mexican labor departments and New York state authorities on finding ways to accelerate claims processing, a key aspect of the complaint.[90]

As these cases and complaints suggest, the past ten years have witnessed a concerted effort on the part of workers rights advocates to use international labor instruments and mechanisms. Some unions are now laying the ground for a next stage: using recent trade agreements signed by the United States including the DR-CAFTA agreement, the U.S.-Australia free trade agreement, and the U.S.-Peru free trade agreement to put U.S. workers' rights violations under international scrutiny in a trade context.

New Labor Scholarship

Another "climate-changing" effect is taking place among U.S. labor and human rights scholars. Many are incorporating human rights norms and ILO core standards in their analyses. Here are three examples involving workplace health and safety, labor arbitration, and the right to work (in its true sense, not the anti-union "right-to-work" fraud).

Many American analysts view occupational health and safety protections and workers' compensation for workplace injuries as strictly economic benefits dependent on a country's level of development or a company's ability to pay for them, not as basic rights. Professor Emily Spieler, a leading expert on worker health issues, noted:

The apparent underlying assumptions are that working conditions, including occupational safety, are context driven, difficult to define, and contingent on local levels of economic development and productivity. . . . This approach relegates subminimum wages, excessive hours, and sometimes brutally dangerous conditions to a lower level of importance in human rights discourse; it ratifies the view that labor is a commodity that is fully subject to market forces, no matter how abusive the resulting working conditions.[91]

Professor Spieler pointed out that workplace health and safety was the subject of the first international labor rights treaty, a 1906 accord banning manufacture and export of white phosphorus matches deadly to workers who produced them. Since then, authoritative international human rights instruments include workplace health and safety and compensation for workplace injuries as fundamental rights. In a powerful analogy driving home her point, Professor Spieler argues, "In view of the egregious health and safety hazards in some workplaces . . . postponing the improvement of health and safety until market forces can effect change is analogous to postponing the release of political prisoners who may die in prison until a despotic government is replaced through democratic elections. It is in fact the right to life that we are talking about when we talk about work safety."[92]

Professor Spieler's carefully constructed argument for workplace health and safety as a human right does not rest at the level of a general proposition. She focuses on three more detailed standards for affording the right:

- Workers' right to information on workplace hazards;
- Workers' right to be free from retaliation for raising safety concerns or for refusing imminently dangerous work;
- Workers' right to work in an environment reasonably free from predictable, preventable, serious risks.

According to Professor Spieler's analysis, "human rights violations occur when employers' deliberate and intentional actions expose workers to preventable, predictable, and serious hazards. The fundamental right to be free from these hazards should be guaranteed."[93]

As well as a renowned labor scholar—the leading historian of the National Labor Relations Board and analyst of workers' rights as human rights—Professor James A. Gross is a nationally prominent labor arbitrator. Among other responsibilities, he was a standing arbitrator for Major League Baseball and the Players' Union for many years.

Professor Gross has developed a creative proposal to bring international human rights jurisprudence into U.S. labor arbitration practice. He writes:

It is only recently that many union leaders and members have come to understand workers' rights as human rights. As unions come to perceive themselves as human rights organizations promoting and protecting such fundamental human rights as the right to freedom of association and collective bargaining, safe and healthful workplaces, and discrimination-free treatment, there will be a necessary carry-over to the grievance-arbitration process. . . .

Unions can also pursue human rights clauses in contract negotiations with employers. Human rights clauses in collective bargaining agreements could become as common as management rights clauses. Since traditional labor arbitrators limit workers' rights to those set forth in collective bargaining agreements, they will have to consider workers' human rights if those rights are written into contracts. . . .

There can be no true workplace justice without recognizing and respecting those rights of human beings that are more compelling than any other rights or interests at the workplace. That will occur only when U.S. labor arbitrators come to utilize human rights standards in their decision-making.[94]

Professor Philip Harvey argues compellingly for application of the United Nations' economic, social, and cultural rights covenant to the right to employment in the United States:

The right to work is expressly recognized in Article 23 of the Universal Declaration [and] in the International Covenant on Economic, Social and Cultural Rights . . . domestic advocacy of the right to work has occasionally been quite strong in the United States, and federal legislation stemming from this advocacy has succeeded in imposing, with one significant difference, essentially the same substantive obligations on the United States government that would flow from ratification of international human rights agreements recognizing the right to work. The difference is that ensuring access to work is not recognized as a human right in this legislation, but merely a desirable policy goal competing for attention with other policy goals. . . .

We shall see that important consequences may flow from this distinction, but at this point I merely want to emphasize that the right to work claim has achieved some recognition in American law, despite the United States' strong resistance to accepting international human rights obligations beyond those already mandated by the nation's Constitution. Whether this recognition will grow with time is difficult to predict, but participants in employment policy debates in the United States should feel some obligation to address the legal mandates that do exist in this area under both international and domestic law.[95]

Conclusion

Reason for Caution

None of this is meant to overstate the impact of the new labor–human rights alliance in the United States. In fact, some labor supporters caution against too much emphasis on a human rights argument for workers' organizing in the United States. They maintain that a rights-based approach fosters individualism instead of collective worker power; that demands for "workers' rights as human rights" interfere with calls for renewed industrial democracy; that channeling workers' activism through a legalistic rights-enhancing regime stifles militancy and direct action. Labor historian Joseph McCartin says:

Because it puts freedom ahead of democracy, rights talk tends to foster a libertarian dialogue, where capital's liberty of movement and employers' "rights to manage" are tacitly affirmed rather than challenged. Arguing in a rights-oriented framework forces workers to demand no more than that *their* rights be respected alongside their employers' rights. . . .

I am not suggesting that today's labor advocates should abandon their rights-based arguments. These have undeniable power, speak to basic truths, and connect to important traditions—including labor's historic internationalism. Rather, I am arguing that the "workers' rights are human rights" formulation alone will prove inadequate to the task of rebuilding workers' organizations in the United States unless we couple it with an equally passionate call for democracy in our workplaces, economy, and politics.[96]

Historian Nelson Lichtenstein argues:

This new sensitivity to global human rights is undoubtedly a good thing for the cause of trade unionism, rights at work, and the democratic impulse. . . . [But] as deployed in American law and political culture, a discourse of rights has also subverted the very idea, and the institutional expression, of union solidarity. . . . Thus, in recent decades, employer anti-unionism has become increasingly oriented toward the ostensible protection of the individual rights of workers as against undemocratic unions and restrictive contracts that hamper the free choice of employees. . . . without a bold and society-shaping political and social program, human rights can devolve into something approximating libertarian individualism.[97]

Historian David Brody suggests that a human rights analysis too willingly accepts the view that collective bargaining is gained through a bureaucratic process of government certification rather than through workers' direct action. "That a formally democratic process might be at odds with workers' freedom of association," he writes, "seems to fall below the screen of 'human rights analysis.' "[98]

These are healthy cautions from serious, committed scholars and defenders of trade unions and workers' rights. They contribute to a needed debate about the role and effectiveness of human rights activism and human rights arguments in support of workers' rights. All three historians agree that human rights advocacy is important for advancing the cause of social justice; that one need not make an "either-or" choice.

Reason for Hope

Conditions have ripened for raising the human rights platform to advance workers' rights in the United States. International labor law developments are fostering new ways of thinking and talking about labor law in the United States—a necessary condition for changing policy and practice.

Arguing from a human rights base, labor advocates can identify violations, name violators, demand remedies, and specify recommendations for change. Workers empowered in organizing and bargaining campaigns are convinced—and are convincing the public—that they are vindicating their fundamental human rights, not just seeking a wage increase or fringe benefits enhancement. Employers are thrown more on the defensive by charges that they are violating workers' human rights. The larger society is more responsive to the notion of trade union organizing as an exercise of human rights rather than economic strength.

This is not meant to exaggerate the effects of the human rights argument. Labor advocates cannot just cry "human rights, human rights" and expect employers to change their behavior or Congress to enact labor law reform. U.S. labor law practitioners need first to learn more about international labor standards. Then they have to make international law arguments in their advocacy work before the NLRB and the courts. The simple step of regularly including international labor law standards, citations, and arguments in their briefs will begin to educate labor law authorities and the judiciary on the relevance of international human rights law to American labor law.

Change will be incremental. Labor and human rights advocates still confront general unawareness in the United States of international human rights standards and of the International Labor Organization's work in giving precise meaning to those standards. Advocates still have an enormous educational challenge of making them more widely known and respected.

Trade unions' use of international instruments and mechanisms and human rights groups' labor rights reporting contribute to this educational effort. At the same time, they change the climate for workers' organizing and bargaining by framing them as a human rights mission, not a test of economic power between an employer and a "third party" (employers' favorite characterization of unions in organizing campaigns).

A human rights emphasis also has alliance-building effects. Human rights supporters and human rights organizations are a major force in civil society, one that historically stood apart from labor struggles, seeing them not as human rights concerns but as institutional tests of strength. Now the human rights community is committed to promoting workers' rights, bringing important addition to labor's traditional allies in civil rights, women's, and other organizations. We cannot foresee in detail how this new alliance will proceed, but it has surely succeeded in reframing the debate, redefining the problems, and reshaping solutions to protect workers' rights as human rights in the United States.

Labor advocates' human rights focus is still new. It is not a magic bullet for organizing or bargaining success; there are no magic bullets for workers in this society. Still, many unions are finding the human rights theme one that resonates and advances their campaigns: the UFCW in that hog-slaughtering plant in North Carolina, AFSCME in its hospital workers' organizing campaign in Chicago, Teamsters in the drive to help port truck drivers stand up to big container shippers; SEIU in its campaign to organize school bus drivers, and many others. Perhaps in years ahead, with some victories to show from a human rights base in its organizing and bargaining campaigns, the labor movement and its allies can advance a rights-centered public policy agenda raising economic and social rights under international human rights standards.

Notes

1. For an account, see Ronald L. Filippelli and Mark McColloch, *Cold War in the Working Class: The Rise and Decline of the United Electrical Workers* (Albany: State University of New York Press, 1995).

2. See Hugh Wilford's study of CIA "front" operations during the early Cold War period, forthcoming from Harvard University Press.

3. See, for example, Leon Fink, *Workingmen's Democracy: The Knights of Labor and American Politics* (Champaign: University of Illinois Press, 1983); Joseph A. McCartin, *Labor's Great War: The Struggle for Industrial Democracy and the Origins of Modern American Labor Relations, 1912–1921* (Chapel Hill: University of North Carolina Press, 1997).

4. For this citation and a discussion of this period and its references to industrial democracy and rights, see Nelson Lichtenstein, *State of the Union: A Century of American Labor* (Princeton, N.J.: Princeton University Press, 2002).

5. For a fuller discussion of the failure of labor and human rights activists to see each other's work as part of their own, see Virginia A. Leary, "The Paradox of Workers' Rights as Human Rights," in Lance A. Compa and Stephen F. Diamond (eds.), *Human Rights, Labor Rights, and International Trade* (Philadelphia: University of Pennsylvania Press, 2003).

6. For extensive analytical treatment of this point, see James Gray Pope, "The Thirteenth Amendment Versus the Commerce Clause: Labor and the Shaping of American Constitutional Law, 1921–1957," *Columbia Law Review* 102 (2002): 1.

7. See Michael H. LeRoy, "Regulating Employer Use of Permanent Striker Replacements: Empirical Analysis of NLRA and RLA Strikes 1935–1991," *Berkeley Journal of Employment and Labor Law* 16 (1995): 169.

8. For two gripping accounts of strikes broken by permanent replacement, see Jonathan D. Rosenblum, *Copper Crucible: How the Arizona Miners' Strike of 1983 Recast Labor-Management Relations in America* (Ithaca, N.Y.: Cornell University Press, 1998), and Julius Getman, *The Betrayal of Local 14: Paperworkers, Politics, and Permanent Replacements* (Ithaca, N.Y.: Cornell University Press, 1998). See also Steven Greenhouse, "Strikes Decrease to 50-Year Low as Threat of Replacement Rises," *New York Times*, January 29, 1996, p. A1.

9. See Joel Cutcher-Gershenfeld, "The Social Contract at the Bargaining Table: Evidence from a National Survey of Labor and Management Negotiators," Industrial Relations Research Association, *Proceedings of the 51st Annual Meeting*, vol. 2 (1999).

10. See Helen Dewar and Frank Swoboda, "Republican-Led Filibuster Kills Striker Replacement Bill in Senate," *Washington Post*, July 14, 1994, p. A7.

11. Workers in right-to-work states earn on average $7,000 a year less than workers in states where employers and unions can agree to "union security" clauses. See Center for Policy Alternatives, "Right to Work for Less," *Policy Brief*, available online at www.stateaction.org/issues/issue.cfm/issue/RightToWorkForLess.xml.

12. See U.S. General Accounting Office, *Collective Bargaining Rights: Information on the Number of Workers with and without Bargaining Rights*, GAO-02-835 (September 2002).

13. See Julius Getman, "The National Labor Relations Act: What Went Wrong; Can We Fix It?" *Boston College Law Review* 45 (December 2003): 125.

14. For a collection of essays on this question, see Michael Ignatieff (ed.), *American Exceptionalism and Human Rights* (Princeton, N.J.: Princeton University

Press, 2005). See also Kenneth Roth, "The Charade of U.S. Ratification of International Human Rights Treaties," *Chicago Journal of International Law* 1 (Fall 2000): 347.

15. The United States has ratified Convention No. 105 on forced labor and Convention No. 182 on worst forms of child labor. The United States has not ratified Convention No. 29 on forced labor, No. 87 on freedom of association, No. 98 on the right to organize, No. 100 on equal pay, No. 111 on nondiscrimination, or No. 138 on child labor.

16. See Appendix B, Senate Foreign Relations Committee, Report on the International Covenant on Civil and Political Rights, S. Exec. Rep. No. 23, 102d Cong., 2nd sess., 25 (1992), reprinted in 31 I.L.M. 645, 660 (1992).

17. See *Second and Third Report of the United States of America to the UN Committee on Human Rights Concerning the International Covenant on Civil and Political Rights*, October 21, 2005. The report did mention, without discussion, the Supreme Court's 2002 decision in *Hoffman Plastic Compounds v. NLRB*, discussed in detail below. A failure to mention *Hoffman Plastic* would have signaled either gross incompetence or deliberate omission.

18. See Cynthia L. Estlund, "The Ossification of American Labor Law," *Columbia Law Review* 102 (2002): 1527.

19. See International Labor Organization, Follow-Up Reports to 1998 Declaration on Fundamental Principles and Rights at Work, United States report, "Freedom of Association and the Effective Recognition of the Right to Collective Bargaining," 1999.

20. See AFL-CIO, "Comments of the AFL-CIO on the Report by the Government of the United States of America, in Accordance with Article 22 of the Constitution of the International Labor Organization, on the Measures Taken to Give Effect to the Provisions of the Tripartite Consultation (International Labor Standards) Convention, 1976," on file with AFL-CIO legal department.

21. For a critique on this point, see Philip Alston, "Labor Rights Provisions in US Trade Law: Aggressive Unilateralism?" in Lance Compa and Stephen F. Diamond (eds.), *Human Rights, Labor Rights, and International Trade* (Philadelphia: University of Pennsylvania Press, 2003).

22. See *International Labor Rights Education and Research Fund v. George Bush, et al.*, 752 F.Supp. 495, 1990.

23. See Petition to the United States Trade Representative, Labor Rights in Chile (1986); Petition to the United States Trade Representative, Labor Rights in Chile (1987) (filed by the UE and the AFL-CIO) (on file with USTR).

24. Paul Adams, "Suspension of Generalized System of Preferences from Chile—The Proper Use of a Trade Provision," *George Washington Journal of International Law & Economics* 23 (Winter 1990): 501.

25. Eugene Robinson, "Chile's Pinochet Beaten in Plebiscite on Rule; Voters Reject Bid for 8 More Years in Power," *Washington Post*, October 6, 1988, p. A1.

26. This does not mean there are not still severe problems with Chilean labor law and practice. For a thorough analysis, see Carol Pier, "Labor Rights in Chile and NAFTA Labor Standards: Questions of Compatibility on the Eve of Free Trade," *Comparative Labor Law & Policy Journal* 19 (1998): 185.

27. Tod Robberson, "Guatemalan President Seizes Decree Power, Dissolves Congress; Moves Follow Talk of Restive Military," *Washington Post*, May 26, 1993, p. A21.

28. Jared Kotler, "Keep the Economic Heat on Guatemala's Leaders," *Miami Herald*, June 7, 1993, p. 11A.

29. Ibid.

30. Tim Golden, "Guatemalan Leader Is Pressed to Yield Power," *New York Times,* June 1, 1993, p. A7.

31. Tod Robberson,"Guatemala Swears in New President, Rights Leader Faces Political Challenges," *Washington Post,* June 7, 1993, p. A13.

32. Tim Golden, "Guatemala's Counter-Coup: A Military About-Face," *New York Times,* June 3, 1993, p. A3.

33. These agreements and their labor chapters are all available on the Web site of the U.S. Trade Representative, www.ustr.gov. Among them, only the U.S.-Jordan Free Trade Agreement makes labor rights guarantees binding and enforceable through trade measures. The others lack an effective enforcement mechanism.

34. *North American Agreement on Labor Cooperation,* Annex 1, Labor Principles.

35. *North American Agreement on Labor Cooperation,* Article 2, Obligations.

36. See Evelyn Iritani, "Mexico Charges Upset Apple Cart in US," *Los Angeles Times,* August 20, 1998, p. D1.

37. For extensive discussion of internal company codes, see Lance Compa and Tashia Hinchliffe-Daricarrere, "Enforcing International Labor Rights Through Corporate Code of Conduct," *Columbia Journal of Transnational Law* 33 (1995): 663.

38. See Mark B. Baker, "Private Codes of Conduct: Should the Fox Guard the Henhouse?," *University of Miami Inter-American Law Review* 24 (1993): 399; Robert J. Liubicic, "Corporate Codes of Conduct and Product Labeling Schemes: The Limits and Possibilities of Promoting International Labor Rights Through Private Initiatives," *Law & Policy in International Business* 30 (1998): 111; David Kinley and Junko Tadaki, "From Talk to Walk: The Emergence of Human Rights Responsibilities for Corporations at International Law," *Virginia Journal of International Law* 44 (Summer 2004): 931.

39. See Web sites respectively at www.fairlabor.org/html/monitoring.html; www.workersrights.org; and www.sa-intl.org.

40. See Web site at www.jo-in.org.

41. For extended discussion, see Lance Compa, "Trade Unions, NGOs, and Corporate Codes of Conduct," *Development in Practice* 14 (February 2004): 210. A shorter version in *The American Prospect* titled "Wary Allies" is available online at www.prospect.org/print/V12/12/compa-l.html.

42. See Marc Lifsher, "Unocal Settles Human Rights Lawsuit over Alleged Abuses at Myanmar Pipeline; A Deal Ends a Landmark Case Brought by Villagers Who Said Soldiers Committed Atrocities," *Los Angeles Times,* March 22, 2005, p. C1.

43. See *Rodriguez et al. v. Drummond Co.,* 256 F.Supp. 1250 (2003).

44. See *Romero v. Drummond Co.,* 11th Cir., No. 07-14090, December 22, 2008.

45. See Michelle Amber, "U.S. Company Agrees in Norwegian Court to Inform Employees of Organizing Rights," *BNA Daily Labor Report,* November 12, 2002.

46. For extensive analysis of cross-border solidarity efforts, see James Atleson, "The Voyage of the Neptune Jade: The Perils and Promises of Transnational Labor Solidarity," *Buffalo Law Review* 52 (Winter 2004): 85.

47. For more information, see Amnesty International USA Web site at www.amnestyusa.org; Oxfam America Web site at www.oxfamamerica.org.

48. See "Unfair Advantage: Workers' Freedom of Association in the United States under International Human Rights Standards"; "Fingers to the Bone: United States Failure to Protect Child Farmworkers"; "Hidden in the Home:

Abuse of Domestic Workers with Special Visas in the United States"; all available online at the Human Rights Watch Web site, www.hrw.org.

49. See, for example, Julian Borger, "Workers' Rights 'Abused in US,'" *Guardian* (London), August 30, 2000, p. 12; Ned Glascock, "Rights Group Targets Firms," *Raleigh News & Observer*, August 31 2000, p. A3; "Study: Labor Law Fails Millions" (editorial), *New York Daily News*, August 31, 2000, p. 84; "Labor Day Finds Some with Old Troubles" (editorial), *Greensboro News & Record*, September 4, 2000, p. A8; Robert McNatt, "The List: Union Busters," *Business Week*, September 11, 2000, p. 14; Steven Greenhouse, "Report Faults Laws for Slowing Growth of Unions," *New York Times*, October 24, 2000, p. A20; Lance Compa, "U.S. Workers' Rights Are Being Abused" (op-ed), *Washington Post*, October 30, 2000, p. A27; "O governo dos EUA tem sido ineficiente na defesa dos trabalhadores," *O Estado de Sao Paulo*, November 1, 2000; Roy Adams, "U.S. Immigrants Being Exploited," *Hamilton Spectator*, November 21, 2000, p. D10; Arvind Panagariya, "Shoes on the Other Foot: Stunning Indictment of Laws Governing Workers' Rights in the United States," *Economic Times* (India), December 20, 2000, p. 1; "Worker Rights," Scripps Howard News Service, February 21, 2001.

50. See, for example, Judith A. Scott, SEIU General Counsel, "Workers' Rights to Organize as Human Rights: The California Experience," Los Angeles County Bar Association Labor and Employment Law Symposium, February 26, 2004.

51. See Rodger Doyle, "U.S. Workers and the Law," *Scientific American* (August 2001): 24.

52. The Reuther-Chavez Award, named for ADA co-founder and United Auto Workers president Walter Reuther and United Farm Workers leader Cesar Chavez, was created by the ADA "to recognize important activist, scholarly and journalistic contributions on behalf of workers' rights, especially the right to unionize and bargain collectively."

53. See Carl Swidorski, "From the Wagner Act to the Human Rights Watch Report: Labor and Freedom of Expression and Association, 1935–2000," *New Political Science* 25 (March 2003): 54.

54. See *Blood, Sweat, and Fear: Workers' Rights in the U.S. Meat and Poultry Industry*; *Discounting Rights Wal-Mart's Violation of US Workers' Right to Freedom of Association*, available online at www.hrw.org.

55. See Steven Greenhouse, "Labor to Press for Workers' Right to Join Unions," *New York Times*, December 9, 2005, p. A18; Alison Grant, "Labor Supporters Take to Streets; Week of Demonstrations Meant to Rev Up U.S. Union Movement," *Cleveland Plain Dealer*, December 10, 2005, p. C2; Tracy Idell Hamilton, "Labor Union Advocates Rally for Better Workers' Rights," *San Antonio Express-News*, December 11, 2005, p. 5B.

56. For more information, see www.aflcio.org/joinaunion/voiceatwork/efca/.

57. See Senator Edward M. Kennedy, "Leveling the Playing Field for American Workers," *LERA Perspectives on Work Online*, Labor and Employment Relations Association, 2005.

58. See JwJ Web site at www.jwj.org.

59. See the ARAW Web site at www.araw.org for detailed information on the group's program and activities.

60. See the NESRI Web site at www.nesri.org.

61. See RFK Center Web site at www.rfkmemorial.org; Coalition Web site at http://www.ciw-online.org.

62. See, for example, Leslie D. Alexander, "Fashioning a New Approach: The Role of International Human Rights Law in Enforcing Rights of Women Gar-

ment Workers in Los Angeles," *Georgetown Journal of Poverty Law and Policy* 10 (Winter 2003): 81.

63. See NELP Web site at www.nelp.org.

64. See Inter-American Court of Human Rights, *Legal Condition and Rights of Undocumented Migrant Workers*, Consultative Opinion OC-18/03, September 17, 2003.

65. See Janice Fine, *Worker Centers: Organizing Communities at the Edge of the Dream* (Ithaca, N.Y.: Cornell University Press, 2006); Steven Greenhouse, "Immigrant Workers Find Support in a Growing Network of Assistance Centers," *New York Times*, April 23, 2006.

66. See International Brotherhood of Teamsters, "Workers' Rights Violations at Maersk: Report and Analysis; Actions by U.S. Divisions of Maersk Corporation in Light of International Human Rights and Labor Rights Standards," June 1, 2004.

67. See Bill Mongelluzzo, "Teamsters Shift Gears: Union Targets Maersk Sealand in Campaign to Organize Port Drivers," *Journal of Commerce*, September 13, 2004, p. 13; Rajesh Joshi and Andrew Draper, "Maersk Target of Protest by Thousands of Truckers: Company Accused of 'Threatening, Intimidating and Terminating Drivers,'" *Lloyd's List*, September 6, 2004, p. 3; "Mærsk ramt af strejke i USA: Mærsk undertrykker og nægter at anerkende fundamentale rettigheder for transportarbejdere, som nu har besluttet at tage strejkevåbenet i brug i havnene Miami og San Francisco," *Netavisen APK*, August 2004.

68. See Bill Mongelluzzo, "Teamsters Pushes Maersk Driver Protest; Union Hits Carrier's Shareholders Meeting," *Journal of Commerce Online*, April 19, 2005.

69. Bill Mongelluzzo, "Teamsters Want Maersk to Abide by UN Workers Rules," *Journal of Commerce Online*, April 11, 2006.

70. See AFSCME, "Freedom of Association and Workers' Rights Violations at Resurrection Health Care: Report and Analysis Under International Human Rights and Labor Rights Standards," Prepared for Worker Rights Board Hearing, Chicago, Illinois, August 26, 2004.

71. See, for example, "Catholic Scholars Call for Hospital Chain to Respect Workers' Rights; Open Letter Cites Resurrection Health Care's Intimidation of Employees," *PR Newswire*, December 14, 2006.

72. *Hoffman Plastic Compounds, Inc. v. NLRB*, 535 U.S. 137 (2002).

73. The four dissenting justices said there was not such a conflict and that a "backpay order will *not* interfere with the implementation of immigration policy. Rather, it reasonably helps to deter unlawful activity that *both* labor laws *and* immigration laws seek to prevent."

74. See "Complaint presented by the AFL-CIO to the ILO Freedom of Association Committee," AFL-CIO, October 2002.

75. See ILO Committee on Freedom of Association, Complaint against the United States, Case No. 2227, Report No. 332 (2003).

76. Ibid.

77. See "Complaint against the Government of the United Kingdom presented by the Association of United States Engaged Staff (AUSES), the International Federation of Professional and Technical Employees (IFPTE), the American Federation of Labor and Congress of Industrial Organizations (AFL-CIO) and Public Services International (PSI)," June 23, 2005.

78. See ILO Committee on Freedom of Association, Complaint against the United Kingdom, Case No. 2437, Report No. 344, *Report in which the Committee requests to be kept informed of developments* (March 2007).

79. Author e-mail exchange with Julia Akins Clark, general counsel, International Federation of Professional and Technical Engineers, March 18, 2008.

80. See *Oakwood Healthcare, Inc.*, 348 NLRB No. 37; *Croft Metal, Inc.*, 348 NLRB No. 38; *Golden Crest Healthcare Center*, 348 NLRB No. 39 (October 2, 2006), called the *Oakwood* trilogy.

81. The AFL-CIO complaint pointed to principles established by earlier CFA cases from other countries involving the status of workers deemed "supervisors": the expression "supervisors" should be limited to cover only those persons who genuinely represent the interests of employers; legal definitions of "supervisors" or other excluded categories of workers should not allow an expansive interpretation that excludes large numbers of workers from organizing and bargaining rights; employees should not be "excluded" to undermine worker organizing or to weaken the bargaining strength of trade unions; changing employees' status to undermine the membership of workers' trade unions is contrary to the principle of freedom of association; even true supervisors have the right to form and join trade unions and to bargain collectively, though the law may require that their bargaining units be separate from those of supervised employees. See Pakistan (Case No. 1534), Dominican Republic (Case No. 1751), Pakistan (Case No. 1771), Peru (Case No. 1878), Canada (Case No. 1951).

82. See ILO Committee on Freedom of Association, Complaint against the United States, Case No. 2524, Report No. 349, Report in which the Committee requests to be kept informed of developments (March 2008).

83. See ILO Committee on Freedom of Association, Complaint against the United States, Case No. 2292, Report No. 343, Report in which the Committee requests to be kept informed of developments (November 2006).

84. Traditionally a manufacturing sector union, the UE began an innovative organizing campaign among low-paid public sector workers in North Carolina, a state that prohibits collective bargaining by public employees. Using state and local civil service procedures, the union has won several grievances and wage increases for workers.

85. See ILO Committee on Freedom of Association, Complaint against the United States, Case No. 2460, Report No. 344 (2007).

86. See North Carolina General Assembly, House Bill No. 1583 (April 2007).

87. Author interview with Robin Alexander, director of international affairs, United Electrical Workers, March 20, 2008.

88. See information on these complaints at the UE website, http://www.ranknfile-ue.org/.

89. See International Commission for Labor Rights, "The Denial of Public Sector Collective Bargaining Rights in the State of North Carolina (USA): Assessment and Report," June 14, 2006. See Web site of ICLR at http://www.labourcommission.org/.

90. See National Administrative Office of Mexico, Submission No. 2001-01 (New York State), 2001. In another case reflecting labor advocates' use of international mechanisms, the Farmworker Justice Fund, Inc., and Mexico's Independent Agricultural Workers Central (CIOAC) filed a complaint in 2003 under the NAALC on behalf of thousands of migrant agricultural workers in North Carolina holding H-2A visas for temporary agricultural labor. The complaint gained widespread support in Mexico and helped H-2A workers win a breakthrough collective agreement in 2004. See National Administrative Office of Mexico, Submission No. 2003-1 (North Carolina), 2003; Kristin Collins, "Farm Union Gets Consent to Recruit," *Raleigh News & Observer*, August 25, 2004, p. A1.

91. See Emily A. Spieler, "Risks and Rights: The Case for Occupational Safety and Health as a Core Worker Right," in James A. Gross (ed.), *Workers' Rights as Human Rights* (Ithaca, N.Y.: Cornell University Press, 2003).

92. Ibid.

93. Ibid.

94. See James A. Gross, "Incorporating Human Rights Principles into U.S. Labor Arbitration: A Proposal for Fundamental Change," *Employee Rights and Employment Policy Journal* 8 (2004): 1.

95. See Philip Harvey, "Taking Economic and Social Rights Seriously," *Columbia Human Rights Law Review* 33 (Spring 2002): 363.

96. Joseph McCartin, "Democratizing the Demand for Workers' Rights: Toward a Re-framing of Labor's Argument," *Dissent* (Winter 2005).

97. Nelson Lichtenstein, "The Rights Revolution," *New Labor Forum* (Spring 2003).

98. David Brody, "Labor Rights as Human Rights: A Reality Check," *British Journal of Industrial Relations* (December 2001).

About the Editors and Contributors

About the Editors

Cynthia Soohoo directs the U.S. Legal Program at the Center for Reproductive Rights. The Center for Reproductive Rights uses the law to advance reproductive freedom as a fundamental right that all governments are legally obligated to protect, respect, and fulfill. From 2001 to 2007, Ms. Soohoo was the director of the Bringing Human Rights Home Project, Human Rights Institute, Columbia Law School and a supervising attorney for the law school's Human Rights Clinic. She has worked on U.S. human rights issues before UN human rights bodies and the Inter-American Commission for Human Rights, as well as in domestic courts, and on issues including juvenile justice and challenges to the Bush administration's antiterrorism policies post-9/11. Ms. Soohoo is on the Board of Directors of the U.S. Human Rights Network and is cochair of the American Constitutional Society's Working Group on International Law and the Constitution.

Catherine Albisa is the executive director of the National Economic and Social Rights Initiative (NESRI) and a constitutional and human rights lawyer with a background in the right to health. She also has significant experience working in partnership with community organizers in the use of human rights standards to strengthen advocacy in the United States. Ms. Albisa co-founded NESRI along with Sharda Sekaran and Liz Sullivan in order to build legitimacy for human rights in general, and economic and social rights in particular, in the United States. She is committed to a community-centered and participatory human rights approach that is locally anchored but universal and global in its vision.

Martha F. Davis is professor of law at Northeastern University School of Law, and co-director of its Program on Human Rights and the Global Economy. Her scholarly writing and legal work focus on human rights, poverty, and women's rights, and she lectures widely on these issues. Her book, *Brutal Need: Lawyers and the Welfare Rights Movement, 1960–1973*, received the Reginald Heber Smith Award for "distinguished scholarship in the area of equal access to justice" and a citation in the American Bar Association's Silver Gavel competition.

About the Contributors

Carol Anderson is associate professor of African American studies at Emory University and has recently completed a fellowship at Harvard University's Charles Warren Center for Studies in American History. Her research and teaching focus on public policy, particularly the ways in which domestic and international policies intersect through the issues of race, justice, and equality in the United States. She is the author of *Eyes off the Prize: The United Nations and the African-American Struggle for Human Rights, 1944–1955*, which was published by Cambridge University Press and awarded both the Gustavus Myers and Myrna Bernath Book Awards.

Elizabeth Borgwardt is associate professor of history at Washington University in St. Louis, where she specializes in the history of human rights ideas and institutions. Her book, *A New Deal for the World: America's Vision for Human Rights* (2005, paperback 2007), garnered the Merle Curti Award for the Best Book on the History of Ideas for 2006 from the Organization of American Historians, as well as the Best First Book Award from the Society for Historians of American Foreign Relations and the Best First Book Award from the History Honor Society. Her current project is on the Nuremberg Trials and the notion of crimes against humanity.

Lance Compa is a senior lecturer at Cornell University's School of Industrial and Labor Relations in Ithaca, New York, where he teaches U.S. labor law and international labor rights. His most recent book project (with co-authors) is the textbook *International Labor Law: Cases and Materials on Workers' Rights in the Global Economy* (West Law Group, 2008).

Margaret Huang is the director of the U.S. Program at Global Rights, an international human rights advocacy organization that partners with local activists to challenge injustice and combat discrimination. She has developed training materials and other resources to help activists engage international human rights procedures in their advocacy work. Ms. Huang also sits on the board of directors of the U.S. Human Rights Network, a coalition of organizations and individuals committed to promoting U.S. government accountability to international human rights standards.

Paul Gordon Lauren is Regents Professor at the University of Montana. He is acknowledged as one of the leading authorities in the world on the history of human rights, has lectured widely in many places and before many types of audiences, has received many awards, and has published extensively, including the highly acclaimed *The Evolution of International Human Rights: Visions Seen* and *Power and Prejudice,* both of which have appeared in various editions and translations. Most recently he has created a Great Course for The Teaching Company on the subject of human rights.

Hope Lewis is professor of law at Northeastern University School of Law and co-founded its Program on Human Rights and the Global Economy. Her textbook, *Human Rights and the Global Marketplace: Economic, Social, and Cultural Dimensions* (with Jeanne Woods) (Transnational/Brill USA, 2005), highlights the human rights implications of globalization. A 2008–9 Sheila Biddle Ford Fellow of Harvard University's W. E. B. Du Bois Institute for African and African American Research, she also co-edits *Human Rights & the Global Economy,* an electronic abstracts journal.

Wendy Patten is a senior policy analyst at the Open Society Institute in Washington, D.C., where she engages in legal and policy advocacy on U.S. human and civil rights issues. Previously, she was the U.S. advocacy director at Human Rights Watch, and she was director of multilateral and humanitarian affairs at the National Security Council from 1999 to 2001. Ms. Patten served for five years as an attorney at the U.S. Department of Justice, including as senior counsel in the Office of Policy Development and as special counsel for trafficking in persons in the Civil Rights Division.

Kathryn Sikkink is a Regents Professor and McKnight Distinguished University Professor at the University of Minnesota. Her publications include *Mixed Signals: U.S. Human Rights Policy and Latin America; Activists Beyond Borders: Advocacy Networks in International Politics* (co-authored with Margaret Keck); and *The Power of Human Rights: International Norms and Domestic Change* (co-edited with Thomas Risse and Stephen Ropp). She is a fellow of the Council on Foreign Relations and the American Association for Arts and Sciences.

Dorothy Q. Thomas is a visiting fellow at the Centre for the Study of Human Rights at the London School of Economics. From 1999 to 2006 she served as an independent consultant on human rights in the United States. She is a member of the board of directors of the Ms. Foundation for Women and sits on the advisory boards of the ACLU Human Rights Project, Breakthrough, the Four Freedoms Fund, the Human Rights Watch U.S. Project, and the U.S. Human Rights Fund.

Index

Acknowledgments

We want to express our deep appreciation to the activists cited in this book, whose work continues to inspire us, and to the authors of these chapters for contributing their experience, insights, and hard work to this effort. Thanks are in order to Peter Agree for his enthusiasm about this project and to Hilary Claggett for encouraging us to pursue it. We are also grateful to Professor Peter Rosenblum, Shana Jones, Elizabeth Potenza, and Lindsay Claire for their support and encouragement.

During the initial stages of this project, we were fortunate to be able to convene two conferences at Columbia Law School, in May 2005 and June 2006, to develop the content and themes for this book. Several conference participants became contributing authors. Other participants, including Clifford Bob, Ellen Chapnick, Rhonda Copelon, Jamie Fellner, Hadar Harris, the Honorable Claire L'Heureux-Dube, Garth Meintjes, Alice Miller, Judith Resnik, Peter Rosenblum, Amanda Shanor, and Steven Watt, provided invaluable comments and suggestions which helped to shape the direction of the project.

We are particularly grateful to Bob Morgado for making these conferences possible and to the Ford, JEHT, Mertz Gilmore, and Shaler Adams foundations, as well as the U.S. Human Rights Fund, for their steadfast support and commitment to human rights in the United States.

We must also acknowledge the significant contributions of Columbia and Northeastern Law Schools, Northeastern's Project on Human Rights and the Global Economy, and the staff of Columbia's Human Rights Institute's Bringing Human Rights Home project, Caroline Bettinger-Lopez and Trisha Garbe, without whom this project could not have been completed. Finally, we thank Samuel Jack, Jan McNew, Richard Doyon, Samuel Fury, Childs Daly, and Karen Lin for outstanding editing and editorial assistance.

Many colleagues and friends provided advice as we were formulating the scope of this project and following it through to completion. Particular thanks are due to Kenneth Cmiel, Barbara Stark, Mary Dudziak, John

Witt, Mark Bradley, Brian Balogh, Hope Lewis, and Richard Ratner for their assistance and consultation.

In addition, each of the editors would like to personally express thanks to the following individuals and institutions:

I am greatly indebted to my colleagues in the Bringing Human Rights Home Lawyers Network for sharing their ideas and projects and providing a continuing source of inspiration. A collaborative project of this scope is by its nature difficult, but it can become an ordeal unless you are fortunate, as I was, to work with colleagues whom you like and respect and upon whom you can depend. I am grateful to Cathy Albisa and Martha Davis for their commitment, hard work, vision, and good humor throughout this project. Finally, special thanks to Sarah and Thomas Creighton for their patience and support and to Daniel Creighton for making this project and everything else possible. —CS

Every social justice effort is by nature a collaborative one. I have many people to thank for making this book possible, starting with my family, in particular my mother-in-law, Dalia Davila, and husband, Waldo Cubero, for their steadfast support for my work despite sacrifices they endure as a result; my children, Gabriel and Dario, for being a constant source of inspiration and wisdom on what is clearly right and wrong in this world; my mother, Gladys Albisa, for her encouragement to commit myself to this work; Larry Cox and Dorothy Q. Thomas for their guidance, leadership, and inspiration; the extraordinary staff at the National Economic and Social Rights Initiative (NESRI) for the depth of their commitment and creativity; my co-founders Sharda Sekaran and Liz Sullivan for their leap of faith in creating NESRI; Laura Gosa and Molly Corbett for their work to ensure the completion of many of the chapters in this book; Tiffany Gardner for her optimism and her commitment to carrying this work into the future; the contributing authors with whom I had the honor of working, who made time in their impossible schedules to make a invaluable contribution; my board members Mimi Abramovitz, Rhonda Copelon, Lisa Crooms, Martha Davis, Dr. Paul Farmer, Patrick Mason, and Bruce Rabb for their leadership and support; NESRI's partner organizations that exemplify the U.S. human rights movement; our funders mentioned above as well as the Public Welfare Foundation, which make the work possible; and most of all our extraordinary colleague Cindy Soohoo, who quietly and modestly developed the vision for this project and generously allowed all of us to become a part of it. Thank you, Cindy, this could not have happened without you! —CA

Thanks to Northeastern Law School and the Harvard Law School Human Rights Program for providing both the support and flexibility for me to devote the necessary time to this project. I am grateful to Kyle Courtney for his unflagging good humor and expertise and to Elizabeth

Farry for her excellent research assistance. My profound thanks to Caroline Davis, Mei Davis, and my parents, Robert and Marian Davis, for their continued support. Finally, thanks to Cindy Soohoo and Cathy Albisa for their invitation to join them in this project, and for being such exceptionally generous and visionary colleagues. —MD